D1639047

Richard Lindley was born in Winchester and educated at Bedford School. After National Service with the Royal Hampshire Regiment in Malaya he went to Queens' College Cambridge, where he ran the University Film Society. After a spell in advertising, making commercials, he became a television reporter, first for ITN's *News at Ten* and later for the BBC's *Panorama* and ITV's *This Week*. He now makes occasional television documentaries. He has two children, Tom and Jo, and lives in north London with his wife, the author and broadcaster Carole Stone.

Panorama

Fifty years of pride and paranoia

updated edition

Richard Lindley

POLITICO'S

First published in Great Britain 2002 by Politico's Publishing

This updated paperback edition published in Great Britain 2003
byPolitico's Publishing, an imprint of
Methuen Publishing Limited
215 Vauxhall Bridge Road
London SW1V 1EJ

A catalogue record for this book is available from the British Library.

ISBN 1 84275 046 1
Printed and bound in Great Britain by Cox and Wyman

Contents

For Carole, who has made the *Panorama* crew so welcome aboard.

⊕ Foreword

by Jeremy Paxman

Just about anyone who has ever worked on *Panorama* in the last quarter-century has called it by its nickname, Paranoia. The joke's well judged.

The programme aimed to make the flesh creep with some disturbing tale of evil, corruption or incompetence. The truth was that often the most acutely disturbed weren't the viewers but the production team. At times in its history you would have had to be very unlucky indeed to find a more poisonous place to work. The motto adopted by one of its producers at the time that I was there was that it was not enough to succeed. Others had to be seen to fail. That competitive spirit was as much a spur as it was unsettling.

But for all that, the programme is a classic of broadcasting. Or, in the cliché of the trade, a 'flagship'. Like one of those Second World War battleships which were still lumbering out to the Middle East 40 years later, the programme began in another era. We imagine families huddled around their flickering black-and-white screens for a communal laugh at the famous 'spaghetti tree' spoof, before Dad in his cardigan suggested a nightcap cup of Ovaltine.

In the succeeding decades the programme has brought the world to its audience, reporting wars, interviewing presidents and prime ministers, confronting criminals, exploring the areas beyond politics. In tone it has ranged from the whimsical to the hysterical. But mostly, it has been urgent, its conviction based upon the old-fashioned journalistic values of an inquiring mind, a suspicion of all spokesmen for vested interests and a refusal to take 'no' for an answer. A stint on the programme was essential for many on their way to the commanding heights of television journalism. In the present world, the question which hangs over the old vessel is whether it simply needs a new lick of paint or an enormous limpet mine on the bottom of its hull. No longer a weekly feature in the schedules and exiled from prime time to late Sunday nights, the signals are not good.

Television is an ephemeral medium in which no individual, and no individual programme, can expect to last forever. Self-important and overblown, it has not always been its own best advertisement. The very expression 'current affairs' seems to belong to another era, when well-educated chaps in corduroy suits made sense of a world in which events moved more slowly. Now, we can switch on channels at any hour of the day or night and hear, live, from the latest corner of the world to be afflicted by natural disaster, war or crisis.

The news maelstrom in which we live has brought benefits. But they have come at a cost. Immediacy is not the same as understanding. The sheer speed with which the news cycle revolves allows the rich and powerful to bury things that ought to be dug up and to announce things which are not all they seem. We need to keep a way of holding these people and organisations to account. All journalistic outlets make enemies. But the worst enemy is indifference.

⊕ Preface

In the early 1970s I followed a television trail first hacked out of the journalistic jungle by pioneers Chris Chataway, Robin Day and later Alan Hart, a trail that led from news to current affairs, from ITN to BBC *Panorama*. There, as reporter and, more briefly, presenter, I worked for fifteen fascinating years.

There are not many jobs where, when you get up in the morning, you can say to yourself: 'Today I'm going to be paid to tell the truth.' Reporting for *Panorama* was such a job, and I was lucky to get it.

When *Panorama* began in 1953 there was a void, darkness on the factual face of television: ITV did not yet exist, and through prejudice and inertia BBC News had failed to develop. It was left to *Panorama* to invent television journalism in Britain.

It was *Panorama* that first found effective ways of reporting and presenting what was happening in the world to the mass television audience: *Panorama* that first made television journalism important. Similar programmes – *This Week*, and *World in Action* – followed, thrived and died. *Panorama* survived, a potent symbol of public service broadcasting.

For nearly fifty years *Panorama* has sought to combine authority and popularity as the BBC's flagship current affairs programme, constantly trying to reinvent itself to reflect a changing social and political climate.

Now, as factual programmes proliferate and audiences fragment, the will to keep *Panorama* afloat seems to be flagging.

In this book I try to chart some of the more significant moments in *Panorama*'s long voyage – half a century of pride and sometimes paranoia; its curious early years; the contribution of Editors, reporters, producers and presenters; the way it has stood up to pressure and complaint from inside and outside the BBC; fierce engagements; times when it has sailed into danger or been ordered back to port in disgrace; its current standing in the BBC fleet.

This book is not a comprehensive account of *Panorama*'s 50-year story. Broadsheet journalists sometimes call their work 'the first rough draft of history'; for this book I prefer a phrase that better suits a current affairs television hack: a stab at the truth.

I apologise to all those many talented *Panorama* people I have failed to include – and all those I have.

⊕ Research note

The BBC Written Archives have been indispensable to me in documenting this history of *Panorama*, and I am most grateful to Jacquie Kavanagh and her colleagues at Caversham Park. The files are not at present open to independent researchers such as myself if they refer to events later than 1979 – just over halfway through *Panorama*'s story. I am therefore particularly glad that successive BBC Heads of Heritage, the late Justin Phillips, Tim Orchard and Robin Reynolds, gave me access to some later files, and at the BBC Photo Archive Gareth Miles has unearthed many historic photographs. Christine Slattery has kindly provided extracts from interviews in the BBC Oral History Collection. At the library of the Independent Television Commission Barrie MacDonald and his colleagues were particularly helpful with press cuttings and television reviews.

I want to thank all those, whether alive or dead, from whose books and articles I quote, in particular Jonathan Dimbleby, the biographer of his father Richard, and Robert Rowland, who has himself written about *Panorama*.

Finally, I owe the greatest debt to the scores of *Panorama* people – past and present – who have so diligently searched their memories and their attics to help me better understand who did what to whom, and when. It is remarkable how many sided the truth turns out to be.

chapter one

⊕ 'This terrible shambles'

At 8.15 p.m. on 11 November 1953, a Wednesday, BBC Television broadcast the first edition of the *Panorama* programme – 'Panorama No.1', as the script is headed.[1]

It was very nearly the last.

Stephen Bonarjee, who as a Television Talks producer was there that night, helping to get the programme on air, later described it as 'the most disastrous single production with which I have ever been associated. Literally everything went wrong. The overall memory is of this terrible shambles.'[2] Watching the programme go out in angry dismay was Cecil McGivern, the Controller of Television Programmes. As the first *Panorama* staggered off the air he telephoned the studios and spoke to the commissionaire on duty. 'He didn't say a word [to us],' Bonarjee recalled:

Not that night – he had plenty to say later . . . What he did was to give orders: that none of us was to be admitted to the Hospitality room after the programme and that the sooner we all cleared off the better. Well, in BBC terms that's a pretty dire punishment, and goodness knows we all needed a drink, although we didn't deserve it. And so we all had to repair to the pub at the end of Lime Grove and drown our sorrows there.

Conception and gestation

Panorama, which had begun life with such a difficult birth, was conceived not in Lime Grove, in that rather tatty area of London immediately west of Shepherd's Bush, but on the northern heights of Wood Green rising loftily above the capital at Alexandra Palace, the original home of BBC Television. The Television Service, closed down for the duration of the Second World War, had reopened in 1946, with Richard Dimbleby giving the commentary on the victory parade. But, far from Broadcasting House in the centre of London, television languished, a poor relation of the mighty BBC Radio. The BBC's attitude to television as a whole remained 'repressive',³ but some could see the possibilities.

Dennis Bardens, now ninety-one years old, has always liked to be ahead of events. His mews home in London's Notting Hill is full of examples of the earliest computers seen in Britain: museum pieces today, but bought at the very beginning of the electronic word-processing age, a time when most journalists were still clinging to their battered portable typewriters, as if to some comforting teddy bear. In the 1930s Bardens had established himself as a versatile print journalist, working across Fleet Street as a reporter and feature writer on papers like the *Sunday Express* and *Daily Mirror*. During the War he'd been attached to the Ministry of Information and afterwards began working for the BBC as a freelance radio producer. Since 1949 he'd been series editor of *Focus*, which week by week on BBC Radio's Light Programme tackled all sorts of topics of general interest in some depth but in a popular way. There were programmes on 'Prisons', 'The English Sunday', 'Sugar', 'Apartheid', 'Pantomime', 'Superstition', and 'Hollywood'.

In 1952 Dennis Bardens told Cecil McGivern that he wanted to work on similar factual material in television. Unlike so many of his radio colleagues, Bardens was interested in what might be done in the new medium. Soon he got a call from Andrew Miller Jones, a staff producer looking for a new television project. Miller Jones, then in his mid-forties, had a reputation for programmes of a scientific bent – *Matters of Medicine, The Limits of Human Endurance* and so on. As Bardens describes him, Miller Jones was an upper-class army type: tall, dignified, with bowler hat, and dark suit: 'He never went anywhere; he arrived. Whenever he stepped from his yellow Rolls-Royce it was clear to everyone that something serious was afoot. And, since he was in the process of changing one wife for another at the time we worked together, he was somewhat tense.'

Through long sixteen-hour days, Bardens and Miller Jones began to shape their new programme, which by July 1953 they had defined for their bosses in the Television Talks department as:

> A magazine of informed comment on the contemporary scene. Emphasis would be on topicality and, above all, quality. The programme would be built around a central figure who, besides being a genial and acceptable personality, should be catholic in his interests and possess a lively and enquiring mind. He should be capable of talking to experts in many subjects on their own ground.[4]

Names under consideration at that time were Graham Hutton, an academic, Sir Gerald Barry, Editor of the *News Chronicle*, and Malcolm Muggeridge, Editor of *Punch*.

'Miller Jones wasn't much of a showman,' says Bardens, 'but I started with the idea of trying to catch people's attention: then, when you've done that, you tell them what you're going to talk about.'

What this new programme should be called had been a matter of considerable discussion. A long list of nearly a hundred titles was produced – none of which was in the event adopted. Since this was to be a fortnightly show there were variations on that theme – *14 Days Journal, 14 Days Review, Fortnightly Witness*. Other suggestions were *Eye on the World, You and the World, It's Happening Now, Eye Witness, Vista, Scope* and *Way of the World*. As the day of the week on which the programme would be transmitted became clear, *Wednesday's World* and *The World on Wednesday* were added. There were other titles one can only be glad were abandoned – *Filed for Reference, Longitude Zero* and, most exciting of all, *One Pace Back*. Some say it was Miller Jones's wife-to-be Daphne who thought of the title that was in the end chosen. But today Bardens insists it was he who eventually came up with the name that stuck: 'I was looking out of the huge window in my office on the fifth floor at Alexandra Palace and enjoying the view, this wonderful panorama spread out before me, when I suddenly thought "Bugger it,

Panorama, that's the title."' And so it was. Indeed, the early *Panorama*'s titles featured an evening panorama of the London skyline.

On 22 September 1953 a document marked 'Confidential' was circulated to interested parties. It was headed '*Panorama*: Preliminary lay-out for a 45-minute Talks Magazine, beginning October 29th., Edited and produced by Andrew Miller Jones. Research Editor: Dennis Bardens.' There was to be a 'Topic of the Fortnight (10–15 mins) providing background to news items, e.g. Publication of the Report of the Royal Commission on Divorce, Earthquakes, Kinsey, An Outbreak of Polio – or similar subjects (not primarily political except when a situation occurs unexpectedly and is of outstanding importance). This item will be illustrated with specially shot film, photographs and animations.'

The other elements were:

Criticism (10 mins), in which there would be reviews of current theatre, cinema, literature, art exhibitions and television programmes by regular critics 'supported by personalities'.

Personality of the Fortnight (5 mins), e.g. Chaplin, Orson Welles, Dior. Either someone in the news or likely to make news – e.g. Sir William Penney.

Under Fire (7 mins): Replies to criticism from viewers by appropriate experts.

In Westminster (5–10 mins): 'An account of the highlights of the fortnight in Parliament',

alternatively

Report from Abroad, when Parliament was not sitting: 'An account of the contemporary scene from regular correspondents in Europe, America or the Far East. Occasionally this would take the form of a transatlantic conversation recorded on film.'

Topical Caricature or Cartoon (3 mins): 'The precise format of this item is still under consideration. It may be either live (Ustinov) or with puppets and light verse (A.P. Herbert, John Arlott, Olga Katzin, Mikes, etc.)'.[5]

These proposals filled Cecil McGivern, Controller of Television Programmes, with misgiving. In an 'Urgent and Confidential' memo to Mary Adams, Head of Television Talks, he wrote: 'I am rather concerned by some aspects of the outline of *Panorama*.' McGivern was worried that the subjects suggested for Topic of the Fortnight were 'all on the grim and morbid side. This is a streak which does exist in Talks Department and I leave you to consider the reason – and the remedy.' On 'Criticism' he argued: 'Our relations with the theatre and the cinema are delicate and difficult . . . I feel it would be very bad diplomacy to include criticism in our programmes until times are more auspicious.' As for 'In Westminster', McGivern clearly thought that any comment on the politicians was asking for trouble. 'Is it wise to include this in a magazine programme, even a serious one?'

More perceptively he pointed to the rather 'talky', non-visual nature of the format:

> The lay-out is not exciting in any way and it does not indicate any new or bright ideas. It mentions 'visual presentation' but otherwise the emphasis is on verbal comment. The lay-out also gives me the feeling that, though thought has been given to the subject of a magazine in television, there just *are* no new ideas forthcoming and that the thing is tending to fall to pieces. We must be sure before we start this programme . . . that it is more than possible that it will grow soon to be a success.[6]

With the first transmission fast approaching, the Music department set about finding suitable title music. Kenneth Wright, Head of Music Programmes, Television, told one of his staff, John Carter, to choose something from the library, since there was no time to record anything original. On 12 October Carter wrote to *Panorama*'s Producer Miller Jones to say:

> I have been exploring a great many orchestral works by Rubbra, Ireland, Tippett, Nielsen, Nystroem, Prokofieff, Glasounov [sic], Jensen, Bartok etc and believe I have found you a fine theme for *Panorama*. It is the last movement from Carl Nielsen's 'Sinfonia Espansiva' . . . I would welcome the opportunity of playing this to you, together with some of the runners-up, when you are next at Lime Grove.[7]

That last phrase reveals a fundamental flaw in plans to get *Panorama* smoothly launched – the same flaw that more than 30 years later was to lead to a planned programme falling off the air. *Panorama* was being put together in more than one place. The initial planning, research and practical preparation had mostly gone on at Alexandra Palace.[8] Now, with only weeks to go before the first transmission, the production team was transferred to Lime Grove and installed in one of the little Victorian houses that had recently been acquired by the BBC just next to the old studio block. Here, Dennis Bardens remembers, he found himself working in the most primitive conditions, without even a phone. 'Television', he reflects today, 'is so stressful; radio is much more civilised.'

Perhaps fortunately, the transmission date for the first *Panorama* had now slipped a fortnight to 11 November, apparently to make way for the broadcast of a farewell concert given by Kirsten Flagstad.

And the big decision had been made. As 'The Scanners' column in the *Radio Times* of 6 November put it: 'The guide, mentor, compere, commentator and interviewer – unless we invent a new word there is no accurate way of describing his many functions which are peculiar to television – will be Patrick Murphy, journalist and author, who brings with him a wide knowledge of life and people.'

You could certainly say that. Murphy was one of the great newspaper characters of the time, a man who had roamed the world and talked to its leaders in what he always claimed were seven languages. As his friends remarked, he was endless in all of them. Before the Second World War Murphy had been friendly with Churchill, and, on his assignments to Berlin, was regularly ranted at by Hitler. He'd saved Albert Einstein from the Nazis by bringing him to Britain, and even claimed to have met Rasputin. This is how in 1987, just before his 90th birthday, he told that story to John Edwards of the *Daily Mail*:

> I was a student in Russia when I met Rasputin at the Czar's palace in Petrograd . . . He was smelly as an old donkey. He had ghastly eyes and a pointed head and a tremendous urge for sex. He used to like to go to bed with two young women, a young man and a black dog. I knew he fancied me to be the young man. He was always touching me. He said: 'Who art thou?' I said I was Murphy.

In his 'Teleview' of 27 October, headed 'They have found their chairman for the diversions of *Panorama*', Peter Black of the *Daily Mail* looked forward to seeing Murphy on the television screen:

> I mentioned earlier that TV was seeking a new type of chairman to lead viewers and visitors through this assortment of diversions. They wanted a man who could talk on any subject whatever, argue with experts without making an ass of himself, be interested in everything under the sun and have a towering personality which he could turn on or off at will like a hose.
>
> TV thinks it has found the man. I think so too, for I know him well. It is none other than Pat Murphy . . . Murphy is by way of being a legend in Fleet Street . . . He is, I suppose, one of the best, as well as one of the most tireless, talkers in London. I can vouch personally for his ability to get you to do or say things which, upon reflection, leave you bewildered, not to say aghast.
>
> I look forward to watching him with great enthusiasm.

Dennis Bardens remembers Murphy as 'tall and confident, with a loud voice and a wildly Irish accent'. But he was not impressed by Andrew Miller Jones's choice of the man to front the new programme: 'Much as I liked Murphy I could never have dreamed of him as *Panorama*'s presenter.' Stephen Bonarjee too had the gravest doubts: 'I warned him that Murphy was too fond of a drink to be reliable. But Miller Jones wanted a hard-nosed journalist because he was very conscious he wasn't one himself.'

The decision was made. Patrick Murphy was hired at a fee of 40 guineas for the first programme, and a rather intense and frowning picture of him appeared in the *Radio Times*. The billing read:

PANORAMA

A fortnightly reflection of the contemporary scene

YOUR GUIDE, PATRICK MURPHY

MATTERS OF MOMENT
Background to important news

WORTH NOTICE
Theatre: *Lionel Hale*
Books: *Marghanita Laski*
Art: *Denis Mathews*

UNDER FIRE
Experts answer your grievances

PERSONAL APPEARANCE
People in the news

AT RANDOM
Reflections by *Patrick Murphy*

STRIPTEASE
A telecartoon of passing events

Directed by Alan Bromly
Edited by Dennis Bardens
PRODUCED BY ANDREW MILLER JONES AT 8.15[9]

The programme had been given a budget of £613 a week, and some things at least had been properly prepared. The Hospitality cupboard was well stocked with whisky, gin, French vermouth, sherry, lager, light ale and a few soft drinks, and a buffet supper was ordered for the studio guests – plus Murphy and Miller Jones – before the programme went on air at 8.15pm.

The title music had finally been chosen – the entr'acte from Sibelius's suite *Pelleas and Melisande* – and props had been requisitioned. There were blocks of ice for an item on the fishing industry, quantities of 'nutty slack' for another about the poor quality of domestic coal, and a piano on which someone would play Noël Coward songs to illustrate the book review item.

But how were all these disparate items to be combined in a coherent television production? Unfortunately, neither Bardens nor Miller Jones was qualified as a studio director – the person who 'calls the shots' to the cameramen from the studio gallery during a live transmission. Alan Bromly, from BBC Drama, had been assigned to direct what was by any standard an extremely complicated magazine programme; but Bardens did not even meet him until the actual day of transmission.

Labour and birth

Technical rehearsals, due to begin at 8.30am in Studio E, started late. As Andrew Miller Jones later wrote reproachfully to the Head of Television Design: 'The set was not complete at the end of the overnight setting period, and the cord curtain which was needed for filming as from 9 o'clock was not delivered until after 9.30 and was not hoisted into position until nearly 10 o'clock.' There were numerous other items that either did not arrive on time or did not work even when they did: 'The hexagonal photograph display stand [which Pat Murphy would have to turn on air to trail upcoming items] arrived minus base. When this was ultimately produced, the display head was found to be unsteady owing to the fact that the resistance between it and the rather primitive bearing was too great for it to be turned easily . . . The bookcase lectern was too flimsy to carry the weight of a book, and was incorrectly hinged so that it swung about.'[10]

As the long day's rehearsal wore on everyone, Murphy especially, began to flag. 'It must have been as painful as a dentist's surgery to him,' says Dennis Bardens. This was Murphy's first time in a television studio. As Stephen Bonarjee points out: 'He had a variety of items to handle without any kind of prompter. So being on the ball was even more critical for him than it would be for a presenter now. Everything depended on his memorising his script.' It was clear even in rehearsal that it wasn't going to work. The only question was how bad it would be. 'In the studio gallery', Bonarjee recalls, 'there was a kind of deathly hush as the transmission time approached.'

To begin with, the programme seemed to go quite well. 'Tonight', said the off-screen announcer, 'we present the first edition of a new fortnightly magazine.' After titles and music Murphy appeared: 'Good evening. In *Panorama* we shall try, fortnight by fortnight, to give a picture of life as it goes by, reflecting the lighter side of life as well as more serious matters which affect us all. We begin tonight with 'Matters of Moment'.'[11] So far so good, and the item Murphy was introducing was in fact an extremely interesting one – 'brainwashing', and how it was done.

The papers had recently been full of stories about how British troops taken prisoner of war by North Korea had been brainwashed to endorse Communism. As the 'Glorious Gloucesters' came home from a gruelling captivity the *Daily Mirror* headline screamed: '250 of the freed British prisoners have gone Red'; *The Times* thundered: 'Indoctrinated war prisoners'. At around the same time, in the Soviet bloc, show trials were featuring accused who confessed with every appearance of conviction that they were traitors, or foreigners who said they had been spying for the West. Using his wartime contacts with the murkier side of the Foreign Office Bardens had got hold of Edgar Sanders, an alleged spy imprisoned in Hungary after a show trial in 1949, but released in August 1953 and now back in Britain. He would be interviewed in the studio by Murphy, while Dr William Sargant, an expert on the manipulation of the mind, would explain how brainwashing worked.[12]

Bardens had uncovered a BBC recording of Sanders's 'confession' at his trial, which had been broadcast by Budapest radio. The idea was that Murphy should play this tape in the studio to introduce the discussion. The playback machine, known as a 'Sound Mirror', was a massive mechanism weighing some 52lb., with a sort of joystick control which could be moved in any one of four different directions.

Inevitably, what could appropriately be called Murphy's Law took immediate effect. 'When the moment came to play the tape,' says Bardens, 'Murphy got into a technical panic and didn't know whether to turn the joystick north, south, east or west.' Murphy grasped the stick and pushed it firmly in the wrong direction. As the tape ran backwards, a ghastly noise assailed the ears of viewers at home and the production team in the studio gallery. 'Instead of a confession', says Bardens, 'we were deafened by Donald Duck squeaks.' Like a pilot struggling with the controls of some doomed airliner, *Panorama*'s first presenter had now started his dive towards disaster.

From time to time other subsidiary interviewers temporarily took the strain for Murphy.

Lionel Hale reviewed a current London production of *The Sleeping Prince*, starring Sir Laurence and Lady Olivier. Marghanita Laski did the book review spot: 'November sees many new books . . . ' and talked about the new *Noël Coward Song Book*. As 'the Master's' regular accompanist Norman Hackforth played some of the familiar tunes.

Then Murphy came out for another round as the programme's referee. In the 'grumble spot', 'Under Fire', he held the ring while an irate housewife attacked Sir Andrew Bryan of the National Coal Board for the poor quality of her coal, and Bryan blandly replied with extracts from an NCB public relations film.

In the 'Personal Appearance' spot George Dawson, a flamboyant millionaire who had made his fortune in war surplus goods, was to explain why he had now turned his attention to fish, which he was buying direct from Iceland. Over a picture of a large cod on its slab of ice in the studio Murphy began in a less than compelling way: 'Tonight we were going to ask along a man prominent in the news. Actually he couldn't come, so we interviewed him this morning.'

But the cataclysm came with the item 'At Random'. This was an attempt at a 'television essay', a series of thoughts on the theme of November, drafted by Bardens and given a final polish by Murphy himself. Murphy was to read this in the studio as an evocative commentary over appropriate silent film sequences. So, for example, as the screen showed pictures of 'winter ploughing and sowing' Murphy was intending to say something along the lines of: 'To the townee, ignorant, as so many townees are, of country life, November may seem the end of things; to the countryman it's the opening of the year.' Over 'lighted streets seen through fog, cars crawling' the script ran: 'To the city worker it means late trains, stumbling about with a torch on the way home, chesty coughs and sore eyes.'[13] But Murphy could no longer cope with the unfamiliar demands being loaded upon him as he strove to save this first *Panorama* from disaster: 'I can only hope the film we took will have arrived by now, because it was difficult to develop,' he began. Says Bardens: 'Still badly rattled by the fiasco of his first item, Murphy got utterly lost. So, as the film flowed on, what he was saying was completely out of synchronisation with the pictures.'

At last it was over. Murphy's pay-off to the programme was optimistic, but seemed to recognise that there might be room for improvement: 'We'll be on the air again in about fifteen days – in fact precisely fifteen days – the 25th of November. And till then I hope, like good wine, we mature.'[14] But *Panorama* No. 1 had crashed; it was indeed a shambles. Cecil McGivern immediately cancelled the next edition, taking the programme off the air for a month. 'We were a bit winded,' says Bardens, 'but there was no name-calling afterwards. After all, where would you start?'

Well, when in doubt, sack the presenter.

The critics, mostly his friends and colleagues, did their best to be kind. Lionel Hale, who – in the studio with him – had watched Murphy self-destruct, wrote in the *News Chronicle*:

> My old journalist friend, Mr Patrick Murphy, strode out in front of the television cameras last Wednesday night, full of blarney and old buck. Mr. Murphy, up and down the choirs and places where they sing in Fleet Street, is known to have the steely assurance of a battle-cruiser . . . After his programme *Panorama*, his Fleet Street colleagues, torn between loving personal loyalty and the truth, had ultimately to confess that the TV camera had robbed Mr. Murphy of some of his breeziness . . . I indignantly deny that Mr. Murphy had stage fright. He resembles rather the child Horatio Nelson who had to ask his mother what Fear was, 'because he had never seen it'. It was just that Mr. Murphy, pitch-forked for his first TV appearance into a programme full of complications, was rapt in delight at the miracles of modern science.
>
> The newcomer stands in the bustling studio, with cameras cruising to and fro like tanks in a desert, with films flashing on screens behind him, with men dragging mysterious cables across his feet, and with microphones dangling over his head like floats on fishing lines; and he thinks: 'All this wonderful paraphernalia for just my mother's son!'
>
> Of course next time the ebullient Mr Murphy, having lost this primal and innocent wonder, will be magnificent on TV . . .

But there was to be no next time.

When the audience research commissioned by the BBC came in it was unequivocal:

> Much of the viewers' adverse criticism was directed at Patrick Murphy, the guide to the programme. They found him uncomfortably nervous, hesitant and fidgetty [sic], but whether caused by lack of experience on TV, or insufficient rehearsal, or sheer incompetence they could not decide. The general impression he made was unfortunate however and many viewers said he was

a very poor guide. Indeed, remarked a Civil Servant, 'the occasion appeared to be too big for him, for instead of guiding, he himself had to be pushed along'.[15]

But this criticism was academic, for Murphy had already been told that *Panorama* would not require his services again. On 19 November he wrote a graceful and apologetic letter to *Panorama*'s Producer, Andrew Miller Jones:

My dear Andrew,

May I puff a little breeze of affection to expel from your heart the ache I clearly detected when you signalled, so honestly, the dropping of the Murphy pilot from *Panorama*. It is the right decision to make. I am sorry I did not rise above the conditions which circumstance created. To have done so would have helped you greatly. But I did not and no one could be more aware of it. Mea culpa, non tua.

The humility which failure induces in sanguine spirits like mine helps to bring truth into focus and who would not be grateful for that? . . .

Count upon me for any help I can ever give and all ideas Panoramic that come to my rag-bag brain I shall pass on to you swiftly. There is no faintness of heart here, just a feeling of guilt that I did not rise to the occasion for you . . .

God prosper your brave ways,
affectionately,
Pat.[16]

In an age when there was no alternative television channel, nearly half the adult viewing public had watched this first *Panorama*. But the reaction had been generally hostile – not just to poor Patrick Murphy, but to almost everything else about the programme. Analysis of the figures 'gives a Reaction Index of 48, an unimpressive figure. There has been no strictly comparable broadcast for which figures are available but it should be noted that the average for talks is 62 and for magazine programmes 67.[17]

'Although a majority considered the idea behind it a good one, viewers were, as the Reaction Index suggests, not at all satisfied with this programme. Even those who welcomed the concept wholeheartedly on the whole qualified their remarks with such phrases as "but it lacks polish", "but it needs pepping up" and "but there's much room for improvement".

Panorama's designer, Frederic Henrion, tactfully let some time go by before he told Miller Jones what he thought of the show, but on 23 November he wrote:

> I have been on this programme from the very beginning, and seen how very much thought and care you have put into its conception, into its development and into all the ingredients, and again into the careful blending of them. The script of the programme which was given to me at the time is ample proof of all this. It makes most impressive reading, but it did not to my mind make impressive viewing. This in my opinion was due to the absolute lack of any visual continuity. Obviously television must be primarily enjoyed and absorbed by the eye, and although there was much co-ordinating brainwork and literary ability and journalistic experience behind it, there was no evidence of a directing eye.[18]

It was very clear to those involved in producing that first *Panorama*, as well as to those watching it, that there was a great deal wrong. But amongst the criticism from viewers the Research department did find some hints of hope that there might be better things ahead:

> A substantial minority, however, undoubtedly think the programme has possibilities: its variety and topicality particularly appealed to them. 'This promises well for future viewing. We look forward to meeting many interesting people and to hearing more "Under Fire" discussions,' commented a commercial traveller's wife, one of the most enthusiastic.

Panorama survived – just – to reappear a month later on 9 December with a new, and much more experienced, 'guide' to help it find its way.

chapter two

⊕ # First faltering steps

Max Robertson was once described as 'every aunt's favourite nephew'. Then (and now, for he remains a man with the most charming manner), Max was an ideal *Panorama* guide – just as long as the path the programme followed was fit merely for a gentle, amusing and generally undemanding stroll.

As a young man Robertson had been a gold prospector in Papua New Guinea, suffering from vitamin deficiency and leeches in a fruitless search for fortune. He had worked in Australia as a radio announcer and commentator, and in 1939 had come to Britain to join the BBC's European Service. He was of the generation that the BBC expected to wear dinner jackets when reading the evening news after 6pm, and which had been taught to deliver every news item in the same tone of voice, whether it was the result of the Cup Final or the end of the world. But as a commentator on live events Robertson became adept at ad-libbing his contributions to match the action and fit the time allowed; and he was enterprising too. Covering the Winter Olympics for the BBC in 1948 he gave a running radio commentary as he hurtled down the terrifying bobsleigh run at St. Moritz.

Increasingly Robertson was asked to do commentaries for the Television Service's *Newsreel* programme at Alexandra Palace. As he recalls it, the pride and pleasure he might have taken in that were somewhat spoiled by the initials SNF against his name on the script – they stood for 'Staff, No Fee'. So Robertson went freelance. Just at the right moment he became available to a Television Talks Department desperate to find a reliable presenter for *Panorama*. As Stephen Bonarjee describes him, Max Robertson was 'the safest pair of hands you can imagine; a kind of neutral personality, who gave offence to nobody'.

Max well recalls *Panorama*'s disastrous start with the wretched Pat Murphy. 'Not only was he new to television, but he was trying to present, or introduce, as it was called in those days, a programme that had never been on the air before. Anyone watching that first hideous display might have laughed or wept, because not a single thing seemed to go right. It was chaos.' Now it was up to Robertson to help salvage the wreck, to pull *Panorama* off the rocks. 'Was I competent and knowledgeable enough to present a programme with a wide spectrum of the arts and world affairs? The answer was undoubtedly "no", if anybody had really thought about it. But desperate measures were needed and I was just becoming free, so I was hired.'[1] Max is modest about his ability to do the job: 'I was really just a link man who didn't think very much about what I was doing'. But he was blithe, insouciant, and confident enough in his ability to earn a living as an outside broadcast commentator not to worry unduly about the perils of presenting *Panorama*.

When the programme returned on 9 December 1953 it included Peter Ustinov talking about his play *No Sign of the Dove*, as well as the footballer Jimmy Hogan, 'the man who taught Hungary how to beat England at Wembley', who gave a demonstration of how to kick the ball in the studio. In the 'Under Fire' item Margaret Lovell complained to a company research manager about the way that nylons laddered all too easily, and in 'At Random' Sir Stephen Talents expanded on the theme of children's toys.

Viewers reported favourably on their new 'guide': 'The general impression he made was good, and many viewers said they much preferred him to Patrick Murphy who took charge of the first edition. Max Robertson was said to have been much clearer, as well as courteous and efficient, and to have given "at least some sense of unity" to the programme.'[2] But if Robertson was an improvement on Murphy as far as presentation went, *Panorama*'s content still failed to excite the audience:

'Although a majority of the viewers supplying evidence look upon the idea of creating a television magazine of opinion and information as having possibilities, there is a strong feeling that the programme will fail to make the grade unless it succeeds in shedding a good deal more of its initial stiffness and acquires some "pep"'. However, the Research Report's conclusion was just enough to keep *Panorama* afloat: 'From general comment it is clear that *Panorama* is still far from giving viewers in this sample just what they would like to see, but there were indications that the items in this edition had gone some way towards this end.'

Attempts were made to liven things up in the next edition just before Christmas with an item about the circus. But Robertson was shaken and the programme thrown into some confusion when Blondie, a performing elephant, anticipated her cue and came bursting out of the Lime Grove scenery lift into the studio, her trunk alarmingly aloft.[3]

It wasn't just the viewers who were dissatisfied with *Panorama*. Producer Andrew Miller Jones had sent Cecil McGivern, Controller of Television Programmes, a memo listing what would be in the programme scheduled for 6 January 1954: 'Mrs Ada Austin will complain about laundries, and Mr Harold Paine, President of the Institute of British Launderers, will reply . . . Mrs Dona Salmon will talk about Twelfth Night customs, and show a number of Christmas cards . . . Lady Helen Nutting will talk about wages for wives,' and so on. Back came the memo with a curt and angry note from McGivern typed at the bottom: 'The above is a fast progression (in the 3rd *Panorama*) towards a minority – a <u>distinctly</u> Minority programme. If it remains like this it will die. Before it dies, I will take it out of schedules.'[4] Dennis Bardens insists that he was always keen that 'the viewers should have something to bite on; not too bland. I was against intellectual pap.' But the early *Panorama*, under Miller Jones and Bardens, was more often whimsical than weighty, a rather lightweight miscellany; as Max Robertson describes it, 'it was a bran tub from which any surprise could be pulled'. But as yet this lucky dip of a programme satisfied nobody.

On 1 January 1954 a new Head of Television Talks, Leonard Miall, took over at Lime Grove. He was told by McGivern that if *Panorama* were to continue it must be 'put on a better basis'. 'It was', Miall says, 'a rag-bag. There was nobody properly in charge'. It was fine to order Miall to do something about *Panorama*, but not so easy to prescribe the remedy: 'This programme could be improved, but it is difficult to say how,' was the way one viewer summed up the difficulty. There were problems of every kind, to do with practical matters as well as content. The first programme of the New Year overran by no less than 11 minutes. Erich von Stroheim, the great Hollywood director and actor, had threatened to walk off the set if his interview was restricted to the four minutes allotted to it. And as for the Russian dancers in the studio, it was apologetically reported after the programme that 'they could not be constrained'.

On 24 January 1955 Maurice Wiggin in the *Sunday Times* wrote:

> *Panorama* is a perfect illustration of what is wrong with television. I make no apology for returning to it: the BBC make no apology (to put it mildly) for persisting in it. Just look what happened last week.
>
>   Mr Max Robertson appeared and blandly reminded us what a daringly controversial argument we had heard last time, when someone had the effrontery to say a hard word about laundries. He promised us equally stirring arguments this time. Then, for a few minutes two men argued inconclusively about amateurism in sport. [It was Harold Abrahams, the only man ever to have won the 100 metres Olympic gold medal for Britain, and sporting columnist Peter Wilson.] . . . Finally, Mr Robertson produced stopwatch, bell and gong and timed a pair of speakers, as if he were timing an egg, through a few minutes of ancient argument about the sex appeal of English women. Mr Robertson then told us, almost in as many words, that we had been privileged to hear such hard-hitting stuff, and bade us *au revoir*.

It was not all trivia and froth: there were some worthwhile items such as the discussion of the 11+ exam, and its alleged unfairness, with the education expert John Newsom; or (at a time when a third of the country's homes still had no bathrooms) an item on housing improvements. And the resources available to the programme makers were fast increasing. The episode on 17 February, for example, included a demonstration of the BBC's Roving Eye, a mobile outside broadcast unit transmitting pictures, and an excited commentary from Peter Dimmock, as it drove down Piccadilly and on to Leicester Square.

Early in February 1954 George Barnes, the Director of Television Broadcasting, had urged Leonard Miall to feature more controversy in his programmes: 'The Corporation's tackling of current controversy tends to be restricted by over-conscientiousness in regard to our role of objectivity and impartiality, but controversy is a fact and can itself be treated objectively.' Calling for a greater use of sound film Barnes went on: 'If it is said that this would be too expensive, I can only reply that film stock is the cheapest of our resources and that it is up to you and Film department to devise a really efficient team instead of taking around a circus.'[5] But the problem here was not so much the size of the film crew as simply the availability of equipment. At that time *Panorama* could never count on getting use of a sound camera at all. 'Under these circumstances', Miall's deputy reported to him, 'it seems difficult to offer topical programmes of the kind that D.B.Tel. requires.' One of Miall's proudest achievements was eventually to get *Panorama* the permanent use of a 35mm sound camera.

In April 1954 Dennis Bardens's six-month contract was not renewed. He went off to work first for the Foreign Office and then, after it began in 1955, for ITV. He became a prolific author. But he has rightly remained proud of his pioneering work as *Panorama*'s first Editor. It should be said that the title 'Editor' did not then mean what it does now – the person in overall charge, who was then called the Producer. But Bardens *was* primarily responsible for finding the programme material, and when his successor Michael Barsley claimed in a book published by the BBC some years later that he was the first *Panorama* Editor, Bardens successfully sued for libel. In 1976 he received damages and his costs, and a clear public acknowledgement that he, and not Barsley, had been 'the first Editor of *Panorama*.'[6]

Barsley was a good ideas man who quickly made a mark with the first *Panorama* special, a programme devoted to one subject. 'Every other item was thrown out or shelved, and we got to work on the tricky job of blending popular exposition with expressions of moral, military, political and religious opinion.'[7] On 13 April 1954 Max Robertson's introduction ran: 'For this edition of *Panorama* we've taken the unusual step of devoting the whole programme to something which (I think you'll agree) is both the topic of the day and perhaps the question of the century – the Hydrogen bomb.' There was film of the first H-bomb test at Eniwetok in November 1952, and a distinguished panel filled the studio. The Archbishop of York, Dr Cyril Garbett, had taken time out of his Holy Week duties and made a round trip of 400 miles to be there; Bertrand Russell represented CND and the Ban the Bomb campaign; Sir John Slessor, retired Marshall of the Royal Air Force, put the conventional military man's point of view; Colonel Walter Elliott and John Strachey were the senior Tory and Labour spokesmen; and Professor Joseph Rotblat, who had worked on the original nuclear weapons programme in America, explained how the H-bomb worked. Following the bomb's fourth test a month before, Robertson gave the reactions of foreign countries, over stills of their leaders, and introduced film of President Eisenhower speaking about America's possession of this new and terrible weapon.

In discussion, Slessor argued that the development of the H-bomb meant the end of world war: 'So long as both sides have them I don't believe either side will force a war. If by an evil chance they were abolished, then I should certainly regard World War III as a certainty within five years.' Lord Russell wanted to persuade the Great Powers, the USA and the USSR, of the evils of war. Wrote Barsley: 'His plume of white hair seemed to shine as brightly as the mushroom cloud of the H-bomb itself.' The Archbishop did not support unilateral disarmament but said that 'deterrence through fear alone is a frail defence against the lunacy of a dictator or the wickedness of a nation obsessed with hatred or blinded by panic'. A conference of the Great Powers was called for, and Robertson summed up (somewhat patronisingly): 'You've heard the views of eminent men on the greatest question of our time. We hope you have learned something from the scientific explanation that went before it.' *Panorama* was beginning to stake a claim to high seriousness. Important people were now prepared to appear on the programme; it was becoming the place to be seen.

On 26 May, following his London Crusade, the American evangelist Billy Graham was interviewed by Malcolm Muggeridge: 'His enquiries were searching, and Billy Graham – taut, nervous, finely-chiselled in face – gave back as good as he got.'[8] This exchange was regarded as a great success, and in June the BBC's Programme Board discussed the possibility of using Muggeridge as a regular *Panorama* interviewer: 'Feelings were divided about his manner and voice', but it was generally agreed that he would be 'a very successful personality'.[9] So Muggeridge was recruited.

The Billy Graham programme also included a live studio item in which a Southend dentist, using hypnosis rather than anaesthetic, extracted a tooth from a young lady called Sylvia Langley. As she assured Robertson afterwards, she 'didn't feel a thing'. A stage hypnotist threatened legal action on the plausible grounds that the BBC had broken the ban on hypnotism as a public entertainment, but after a chat with *Panorama* the police took no further action. In that same edition Dilys Powell reviewed the brilliantly effective French film *The Wages of Fear*, which had just won first prize at the Cannes Film Festival, and Sir Compton Mackenzie interviewed Dame Sybil Thorndyke, celebrating her fifty years in the theatre. These all sound excellent individual items – they illustrate the enormous range of the early *Panorama*. But what an extraordinary mix; and how difficult to define what kind of programme *Panorama* actually was!

Certainly, foreign items were not often seen on *Panorama*. Wrote Barsley: 'Compiling it on a shoestring basis, we could never afford to fly showgirls over from Paris or Miss [Gracie] Fields from Capri or get a Eurovision link. We could very rarely send cameramen abroad to follow up on a story on which we had an exclusive lead, but on one remarkable occasion luck was with us.'[10] Siamese twins had been born in Britain. In Holland an operation had just been carried out to separate a similar pair. Showing considerable enterprise Barsley flew over, hired a local camera crew, filmed the doctor who had carried out the operation in a demonstration of how he'd done it, and then talked his way into the ward to film the separated twins. The hospital, an austere Protestant institution, had previously refused $1,000 from an American news agency for similar access. Such was the BBC's reputation (if not yet *Panorama*'s) that the hospital charged Barsley nothing for his scoop.

Reviewing the first complete *Panorama* season in the autumn of 1954, and looking forward to the next, Barsley wrote:

> Max Robertson will continue to guide the viewer through the programme – a tricky job when the subjects and material are so varied. Malcolm Muggeridge (who, if there were ever a *Panorama* pantomime, might play the Demon King to Max's Prince Charming) will have a single item to himself each time. His first appearance on *Panorama*, when he was confronted with Billy Graham, revealed the sort of 'Enquiring Layman' mind which can tackle famous personalities, without fear or favour.[11]

Panorama was beginning to establish itself as a feature of the television landscape. On 5 August, as the season ended, Leonard Miall, Head of Television Talks, wrote to Andrew Miller Jones:

> I agree with Peter Black's view in today's *Daily Mail* that '*Panorama* has won its place as a responsible Television Magazine.' Now that the current series has come to an end I would like to congratulate you, and all the team working regularly with you, on a really solid achievement. When I arrived here, *Panorama* was a despairing headache. It is now an excellent Television property. We shall miss it during its rest.[12]

Miller Jones replied thanking Miall for his kind words, but adding: 'I should cavil slightly at one thing – namely, I disagree that *Panorama* was "a despairing headache" when you arrived. The audience reaction indices show it was on the up as early as the beginning of February!' He continued:

> I hope that the second edition will come a little nearer to the original blue-print for the programme. This of course depends on a good and reliable central figure. If one is not forthcoming, it might be worth while to consider having regular contributors to particular sections of the programme, and thus achieve some sort of editorial responsibility and continuity, without losing the very efficient Max Robertson.[13]

A difficult toddler

In the event, when the new *Panorama* season began, Michael Barsley had taken over as Producer, and Andrew Miller Jones had left the hurly-burly of Lime Grove for the academic calm of Manchester University, given a year's leave of absence to write a thesis on 'the psychological impact of visual stimuli'. He did not return.

Panorama was not yet safe. The first edition of the new season, on Wednesday 20 October 1954, 'was far from giving viewers just what they wanted to see of topical moment and interest'.[14] When the programme majored on sculptural finds at a Mithraic temple site and a discussion of National Savings, one can understand why those viewers found it 'stodgy' and 'boring'. The next day Leonard Miall wrote in head-masterly admonition to Barsley:

I never hesitated to give critical comments on *Panorama* to Andrew. I propose to do the same to you ... *Panorama* had, in my view, only what could most generously be described as a moderate success as it started up again ... the zoetrope was a total failure ... the cartoon item was a flop ... the modern Bachus item did not, I think, come off . . . the Muggeridge/Mackintosh interview was badly produced.

Miall could find only two things worthy of praise. First, the programme had actually ended on time; second, the team deserved congratulations on choosing significant subjects (in his view, at least), however badly they had been done. 'Don't be distressed unduly by this criticism,' Miall concluded, perhaps worried he might utterly destroy the new Producer's confidence; '*Panorama*, after a bad start, reached a high level when it was rested for the summer. We must get back to that level as fast as possible.'[15]

Over the following months Miall's priority remained the improvement of *Panorama*. It had now become a regular feature of the schedule, but what kind of programme was it, and how should it develop? It was the failure of another BBC department that left room for *Panorama* to grow, and flourish.

chapter three
⊕ # Finding a role

Leonard Miall had become Head of Television Talks at the beginning of January 1954. He had previously worked in the BBC's European Service and, during the 'hostilities', had been in the Political Warfare Executive. Later he'd gone as special correspondent to Czechoslovakia, and then, after the War, become the BBC's Washington correspondent. When he arrived at Lime Grove he knew nothing about making television programmes, but he'd seen plenty of them in the States. An experienced journalist, he was interested in giving people news about the important things that were happening in the world.

Unfortunately, BBC television was not.

The BBC's overall Head of News at that time was the improbably named Tahu Hole, a New Zealander brought up in Australia. Very tall, with a bloodhound face and an aloof sort of dignity, Hole ruled his news empire (which Hugh Carleton Greene, the future Director General, called 'the Kremlin of the BBC') with a brooding gravity. He saw himself as the custodian of the Corporation's wartime reputation for accuracy and impartiality. 'Determined that this reputation should remain inviolate he followed a line of hyper-caution. The bulletins under his directions became colourless, long-winded and dull. Editors seethed with frustration.'[1]

When he was in America, Leonard Miall remembers, his eyewitness report of a major story – the announcement of the Marshall Plan for the rebuilding of post-war Europe – had been 'spiked' by Tahu Hole. BBC reporters were actually told *not* to file exclusive stories, for they would not be used. Were BBC men stupid enough to be the first with the news their only hope of getting it on air was to give it to one, or preferably two, news agencies. Only when the agency teleprinters had chattered out the story in the BBC newsroom would Tahu Hole and his team be prepared to listen to 'our own correspondent'.

Hole's motto was, quite simply: 'When in doubt, leave out.' As an admonition not to embellish a story with detail that cannot be substantiated, that is no bad injunction. To apply it to the BBC's entire news service was stultifying. And if there was anything Tahu Hole was more opposed to than BBC correspondents bringing him their own news stories, it was the idea that news on television should have anything visual about it.

On BBC television news bulletins nothing moved. The news was received and edited in central London, in a building opposite Broadcasting House; then newscasters such as Robert Dougall, Richard Baker and Kenneth Kendall would be driven all the way to Alexandra Palace where they would read their bulletins in a television studio. But they would not be in vision, nor would they be identified. The cult of personality was not to sully the news. All that television was then allowed to add to a radio broadcast were a clock, a few tedious captions and some still photographs. 'Don't let anybody tell you, Mr Wheeler, that stills don't make good television,' was what Hole told the young David Wheeler, soon to join *Panorama* as a producer. BBC News was, as the *Star* newspaper described it in 1954, 'about as impressive visually as the fatstock prices'. Not until 4 September 1955, three weeks before ITV began, were BBC newscasters actually seen by viewers. Even then, though they were familiar faces, often written about in the press, they were still not named on air.

The BBC's attitude to television was dismissive: 'Television won't matter, in your lifetime or mine,' a pre-war Editor of the *Listener* had said to one of his reviewers,[2] and in the early 1950s it still didn't matter much. In the Corporation the Word was god. BBC bosses brought up in the tradition of Lord Reith were wizards with words: indeed there was a Director of the Spoken Word. They knew nothing of television, and despised it.[3] To them television was about pantomime horses and chorus girls; much more a medium of entertainment – light entertainment – than of information and education. It was therefore not surprising that what television still lacked was any sense of being important. And as a source of news it carried no authority. At Alexandra Palace attempts to fill this vacuum were 'disdainfully permitted'[4] by the then BBC Director General Sir William Haley.

Out of the darkness

A.A. 'Tubby' Englander (later to be the lighting cameraman on Lord Clark's great BBC series *Civilisation*) joined *Newsreel*, produced by the BBC Film Department under Philip Dorté. The two men had known each other at Gaumont British before the War. So now, when an American company he had been shooting for in Britain went bust, leaving him his camera equipment in lieu of the money it owed him, Englander found himself one of half a dozen cameramen on television's *Newsreel*. Each of them normally worked as a 'one-man band', dispatched with a subject and the name of a contact to go and get a story.

Often these stories were shot silent – indeed, Englander remembers only one sound camera in the *Newsreel* unit, though there may have been more. Back at Alexandra Palace writer–producers like Paul Fox and David Wheeler (both later to be Editors of *Panorama*) would view the rushes, knock out a running-order, write a commentary, see the story cut and dubbed and get it into the next *Newsreel*.

By 1952, in the absence of any decent news programme, there were five *Newsreel* transmissions a week, plus a weekend edition. But they were made up mostly of feature stories. Occasionally there was some real reporting – of the Korean War for example – which put *Newsreel* in a different category from the cinema's *Look at Life*; but that was the exception.

Dorté, backed by Television's Controller of Programmes Cecil McGivern, decided that there must be more real news in *Newsreel*. Eventually, in 1954, he won his case, but it was a Pyrrhic victory: control of the news content within *Newsreel* was given to Tahu Hole. If he could help it, Television News would not be allowed to develop its own way of telling viewers – in sound and vision – what was happening in the world.

And so it was left to Television Talks to do the job instead. At that Appointments Board just before Christmas 1953 when Leonard Miall had been chosen to head the department there had been another contender, a woman. Shortly after *Panorama* first staggered incoherently on to the screen, and Miall got the top job, she became Assistant to the Head of Television Talks – in BBC parlance A.H.T.Tel. Her name was Grace Wyndham Goldie.

Miall's predecessor Mary Adams had disliked and distrusted Wyndham Goldie. To stop her having anything to do with the beginning of *Panorama* in 1953 she had sent her abroad on a tour of American broadcasters. But now Wyndham Goldie was back at Lime Grove, and after its desperately shaky start *Panorama* had improved. By 1955 the option of axing the programme had been abandoned; instead it was now to be transformed, and Leonard Miall gave Grace Wyndham Goldie the job.

Into the light

This is how Sir Geoffrey Cox (in 1955 about to become Editor of ITN) puts it:

> Chance had thrown up, in the person of Grace Wyndham Goldie, a character quite as strong as Tahu Hole, and one who not only saw the wide horizons stretching ahead of television journalism but had the drive and talent to move towards them. In her role as Talks producer she moved swiftly and confidently into the no man's land between current affairs and news which the BBC News division was leaving unoccupied, until she gathered for the Television Service areas of analysis and interpretation that in radio as well as newspapers were seen as the province of those engaged in the daily coverage of hard news.[5]

Before the War Wyndham Goldie had been television critic for the *Listener*, and in 1936 had seen the first television transmission go out from Studio A in Alexandra Palace. She had joined the BBC staff in 1944, when her predecessor in Radio Talks, Guy Burgess, later revealed to be a Soviet spy, managed to get himself transferred to the Foreign Office.[6] In 1948 she became a television producer – one of the few able people ready to take radio's poor relation seriously – and started to show what the medium might be capable of doing.

At Alexandra Palace in the early 1950s Wyndham Goldie had made some pioneering programmes about the contemporary world. Her series *Foreign*

Correspondent used experienced and authoritative journalists like Chester Wilmot to go and find out how people in other countries lived, for the benefit of British viewers. 'Tubby' Englander travelled with Wilmot to Indo-China, for example, to look at the advance of Communism there. While Englander returned to London with the rushes, Wilmot flew on to Australia, only to die when the Comet he was in crashed as a result of catastrophic metal fatigue.

For other series, *Viewfinder* for example, Wyndham Goldie hired rising young politicians, including former junior ministers Christopher Mayhew, John Freeman and Aidan Crawley, to go abroad and report on what they found – 'illustrated reports on world affairs', they were called. She wanted to move away from the style of *Newsreel*, where commentaries were normally written back at base to fit material produced by other hands. Grace later described[7] how concerned she had been to discover film shot for one particular story turning up in another to illustrate something completely different – shots of some sleazy nightclub in Prague had later been used to illustrate a story about attractive weekends in Paris. She wanted to do better than that. And now she did.

chapter four

⊕ Bumble and the whim of iron

At Alexandra Palace Grace Wyndham Goldie had discovered some able young reporters. Now in her new management role at Lime Grove, she recruited an even younger group of people – reporters and potential presenters like Geoffrey Johnson Smith, and producers like James Bredin and Michael Peacock. Wyndham Goldie and Peacock worked together on the first television results programme following the 1955 General Election, and when that was over they began planning a brand-new *Panorama*.

It was soon clear that *Panorama*'s transformation scene from fortnightly miscellany to weekly current affairs programme would bring a final curtain for Prince Charming as its leading man.

Max Robertson, the debonair presenter of the current *Panorama*, quickly discovered that, as he puts it, 'Grace had a whim of iron'. He realised that, for him, the game was up. Ruefully he wrote: 'Not much could be done, or preferment won, except by the grace of Goldie.' Grace was not for him; she was determined on radical change with her own protégés: 'I had already been discovered,' wrote Max, 'nor had I the new liberal, anarchic, searching mind that would appeal to her. The new *Panorama* was to be more "significant", a favourite word with Grace. It would deal with important topics of the day.'[1]

So Max, until this moment the programme's regular 'guide', would be demoted to a lightweight interview spot – for example, talking to children at Christmas time while dressed in a Santa Claus outfit. 'And what do you want?' said Max kindly to the little girl perched on his knee. 'I want a doll that wees,' she loudly responded.

Michael Barsley too disappeared through the television pantomime trap-door to clear the stage for this new, more serious, *Panorama* production. During the programme's last run, in April 1955, John Betjeman had been allowed to review a book which Barsley himself had edited. Leonard Miall had been furious: 'This seems to be a most unethical abuse of your position as Editor of *Panorama*.' And there had been complaints that Barsley was sloppy with studio rehearsals: they took much longer than they should have done – and therefore cost a good deal more. 'He does a good deal of planning on the floor' had been the acid comment. Barsley, recalls Robertson, 'had a good journalistic flair, but a terrible incapacity to make up his mind; he always waited until the last possible minute to do so. It was nerve-wracking'. Fundamentally, it was Barsley's rather whimsical temperament that made him ill-suited to a programme which was now, week after week, to include serious items on what was happening in the world. And so he left the stage.

Panorama's first producer, Andrew Miller Jones, had (perhaps unwisely) taken a year off to write his academic treatise. Grace Wyndham Goldie had no difficulty in installing her own protégé, Michael Peacock, to run the programme in his place.

On 3 June 1955 Wyndham Goldie wrote a confidential memo to Miall: 'We think an attempt should be made to start a one-hour weekly *Panorama* in September. I will as agreed, be responsible. Michael Peacock will produce.'[2] There followed lists of staff and facilities required.

He might have wanted to improve the programme, but Miall was obviously nervous at the prospect of 'revving up' *Panorama* in this ambitious way. On 22 June Wyndham Goldie wrote again to her worried boss in tones of exasperation:

> You asked me whether I was 'quite happy' about this. I can only say that it is quite impossible to be 'quite happy' about so difficult a project at this stage. If the only conditions on which I think it can even be undertaken can be

fulfilled, I think it will still be a risk, but a risk worth taking. The conditions without which I do not think we should attempt the programme at all are those which I outlined in my memorandum of June 3rd.

These conditions included Michael Peacock and Richard Cawston as joint Producers (it was intended that Cawston would mostly look after the film items); two production assistants and one research assistant; two cameramen and two film editors with assistants; plus secretaries and graphics/design people as required.

At the end of her memo, almost as a throwaway line, Wyndham Goldie added a paragraph that was to prove more important in this new chapter in *Panorama*'s history than any other: 'With these facilities, and with an agreement that the staff working on the programme should be really full-time and not diverted to any other projects, however urgent, I think we should get Richard Dimbleby to be the "anchor man" and that we should be able to turn out an important programme.'[3] She was right on both counts, and her first proposal led to the second. Hiring Dimbleby made *Panorama* for the first time both popular *and* important.

Dimbleby was already broadcasting's heavyweight hero. Two years before, in June 1953, it was he who had finally demonstrated the dominance of television over radio with the BBC's outside broadcast of the Coronation. In every region but one viewers outnumbered listeners. Fifty-six per cent of the adult population, more than 20 million people, watched the ceremony in Westminster Abbey and listened to Dimbleby's authoritative and moving commentary. As many at the time remarked, it seemed that Dimbleby, rather than the Archbishop of Canterbury who conducted the ceremony, was in charge of the occasion. Now in the summer of 1955 he was fresh from a masterly performance in the studio as presenter of the BBC's first General Election results programme on television.

Dimbleby had joined the BBC in 1936 as a Topical Talks assistant – in radio of course. From the start he had had ideas on how to improve the way the News was delivered. In his first job application he had written: 'It would be possible to enliven the News to some extent without spoiling the authoritative tone for which it is famed . . . I really believe that News could be presented in a gripping manner, and at the same time remain authentic.'[4]

Nicknamed 'Bumble' because he was fat and buzzed with ideas,

Dimbleby pioneered the first-hand radio reporting that banished the BBC's Olympian tone of detachment. He became the first reporter to be named in a BBC bulletin – 'our observer, Richard Dimbleby'. During the War he had made an impact not just because of his reports but because it was he who was making them. He had already become something of a story in himself. His successor with Middle East Command in Cairo, Godfrey Talbot, remarked tartly: 'I was a journalist succeeding a personality.' Some of his future *Panorama* colleagues were also to have reservations about Dimbleby the journalist, but there was no doubt that he gave weight and importance to whatever story he covered. His biographer, his son Jonathan, concedes that Richard Dimbleby was at times 'without sophistication and even naïve . . . but he broadcast with such authority (more in the manner of a statesman than a reporter) and he alighted with such unerring instinct on the right tone, that he evoked a response in the listener of much greater intensity than the bare words might have deserved'.

In his ten years on *Panorama* Richard Dimbleby's essential role was to be the solid presence in the studio. He was that calm authority at the centre of the whirlwinds of the world which the programme's correspondents would ride so dashingly. The reports that they sent back Dimbleby presented to the viewers. Although he liked nothing better than introducing a programme in an outside broadcast from some location far from Lime Grove – whether at home or abroad – it is as *Panorama*'s studio presenter that he is best remembered. But it was surely because he had so much experience in the front line of life that he was so good back at base, briefing the viewers on what was going on 'out there'.

As a war correspondent Dimbleby had often flown with Bomber Command on their desperately dangerous raids over Germany. Former *Panorama* reporter Michael Charlton remembers Dimbleby describing to him ruefully how, after an all-night raid on Berlin, he had landed at an RAF bomber base and then travelled back to London by train, slumped in his seat, dishevelled and utterly exhausted. A woman passenger had snorted disapprovingly: 'I do think you might get up, young man, with all those poor men in uniform having to stand in the corridor.'

As a journalist Dimbleby had had a 'good war'– most memorably as the first correspondent to enter the Belsen concentration camp and describe to a horrified world the truth of what had happened there. But it didn't at first advance his civilian broadcasting career. With the end of the fighting the BBC reverted to its pre-war editorial posture – prone – in which news agency reports were absurdly and humiliatingly preferred to those of its own correspondents. Frustrated, Dimbleby resigned from his staff job with News. In the War, his reporting had had a positively Churchillian quality to it. Now in the peace, like Churchill, he felt rejected, his achievements and talents undervalued.

As a freelance Dimbleby soon made a great success for himself in radio and television programmes which were essentially entertainment – *Twenty Questions*, *About Britain*, *At Home* and *Down Your Way*. His presentation was easy, his interviewing deft (if sometimes too deferential), and, as television began to spread across Britain, he became a national celebrity. Jonathan Dimbleby describes how 'in one northern town, where television had newly arrived, a woman stopped him and said: "Mr Dimbleby, do you mind, I just want to say I have touched your coat."'

But, though he enjoyed his starry celebrity status, Richard Dimbleby was much more than an entertainer. In 1950 he had written to Philip Dorté, who was producing *Newsreel* – the nearest thing to a television news that then existed. Dimbleby was looking far ahead, further even than straightforward 'news'. To Dorté he explained his concept of 'current news', as distinct from what was either 'immediate' or 'permanent'. He argued that such programming would include those events which were either not dramatic enough for inclusion in a news bulletin, or which started as 'immediate' news but were worthy of treatment in greater depth. And he identified what would become the essence of the typical *Panorama* package of the future:

A well-known observer, accepted by the viewer, should be the central figure of each report . . . It is an on-the-spot investigation, presented as a connected whole . . . It must come back to the studio complete and ready, but for the trimming. Most important of all, the observer must lead, point and explain throughout. He is guiding the viewer's eye in his capacity as a trained newsman; he is NOT a commentator talking to suit the requirements of a cut and tailored picture. I believe that this scheme . . . offers something that television does not yet have – a regular, authoritative report on news of common interest in which the viewers can be made to feel that they have gone out from their firesides to see and hear for themselves.[5]

Dorté's response to this brilliantly far-sighted note was enthusiastic, and Cecil McGivern, the Controller of Television, liked it too; but for the moment nothing further came of it. The Television Service had neither the resources nor the necessary clout within the Corporation to develop such an ambitious idea. Indeed it was not until July 1955 that the BBC, realising that ITN would shortly be on the air with news programmes for the new ITV, grudgingly set up its own Television News department.

By then, down at Lime Grove, Grace Wyndham Goldie and the young Michael Peacock had discovered for themselves Dimbleby's worth as a studio presenter of 'current news'. As the main presenter of the first ever BBC television results programme, following the 1955 General Election, Dimbleby had done an excellent job, demonstrating his mastery of all the skills required to present a complicated live television programme. On 2 June Wyndham Goldie wrote to him: 'I was more delighted than I can say by your unfailing good humour in circumstances that were often, I know, very trying, and the confidence which your combination of profession-alism and ease gave to us all . . . It is pleasant to go around and see beaming faces and be stopped in the corridors by engineers and studio hands and hear "it was a jolly good show" . . . I hope we may work together again some day.'[6]

Peacock wrote in the same strain: 'The letters are still pouring in congratulating you and the rest of us on the success of the programme . . . Grace and I could never have done the programme without you.'[7] There was no question in their minds: in Richard Dimbleby they had found the man to present the revamped *Panorama* they were planning. And when Dimbleby received their invitation he accepted with alacrity.

By 4 July Wyndham Goldie could write to Peacock to say: 'He is prepared, given an adequate contract and other arrangements, to be the "Anchor Man" for the new *Panorama* programme starting on September 19th. This will mean his being available each Monday all day, for rehearsal and transmission. He would also arrange to be available every Friday afternoon for an editorial conference.'[8]

Panorama's joint Producer Richard Cawston had Dimbleby in his proposed programme budget at £100 a week. Wyndham Goldie wrote to Bookings that she would prefer to pay him 75 guineas 'but I don't want to lose him. As with the Election, he is a key figure in this forthcoming important news service'. In the event they got their new presenter for 80 guineas[9] a programme, plus extra fees if he was also required for film reports.

Like Dimbleby, Grace Wyndham Goldie too had seen the future, had seen television moving towards 'something quite new, for which no name has yet been found; whose form is only just beginning to emerge; which has to be shaped; to be invented; to be created; and which is going to be of the greatest importance'. The keel of current affairs television in Britain was being laid, with Wyndham Goldie as chief naval architect.

chapter five

The window on the world

Fitting out a flagship

Working with Grace Wyndham Goldie, said Huw Wheldon later, was 'both a nightmare and a pleasure'. That was a common experience. As the man who had beaten Wyndham Goldie to the Head of Talks job Leonard Miall was never going to find it easy to manage this defeated rival, who was 14 years older than he was. She was, as Miall readily admits, 'the deputy from hell'.

Margaret Douglas, later Chief Assistant to the Director General, was then *Panorama*'s secretary. She recalls typing memo after memo – salvo after salvo – in 'a huge turf war' between Wyndham Goldie and Miall. Says Miall: 'Grace had to be totally in charge of whatever activity she was engaged in, which did not make her a natural deputy.' His solution, he says, was to give her responsibility for launching new projects and programmes – such as *Panorama* – but then move her on before she became bogged down in day-to-day management.

Grace Wyndham Goldie was indeed formidable. As Ian Trethowan, political interviewer and future BBC Director General, later wrote: 'Her sharp tongue and angry snapping eyes were feared and disliked by newer and more junior members of her staff, but the older hands held her in deep respect, even awe.'[1] Wyndham Goldie told the team of young producers and reporters she was recruiting: 'If you don't dream about television every night you're no use to me.' What appealed to Alasdair Milne, another future Director General, was her sharp, rigorous mind: 'In whose name are we making this programme?' she would demand fiercely. She wanted everyone working at Lime Grove to recognise the responsibility they had to the viewer to make the best television they could.

Not everyone was an out-and-out fan. John Grist, later to run what became the Television Current Affairs Group, arrived in 1957, when Wyndham Goldie's glory days as the inspiration of the new *Panorama* and then *Tonight* were nearly over. 'She was a formidable and dynamic woman, but not truly likeable' wrote Grist:

> She carried an aura, and senior men shuffled their papers when she came into a meeting and moved their bottoms in their chairs when she interjected some comment, looking uneasy. She talked very well and laughed a lot with her young men. She was immensely proud of 'her boys' and would defend them against all comers, but would box their ears, figuratively, and glare in a steely way. I confess I did not like her, but, like everyone else except perhaps Huw Wheldon, was frightened of her.[2]

In later years, as her Chief Assistant, Grist found himself informally appointed Wyndham Goldie's 'minder', impatiently waiting as she sat late in the Hospitality room, glass in hand, arguing about some programme. 'It was not so much that she drank,' he writes, 'she only had to smell the cork of the bottle to come under its influence.' Having at last seen her off the premises, he would watch in exasperated alarm as she drove off in her Morris Traveller down Lime Grove – a one-way street – in the wrong direction. But Grist did admire her ability to make programmes like *Panorama* happen: 'Grace understood real estate; that once you had the staff, the money and the studio, you could tell other people to bugger off.'

Rex Moorfoot, who was to become the Producer of *Panorama* in April 1958, inevitably had a great deal to do with the difficult Mrs Wyndham

Goldie. 'If you went in to see her and she was in a bad mood, sit it out,' he wrote:

> because in 10 minutes she'd come round. Equally, if she's in a good mood, make sure you get out in 10 minutes, because she'd sour. She'll find something wrong. If you wanted to destroy Grace, you used to say, 'Have you got something wrong with your feet?' because she liked 'comfortable' shoes. But she had the most delightful hats, and if you wanted to get round her, 'What a lovely hat, Grace!' She was analytical rather than creative. She used to come down to look at rough-cuts of documentaries and we always used to put a bad shot in. It was called a 'Goldieism'. I used to say, 'What do you think of it, Grace?' 'Well, that shot in reel 2, you really . . . it shouldn't be there . . . there's no justification . . . ' 'Oh you're quite right, Grace.' Out it came like a flash![3]

She could be rough. Margaret Douglas remembers Wyndham Goldie as having the unattractive habit of looking round a room to find someone weak, particularly a woman, to pick on: 'She was into beating people up'. And Charles Wheeler recalls being quite viciously attacked by Grace as 'a traitor' when he left *Panorama* in the spring of 1958 to go and work for BBC News, as it struggled back into the ring.

Catherine Dove, a young arts subjects producer, who first encountered Wyndham Goldie in the Lime Grove ladies', quickly found herself bullied into starting on time and working late. Wyndham Goldie, she says, was often over-critical, once telling John Freeman, the distinguished interviewer of *Face to Face*: 'Mr Freeman, I can't tell you how bad you were tonight.'[4] But, Dove says, 'Grace was decent and kind, as well as terrifying', and she took Dove – the first woman producer on *Panorama* – seriously, as the men sometimes did not.

In 1958, in a book he wrote after a whirlwind career as *Panorama*'s first current affairs reporter, Woodrow Wyatt contrasted his admiration for Wyndham Goldie with what he saw as the dead hand of Sir Ian Jacob, then the BBC's Director General. Wyatt had no doubt where honour was really owed:

> The successes of BBC Television in dealing with subjects on an intelligent level are not due to the active participation of Sir Ian. The chief credit belongs to a

remarkable but little known lady, Mrs Grace Wyndham Goldie . . . Mrs Goldie was born at the turn of the century, but in attitude she is the most youthful of the important officials. Long before Sir Ian or most other high-ranking executives, she realised that television would quickly displace sound broadcasting and become a far greater influence than radio had ever been. She grasped that presenting serious subjects to huge audiences needed imagination, detailed preparation, energy and hard work. It might be possible to have one person lecturing on a subject on the wireless – it was quite impossible to capture the attention of millions on television for adult ideas unless they were presented in varied and exciting forms. Making no sacrifice of accuracy she introduced a brightness and speed quite new to the BBC.[5]

The BBC tried to have Wyatt's book stopped. It alleged he had broken his contract with the BBC by writing so rudely about the Director General. It was an excellent irony that it fell to Tahu Hole, finally kicked sideways to be Director of Administration, to deal with the matter, and report mournfully that the BBC's lawyers could find no grounds for preventing publication.

Sea trials

When Grace Wyndham Goldie launched the new *Panorama*, she had put Michael Peacock on the bridge. While still a student at the London School of Economics, Peacock had been suggested to Wyndham Goldie by his professor, Robert McKenzie, himself a very considerable broadcaster on political programmes.

At 25, the programme's new Producer was young and inexperienced, but gruff, tough and serious-minded: 'Commanding, you could say arrogant', is how Peacock's co-Producer Charles Wheeler puts it. Wheeler recalls Peacock telling him brusquely to go and get the tea – something he thought he'd stopped having to do when he was on the *Daily Sketch* 10 years earlier. 'Michael Peacock was not a man who said "thank you" very much', says Charles's colleague of that time (but no relation), David Wheeler.

On American television Peacock had already seen the kind of thing he wanted to do himself on *Panorama*. In Berlin, making some programmes about Europe, he recalls being introduced by Charles Wheeler (then the BBC's European Service radio correspondent there) to Ed Murrow and the

See It Now team from CBS. Back at Lime Grove Peacock ran what was quaintly called – in the days before video recording – a 'kinescope' of *See It Now*. 'I realised this was it,' he says, 'reporters addressing people from the location.' After the British General Election in 1955 the BBC broadcast an edition of *See It Now*, in which Ed Murrow did what no British television programme team had so far dared to do – actually report on the election campaign itself. 'The earthy candour of the muscular slum housewife, the lady-like reasonableness of the suburban shopper, the cynical distrust of the two slightly drunk men in the pub; this, one suddenly realised, was what the television camera was meant to capture,' wrote Alan Brien in the *Observer*. 'This was a brilliant piece of journalism. What has Murrow got which the BBC couldn't buy with our money?'

The purpose of *Panorama* now was to show what could be done. Though Wyndham Goldie remained 'responsible' for *Panorama*, Peacock had day-to-day charge of a programme which would do what television news had so signally failed to do: report regularly on significant events both at home and abroad.

Peacock recalls another, earlier experience in his short television career, which had shown him what *Panorama* might be. The Ministry of Defence had agreed that BBC cameras should cover a NATO exercise. In fact there was only one camera, which had to change sides half-way through the make-believe battle. But that didn't matter: nor did the seasickness that affected Geoffrey Johnson Smith and the BBC team aboard a minesweeper. What worked was the way journalists were seen to be reporting from the scene of the action, while back in a command centre in Portsmouth Richard Dimbleby deftly drew their different reports together to make a complex story comprehensible to the viewers.

So now *Panorama* was relaunched. Wyndham Goldie had tried to get the name of the new programme changed, but that was a skirmish she lost. Cecil McGivern recognised that the *Panorama* brand was already worth too much to discard. But to emphasise that this was to be something very different to what had gone before, Grace did get agreement to add to the title the famous phrase 'television's window on the world'.

The aim now was to take an often serious look outside the confines of the studio, and outside Britain too, on a regular weekly basis. A new studio set was devised where Dimbleby would sit in a sort of tower and summon up film reports from different corners of the earth. The tower itself got in the way and was soon abandoned, but the concept remained: *Panorama* would bring the world into the studio, where Dimbleby would make sense of it all. 'Let me see if I can simplify,' he would say. The *Radio Times* ran a short article about the revamped programme:

> When *Panorama* returns to television on Monday it will have a new look and a wider horizon, helped by the fact that it is now to be weekly. As viewers' 'Window on the World', it will aim at bringing the news to life with illustrated reports, personalities and comment on what is going on not only in this country but all over the globe. Its shape is likely to be as variable as the patterns of a kaleidoscope.
>
> Michael Peacock, who shares the production with Richard Cawston,[6] tried to put it in a sentence when he told us: 'It will be a reflection of everyday life – ships, jazz, people, ploughing, theatre, industry, art, books, buildings, or bulldozers'.
>
> To embrace so much, *Panorama* will be drawing on the full resources of the BBC Television Service. Outside broadcast units, film camera teams, Roving Eye cameras and Regional studios will all play their part, and with the Eurovision link now operating on a permanent basis, the *Panorama* network will include live broadcasts from the Continent.
>
> Richard Dimbleby will preside in the studio.[7]

On the programme page there were photos of Dimbleby, Max Robertson and Malcolm Muggeridge and, framed in a television screen, the image of a globe – an image which today's *Panorama* still retains.

Setting sail

The new *Panorama* went on the air on Monday 19 September 1955, three days before the start of ITV. Starting at 8.15pm, it was sandwiched between *Pocket Edition*, 'the pages turned by Jimmy Young', and *Garrison Theatre*, from Biggin Hill, featuring Vera Lynn, Bob Monkhouse and the Squadronaires. 'We set out to explore the virgin lands of weekly television journalism,' said Michael Peacock.

Well, up to a point.

From Moscow there was film of Japanese *kabuki* dancers. There were two studio interviews, one with Lord Harewood, another with the Reverend Marcus Morris; Max Robertson reported on visitors to Britain; Woodrow Wyatt presented a film report from Malta; in the studio again Richard Dimbleby demonstrated a radio-controlled tractor. If change was apparent, it was scarcely startling, but for the first time BBC television was broadcasting a weekly current affairs programme. If there were still many soft, *Look at Life* feature items, there were harder elements too. Thanks to what Grace Wyndham Goldie later described as 'the laggardly start and incompetent presentation of BBC News'[8] *Panorama* had the whole field of human activity from which to choose its coverage: it was the only BBC television programme making a serious attempt to inform the nation of important developments in the world about it.

Panorama's magazine format typically contained five items in each 45-minute programme. In its first few months after the relaunch it covered unemployment in Northern Ireland, the housing shortage in Britain, the revels at a hunt ball, and the situation in the Middle East. There were reports on the mood of the Welsh coal miners and the colour bar in British Rail; Dimbleby interviewed the Prime Minister of Northern Ireland and, after Princess Margaret broke off her engagement to Group Captain Townsend, the Archbishop of Canterbury. The audience rose quickly, until eight million viewers were looking through their window on the world every week. 'What was said on *Panorama* on Monday evening came increasingly to be headlined in Tuesday's morning newspapers,' wrote Leonard Miall. '*Panorama* deals million pound blow to British car industry' was the Fleet Street reaction to a story about British drivers' dislike of British cars.

At the Lime Grove studios on Monday nights 'there was always a knot of schoolboys with autograph books in the darkness outside the main door on the lookout for visitors whose names were in that day's headlines, or would be in the morning's'.[9]

Robin Day later wrote of the programme he was soon to join: '*Panorama* was a major event of the week, keenly awaited by press, politicians and people alike . . . It was the TV forum where national issues, political, economic, moral, were debated.'[10] Wyndham Goldie agreed: 'The style of *Panorama* was to be authoritative . . . Like any serious weekly, it could not afford to omit major developments at home or in international affairs.' Says Margaret Douglas, then the wide-eyed young programme secretary, watching *Panorama* make its mark: 'You felt you were at the epicentre of the world. The programme knew what it should be doing, and what to do about it.'

For Miall, *Panorama*'s finest hour in those early days came in 1956, the year of Suez, as the Soviet Union took advantage of the West's preoccupation with war in the Middle East to crush the uprising against Communist rule in its vassal state of Hungary. As Sir Geoffrey Cox records, neither BBC News nor ITN got their cameras into Hungary. *Panorama* did – against orders.

In 1956 there were only two sound cameras in Lime Grove, one assigned to Paul Fox and Ronnie Noble on *Sportsview*, the other to *Panorama*. Appalled at the prospect of losing the one piece of equipment that was absolutely essential to keeping the programme on air at this time of crisis, Miall forbade the *Panorama* team to go into Hungary itself. While *Panorama* people could always be replaced if somehow they disappeared in the tumult of Hungarian revolt, the camera could not. Instead they were sent to Vienna, to film whatever news might filter across the border into Austria. But the team was not about to settle for this. The producer in the field was Charles Wheeler, and his reporter George Mikes, a native Hungarian who had been working for the BBC's foreign language radio broadcasts at Bush House. With them were cameraman 'Tubby' Englander and sound recordist Robin Green. Not content to wait for the story to come to them in Austria, the team headed for the frontier. The Austrian border guards told them that if they took their car across they would not be allowed to bring it back, but, undeterred, they negotiated a deal. They were allowed to take their vehicle into no man's land and there transfer into the back of a lorry brought up from the other side by Hungarians desperate to tell the world about their revolt against their Communist overlords. Once in Hungary the team would film all day and then return at night, in the same way, to Vienna, clutching their rushes and their precious camera.

Wheeler and Englander recall that, travelling in the back of a coal lorry, Charles dropped the tripod, the 'legs' that stop television film wobbling around all over the place like most home movies. The pan and tilt head was smashed. 'Tubby' Englander had to 'hand hold' the heavy Camiflex camera on his shoulder for the rest of the trip.

They were filming in the university town of Sopron when news came that the Russians were coming, invading to crush the revolution, taking advantage of the way the eyes of the West were on the Middle East, not Eastern Europe. 'You've wrecked our revolution with your Suez adventure,' said the Hungarian students bitterly to Wheeler. Racing back across the border into Austria, the team hurried home to London. As they watched the rushes in the cutting room they were at the same time hearing the Hungarians' desperate appeals for help from the West, rebroadcast by BBC Radio. Margaret Douglas remembers being in tears at the pity of it.

Then there was an argument. While Michael Peacock wanted to lead the programme with Hungary, Grace Wyndham Goldie insisted that the Middle East crisis must come first: 'Our boys are dying in Suez,' Charles Wheeler remembers her saying.

For *Panorama* on 17 November Richard Dimbleby, Wheeler and another producer, Tony Jay, were dispatched back to Vienna to present the programme live. They set up their three-camera outside broadcast in a basement *bierkeller*. There, talking to despairing Hungarians who had just escaped across the border, Dimbleby was at his best. The Eurovision link was late coming through, but on the telephone from Austria he urged London to hold on. Cliff Michelmore, presenter of the new programme *Tonight*, was pulled out of the Lime Grove Club bar by Catherine Dove and hurried to the *Panorama* studio to keep the programme on the air. The 'feed' from Vienna came through at last, and in his interviews with the desolate Hungarians, Dimbleby movingly conveyed the tragedy of liberty lost, of a sudden joyous blaze of freedom just as suddenly snuffed out.

An early engagement

In this year of major international news Cecil McGivern, now Deputy Director of Television Broadcasting, told Grace Wyndham Goldie that he wanted *Panorama* 'to take on a more urgent appearance in view of the world situation'. But, in common with the nascent news programmes, *Panorama* still laboured under formal political restrictions we can now hardly imagine.

Back in 1946 Sir William Haley, then BBC Director General, had said that television could 'add nothing' to political discussions, and should not do them. Unsurprisingly, that was a view widely shared by Government ministers. The BBC had long connived at what was known as the '14-day rule', which meant that nothing due for debate in Parliament in the next fortnight could be discussed on television. Originally introduced under a wartime coalition government, ostensibly to prevent politicians saying anything on air that might damage national unity, this piece of censorship had come to be embraced by a timid BBC management as a convenient shield against charges of political bias.

In 1955 Prime Minister Anthony Eden, supported by Winston Churchill and by Clement Attlee for the Labour Opposition, made the convention official. The Postmaster General, Charles Hill, delivered a formal instruction to the BBC. Said Churchill: 'It would be a shocking thing to have the debates of Parliament forestalled on this new robot organisation of television and BBC broadcasting. The right of Members of Parliament must be protected against the mass and against the machine.'[11]

But the '14-day rule' was, as MPs taking part in the television discussion programme *In the News* described it, a 'lunatic restriction'. When in November 1956 the British Government sent an invasion force to Egypt to try and reassert its control of the Suez Canal the rule prevented the broadcasters giving any reaction from Britons to what was being done in their name. Earlier that year viewers had heard Richard Dimbleby open the programme by saying: 'We can't tonight discuss the rights and wrongs of the situation,' and now, when the crisis had come, no hint of the controversy that British intervention had provoked in Britain itself was allowed to enter the studio. Dimbleby could only conduct Rear-Admiral Nichol round his relief maps rather as if he, Dimbleby, were in charge of the landings at Suez that morning. As the Government threatened to bomb Egypt into surrender, *Panorama* was reduced to reporting world, rather than British, reaction to this dramatic display of imperial power: forbidden to discuss directly with responsible British ministers a crisis that was dividing the nation. The BBC hierarchy stopped Michael Peacock even asking the Foreign Secretary for an interview.

As a BBC briefing document later put it:

> The editions of *Panorama* of both 5th. November and 12th. November were restricted by the '14-day rule'. A request to approach the Foreign Secretary for

an interview had been turned down by the Board of Management. *Panorama* was reduced to reporting events, and reporting reaction to those events abroad. The discussion of British reactions to the action in Egypt was ruled out. The mounting of the programme on 12th. November with filmed reactions from places as far away as Australia, India and New York was an extremely fast piece of work.[12]

But this strict observance of the '14-day rule' did not prevent *Panorama* being attacked by politicians who supported the Suez invasion, like Peter Rawlinson. It transpired – as it was so often to do in the future – that the outraged MP had not even seen the programmes of which he was complaining. The BBC investigated itself – again, as it was so often to do in the future – and repudiated the charges of 'socialist' bias. The programmes 'fulfilled the BBC's obligation for impartiality, objectivity and telling the truth', the Corporation insisted.[13]

Suez exposed the '14-day rule' for what it was: an absurd and disgraceful restriction on free speech, and a denial of the right and duty of the broadcasters to give that free speech airtime. On 18 December, when passions had somewhat cooled, the politicians graciously agreed a face-saving formula: the rule would be 'suspended' for an 'experimental period'. Though not finally lifted (or rather 'permanently suspended') until July 1957, the '14-day rule' was never again applied.

For *Panorama*, the autumn of 1956 had been a testing time. Restricted both by arbitrary censorship and by its limited resources it had faced up to covering two major events in world history simultaneously. This is Richard Dimbleby speaking in his inimitable style to the studio camera in *Panorama* on 5 November:

> We shall presently, I hope, be talking to Vienna for the latest news of Hungary. You know, it's difficult to comprehend, isn't it, that both these crises and all the events of them that have developed in Hungary and the Middle East have all virtually happened in the last fortnight, or even less than the last fortnight. But here is the diary of events of those particular days. Ten days ago Gomulka was in power in Poland and the Hungarian revolution was in full swing. Eight days ago Nagy pressed for Russian troops to leave Hungary. Seven days ago Israel invaded Egypt. Six days ago Britain and

France sent their ultimatum to Egypt and Israel, and used their veto in the Security Council. Budapest fell to the rebels. Five days ago Britain and France began bombing Egyptian airfields. Four days ago, in Hungary, Nagy appealed for United Nations support. Three days ago the United Nations General Assembly condemned the Anglo–French action in the Middle East. Soviet troops reoccupied Hungary. Two days ago Israel announced the defeat of the Egyptian army in Sinai. Russia vetoed the Security Council resolution on Hungary. Yesterday a thousand Russian tanks attacked Budapest. Nagy's Government surrendered. Today our paratroops dropped on the Port Said area – surrender talks are going on. Communication with Hungary we think, is cut off. And tomorrow, almost unnoticed, the American election.[14]

Turbulent days, at a time when everyone still felt that the Third World War might be waiting round the next corner. Coming as they did just a year after the programme's relaunch, the crises of Hungary and Suez did a good deal to establish *Panorama* as *the* place to find out what was happening in the world. After 1955, as former *Panorama* Editor Robert Rowland says, '*Panorama* rapidly became the vehicle of authoritative opinion, with very little competition . . . It took root in the nation's mind as the place to hear what important people had to say.'[15]

Alarms and excursions

But much of the world that flew in through *Panorama*'s window was still far lighter than the heavy drama of major political events. With as yet no *Monitor* to cover the arts, no travel programmes, no *Tomorrow's World*, no *News* worth the name, *Panorama* could and did cover all the territory these programmes would one day make their own. *Panorama* as a magazine programme still had room for great variety of tone and subject. And Max Robertson's light touch still had its admirers in high places. On 12 March 1957 Kenneth Adam, Controller of Programmes, wrote to Leonard Miall, Head of Talks, telling him Richard Dimbleby should be 'rebuked' for mentioning the name of his tailor in a *Panorama* programme. By contrast: 'I thought the Rag-and-Bone item was superbly handled by Max Robertson. Why don't we use him more?'[16] Miall wrote back: 'I entirely agree that Max Robertson's Rag-and-Bone item was a very good one. We have used him a good deal in the past, he is very good with certain types of people and on certain subjects. With others he is absolutely ghastly. We have to be careful how we use him to get the best out of him. He is good with "characters" but is awfully slow at thinking on his feet.'[17] Poor Max: Television Talks had decided that he was not serious enough, not sufficiently interested in the issues, to play a greater role in the new *Panorama*. Not long afterwards he left the programme to develop his broadcasting career elsewhere. He became the chairman of the antiques programme *Going for a Song*, and for 21 years was BBC Radio's main commentator at Wimbledon.

In June 1956 a rash decision had been made to interview the Irish playwright Brendan Behan in the studio. This would be the first occasion the 33-year-old Behan had been allowed back into Britain after serving time for IRA-connected offences. His play *The Quare Fellow*, about his prison experiences, was having a successful run at the Theatre Workshop in east London, and extracts were to be screened in *Panorama*. Aware of Behan's reputation, Charles Wheeler, in charge of the programme during Michael Peacock's temporary absence, had hired a young researcher to go to Ireland, bring Behan to London, book him into his hotel and then deliver him safely to the studio. In order to catch the only available plane from Dublin, they'd had to make a 4am start, so Behan had enjoyed a long day's drinking. On arrival at the BBC he was very much the worse for wear – virtually comatose, according to Catherine Dove, the producer and studio director.

After four hours in the Hospitality room where, says Wheeler, 'he drank everything', Behan emerged for a rehearsal with his interviewer, Malcolm Muggeridge. It did not bode well for the live transmission to come. Though Behan was just able to speak, he was incoherent. Nicely brought-up teenage girls involved in another item about finishing schools looked on aghast. Hovering in the studio like an anxious Alastair Sim, Leonard Miall asked nervously: 'What if he says fuck?' 'My dear Leonard,' replied Muggeridge, 'nobody is going to understand a word; everything will be fine.' It was not. Though drink and a thick Irish accent made Behan unintelligible to most viewers, *Panorama* became the first programme in which an interviewee used this particular four-letter word on television.

'Millions see drunk man on TV show' was the delighted headline in the *Daily Sketch* the next morning. The article continued: 'Behan slumped in a chair like a heavyweight boxer. He wore no tie, puffed at a cigarette butt, and was completely unintelligible. A BBC official said: "Mr Behan was extremely nervous and had a few drinks before the programme. He was a bit drunk, but we didn't think he'd be as bad as he turned out to be.'"

A solemn inquest on the incident was conducted by Harman Grisewood, Assistant to the Director General. Charles Wheeler was threatened with the sack, but his account of how he had done his best to save the day by hero-ically pouring the remaining 'hospitality' gin and whisky down the sink secured his reprieve. The whole incident was an early example of how *Panorama*, in so many different ways, would give the BBC hierarchy heartache. *Panorama*'s zeal to extend the boundaries of television, to go where none had gone before, to reveal what had until then remained hidden, was often self-consciously in conflict with contemporary convention. The Swinging Sixties were yet to come: sex had not yet been invented.

According to his co-Producer Wheeler, Michael Peacock, for fear of interference from the Head of Talks, would hold his programme running order very close to his chest. As the weekend approached, an under-standably nervous Miall would try to discover what exactly would feature in Monday night's programme. Peacock would do anything to avoid revealing his hand.

On Monday 4 February 1957 the front page of the *Daily Mirror* informed a shocked Sir Ian Jacob, the Director General, that *Panorama* was that night to feature for the first time the birth of a baby on television. Excerpts of a film made by the pioneer of 'painless childbirth' Dr Grantly Dick Read, showing a mother actually giving birth, were to be included in the programme prior to a studio discussion. Dr Read was quoted as saying: 'This really is a most attractive sequence. The mother is seen to be happy and contented in labour, and there is a complete absence of fear and discomfort. This is followed by the supreme happiness and joy when she holds the child in her arms. The scenes provide an excellent illustration of natural childbirth.' But not after *Panorama* had finished with them.

Thoroughly alarmed, Jacob sent his Broadcasting House apparatchiks down to Lime Grove to view the film before transmission – the first occasion, according to Wheeler, that such a visitation had occurred. In the cutting room they argued about how much pubic hair the *Panorama* public could be allowed to see: 'We must lose that hairy-arsed shot and then it will be all right,' Wheeler remembers Miall suggesting hopefully. But by the time all the BH bosses had had their say there was not much left of this natural birth. 'Now you see a baby's head, now it's in her arms,' says Wheeler. The BBC's regard for respectability took precedence over reality; in the process, the point the film was trying to make was completely lost.

The papers had a field day anyway: 'Revolting. Beyond the pale. I condemn the BBC for the worst display of taste ever,' wrote Alan Gardner in the *Daily Sketch*. 'No, No, No and No again,' said an article written by 'A Mother'. 'The moment of birth was related to nothing at all. The succeeding moment of the baby in his mother's arms seemed unrelated even to the birth. There was no message. Nothing to move us. Nothing, really to horrify. It was merely tasteless. . .it reduced the whole process to farmyard level.'[18] Said a Mrs Elspeth McNeil, awaiting the birth of her baby in a Glasgow hospital: 'I was just getting the hang of what was going on . . . then it ended. I know no more now than I did before.'[19] In an editorial, the *Daily Mail* concluded: 'As a contribution to the discussion which it professed to point it proved nothing at all . . . One does not need to be a prude to conclude that the BBC made a serious error of taste and judgement in this. It should never be repeated.'[20]

As for Dr Grantly Dick Read, he was furious that his film of a happy and relaxed birth had been reduced to an abrupt and meaningless 30-second clip.

Quite soon, *Panorama* had become so sure of its place in the nation's heart that it felt able to play tricks on its audience. 1 April 1957 fell on a Monday, by now *Panorama* night. The team had been waiting for just this conjunction to perpetrate a classic April Fool's Day joke. Cameraman Charles de Jaeger, whose idea it was, was working on another story in Switzerland near Lugano. Carefully he draped 20 pounds of cooked spaghetti on a cluster of laurel bushes and then shot silent film as smiling peasant girls in traditional costume 'harvested' the dangling strands of pasta. Back at Lime Grove *Panorama*'s David Wheeler cut the material together and wrote a commentary for Richard Dimbleby, in which the great presenter described the whole fictitious process of growing, collecting, drying and packing spaghetti in his usual genial, authoritative and helpfully informative style: ' . . . plant breeders have produced spaghetti all of the same length . . . ' Miall, for once forewarned of what *Panorama* was up to, attempted to alert the Director General, but his message did not get through. Sir Ian Jacob later admitted that, watching television at home, he had consulted three different reference books before he had reassured himself that the *Panorama* report was indeed a hoax. Telephone calls to the BBC insisted that if Richard Dimbleby said this was how spaghetti was produced it had to be so. Today it seems curious that *Panorama*, as the trusted current affairs programme, should set out to make fools of its loyal audience, but Miall says: 'All of us involved with *Panorama*, including Richard himself, felt it was high time that television was taken with some critical scepticism.'

The fact is that *Panorama* was so far ahead of the field it could do anything. As Jonathan Dimbleby puts it in his biography of his father: 'For the next ten years, sometimes glib and occasionally ponderous, *Panorama* would lead its huge audience from crisis to catastrophe with a flair and authority that its rivals could rarely match.'

By 1958, only three years after its relaunch, one in four adults was watching *Panorama* every Monday night. That was a great tribute to the young Michael Peacock, the programme's Producer during its reincarnation. Even more perhaps, it was Grace Wyndham Goldie's determination to make something important of the programme, and Richard Dimbleby's supreme skill at presenting it, that had now made *Panorama* such an enormous success. Woodrow Wyatt, the revitalised programme's first real reporter, recognised the contribution the two of them had made. 'Mrs. Wyndham Goldie's determination to have clear and fair expositions of current affairs', he wrote, 'and Richard's comforting mantle suggesting that anyone with common-sense would enjoy and understand them, were the major reasons for *Panorama*'s vast audiences.'

In 1962, when there was talk of amalgamating *Panorama* with the upstart *Tonight*, Richard Dimbleby could justly assert that '*Panorama* has an authority that has not been equalled by any current affairs programme since broadcasting began'.[21] For this he and Grace Wyndham Goldie deserved the principal credit. But they could not have done what they did without those who went out and brought material back for the programme to present – the reporters.

chapter six

🌐 They were giants . . .

And like giants, they were sometimes prone to boastful exaggeration. 'Began *Panorama* with Richard Dimbleby 1955', said the late Woodrow Wyatt's entry in *Who's Who*. Wyatt didn't 'begin' *Panorama*, nor was he in any way responsible for planning its transformation into a serious programme. He was, however, its first regular reporter, and the man who developed what was quickly recognised as the current affairs television reporter's role – to go out into the world and show the viewer what he found there, in sound and pictures, and then tell them what he made of it. Wyatt had no need to claim credit for what he had not done, for what he did achieve in a few frenetic years was quite extraordinary enough. He set the entry standard which others had to meet before they could join that fairly exclusive set, the *Panorama* reporters' club.

Like so many other of Grace Wyndham Goldie's recruits, Wyatt came to television from politics, though he was a prolific print journalist too. A Labour MP, he had been made a junior War minister in 1951, the youngest member of the Government. But his Aston seat disappeared in a boundary revision and when he stood for Grantham in 1955 he lost. So in the summer of 1955 Wyatt was ready for offers. He'd previously made some approaches to BBC Radio, offering himself as a panel member of *Any Questions?*, and in June 1955 he had suggested to Television Talks a programme on book collecting.

Along with Brian Connell, who was to make his television career largely in ITV, Wyatt was given a screen test. 'When the rushes were shown I was horrified,' he wrote later. 'I looked and sounded like a stuffed pig.' It is true that Wyatt was not a particularly handsome man. Neither he nor Robin Day (who was at the same moment being hired as a newscaster for ITN) were of the traditional matinée idol type – familiar television faces like Peter Haigh and Macdonald Hobley. But Wyndham Goldie and *Panorama* Producer Michael Peacock were in no doubt that Wyatt could help them make their Window on the World worth looking through.

Wyatt's first *Panorama* assignment was to make a film report in Malta. There was talk of a new status for this strategically placed island, and a forthcoming contest between Dom Mintoff, the Labour Prime Minister, and Borg Olivier, the Nationalist Party leader. A rough running order sketched out by Peacock survives:

1. Wyatt standing on a high rock saying 'I am standing in Malta . . . over there is Italy, over there Cyprus, etc., etc . . . Down there is the harbour . . . so you see why the strategic position of Malta is so important . . . refer to the importance of the future of Malta.' Go on to say 'I have come to Malta with one of our film camera-men to investigate this problem on the spot and see what the Maltese people themselves think about it.'

2. Silent sequence shot to illustrate commentary which will say who the Maltese people are, what Malta is, how it is made up, etc. Explanation of the problem.

3. Interviews with typical Maltese people (Approximately one minute each).

4. Silent shot (such as Olivier's house or garden) to carry the commentary introducing Olivier.

5. Interview with Olivier.

6. Silent sequence to introduce the interview with Mintoff.

7. Interview with Mintoff.

8. (In the studio). Summary.[1]

Peacock sent a further memo to Charles de Jaeger, the cameraman who was to accompany Wyatt to Malta:

> I attach a list of sequences that I have given to Woodrow Wyatt. Please make sure you get suitable shots to cut in as he points in the various directions mentioned in sequence 1. These shots may only show a little land in the foreground with the Mediterranean beyond and then sky but we want them nonetheless. If possible they should be shot from exactly the point on which he is standing for sequence 1. Sequence 2 will also need some careful silent camera coverage. I suggest you ask Wyatt exactly what he's going to say when he starts The Problem of Malta and coverage must be suitable to use for this important piece of commentary. For example, when he says that one of the problems is unemployment in the dockyard area, we should see shots of men standing around the docks, etc., etc.[2]

So the basic grammar of this new language, current affairs television, was laboriously being invented. Wyatt, just like any other reporter, remembered this as all his own work:

> Ignorant of television I decided on a direct approach to attract the viewers' attention. I stood on a promontory with the sea behind me. 'To my right', I yelled, 'are Africa and Egypt. On my left are Sicily and Italy. In front of me is Cyprus. Behind me is Gibraltar. That is why for centuries Malta has been of strategic importance to anyone who wants to control the Mediterranean.' It was not polished, but I had to start somewhere.[3]

Whatever her own determination to make *Panorama* more serious, Grace Wyndham Goldie seems to have been conscious that her BBC bosses were nervous about the current affairs element. Just before the first programme in the new series, following a telephone conversation she'd had with

Harmon Grisewood, the Director General's Assistant, she wrote a confidential memo to him:

> Included in our weekly magazine programme *Panorama* will be a section in which three or four items of interest in the Current Affairs field will be covered; e.g. in the first edition on Monday 19th. September, we shall be covering briefly the opening of the UN Conference in New York, with reporting on film from Patrick O'Donovan; an assessment of Dr. Adenauer's reception in Bonn (This was to have been done on film by Brian Connell, but it was technically not very good and it may now be done in the studio by Richard Scott); a report on film of the situation in Malta by Woodrow Wyatt. This includes a brief interview with Mr. Mintoff, an equally brief interview with Mr. Borg Olivier, some purely descriptive material about Malta, and two or three interviews with men in the street ... It is our plan to use this type of visual reporting regularly as an ingredient in *Panorama*. Current Affairs occupy a section of approximately 15 minutes out of the 45-minute programme.[4]

'So don't worry', seems to be the message here. 'Please tell the D.G. that we are not going to make any waves at *Panorama*.' Of course, for a BBC that had always thought discussion of serious issues dangerous, this new current affairs feature in the *Panorama* magazine must have been a worry to Broadcasting House. And it rather looks as if Wyndham Goldie was trying to play down the perceived danger of relying upon a former Labour minister as a reporter by reference to other, some of them more Conservative, figures:

> No opinions are expressed by Woodrow Wyatt, who is simply acting as questioner and factual reporter ... We shall have a team of reporters who will change from time to time and from week to week. Among them are William Clark (who will not now, alas, be able to undertake it and whom we shall have to replace), Patrick O'Donovan, Brian Connell, Richard Scott and Geoffrey Johnson Smith. We shall add to this list as we go on. The reports will be objective and factual; personal opinions will not be expressed. The object is to give viewers a visual impression of the places which are being talked about in the news and also to get answers to questions from a representative cross section of both important people and men in the street.

We tried Woodrow Wyatt out a little while ago in a programme which may not appear, about the work of N.A.T.O., and he was extremely good – fair and objective. When we considered having him from time to time in our programmes this winter I discussed very carefully with him the terms on which this would be possible. They were that he did in fact act as a reporter, did not state opinions, was objective in his handling of material . . . He was not only willing to accept this but delighted to do so. I have seen the first of his reports, on film, on Malta, and it seems to be exactly what we intended.[5]

Wyatt's first foray into television reporting, his Malta story, was judged a considerable success. As he wrote: 'Accustomed as a journalist and politician to getting all the main points into a short space I developed new techniques for television reports which were later much copied.' But, like Wyndham Goldie, Wyatt too seems to have realised how carefully he had to tread if the BBC was to allow the development of this daring journalistic initiative. On 16 September, before his next foreign assignment in Cyprus, he actually sent his proposed line of questioning to the Director General, Sir Ian Jacob: 'Of course, this will not be the exact form of the questions and there may be alterations as a result of talking to the interviewees first. But this is the general trend . . . What I hope to do in general is to give the public the basic facts in serious and balanced, but I hope interesting, form, without pretending to give a large scale comprehensive survey of Cyprus.'[6]

With Wyndham Goldie's sharp eye always upon him Wyatt was highly conscious of the need to be non-partisan, and be seen to be so. 'I was determined that everyone's case should be put properly,' he wrote; 'when someone significant to the story in Cyprus reneged on an interview I pointed to the seat where he would have sat, asked the questions I would have asked him, and gave the answers I thought he would have given, possibly better than he would have.'

Wyatt's value to the new *Panorama* quickly became obvious and the BBC hurried to contract him on a longer term basis before the rival ITV snapped him up: 'He has shown himself to be an extremely valuable political commentator who can organise and direct his own filming. We know that Aidan Crawley[7] is angling for him, and it would be uneconomic to offer him a three months' contract with *Panorama* if at the end of it he went over to the other side.'[8] Offered a one year exclusive contract in December 1955 for £2800 ('first class travel throughout'),[9] Wyatt was finally signed up at the end of January 1956.

Soon he was a star: 'My television appearances catapulted me into fame. *Panorama* was the best and most popular current affairs programme on BBC or ITV. We had an audience of between 9 and 14 million. When I walked in the street or went into any public place I was recognised and my autograph sought . . . my erstwhile companions in Parliament were amazed'; and, as Wyatt noted, a touch jealous and resentful: 'Michael Stewart, at the end of a speech I made at a Fabian conference, said "Woodrow will now return to being a television star, while I return to the humble obscurity of the House of Commons."' Wyatt was justified in thinking that it was he, as a reporter, who had made the greatest contribution to the current affairs element in the first year of the new *Panorama*.

New techniques that would become as familiar as the PTC, the 'piece to camera', that Wyatt delivered in that first report from Malta, were being discovered all the time. In January 1956, after a Middle East trip in which he had talked to the leaders of both Israel and Egypt, Wyatt sharply contrasted the differences between them by intercutting their interviews. Wyndham Goldie at once saw how well this new technique had worked: 'The effective portion was the final inter-cutting between Nasser and Ben Gurion, which was very good.'[10] The *Evening Standard*'s Tom Harrison liked it even more:

> In BBC's *Panorama*, Woodrow Wyatt's report on the Middle East was beautifully done. He did not try to show himself off much, yet he made the essential link to fascinating film reportage. This depended strictly on his sense of news, pace and poise. Closely knit sequences pushed the viewer almost painfully to and fro across the Israeli border or between slick Nasser and weary-wise Ben Gurion.
>
> This report could have been done no other way.

'In eight months', wrote Philip Purser of the *Daily Mail*, 'he has become Britain's most influential television commentator. In fact Mr. Wyatt himself is the first to admit that he is now exercising more influence in public affairs than ever he did as an M.P. or junior minister.'

In his article Purser referred to Wyatt's 'dry and unmusical voice', and this was obviously a matter of concern to the *Panorama* production team.

A memo from Michael Peacock dated 4 April 1956 says: 'Wyatt is not getting voice production. I will see whether this can be arranged.'[11] This got Catherine Dove into trouble. As 'the only girl on *Panorama*' she was taken out to lunch by the journalist Eve Perrick for a nice relaxed interview. Next day, to her embarrassment, Catherine found herself quoted as saying of Wyatt: 'He knows he's got a problem with his voice, but he's working on it.' Wyatt telegrammed furiously to Catherine: 'Insist you retract foolish interview *Express*.' Nervously she rang up the *Daily Express* to do so. The following week Eve Perrick's column carried the line: 'I gather Woodrow Wyatt is not taking voice lessons – I wish he would.'

For months at a time Wyatt would set off somewhere on a Tuesday – often abroad. He would film frantically for two or three days, return with the rushes on Saturday, edit through the weekend and Monday, and then appear in the studio live on Monday evening with an upsum to his film report. It was an exhausting schedule that left him distinctly tetchy – and his expenses in disarray. 'I am fed up with these constant irritating enquiries from the accountants,' he fumed in September 1957; 'if the BBC's position is that I am to do these ever-lasting and time-wasting sums then I shall have to decline to do any further television programmes.'[12] Like some of his successors, Wyatt also became very irritated at the way *Panorama*'s presenter seemed to reap the reward of his reporting efforts. Two days before Christmas 1957 he wrote resentfully to Leonard Miall: 'I am constantly getting letters, reading in the newspapers, and hearing from people who are otherwise well-informed, that Richard Dimbleby is responsible, has directed or supervised or in some other way fashioned the items I do.'[13] 'I don't like it either,' replied Miall:

> and neither does Michael Peacock, when otherwise well-informed people think Richard Dimbleby is responsible for planning and shaping the whole of *Panorama*. But I think as long as we have anchor men for programmes there will always be people who assume that the anchor man plans the whole programme, just as other people assume the announcers make up the news, or the weather men cause the rain ... Once one starts saying 'this item on so-and-so was devised by Woodrow Wyatt' then in justice one must add 'discussed in detail with Michael Peacock, forced through against Leonard Miall's better judgement, referred to Kenneth Adam, etc', and where would that stop?[14]

As other reporters joined the team Wyatt began to feel cross that he no longer did all the best stories. On a Pan American flight to the States he smouldered, and, unable to contain himself, eventually scribbled an airmail letter to the Head of Talks, Television:

Dear Leonard,

Without rancour I wish to make a complaint. I have worked loyally for *Panorama* for a year and two months. I have taken on many dull subjects and tried to make them interesting – things like Civil Defence for instance, or even the broadcast on the A.E.U. which when it was first propounded everyone thought was certain to be very dull. Time and again at short notice I have done items because of their inherent importance and not because of the attractiveness of the subject matter. I think it would also be agreed that I was the first person to demonstrate that important and heavy subjects could be made widely interesting and treated adequately in 15 minutes or less. I have certainly done what I could in building *Panorama* up – not without success might be the general opinion.

Frequently it is necessary to do a series of non-peak subjects as far as excitement goes. One takes these with the knowledge that one must accept the rough with the smooth. But one expects the smooth as well to make it possible to give the items one does a real lift from time to time . . .

Now comes Poland – an obvious subject of the kind I am talking about, in fact the best since September 1955. When I rang [Cecil] McGivern about Europe, having heard you were away, you were annoyed. This time I rang Peacock on Saturday 20th. October; he agreed this was an excellent [assignment] for me . . . On Monday I am told the BBC certainly approves of the idea and will send someone else to do it for the *Panorama* programme for which I have worked in fair weather and foul – without having any series of programmes of my own – since September 1955. This is extremely unfair, unethical and a very poor reward for all I have done for *Panorama* . . . I would be glad of your comments. I cannot let the matter rest here.[15]

Nor could Miall, who could not afford to let a reporter, however important to *Panorama*, start calling the shots. He soon replied making it quite clear that it was the BBC and not Wyatt which would decide whom to send on any particular story. And there was now a choice.

Panorama was beginning to build a team of giants – reporters and interviewers who stood, like basketball players, head and shoulders above the ordinary. 'By 1959', Grace Wyndham Goldie later wrote, 'these men (there were still few women among them) had become part of the political scene. They appeared constantly on television, they were known to millions, and often seen to have more political significance than the majority of back-benchers.' So who exactly were they – these giants among men? 'The short answer is that they were selected by television current affairs producers and paid on contract for their appearances in specified television programmes ... Their contracts could be removed or terminated. Their fees were subject to negotiation. Their position in fact was very like that of actors and actresses in television drama and of performers in programmes of television light entertainment.'

A salutary thought, typical of Wyndham Goldie's tart telling of the truth. For she was right, of course; that is how it was then, and that is how by and large it remains. These current affairs reporters, these people on whom we depend for accurate information about the world we live in, are hired and fired just like any other television performer. Unlike their producer colleagues most *Panorama* reporters are not on staff, but self-employed. They have no guarantee of work beyond their current contract, which may well run for no more than a year at a time. The restrictive terms of that contract make it difficult, almost impossible, to develop other kinds of television work with which to bargain successfully with the BBC for better terms and conditions. And while their producer colleagues may go on to become Director General of the BBC, reporters, with rare exceptions, do not.[16] Instead, all but a tiny number eventually wear out their welcome and go.

Is there anything to set against this? Well, in general, reporters are paid more than their producer colleagues to compensate them for their insecurity. And for a reporter there's a certain satisfaction, when he is first hired, or his contract renewed, in knowing that it is because he is valued for what he does. But what *is* that exactly, and how is it different from what BBC staff journalists could themselves offer?

'The practice by which broadcasting organisations selected a number of interviewers by methods which seemed arbitrary and were seldom disclosed caused legitimate resentments among politicians and the public,' wrote Wyndham Goldie. Again, she was right. While BBC producers had typically been appointed by selection boards, it was a much more arcane process as far as reporters were concerned. A name was canvassed by a producer; somebody higher up decided that they would do; and after a drink over lunch to discuss terms they were contracted.

Wyndham Goldie had a clear idea of the sort of reporters she wanted for *Panorama*. She preferred her producer protégés very young: Michael Peacock for example – only 25 when put in to run *Panorama* – would do her bidding in the new way she wanted, building the television machinery of *Panorama* according to her blueprint, to make the window on the world work. But to explore that world and report upon it with authority Wyndham Goldie wanted grown-ups, men of experience. For other programmes in the early 1950s she had hired politicians like Christopher Mayhew, Aidan Crawley, and John Freeman. Now in the autumn of 1955 Woodrow Wyatt had become *Panorama*'s reporter. All of these had had experience of government as junior ministers. They were no longer simply naïve young enthusiasts; as well as having had a chance to develop their own ideas they now had some experience of real life; they understood what it was like for people in power to have to make hard decisions, for they had had to make some themselves. And they had learned, once they had made up their minds, how to express their opinions and not to be afraid of doing so.

So on *Panorama* these people would use their experience of the world, and speak their own minds.[17] At the same time, they would be self-employed individual 'acts' who, when they came to a particular conclusion about something, would not be editorialising on behalf of the BBC. They were 'guest stars' who, if they overstepped the mark, could be disowned and dispensed with much more easily than any staff person. In fact the first to follow Wyatt to *Panorama*, in 1956, had not been a minister, though he would one day become one. He had however already achieved considerable success in quite another field.

The golden boy of athletics, Christopher Chataway had in 1954 taken the 5000 metres world record. A year later, as ITV began broadcasting, he had become ITN's first newscaster, smiling pleasantly alongside the tense and frowning Robin Day. But Chataway, who had interests and ambitions outside television, was keen to show he was more than a pretty presenter. When his hopes of doing more political television programmes faded – ITN was having arguments with the ITV network about its budget – he seized the chance to join *Panorama*.

In the mid-1950s, Chataway recalls, there was still some intellectual snobbery about television in well-to-do families: it had not yet arrived as a serious medium.

> You might hear people say 'We can't afford it but cook's got one', so everybody on *Panorama* was anxious to be taken seriously. We were trying to make a serious medium out of something that had been mere entertainment and frippery. We didn't go for sensation, and it didn't have to be 'shock, horror'. We could be 'on the one hand . . . and on the other'.
>
> It was a very exciting atmosphere indeed, and what was most exciting for me was having a different topic every week. I worked very hard; I wanted it to be even more serious than the producers did. Grace Wyndham Goldie would come and watch a rough-cut of your film story. 'What do you mean by that?', she would demand, 'What is the point of that? Why have that there?'. You knew you'd be facing that interrogation. That was what you had in your mind all the time as you worked.

Panorama reporters working on a magazine programme where they were seen week after week quickly became familiar figures. Says Chataway: 'You were vaguely surprised if you met anyone who *didn't* know who you were.' His athletic celebrity helped him there. He was on leave from *Panorama* representing Britain in the Olympics when the Suez crisis broke in 1956, quickly taking the train from Budapest to Vienna and on to Blackpool in order to report the ensuing row at the Tory Party Conference.

One of Chataway's most telling reports was on the 'colour bar' operating on the railways. Workers in some depots were refusing to have 'coloured' men work with them. Having established in an interview with a manager that jobs were available Chataway returned to ask him why he had just rejected four black but otherwise suitable candidates. 'The fact is', said Chataway to the manager, Mr Campbell, 'you don't want to see too many coloured men working in British Railways.' 'Yes, I think you can say we don't,' was the reply, 'because it can create special difficulties and can exaggerate the difficulties that we have at the present time.' Chataway didn't leave it there; at the end of his report he gave his own conclusions:

> What is disturbing, I think, is that the men at Smithfield, and at depots like it, should deprive West Indians of any chance to prove themselves simply because of their colour. The excuses that they give are that they are too slow, or that they're hard to understand; and these excuses can't in fact be valid because these West Indians do work well and are accepted in other depots; because British Railways by and large has done very well by the coloured man and has offered them thousands of jobs.
>
> But it does seem that the unions should 'crusade', to use Mr Campbell's word, and that the management should be more courageous in trying to persuade these backward depots to be more broadminded and civilised, because if this colour prejudice persists, then there's going to be a great deal of unemployment among coloured men.
>
> The only other alternative is to ban West Indians from coming into this country, and if we ever decided to do that, we should certainly have forfeited the right for good and all to criticise South Africa or the extremists in the southern States of America.[18]

Here is a reporter producing evidence and offering the viewer a judgement based upon it. That was what Grace Wyndham Goldie and Michael Peacock seem to have expected from their reporters, whatever the subject.

Chataway didn't stay long on *Panorama*; in 1959 he was elected to Parliament.[19] He remembers that on *Panorama* he was the lone Conservative: 'There were lots of political arguments.' But that did not invalidate or bias his reporting.

None of these early *Panorama* reporters was afraid to express an opinion. Ludovic Kennedy, who joined *Panorama* after failing to win a parliamentary seat in 1959, reported on the hardship caused in compulsory purchase cases: 'My sympathies – and I dare say yours too – were almost equally divided between on the one hand Mr Smith, who has after all lost his home and his farm, and on the other hand all those hundreds of people, many of whom have come from slums in London, who for the first time in their lives have been given a decent place to live in.' But, Kennedy continued:

If a man is going to lose his home, then surely he should deserve very special treatment. Why, if he is going to lose his home, can't the local authority send down someone to see him in an informal way and give him some kind of warning of what is going to happen? Why can't he get friendly letters starting off 'Dear Mr. Smith, We are very sorry to tell you' rather than letters which start off 'Dear Sir, With reference to X, Y and Z'? And why, above all perhaps, cannot compensation be both speedy and generous? In other words, if the local authorities and other authorities cannot prevent the blow, then they should do all that is in their power to soften it.[20]

Panorama wanted its reporters to state their conclusions, but Broadcasting House was not always so sure about this departure from an older BBC model. On 21 March 1960 the Board of Management considered an edition of *Panorama* that had included an item about the Dominican Republic. The minutes report the Director General like this:

In his opinion the broadcast had departed from strict impartiality, in as much as the views to which James Mossman had given voice had been presented as though they were his own and not, as they should properly have been, as those of well-informed quarters on the spot. The case was in some respects similar to that of the Wheeler despatch from Ceylon. There was a need for greater vigilance in handling material of this nature.[21]

In May 1956 Woodrow Wyatt had taken his remit to look at the evidence and tell the viewers his conclusion further than ever before, speaking out in a *Panorama* programme in a most dramatic way. He had used the power of the personality he had built up in a few short months of frequent television appearances to try to influence an election. Some saw in the way he went about it a British Joe McCarthy in the making; others believed that this was a demonstration of the way that television could contribute to democracy.

The transcript of *Panorama* on 14 May reads:

Dimbleby: Well, now we have something which we hope will start you all thinking. Woodrow Wyatt reports.

Wyatt: Well, tonight I'm going to do something that I've never done before on television. I'm going to talk to just one group of a community only – the members of the Amalgamated Engineering Union, or the AEU for short, and I'm going to ask you to take part in your own elections, the elections which decide who shall be the full time officials who run your union. And I'm going to do that because your union is not only the second largest, with nearly a million members, it's also perhaps the most important in the entire country. You're the backbone of the British engineering industry; you're at the heart of the British export trade; and at this very moment your union is just on the verge of coming under the control of the Communists . . . The Communists don't have any members of parliament, but if they could get control of the AEU that would be more useful to them in the effect that they could have in and on Britain than having 50 members of parliament. Now of course if you want a Communist-dominated AEU, well, that's entirely your affair. This is a democratic country and you've the right to vote in as many Communist officials as you like. But do you really want your union to be run by the Communists?

Wyatt went on to say that, because of apathy, officials were being elected by a tiny number of members: 'The Communists and their friends, they always vote; it's the non-Communists who don't seem to bother.' His film report which followed demonstrated clearly and convincingly how apathy was allowing Communist activists to win power in the union out of all proportion to their actual numbers. Members of the union told Wyatt how they just didn't bother to take the time to sit through meetings and vote in elections that were often decided by a show of hands. Wyatt concluded with a warning about what might shortly happen. If in the election currently going on a Communist-supported candidate should win:

. . . then that seat will change over to being a Communist one, and the Executive Council of the AEU will become dominated by the Communists. And if that should happen, then the AEU will be the largest and most important union in the whole of the free world to come under Communist control. It's your decision.

Dimbleby: Now, I know that nine million people watch our *Panorama* programme each Monday. It will be interesting indeed to see whether

Woodrow Wyatt's report tonight does have any effect on the numbers who vote in the AEU ballot.[22]

Now I want you to meet one of Britain's best known newspaper cartoonists. . .[23]

This was stirring it indeed: 'Woodrow Wyatt's direct address to A.E.U. members from *Panorama* last week was yet another instance of the immediate power TV could have in the nation's life,' said *Time and Tide*. 'Let Communists answer Wyatt,' demanded the *Daily Worker*, while in Parliament Labour's George Wigg asked the Postmaster General 'if he is aware that the British Broadcasting Corporation have recently departed from the code of political impartiality by making attacks on members of minority political parties by paid broadcasters speaking outside the agreed programmes of party political broadcasts'.

Grace Wyndham Goldie wrote a background briefing note to help the BBC Press Office deal with the furore following Wyatt's programme. First of all came the usual 'keeping the reporter separate from the Corporation in case we have to dump him' paragraph: 'Reporters are employed by the BBC on contract; they are not members of staff. They use their own individual approach to each subject but are prohibited from using their position as reporters to advocate their own party political views. The responsibility for seeing that they do not do so rests with the BBC.' Then she went on to deploy her main argument: it would have been disingenuous to ignore the fact that dealing with the AEU elections might affect the vote – better to be quite open about it. She concluded:

'In general terms we felt it was important to keep a clear distinction in our minds between

a) An attempt to bring political pressures, or allow commentators to bring political pressures. This we should and must not do.

b) The advocation of democratic action, and/or reporting, which though fair and allowable might have political consequences. These we should not be afraid to do.[24]

What did Wyndham Goldie mean exactly? She seems to be saying that arguing in favour of democratic action is fine for a *Panorama* reporter. But was it proper for Wyatt to lean out of the screen to buttonhole AEU members, telling them to go and vote? This is getting close to advocacy journalism – on behalf of democracy and casting your vote today, but what cause next? Give your children the MMR vaccine? Demand fluoride in the drinking water? March against paedophiles? Ban the Bomb? Boycott Burma?

Wyatt's AEU story could have been covered in a more straightforward way in which all the facts he presented in his report would still have featured. Was it really proper, as Wyndham Goldie argued, for him to tell his audience so loudly to go and act on them? Current affairs reporters should go beyond the bare bones of the news story to indicate clearly where they think the truth lies, and lay out the likely consequences of one course of action or another. But campaigning journalism wants to go further than that. There may be a place where television journalists who feel strongly about an issue can tell us what we should do about it, but a programme like that should be, as it were, within inverted commas, in some series in which viewers will expect to hear a vigorous call for action – let's call it the John Pilger Pulpit.

While the big broadcasters still dominate television viewing, while the BBC Licence Fee and the idea of public service broadcasting prevail, then these broadcasters should normally avoid advocacy in mainstream programmes. *Panorama*, or any similar current affairs programme, or any individual reporter, must be wary of demanding specific action in the wake of some investigation: Free the prisoners! Ban the gun clubs! Provide the lifesaving drug! – that must normally be a matter for viewers to make up their own minds about. But it need not blunt the cutting edge of good journalism; by putting the emphasis on gathering and presenting the evidence rather than banging a drum or leading a crusade a programme may deliver the message with even greater impact.

Eighteen months after Wyatt's AEU campaign he returned to the subject of Communist-dominated unions – this time the ETU. It was, for a BBC dependent on strongly unionised electricians to get its programmes on the air, a highly sensitive issue. In response to a request from Leonard Miall for guidance, S.G. Williams, the Controller of Television Administration, said a programme like that envisaged might open the BBC to charges of libel; and it might upset not only the ETU but the TUC as well: 'I doubt the propriety of an examination of alleged corruption over the air.' Miall persisted, sending the proposal to the Board of Management. The Director General said he had 'no objection', and the *Panorama* investigation went ahead.

This time there were no studio histrionics from Wyatt, just an extremely effective film which detailed the way in which Communists were manipulating union elections. 'In last week's sizzling *Panorama*,' wrote Maurice Wiggin:[25]

> Mr Woodrow Wyatt's interviews with members of the Electrical Trades Union gained a huge increment of drama from the fact that several of them were not seen . . . In its strange, chilling way this was one of the most dramatic things I have seen. In your quiet insulated room you felt the weight and swirl of

> the dangerous flood
> Of history, that never sleeps or dies,
> And, held one moment, burns the hand.

Another commentator talked of the 'instantaneous impact of the programme . . . For this the credit must go in equal parts to *Panorama*'s Editor, Michael Peacock, and Woodrow Wyatt, who conducted the interviews. Editing and production held a note of controlled passion which exactly matched the occasion. The hidden faces and disguised voices, which might have been merely melodramatic, added a chill of fear . . . In such a setting Woodrow Wyatt's bland spectacles and clubroom drawl were doubly emphatic. He resisted any temptation to jog the viewers' attention with interjections of his own: the graphic, impromptu stories of the union men were in any case quite sufficient. I call this television journalism of a high order.'[26]

Wyatt left *Panorama* in 1958 to return to politics.[27] But his bold ETU programme eventually bore fruit. On 22 February 1960 Frank Foulkes, the Communist President of the ETU, finally came into the studio to answer allegations made by some of the union's local leaders in the previous week's programme. They had claimed that Frank Haxell, another Communist, had only been re-elected General Secretary because of widespread ballot-rigging. In a powerful interview that was certainly worthy of Wyatt's original report interviewer John Freeman said to Foulkes: 'You do realise, don't you, that these charges concern you personally? . . . If they are not charges of administrative inefficiency then they are charges that amount to charges of fraud, perhaps of criminal conspiracy. What do you feel about that?' Foulkes replied that he was quite well able to stand up to any charge of criminal conspiracy. Freeman continued: 'You have a very simple remedy. You can go to the courts tomorrow morning and issue writs for libel against me, against the BBC, against all the papers that have attacked you and against the four gentlemen who appeared in last week's programme.'[28]

In letters to *The Times*,[29] such Labour luminaries as George Brown and Patrick Gordon Walker leaped to Foulkes's defence, accusing *Panorama* of unacceptable behaviour. 'We wish to express our grave concern at what we regard as the dangerous implications of the recent BBC programme in which Mr. Foulkes was interviewed by Mr. John Freeman. If this kind of programme spreads, it seems to us that there is a danger of a new form of procedure in public affairs – namely, trial by television.'

Saying that Foulkes had been virtually forced to appear, the politicians (who had themselves signally failed to secure any effective investigation of the ETU) continued:

> We wish to protest before this kind of thing is carried further. We don't want to see in Britain the abuse of trial before television cameras that has occurred in other places. We hope that the convention of public life will be firmly established that it is not part of the function of television authorities, BBC or commercial, to set up their own form of tribunal, or to use their great power of public appeal to coerce people to subject themselves to inquisition by spreading abroad accusations against them.

Oh dear! What barely concealed anger at television as a rival power in the land, a medium prepared to set its own agenda, rather than await instruction from Westminster as to what was proper for discussion.

The BBC Board of Management was nervous but firm. In an important minute on 29 February 1960 it said:

The question of principle posed in the M.P.s' letter was further discussed. It was felt to be a legitimate and undeniable part of the BBC's informational function to pursue the search for truth in matters of controversy where the public interest was clearly involved. The case of the E.T.U. elections was precisely such an issue, and *Panorama* had been right to handle it. The charges made against the manner of its handling could not be sustained. The letter had however been useful in pointing to certain dangers that could be incurred unless the proper precautions were taken. The interviewer, in particular, must be a man who, while fearless in questioning, could be relied upon not to assume too patently the gown of the prosecutor, and who could preserve objectivity in all circumstances. The question of victimisation, though it did not arise in the E.T.U. instance, was also one that needed to be carefully watched. Above all, the BBC must be quite clear as to its purpose on embarking on these controversial issues and be prepared to justify it.[30]

Panorama had not usurped the courts' functions. After John Freeman's interview Frank Foulkes did not leave the studio and go directly to jail. There was a lengthy hearing in the High Court before, in June 1961, the judgement of the court confirmed that there had been a ballot-rigging conspiracy organised from the headquarters of the Communist Party. Frank Haxell was removed from his post as the ETU's General Secretary, and so, after an appeal, was Foulkes, its President.

A single *Panorama* – or any other television programme - can rarely change the world, move mountains, bring down governments, make or break people, nor should it be able to do so. After all, as politicians sometimes quite reasonably say to *Panorama* reporters, 'Who elected you?' What a programme like *Panorama* can do is bring before viewers new information which will begin to change public opinion, or, with proper analysis, help people make up their own minds on a difficult issue. In the AEU and ETU cases Woodrow Wyatt and *Panorama* contributed to a process in which some of the truth, hitherto concealed, was exposed. It was to happen on many occasions subsequently. The denial of democracy in some trade unions, the fraudulent manipulation of newspaper competitions by Robert Maxwell, the concealment of evidence by tobacco companies, the callous injustice in the case of three Cardiff men wrongly convicted of murder or the links between the security forces and political assassinations in Northern Ireland – this was all *Panorama* territory, where journalists who would come after Wyatt could ferret out the truth and turn it over to public view. The revelations themselves were rarely complete or conclusive, but they led on to further enquiries and subsequent action.

That sounds pretty good: a round of applause please for the People's Champion *Panorama*. But it rather ducks the question raised by Wyatt's original programme on the AEU: how far is the *Panorama* reporter entitled to go in giving us his opinion, whether he lectures us directly 'to camera', or puts it in his commentary? And if he is going to give us that opinion – and even start telling us what to do – how can we trust him not to be biased in some way that is unknown to us?

Reporter bias: where are they coming from?

There's no getting away from it that current affairs journalists do want to tell us what they think – and so they should. In the beginning, that early generation of *Panorama* reporters felt their experience of life, of government even, entitled them to give their opinion, as long as they did so in a personal, non-party way. And in those far-off days the fact that someone had served as a minister of the Crown, had been in authority, might in itself have added some weight to that opinion. But it's not just politician reporters who want to tell us what they think: others too have their own reasons for thinking we should welcome their views.

Many *Panorama* reporters have acquired their experience of journalism working for the news. For some time they have covered 'on the day' stories which have been broadcast quickly, at no great length. There's been no time, whatever other elements the news bulletin editor may add to the package, for the individual reporter to dig deep into the story, put his news in context, or try to explain the often complex background to the simple tale which is all he has time to tell. This can be frustrating, particularly when that background might make the story more interesting, or when it has been difficult or dangerous to get. To give an example: in Vietnam in the 1960s and 1970s, television news reporters would routinely leave their hotel in Saigon early in the morning and drive up one road or another with their camera teams looking for action. Or they might take a helicopter ride with the US forces to some potential trouble spot. There they would hope to get some 'bang-bang' action. If they were lucky something exciting would happen in front of the camera. Then, sweaty, exhausted, and probably very frightened, the reporter and his camera crew would hurry back to Saigon, write and record a brief commentary, and ship their film on the evening Air France flight en route to Britain. If there was some particularly exciting footage, with soldiers firing, casualties bleeding, villages blazing, Vietnamese women weeping, or napalm dropping in a colourful way that justified the extra expense, then the 'rushes' would be flown to Hong Kong, edited there and a package sent by satellite to London for transmission that same night.

But next morning there would often be a telex from the foreign desk: 'SORRY YOUR EXCELLENT DA NANG STORY OUTHELD STOP GEORGE BEST SNEEZED' or 'REGRET DUE BIG HOME NEWS DAY YOUR PIECE RAN 27 SECONDS'. This could be frustrating. After several assignments to somewhere fascinating – like Vietnam – some news reporters would begin to feel they had a bit more to say about what was really happening there than a few words of commentary over an isolated incident, however exciting. And they might reasonably come to the conclusion that the news would never have time for that. Rather than leave a sub-editor (who had probably never been anywhere near Vietnam) to write a paragraph introducing his short film package, the reporter decided he could do the job better himself – if he was only allowed a longer film, and a longer time to make it in. And so he became a current affairs reporter – perhaps for *Panorama* or ITV's *This Week*. Now at last he had the time and space to tell the viewer a bit more about what was happening: to explain why it was, for example, that though this ARVN battalion had wiped out this Vietcong unit in these exciting pictures, the South Vietnamese might not necessarily win the war.

But if current affairs reporters want to tell us what they think, how far should they really be allowed, let alone encouraged, to do so? Were those early *Panorama* pioneers right to tell us directly and clearly what they thought was the truth of the matter? Yes, for that is the essence of current affairs television: telling viewers a fuller and therefore potentially more accurate story than the News will ever have time or opportunity to do. The *Panorama* reporter's job, as Grace Wyndham Goldie rightly saw it, was to help the viewer to get the best possible look through that window on the world. If the viewer could not himself go abroad to Malta, or Vietnam, then he should feel able to rely on the account of it that the *Panorama* reporter brought back to show him.

That account is inevitably going to be a personal one, a tale told by one person rather than another. By Charter there cannot be any such thing as a 'BBC editorial opinion', nor should a mainstream current affairs programme adopt an editorial line. *Panorama* never has. But individual reporters are just that, individuals.

Reporters are called on to decide what, in their own opinion, are the important elements of a story; then, if they are to be of any use to the viewer, they must indicate what they think is more important to consider than something else – and tell us why. Finally, having decided on the more important elements in the story, the bits that must be dealt with, the reporter must try to make his own judgements about where the weight of the evidence lies. It's not enough to report that 'Galileo says the earth goes round the sun; the Holy Office says the sun goes round the earth'. A *Panorama* reporter's job is to decide where, in his opinion, and on the evidence he offers, the balance of the truth lies. Unlike the Pope speaking *ex cathedra* he is not laying down his interpretation of the facts as something that must be accepted. He is suggesting that his opinion is worth considering seriously. And whether we agree with him of course depends on the quality of the reporter, the evidence he has produced and the way he has presented it.

By the late 1950s *Panorama* had assembled a team of reporters whose quality could not be denied. Woodrow Wyatt had opened the window on the world and stepped out to explore it; Chris Chataway had joined him; and now, as the current affairs element in the programme grew, others arrived to report. Robert Kee, Jim Mossman and John Morgan came, not from politics or television but from print journalism. They too were real giants.

Kee had been an RAF bomber pilot, a prisoner of war in Germany and later special correspondent for both the *Observer* and the *Sunday Times*. Even more significant, he had for three years worked for *Picture Post*. This magazine was a model for aspiring television journalists. In its marriage of strong, simple but well-written popular journalism and gritty, powerful pictures it had huge impact. That's what the new medium of television wanted to be like.

Kee was a highly intelligent and cultivated man, who would later write a definitive history of Irish nationalism, translate innumerable German texts, and could still be found in the British Library at the age of 80 researching a book on François Mitterrand. But no one who ever saw him in action could ever think of Kee as an ivory tower academic, rising serene above the mist of battle. In 1968, following the Soviet invasion and occupation of Czechoslovakia, the author glimpsed Kee weaving though the crowds in Prague's Wenceslas Square. Dodging in and out of doorways with his cameraman, as occasional warning bursts of Russian gunfire reasserted Soviet control over its rebellious satellite, Kee was thumbing through a notebook bulging with invaluable Czech contacts he had previously made. His reporting was always intelligent because it was based on a thorough understanding of the background to events.

Like Kee, Jim Mossman was not just extraordinarily bright, but vastly experienced. 'A careworn figure in a white suit', as Jonathan Dimbleby remembers him, he had worked for the *Observer* in the Middle East and also for MI6, the foreign intelligence service. Mossman, the world-weary cynic, warned the young Dimbleby off television reporting: 'Don't ever do it,' he said, 'we're just old whores.' Says Chris Ralling, a *Panorama* producer with whom Mossman was often teamed: 'Jim was effortlessly brilliant, a cross between Lawrence of Arabia and Cassius. He was almost too good for what he was doing. When it came to writing the script he was superb, and he wasn't afraid of anybody or anything.' Ralling vividly recalls a trip to interview Ethiopia's Emperor Haile Selassie – not least because one of the Emperor's tame lions took a bite out of his trousers while they were waiting. As they were ushered into the presence of the Emperor, who understood English perfectly well, Mossman said in a loud stage whisper: 'He reminds me of a third-rate London actuary.'

The freelance cameraman Erik Durschmied first encountered Mossman when they met each other at the airport in Paris, en route to Hong Kong. Durschmied's first impression was of a cold man: 'He was a tall scarecrow, thin and bony. A mouth twisted into a grin of cynicism and perhaps contempt.' But, he says, Mossman was just brilliant, a cameraman's dream of what a reporter should be. Durschmied gratefully recalls Mossman coming vigorously and effectively to his rescue on their first trip together, when he was set upon by a gang of thugs one dark night in Macao.

A homosexual at a time when it was not possible to be open and relaxed about it, Mossman led a rather tortured private life. Though a favourite lunch guest of society hostesses he rarely came to *Panorama*'s Lime Grove offices. He could not bear to linger in London any longer than was necessary to prepare for some new assignment.

And then there was John Morgan: Welsh, much more heart on sleeve and raffish than his colleagues; like them, a wonderful writer; unlike most of them very much not the product of an English public school; happy to down a lunchtime pint or two in the BBC Club bar as he held forth, full of ideas about building the New Jerusalem. Of all the new arrivals, Morgan, a major contributor to the *New Statesman*, was the most overtly political. Says Chris Ralling: 'John Morgan was a boy from the Welsh valleys who'd made good and gone to college. The rest were silver-spoon boys; he was more down-to-earth – and very convivial.'

Woodrow Wyatt and Christopher Chataway left *Panorama* to stand at the 1959 general election. They were successful, and left television for political careers. But two political hopefuls who had not been so lucky came to replace them.

Robin Day had been turned down by Leonard Miall when he first tried for a job with the BBC's Television Talks department in 1954. The following year he and Chataway had been hired as the first newscasters at ITN. There, after a rather shaky start, Day had made a considerable mark, particularly with important interviews. In Cairo, a few months after the Suez fiasco, he had quizzed President Nasser about relations between Britain and Egypt; in the studio in London he had asked Prime Minister Harold Macmillan whether he would sack his Foreign Secretary.

The way Day had conducted these interviews, like the barrister he had trained to be, was a very significant development. Gone were the fawning, unctuous questions and, as a result, the patronising, condescending answers that had been typical of previous political interviews on television; in came direct effective questioning that revealed more than the general public had ever known before about the world's leaders. It swept away unnecessary deference and replaced it with man-to-man encounter. As Day later put it: 'When I interview a king I am on a level with the king. When I interview a dustman I am on a level with the dustman.' But now, in 'a reckless and ridiculous gamble', as he later described it, Day stood as a

Liberal candidate at Hereford in the 1959 election. He was defeated. So too was Ludovic Kennedy at Rochdale.

The dashing, rather aristocratic 'Ludo' had been presenting ITV's current affairs programme *This Week*.[31] 'In those days', he says, it was 'a scrappy affair, known as "the poor man's *Panorama*".' Kennedy had grown tired of a programme which he felt included too many items that were simply silly. Now, after the election, he did not want to return to it.

Neither Kennedy nor Day could easily take up newscasting again so soon after they had both stood for Parliament and so clearly declared their party-political allegiance. Both were delighted when Miall saw his opportunity and signed them both up as *Panorama* reporters.

So when Day joined *Panorama* in November 1959 his colleagues were Robert Kee, Kennedy, John Morgan and Jim Mossman. This, as Michael Peacock rightly boasted, was 'the strongest reporting team ever gathered together for one television programme'.[32] It was a magic moment in television, though these distinguished reporters would no doubt have deplored a phrase of such banality. A few weeks before his death[33] Day was still irascibly trying to impress on the author how truly extraordinary was the place *Panorama* held in the nation's consciousness as the 1960s began.

In five years the 'new' *Panorama* had become part of the fabric of the nation. Every Monday night eight million people or more tuned in to it. As Day had written:

> *Panorama* was a major event of the week, keenly awaited by press, politicians and people alike . . . it was the TV forum where national issues, political, economic, social were debated. *Panorama* was also, as its sub-title 'Your Window on the World' suggested, the programme whose celebrated reporters brought dramatic film of foreign happenings, revolutions, crises and upheavals into the living rooms of Britain. *Panorama* was the flagship of BBC television's journalistic fleet.[34]

How often have *Panorama* people of later generations reminded hesitant interviewees that, if they agreed to talk, they would be appearing on the BBC's 'flagship' current affairs programme? In 1960 there was absolutely no doubt about it at all. *Panorama* was as dazzling a flagship then as Cleopatra's barge.

It's true that for *Panorama*'s crew of reporters it was easier to make an impact than it is today: 'Then', wrote Ludovic Kennedy, 'it was a novelty for viewers to see one of us addressing them from the fringe of some desert or jungle, knowing he had been there only days before.' In a nice piece of self-deprecation Kennedy described the rather simple, indeed formulaic, *Panorama* foreign report typical of the time:

> It was usually a four to five days' shoot in countries the size of Mexico or the Philippines, for a fifteen to twenty minute report. The ingredients would include the Prime Minister and the Opposition leader (assuming there was one). There would be a run-down on the country's economy and a brief look at some singular aspect of it (the French Legion in Morocco, white settlers in Kenya, clocks in Switzerland). And in the Third World there would be a day in the country shooting local crops and a man ploughing with a pair of oxen. The standard commentary for the above would go 'for hundreds of years now the country's peasants have been tilling a frugal living from the always inhospitable soil'.[35]

For reporters who came later to *Panorama* this makes rather uncomfortable reading. Too often in the 1970s a *Panorama* shooting order looked too much as it had a full decade before. The only difference was that, at three times the length, the report was now likely to be much more boring. But in the days of Kennedy and Kee, Mossman, Morgan and Day, the simple format was sufficient framework within which to tell – and show – the viewer something new and interesting. As Trevor Phillpot of the rival *Tonight* programme is said to have remarked: 'The world was a virgin and we had our way with her.'

When it was still relatively rare for any British broadcast journalist to express an opinion some viewers soon found *Panorama* reporters out of order. As colonialism began to unravel in Africa, Robin Day came under attack from the *Daily Mirror* after his report from the Congo, in 1961:

> *Panorama* kicked up its heels last night in a wild and coltish gesture completely divorced from objective reporting . . . Remembering that the programme serves 12,000,000 viewers with information, it was startling to find Robin Day suddenly given his head for personal comment . . . Back from Katanga's

stricken Elisabethville where he stalked the streets to show the city under fire, Mr. Day could not contain himself with plain reporting. He said: 'With the situation loaded with political passion . . . the only useful and honest thing for a reporter who is just back from Elisabethville is to state his own independent conclusions.' The conclusions amounted to an attack on the United Nations for 'imposing a political situation by force' . . . For a reporter to switch abruptly from straight news to political comment is not only dangerous but confusing, biased and disturbing. Are we to expect loaded argument now from *Panorama*? If so, its claim to be a window on the world is shattered.[36]

Leaving aside the *Daily Mirror*'s own potential bias on an issue that was almost as politically divisive as Suez, this criticism misses the point. *Panorama* was not offering 'straight news' but sending a current affairs reporter to try and make sense of the situation. Some viewers will have disagreed with Day's conclusions, but he showed them what he had seen and then gave them his personal judgement on what it meant, the judgement of an intelligent, experienced journalist. And he made it plain which was which.

What can be wrong with that? How infinitely preferable to so much extended news which shows everything, often at length, but makes sense of nothing; news 'reporting' which often means no more than an inexperienced writer sitting in some newsroom cobbling together commentary culled from agency reports to fit pictures shot by heaven knows whom! As Day had himself written a little earlier that year in his book *Television: A Personal Report*:[37]

Panorama is not a news programme, though it often covers big news in its own way. The team of reporters is encouraged to take a critical approach. It is not enough to state a problem or present an individual with a platform.

The reporters are not pundits, nor are they presented as pundits. The idea is that they should become familiar figures to the viewer; not as experts but as men whom viewers get to know as their enquiring representatives in strange places, their persistent fact-finders in confused situations.

The programme looks at events through the eyes of the reporters associated with the programme. This does not mean that the reporter can editorialise or air his own prejudices. It means that, subject to showing the issues fairly, he can interpret these issues according to his own knowledge and judgement.

One of the healthiest developments in British television during the last few years has been the increasing freedom and independence given to (or taken by) television reporters and the editors in charge of programmes.

Michael Peacock, who had returned to lead the *Panorama* team again in November 1959, explained to Michael Wall of the *Listener* magazine just how important his reporters – and their own personal judgements – were to the programme's success. 'The secret of *Panorama*', he says, 'is to build up a team of personalities who are identified with the programme. Thus we do not just show, for example, the riots in Nyasaland, but Chataway in Nyasaland – not just Cairo today, but Day in Cairo. We are looking at news through the eyes of a person identified with the programme.' The image that the Editor wants *Panorama* to have is a 'vigorous, topical and imaginative programme recognised as carrying integrity and authority. But the programme must have edge and bite. It must make people sit up, and at least once a fortnight we should have an item which makes a real impact . . . The success of *Panorama* in living up to this image depends on the men who have to put each item across. They have to be more than news reporters, they have to have more than competence and a presentable appearance.'

Michael Wall could see the dangers of Peacock's emphasis on personality:

> Quickness and edge are only a short step from aggressiveness and even rudeness; a keen mind can lead the interviewer to do more of the talking than the man he is interviewing; success and popularity can breed pomposity or condescension, and perhaps the greatest danger of all for the man with his own views is to tell the viewers what he thinks they should think. *Panorama*'s commentators have never been political neuters – they would be unlikely to meet the requirements if they were – but as long as the team is well balanced politically that should be an advantage. There would seem to be a place now for a bright young Conservative.[38]

In the early days *Panorama* reporters like Woodrow Wyatt were typically party politicians between seats. They moved in and out of television depending on whether or not they could persuade the voters of this or that constituency to send them to Parliament. Wyatt himself was a former junior minister in a Labour Government. But though he was expected to form and express his own opinion on the stories he was assigned to, any hint of party political bias would have meant the end of his contract. Looking back a decade later on his two ground-breaking years reporting for *Panorama* Wyatt praised 'Mrs. Wyndham Goldie's determination to have clear and fair expositions of current affairs . . . She was the last senior official of the BBC who cared deeply about impartiality and insisted on having it. No one was allowed to slant, right, left or liberal, in the programmes she controlled, though they could have what politics they liked provided they did not show.'

Nonetheless, in the early years, when reporters were often people who had been or would again be professional politicians, BBC bosses were concerned about demonstrating a party political balance in the team. As *Panorama* went off for its summer break in 1956 Michael Peacock gave the programme staff a list of things to think about for the new season, among them: 'Reporters: We must find new faces. We need another Current Affairs reporter to balance Wyatt. Chataway will only be available for the first two programmes.'[39] Later, as the team expanded to match the increased commitment to current affairs, there was a renewed effort to recruit overtly Conservative people.

In 1962 there began to be rumblings from the Conservative Party to the effect that *Panorama* was politically unfair and unbalanced. Lord Aldington, Deputy Chairman of the Conservative Party Organisation, had a chat about it with the Director of Television, Kenneth Adam. Because the Conservatives Chris Chataway and Geoffrey Johnson Smith had been so long gone without replacement, Adam told Grace Wyndham Goldie, there was a suspicion (at Central Office) that *Panorama* had not even been trying for a politically balanced team.[40] The suggestion being made by the Tories was that 'the team and those who direct it are estranged from Conservative ideas and the Conservative world, where they are by no means estranged from the ideas of the other two parties. . .[Richard] Dimbleby has become infected with a feeling of being censorious or suspicious towards the Conservatives.'

Wyndham Goldie wrote back robustly saying that this was just an old

Conservative trick designed to make the BBC nervous about doing programmes which might become the subject of a further complaint:

> The suggestion that Richard Dimbleby was in any way turning against the Conservative Party was entirely lacking in any sort of truth. I do not know what his political affiliations are but his general attitude to life is one which embodies a respect for tradition of a kind which is so deeply felt that he must be in general conservative (with a small c) even if not with a capital C.

That was easy, but what about the rest of the team?

> Reporters on *Tonight* and *Panorama* are questioning characters – this is part of their function. One of the matters they question is the use of authority. This may, wrongly, from time to time give to people in authority, if they happen to be Conservatives, a feeling that the questioners are hostile to Conservatism. It is difficult to get this point across, but it is one which I think it important to try and get people to understand.[41]

In May 1962, Leonard Miall, now Assistant Controller, Current Affairs and Talks, Television, wrote to the Editor, News and Current Affairs, Donald Edwards. He sent a copy to the Director General's Assistant, Harmon Grisewood: 'I have again asked Editor *Panorama* actively to search for a professional reporter with known Conservative leanings in order that the stable may be a balanced one.'[42] Negotiations with Ian Trethowan, who was already a well-known BBC presenter, had broken down. According to another memo from Head of Talks, Staff, other names now being considered included Nicholas Harman (then working on the *Economist*); Norman St. John Stevas ('a promising and improving performer'); Peregrine Worsthorne of the *Sunday Telegraph* ('a fair performer only with a rather academic manner'); and William Rees-Mogg, 'reliably tipped' as next Editor of the *Sunday Times*. 'Other possibilities' were Nigel Lawson, then the City Editor of the *Sunday Telegraph* ('very photogenic, slightly superior manner which might be cured'), and Andrew Gardner, the ITN newscaster ('might be won away if thought suitable').[43]

Some of the candidates were not interested, but in August Paul Fox, *Panorama*'s Editor, reported that six hopefuls had now been auditioned. In particular he had liked David Coleman ('Highly competent television performance – must polish up his current affairs (and will do so)'), Peter Lewis of the *Daily Mail* ('Best user of words; light on politics – worth another look') and Roderick McFarquar of the *Daily Telegraph* ('A good performance, both as interviewer and in his piece to camera. Intelligent, persuasive and keen').[44] Fox remembers one particular would-be reporter who applied to him for a job on *Panorama*. He had, it appeared, just 'come down from Oxford'. But Fox decided he was just too brash, without sufficient experience, 'a whipper-snapper trying to bullshit his way in'. His name was Jeffrey Archer.[45]

Of all the possibles named two eventually came to *Panorama* at different times – Roderick McFarquar and Nicholas Harman – but neither stayed for long. Harman came to feel that though television might be good with people it was hopeless at dealing with the issues; after a spell presenting the *Midweek* programme he left the BBC to run the Commonwealth Secretariat. McFarquar, China expert, as much academic as journalist, went to work for BBC Radio before becoming Professor of Government at Harvard University.

At a time, in the 1960s, when the old order, the 'Establishment', was being challenged in an almost revolutionary way the BBC was clearly concerned at the highest level by accusations of political bias. The Conservative Party's private complaints were taken seriously. In the autumn of 1962 a paper commissioned by the Director General came to the conclusion that 'a combination of incidents produced the impression of some anti-Government, or anti-Conservative animus, among those responsible for the programme. Our position is no easy one. We have laudably sought to detach an 'Establishment' label from the BBC, and not to discourage idealism. This has promoted good staff relations with young producers, who (as D.G. [Hugh Carleton Greene] has remarked) are generally Left-wing – if at the expense of a vital sector of public relations on occasion. But it is consequently no less necessary for the national instrument of broadcasting to maintain objectivity and impartiality.'[46]

Later in *Panorama*'s history the BBC – though not the politicians – seemed less concerned about a reporter's specific party allegiance. The most obvious reason was that these people were no longer treating television as simply an interlude in a political career; the era of reporter as professional-politician-in-waiting had ended. Reporters were earning their living entirely in television; they no longer had the problems of men like Woodrow Wyatt, consciously excluding from his work for *Panorama* the party line that he was committed to as a past and future Labour MP.

But in Wyatt's own opinion the disappearance of reporters with a well-known political allegiance only increased the danger of bias. As he moved across the political spectrum from Labour to the Thatcherite wing of the Conservative Party Wyatt became more and more convinced that *Panorama* and the rest of current affairs television had been secretly taken over by extreme socialists. *Panorama*, he said, had 'shrunk to a vestige of its former self, because left-wing, often very left-wing, producers, presenters, directors, reporters and editors and researchers were allowed to take over and slant it in line with their political bias'.[47]

In an article entitled 'It's time to nail your colours to the screen' Wyatt argued that 'the general public watch and listen to TV and radio programmes which they suppose, from the august authority of the organisation sponsoring them, are impartial, whereas frequently they are highly slanted expressions of political views masquerading as impartial'. You knew where you were with newspapers, said Wyatt;

> Not so with the presentation of current affairs on BBC and ITV, where no guide is given as to the political motivation of those who compile or broadcast the material . . . Certainly the ballot is secret. But that is a rule which can apply only to those who do not covertly peddle political viewpoints as though they were apolitical under the banner of the BBC and the IBA [Independent Broadcasting Authority], on whose political impartiality the public are entitled to rely.[48]

Then came Wyatt's modest proposal:

> *Panorama* should tell us how Mr. Fred Emery and Mr. Richard Lindley, regular presenters, voted last time and how they intend to vote next time, as well as revealing the political inclinations of the editors, producers, research workers and so forth of the programmes . . . Those who revel in investigating

the predilections and activities of others should not be ashamed, or too coy, to declare theirs; and the BBC and the IBA should compel them to do so. It is not possible, to have an accurate balance in current affairs programmes, either within each one or taken as a whole, but it is possible for the IBA and the BBC to indicate the partialities of those involved and leave the public to judge the merits of what they put out accordingly, instead of being deceived by subliminal party political broadcasting.

It's an interesting idea: if politicians have to declare their interests, and how they vote in Parliament, on issues that concern us all, shouldn't current affairs broadcasters, particularly those working for the BBC at the licence payer's expense, do the same?

What would happen if they did? First, of course, you would have to decide which people you needed to know about: reporters? presenters? producers? researchers? editors? cameramen? managers? directors general? Where exactly would it stop? And then of course you would have to find some Orwellian way of discovering with certainty how these people had actually voted – or had not. It sounds impractical; is there a better way to ensure that reporters don't apply political spin to their stories?

First, reporters working in current affairs television in Britain know themselves to be pretty lucky people. There are not many jobs where you can say to yourself as you get up in the morning: 'Today I'm going to be paid to tell the truth.' It really is an extraordinary privilege, and it helps explain why people are prepared to work long, exhausting hours for less money than some of them at least might well get doing something else. Those with this enviable role to play are likely to think at least twice before substituting political propaganda for fair reporting. But of course that's not good enough. Wyatt and, it has to be acknowledged, quite a number of viewers, became convinced that current affairs television is simply so over-whelmingly populated by left-wingers that there is no need to apply a conscious spin – it just comes naturally.

The former *Nationwide* presenter and *Panorama* reporter Michael Barratt remembers a very private poll being taken in the *Panorama* office at the time of the 1964 election, when the country was evenly divided between Labour and Conservative. 'There was a widely held view then', says

Barratt, 'that *Panorama* was full of fellow-travellers and pinkos.' In the *Panorama* poll 48 per cent said they would vote Labour; 52 per cent Conservative. Later, in the real election, Labour, under Harold Wilson, was victorious. 'Joy was unconfined in the *Panorama* office,' says Barratt, 'not because the left had won but because it gave us a whole new raft of new issues, new material to get into.'

Barratt's experience, as a reporter in the 1960s, was that 'you were encouraged to make up your own mind'. When apartheid South Africa was banned from taking part in the Olympic Games he was dispatched, and told to come back with his own conclusions. He returned with a report which said South Africa should be allowed into the Games because there was still a chink of light, a gleam of hope that political change might yet come about through greater contact with the rest of the world. Right or wrong, he says, 'you came to your conclusions from what you saw, not from any preconceived political position, or the cuttings you picked up in news information'.

An illustration of this, and of *Panorama* people's political prejudices after the Thatcher era, occurred in 1993. John Redwood, the Secretary of State for Wales, had pointed to what he saw as a disastrous situation on a Cardiff housing estate. There, it was alleged, young, unmarried girls were having babies in order to get social security benefits and council accommodation. *Panorama* producer Barbara Want and reporter Margaret Gilmore set out to investigate. 'The point about doing a programme is to ask "how?" and "why?",' says Want, 'but I probably assumed I would go to the St. Mellon's estate and find that Redwood was wrong.' But they discovered that Redwood was essentially right. The young single women on the estate made no bones about the fact that they got pregnant to get a flat, because they would have been worse off marrying the useless unemployed men that were the only ones available. And so Want and Gilmore duly reported. But many of their colleagues were unhappy. 'At a programme meeting after transmission', says Want, 'I was staggered at the hostility; I've never met anything like it before; it was really quite nasty. Glenwyn[49] put up a stout defence of it, but I certainly felt that the majority disapproved of it: "How could you have said this?" I was gobsmacked. I had upset the apple cart, but not the way people wanted it.'

So here is ammunition for both sides of the 'bias' argument. On the one hand many *Panorama* people seemed to feel it impossible to agree with the analysis of a right-wing Conservative minister and be critical of a system which rewarded unmarried mothers. That sounds blinkered. On the other, the *Panorama* team actually charged with making the film had looked at the situation on the St Mellon's estate and reported it as they found it. That's as it should be.

It would be plain silly to suggest that *Panorama* reporters – or any other kind – start out on a story as a *tabula rasa*, a blank notebook on which nothing has ever been written until they started this assignment; they'd be useless if they did. The important thing surely is not to let prejudice blind you to what you find on the ground. Charles Curran, who became Director General of the BBC in 1969, put it like this: 'When answering the question "why" a current affairs man may start with a hypothesis but not with an evident commitment.' The fact is that any reporter in any medium has to start from somewhere; it's impossible to do otherwise. Whether you are a newsman grabbing a couple of cuttings from the library or a print-out from the internet as you dash from the office, or a *Panorama* reporter with the luxury of time to research thoroughly before you set off, you will always have your own idea of what the story is about – even a preconception of what your report will be saying when you bring it back. But the crucial thing is to recognise that you *do* start out with a preconception – and that it's no more than that. It will have been formed by prejudice, previous experience, particular interests and yes, of course, political inclination – as well as a host of other factors. It doesn't matter – indeed, it's essential – just as long as when you arrive at the scene you start testing your preconception of the truth against the reality you discover. That is what a good reporter does; with rare exceptions that is what *Panorama* reporters do.

Sometimes you will need to revise not merely your preconception but your first report on what you find. Take for example Peter Taylor, who has done so much reporting for television, and *Panorama* in particular, on Northern Ireland.

John Stalker, the Deputy Chief Constable of Greater Manchester Police, had been conducting an enquiry into three 1982 incidents in which IRA and INLA men had been shot dead in Northern Ireland by the security forces, allegedly without warning. Then Stalker was taken off the case. The general assumption was that he had been 'nobbled', and in his *Panorama* programme about the affair[50] Taylor decided, on the balance of probability, that that was indeed the case. As the reporter who 'stood up' this popular assumption he was cheered to the echo by left-leaning liberals: his programme won a Royal Television Society Award.

But Taylor wasn't completely satisfied. Returning to the story later that year, he eventually came to the conclusion that Stalker had been removed from the enquiry for perfectly proper reasons. His second programme[51] said so, even though it did not arouse the same degree of enthusiasm among some of his colleagues as had the first. As Taylor says: 'You go out for the truth. And if you have to change your mind because it's not what you thought, then you must do it.' In fact the second programme was not a climb-down, an apology for getting it wrong first time: 'What it said was "there's more to this than meets the eye." In the end you make judgements on facts and on people – are they telling you the truth? It all depends on your knowledge of the person and your judgement.' Not many television programmes have been prepared to give reporters scope to make investigations sufficiently deep or thorough to justify these difficult judgements. *Panorama* has.

None of this would persuade the convinced sceptic that *Panorama* has not been politically prejudiced. In his recollections of the Thatcher years Sir Ronald Millar (who wrote some of Prime Minister Margaret Thatcher's speeches) well expressed that paranoia about the BBC's reporting that politicians of the right so often suffer from: 'One had to watch and listen carefully over a period to understand subtle techniques employed by some of the news and current affairs programmes of the BBC: the nuances, the delicate juxtapositions, the creative editing, the occasional making of news rather than the reporting of it, that leaned left because it was the right way to think.'

There will always be those who see left-wing subversion in any questioning of the status quo, any challenge to authority: apparently Winston Churchill believed the BBC to be a nest of Communists.[52] The fact is that in any age and under any administration journalists have always wanted to find things out, to question assumptions, to ask whether what they are being told by those in power is true. Increasingly, the temper of recent times has allowed and encouraged them to do so – even at the BBC. In 1963 Hugh Carleton Greene, the Director General, talked to the Commonwealth

Broadcasting Conference about what he thought was the BBC's obligation to reflect a changing society: 'I only want the mirror to be honest, without any curves, and held with as steady a hand as may be . . . We think it is an important part of our duty to enquire, to question authority rather than accept it. To ask in fact whether the emperor has any clothes.' So it doesn't make you a Communist or even a left-winger to want to uncover the truth of a situation. But even if most reasonable people now accept the right of television to enquire and question, how can we be sure that those who do the job are really interested in the truth? Is there any real protection for the viewer against political propaganda instead of good reporting? There is. It lies in seeing on the screen the people who are telling you their stories, hearing what they say and making your own judgement about them. It is the use of reporters who are seen and heard in a succession of programmes that best protects us against those of them who might be tempted to be less than honest.

The whites of their eyes

As the former *Panorama* reporter Julian Pettifer succinctly puts it: 'I know where I am when I listen to individual people – even those I don't like.'

The on-screen reporter, doing his own interviews, reading his own commentary, delivering his own conclusions directly to camera – these are the best guarantors of fair and honest current affairs. Where the interviewer is never seen (and often even his questions never heard), where the commentary is written by an off-screen producer and read by an actor – that is where the danger lies; not that the programme will definitely be biased, but that the viewer has no way of knowing. Whose views exactly is he hearing? Who is it who actually went to that place or did that interview? What does the person or persons who did all these things look like? If the reporter is there, in shot, where you can see him, you can make a judgement about him and the worth of what he has to offer. That is the best way of refuting those who see a hidden hand behind every report they don't like. That is the point of a reporter. That's why it's so important to get the best: giants if you can. And on *Panorama* in the late 1950s and early 1960s that's what they did.

In June 1960 the *Daily Mail*'s Peter Black wrote a piece to celebrate *Panorama*'s 200th edition since the programme was relaunched in 1955:

> *Panorama* has become an unbreakable Monday night fixture for between six
> and eight million people, and the 'hard element of current affairs' has
> become its dominant quality . . . It has specialised in finding interviewers
> whose temperaments are individual and contrasting. The current muster has
> Robin Day, tenacious as a badger; Ludovic Kennedy, whose line is artistic,
> faintly raffish melancholy; James Mossman, the ardent Galahad who will
> never take for granted that men are sometimes wicked on purpose; Robert
> Kee, the hot-eyed public prosecutor of the outfit, who specialises in political
> subjects with undertones of conscience, such as colour bar, flogging, the
> betrayal of old horses.

These reporters, said Black, had an enviably free hand, coupled with the
rewarding knowledge that 'they are rated as persons doing a job that is
more important, not less, than quiz and leg shows'.

While Black was writing his celebration of *Panorama*, the team had been
preparing some ambitious coverage – the American Democratic
Convention in Los Angeles, at which John F. Kennedy would be nominated
as the Party's presidential candidate. Four different items were planned
with two reporters, Day and Kennedy. For the programme on 11 July there
would be a short item in which Robin Day would set the scene the day
before in the Convention arena. His report would be fed across the States,
recorded in New York and shipped to London. There the video tapes
recorded on the American video standard would have to be converted for
the British system before being edited in time for Monday's programme.

Meanwhile Ludovic Kennedy would be filming at Forest Lawn, the
extraordinary Hollywood cemetery so satisfyingly satirised by Evelyn
Waugh in *The Loved One*. This report would be shipped, and edited in
London for use in a future *Panorama* in September. Then Kennedy and Day
would team up for '*Panorama* Goes to a Convention'. Film and tape would
be shipped daily to London during the week and rough assemblies put
together in Lime Grove. Michael Peacock, who as *Panorama*'s Editor had
overseen the filming in the States, would return on Sunday morning to
supervise the final stages of editing this 30-minute story for transmission
in *Panorama* the following night.

In an exhilarating opening, which sets the tone for the rest of the film,
Day and Kennedy arrive flamboyantly at the Convention in an open-

topped Cadillac. With confidence and zest they explore and explain the Convention proceedings, and interview the participants.[53] Getting in amongst it all they communicate the razzmatazz, as well as the political importance of what is happening.

At a press conference Ludovic Kennedy entertainingly questioned JFK 'as one Kennedy to another', and Robin Day demonstrated the good-humoured showmanship that so often saw him, on social occasions, break into his soft-shoe shuffle routine. The whole affair was thoroughly enjoyable, as well as interesting and informative, to watch.

There was indeed an exhilarating, satisfying self-confidence about the reporting of that time. As Jonathan Dimbleby rightly says: 'In those simpler days, *Panorama* reported with assurance and individuality. It sought to unravel big issues, and it assumed that the public cared . . . All of *Panorama*'s reporters were men of strong personality and independent opinion, and their films reflected their own personalities; none of them succumbed to the rule of the back room.'[54]

The reporters of that time were seen as essential to the success of *Panorama*. As Michael Peacock had said, the programme made sense of the news by sending its reporters there to experience for themselves what was happening, and explain it to the viewers. And the viewers, from what they saw of those reporters in action, were free to decide how far they could trust them to tell the truth. But if this is to be the fundamental guarantee of a reporter's honesty, his lack of bias, then the viewer must have sufficient opportunities to see that reporter in action. Quite simply, if he only appears four times a year that will not be enough for the viewer to make a judgement about him, and not enough for the reporter to demonstrate that the way he responds to situations makes him worth watching. If the viewers don't see much of the reporters then there's no reason for them to trust them, like them or want to see more of them; and that will be reflected in audience research. So that having reporters on the screen comes to seem unimportant to the *Panorama* Editor, irrelevant to the success or failure of his programme.

But why should reporters now appear so infrequently? Because the shape of *Panorama* has changed. Instead of a magazine programme with three, four or even five items *Panorama* has now for many years dealt with but a single subject. How that happened is for another chapter, but the effect on reporters has been profound. In the 1950s and first half of the 1960s they would be likely to appear week after week in one or other of the relatively short reports in that programme. When single subject *Panorama*s came in it meant that a reporter might easily take six or eight weeks or even more to research and film before his much longer report finally reached the screen. And that meant that his rapport with the audience, his claim to represent them as a familiar figure regularly setting out to explore the story on their behalf, was much reduced.

How many *Panorama* reporters would viewers today be able to name? There is of course Tom Mangold, who has (with a little bit of broken service) worked on the programme for longer than any other reporter. It would be amazing if, after a quarter of a century – half the history of *Panorama* itself – he was not well known to the television audience. But it would be difficult to call even Mangold a household name in the way that Day or Kennedy were. As for Mangold's *Panorama* colleagues, Sarah Barclay, Steve Bradshaw, Shelley Jofre, John Ware, Vivian White, they are still less well established in the public mind. The reasons are obvious: they are not on the screen very often, and when they are, they don't feature very much in vision as an integral part of the programme; it is not very likely that they will be memorable. This is a waste of talent – and money.

But perhaps BBC attitudes are changing. Richard Sambrook, the BBC's Director of News (which includes Current Affairs) recently talked about the importance of first-hand, eyewitness reporting: 'There is no substitute for a trusted reporter saying: "I went there, I saw this." And audiences – especially the elusive younger ones – respect that too. They recognise its integrity. To be able to say, in a crowded market, that "we know because we were there and saw for ourselves" – that's gold dust.'[55]

When *Panorama* hired Jane Corbin from ITN in early 1988 Editor Tim Gardam acquired a rare asset: a woman television journalist whose work already suggested that she would be as good in current affairs as she had been in news. With long reports on ITN's *Channel 4 News* Corbin had already won three Royal Television Society prizes for domestic stories. Determined to become a *Panorama* reporter ever since she was 13, she soon showed she could find a good subject and report it effectively abroad as well as at home. She went on to win prizes for *Panorama* as she had done at ITN.

There are not enough women on *Panorama*, Jane Corbin says, because of the lunatic hours of work. She had both her children while reporting for the programme, and remembers running for a plane with a voluminous coat wrapped around her to disguise the fact that she was eight months pregnant. Later, she finished dubbing her commentary to a film at 1am on a Monday, went straight to hospital, and had her baby by Caesarean section at lunchtime: she did not even see her film transmitted later that evening. Corbin is tenacious and determined. But she feels that *Panorama*'s reporters in recent history haven't always had the full-hearted backing they need if they are to become people with on-screen authority. 'Authority comes', she says, 'with the way you look and the way you question people.' But if you are not being promoted on screen, seen as an important part of the programme, it's that much harder to establish that authority. 'There *is* such a thing as a *Panorama* reporter. The BBC has been increasingly fixated on the "news machine". It has never wanted to promote reporters who don't fit in to that pattern. It's no longer fashionable to be complicated or difficult, so *Panorama*'s own reporters have often received only grudging support.' Corbin thinks John Birt's idea of importing visiting 'specialist' journalists to make occasional programmes for *Panorama* was not necessarily helpful, because their films often turned out to be rather boring lectures – however well-informed. There is also a feeling among the *Panorama* team that the programme has risked debasing the reporters' coinage by using a succession of less experienced, visiting reporters who are not really ready for service on a flagship. One of the problems here is that there are fewer programmes now where reporters can learn how to make current affairs films.

It is perhaps because of all this that some recent *Panorama* Editors have ceased to see on-screen reporters as vital to the programme's success. Says Peter Horrocks, now Head of Current Affairs: 'If they are people who convey authority when you see them, then that's OK; but the strength of the reporters is in their journalism, not in how they look or speak or write. It's the subject matter – not the programme brand or the reporters – it's the journalism that matters.'

The less reporters are valued by their bosses, the less impact they will be able to make upon the public – and so they are valued still less. *Panorama*'s own reporters, unlike the giants of the 1950s, 1960s and even

1970s, have in recent years been treated as relatively unimportant on screen; their journalism is valued when it comes to finding, researching and making the programme, but their worth as *Panorama*'s human face – telling the story, explaining the issue – has often gone unregarded. Inevitably, as the television executive David Elstein, who briefly worked on *Panorama* in his youth, puts it: 'Lesser talents were required; lesser talents were available.'

On *Panorama* in recent years new faces have come and gone, a specialist this week, an unknown regional reporter with a good story next – all intermingled with *Panorama*'s more permanent team. Even more extraordinary, a 'celebrity guest reporter' may be hired – like Mariella Frostrup. However excellent these people may be in their own field (as Frostrup certainly is) this is an admission of defeat, and a misunderstanding of what *Panorama*'s reporters should be.

In the late 1980s/early 1990s a *Panorama* 'mission statement' (how the heart sinks!) admitted to 'a prejudice in favour of approaching our big names to do *Panorama*s . . . for example, [Peter] Jay, [John] Simpson, [Polly] Toynbee, [Mark] Tully, [Brian] Hanrahan, [Jeremy] Paxman, [Michael] Buerk, [Charles] Wheeler, [Nicholas] Witchell, [James] Naughtie, [Peter] Sissons, [Carole] Walker, [Peter] Snow, [Martyn] Lewis'.[56]

According to this model the ideal *Panorama* reporter would be a visitor from somewhere else – television and radio news programmes for example. It doesn't seem to leave much room for building up an authoritative team of current affairs journalists who would be known as regular *Panorama* reporters. It seems that even while the BBC had understood that recognisable people were important to *Panorama*'s success, it was reluctant to let the programme build its own stable of stars. Gavin Hewitt, a former *Panorama* reporter who now works mostly for BBC News, says:

> The idea of having people with ready-made reputations is a new one. Once you had a team: now you bring in stars. When I was young and watched *Panorama* I knew the difference between a [Michael] Charlton *Panorama* and a [Julian] Pettifer *Panorama*. I knew they were individuals; the sense of personality was a strong part of the programme. Clearly, to enhance the reporters' profile was to increase their power, and this was very much a matter of debate about the programme. And that ambivalence about

reporters has continued. Now that I work as a special correspondent for News, *Panorama* wants more of me. They want 'big-hitters' to be seen.

But they don't seem to want *Panorama* to grow their own.

Instead of trying to attract viewers with a celebrity, or a 'big-hitter' from another programme stuck on the package, wouldn't it be better to promote and feature *Panorama*'s own people, so that through their on-screen presence and authority they can bring the viewers in on a regular basis? If they can't do that, then fire them. If they can, then give them the support they need to do it better. If you don't, it's not very likely that they will ever be sufficiently memorable to play a positive role in building the audience. As Gavin Hewitt says: 'The worst way is to be middle-of-the-road about reporters.' That way you get dull reporting. So the answer to the *Panorama* reporter problem is simple: use them or lose them; back them or sack them.

Of course, sacking them is exactly what some people think should happen. Over the years occasional commentators have certainly found reporters a turn-off, their individual presence, their personal style a hindrance, not a help, to understanding. Here for example is a wonderfully disparaging piece by Dennis Potter in the *Daily Herald*. Clearly provoked by Richard Dimbleby's interview with the King and Queen of Greece ('a creaking exercise in the art of curtsying') Potter laid into Dimbleby's colleagues, *Panorama*'s reporters:

> The old authority is missing, the weighty asides inflate into elephantine pomposity, the generalisations sound tatty rather than startling. The harsh truth is that *Panorama* is relying on a technique of TV reporting which is becoming stale and irrelevant. Those brisk, hard-eyed reporters now appear to be chained to their blown-up personalities like tarnished spoons tied to a railway refreshment-room counter. The TV interviewer will one day be regarded as a primitive kind of animal. He admirably suited the early and uncertain days of the medium; but now he is often a hindrance to honest reporting – his face gets in the way. His carefully cultivated mannerisms intrude. His presumptuous impartiality clogs up the screen.[57]

That most professional of all reporters turned presenter, Michael Barratt, does not agree: 'I strongly believe that if you want to get particular thoughts across there is only one way to do it,' he says, 'tell it to the viewer in vision. People do not listen to voice-overs.'

That may be too sweeping: there have always been wonderfully effective out-of-vision commentaries over sequences that would have been ruined by a reporter intruding into view simply to demonstrate that he was there. And documentaries are anyway different – who could say that Sir Laurence Olivier's magnificently delivered commentary to *The World at War* was ineffective? But Olivier was talking over historical archive material. That's a rather different matter from exploring the contemporary world. In current affairs at least, commentaries are less likely to have their full effect if the viewer can't, from time to time, see who's doing the talking.

There are some self-effacing *Panorama* reporters today who prefer to keep their faces off the screen. Sarah Barclay's fascinating film 'The Story of Child B'[58] was about a father's fight to get his 11-year-old daughter – very ill with cancer – the expensive treatment the NHS did not think justified. Barclay herself was never seen: 'I don't feel I have to appear,' she says. 'I can tell a story without showing my face in front of the camera. I can have a presence in my interviews, in the questions that I ask. I do feel uncomfortable popping up every two or three minutes. I think the on-screen reporter is overused. Just seeing the reporter doesn't necessarily suit. I think I feel that tension more than most people; I feel more uncomfortable about it.'

But whatever Sarah Barclay feels, surely the viewer does want to know who is telling the story and asking the questions – particularly when they are good ones. Of course there have been programmes where the absence of the interviewer is seen as one of the reasons for its success – John Freeman's series *Face to Face* is the classic example here. But those interviews each concentrated in a deeply personal way on one individual. Surely, in a *Panorama* programme dealing with many interviewees and many issues that have to be analysed and explored, an on-screen reporter must be helpful. It seems positively perverse for *Panorama* reporters to want to be invisible in what is a visual medium.

In a *Panorama* programme on the floods that inundated Britain in January 2001 the reporter Vivian White was heard in commentary from the start, but not seen for a good 10 minutes; a programme on match-fixing in cricket (in the middle of the General Election campaign in May 2001) had David Lomax sidle into view long after the first ball was bowled. How were these reporters supposed to persuade the viewers that they were good guides to where their programmes were going when they couldn't even be seen?

Jonathan Dimbleby, who, unlike his brother David, has never worked on *Panorama*, thinks the programme has, over the years, allowed its reporters to become devalued. 'First of all *Panorama* was thoughtful, intelligent, with named reporters taking us on a voyage of discovery,' he says:

> Of course it was easier in some ways then; the huge expansion in broadcasting and the development of technology has been an important factor. But *Panorama* has not responded well. It did not promote its stars, it did not sell its stars. It did not say they were the people to be trusted. Even though the news bulletins got better there was always the appetite for one big programme to say 'we will make sense of the big story of the week.' Reporters have to be people who add value, but you cannot buy stars off the shelf, you have to make and promote them.

Paul Fox, former *Panorama* Editor, former Head of Television Current Affairs and former Managing Director of BBC Television agrees: '*Panorama* has been deprived of star names; you never know who you will see. As you look around the world you need named reporters who you see week after week, whom you can trust to be fair and impartial and tell you the story as it is.'

The shape of *Panorama*, and the way the format of the programme has changed over the years under different Editors is obviously another major factor to be considered; but compare for a moment the relative importance of the reporters on *Panorama* and on the American CBS News programme *60 Minutes* - and the current status of the two shows.

60 Minutes, which began in 1968, adopted the reporter-led magazine style that *Panorama* had developed; there are several stories in each programme. Of its current reporters, Mike Wallace has been there since it began, Morley Safer since 1970, and Ed Bradley since 1981. *60 Minutes* reporters appear frequently, and are prominently featured as the people you've got to know well, the people you can rely on to tell you, face to face, what it all means. Don Hewitt, now aged 79, is the creator of *60 Minutes* and still remains its Executive Producer. 'I never understood,' he says:

> why the BBC kept their reporters anonymous – the only name that came out of London was Richard Dimbleby. Why weren't they hungry to build other people up in the same way? Why not capitalise on their person-alities? What I wanted was 'the adventures of five reporters', and I wanted viewers to feel that those reporters were taking them along on a journey of discovery. Certain people leave the TV set and come right into your living room . . . My reporters say to the viewers: 'Come here; I want to tell you something.'

In an era of constant rolling news, says Hewitt, the thing that makes a programme like *60 Minutes* or *Panorama* stand out is the personality of the reporters: 'It's a mystery to me how they've watched the success of *60 Minutes* all these years and didn't ask why it worked.'

Since it began *60 Minutes* has been one of American television's most popular programmes, so successful that a midweek spin-off, *60 Minutes* II, was started in 1998. For 22 consecutive years *60 Minutes* was in the top 10: *Panorama*, by contrast, no longer makes it into the top 100 programmes on British television. For example, analysis of viewing figures (by Peaktime UK) for the week ending 11 November 2001 shows *Panorama* in 146th place, with an audience of just under three million.

Why is *60 Minutes* so much more obviously successful than today's *Panorama*? Why has its audience remained so large while *Panorama*'s has dwindled away? No doubt there are many reasons; but could it have anything at all to do with how the use of on-screen reporters has always been so central to *60 Minutes*, but on *Panorama*, in recent years, so perfunctory?

Mike Robinson, *Panorama*'s current Editor, doesn't accept that *Panorama*'s reporters must necessarily appear on screen at all. But, since he took over in October 2000, *Panorama* programmes that have allowed the reporter to appear have done so in a much more obvious way – as with Jane Corbin in her programme about the National Front,[59] or her special programme on the September 11 terrorists.[60] And this has been true for other *Panorama* stalwarts too – for instance Tom Mangold, as he strode across America discovering ways in which British policemen could learn to avoid shooting dead quite so many people.[61] This is a deliberate shift in policy. 'Let's feature them, or not see them at all,' says Robinson, who doesn't want *Panorama* to give up its reporters. 'There's no doubt that for the stories we do, stories that require considerable research, you want your own reporters . . . News stars who are spread very thinly, with so many demands made upon them, just can't give us the time for the more considered view we need to take.'

In the wake of September 11, the world's worst terrorist attack, Robinson twice turned to the BBC's top News star John Simpson for *Panorama* programmes about Afghanistan. He was there, in position, a reporter with considerable understanding of the situation – and previous experience of *Panorama*. But Simpson was under great pressure to deal first with the incessant demands of the news machine. He had little time to dig out new stories, or dig deeper into those already uncovered. That depth didn't come until a regular *Panorama* team produced a special programme – transmitted at 9pm on a Wednesday evening. Then, in the course of an hour, Jane Corbin and her producers[62] were able to explore in some detail the background to the terrorists and the atrocity they had committed in the name of Islam.

There may sometimes be good reasons for *Panorama* to work closely with the best of the news reporters, giving them a chance to do at greater length and more coherence what they are already doing for the news bulletins – and giving time for *Panorama* people to get to grips with the story and produce something altogether deeper. But unless *Panorama*'s reporters are seen more often, and seen to be good at what they do, they will always be at risk of being supplanted by colleagues from the news. At a time of crisis in particular *Panorama* will be in danger of becoming just a series of news specials – good on the bare bones of the story, the events, but short on the analysis and depth that *Panorama*'s own reporters should be able to offer.

Too big for their boots

If using reporters prominently on screen is at least arguably the best way of doing current affairs, that doesn't mean that they should rule omnipotent.

Giant reporters can get too big for their seven league boots, and it happened on *Panorama*. In 1962 there was a revolt. Led, it has to be said, by a producer, Jeremy Murray-Brown, most of *Panorama*'s star reporters left the programme to set up in business for themselves. They thought they could do it better on their own. They called themselves TRI, Television Reporters International, and their idea was to make their own brilliant current affairs programmes that ITV or the BBC and indeed broadcasters around the world would be only too grateful to buy.

As he later explained, Jeremy Murray-Brown thought they were right to try to go it alone:

> As reporters become more experienced in the not esoteric techniques [of television current affairs film-making] they naturally feel less need for producers. Why should not the reporter shape the feature in his own way? If his experience and integrity justify it, it is the logical development. Some producers have wondered if it would not be better for the personalities to be dropped instead. But they cannot be sure that their programmes would be so popular like that . . . To exploit even further the personality of the reporter seems a better alternative for the future . . . without the 'blurring' caused by producers, the technical roles of director, cameraman or film editor would fall more easily into place. Television reporters need not fear that they are being type-cast as soap opera heroes and the viewer would get a better programme – one that had a definite personal approach.[63]

Murray-Brown had first met James Mossman in Taiwan – Formosa in those days – while Mossman was still a print journalist. Later they would often work together for *Panorama*. It was out of conversations on those foreign trips, says Murray-Brown, that the TRI idea had grown, and he and Mossman persuaded the others to join them.

Ludovic Kennedy says today that there was no great row when he, Mossman, and Kee, together with other reporters who had worked on *Panorama*, like Malcolm Muggeridge, announced that they were setting up TRI. They had simply had enough of 'the dead hand of the BBC', and perhaps of Grace Wyndham Goldie too. She was 'a bossy woman', says Kennedy; 'there was a feeling of "fresh woods and pastures new".' And a bit more money too. The reporters paid themselves £6000 a year. That was

£1000 more than Kennedy had been getting at the BBC; it nearly doubled what Kee had earned there.

With Michael Astor as its Chairman and financial backing from businessmen like Miki Sekers, the silk magnate, TRI signed an initial contract with ITV's Lew Grade. They were to supply four one-hour and nineteen 30-minute stories to ATV over the coming year. The first three films were entitled 'The Arab Ferment', and saw Kee in Jordan and Egypt, and Kennedy in Israel and Saudi Arabia. Later there was another trilogy – 'The Jew in the World'. Kennedy said later: 'I look back on my time with TRI as the most professionally satisfying in a long television career.' But the TRI enterprise foundered when its contract with ATV was not renewed. ITV had been reluctant to network their programmes, and the BBC did not want them either. At a time when the Corporation still had a powerful sense of its unique position in broadcasting, it was never likely to compete with ITV for the films TRI had to offer.

Says Ludovic Kennedy now: 'We really were an idea ahead of its time', and it's true that today independently made current affairs programmes are seen on all television channels. But it's not normally a matter, and nor should it be, of the broadcaster simply transmitting a finished programme with which it has had virtually nothing to do. A programme like *Panorama* in particular, flagship of the BBC's journalistic fleet, cannot afford to take on trust what some independent offers. There must be editorial control of the programme-making process so that the viewers can have confidence in what they see. That is something the distinguished reporters who set up TRI seem rather to have overlooked.

Perhaps they assumed that since they were already well known to the BBC their independently made films would be gratefully received there. Perhaps the BBC turned them down out of pique that their star reporters had gone off on their own. But no reporter, however distinguished, should be able to say simply: 'Here's my film, now run it.' In that situation there will inevitably come a moment when some reporter cuts a corner, leaves fairness and objectivity behind and destroys the viewer's faith not just in him but in reporters as a breed. Reporters are not elected, they are not directly accountable to the viewers as MPs are to their constituents; they must therefore accept that some Editor figure will, on the viewer's behalf, want to be sure that the film he is about to take responsibility for and transmit is soundly based.

Today it remains a matter of principle that whenever current affairs programmes are made by independent companies it is the broadcasters who must take responsibility for them, ensuring that they are fair and honest, that those corners have not been cut, and that the research stands up to scrutiny.

With the collapse of Television Reporters International, Ludovic Kennedy became a writer, a campaigner for euthanasia, an investigator of miscarriages of justice and later a presenter for many television series, including the BBC's current affairs programmes *24 Hours*, *Midweek*, and *Tonight*. He was knighted in 1994. Robert Kee too developed his writing career, but also worked as a television reporter for various ITV companies, and as a newscaster for ITN. A later stint on *Panorama* as its presenter was to end dramatically.

James Mossman returned to *Panorama* in his old role as reporter, and resumed his hectic travelling life. In May 1963 a list of 'Highlights from Recent *Panoramas*' showed that Mossman had reported from Singapore, where he had interviewed the Prime Minister Lee Kuan Yew on the projected Malaysian Federation; he had been to Somalia to investigate the border dispute with Kenya; he had made a dangerous visit to the new and highly unstable Federation of Aden; in Southern Rhodesia he had examined the threat to racial harmony posed by the election of Winston Field as Prime Minister; and he had been to Baghdad, following the revolution there. He had been back to Kenya as elections loomed, and had ended up in Miami in a Playboy club to report on this new phenomenon, soon to come to Britain. In the studio he had used his expertise as a Far East specialist to interview the legendary Edgar Snow, following Snow's film report about life in China over the past 25 years.

Mossman's prestige was by now immense, but he grew tired of it all. 'I don't think I can cry for the world any more,' he told producer Jack Saltman. In 1969 Mossman left *Panorama* to present an arts programme, *Review*. Two years later, on 6 April 1971, the papers reported: 'Mossman, tough man of *Panorama*, found dead.' His great collaborator, the cameraman Erik Durschmied, remains sceptical of the official view that Mossman took his own life; he still believes that some unfinished business from Mossman's secret service past caught up with him. But the verdict was suicide. 'Bachelor Mossman', said the *Sun*, 'built a reputation for tough, probing journalism in ten years with *Panorama*. He feared "ending one's days alone in a bed-sitter in Bayswater . . . "'.

A new team

The departure of some of *Panorama*'s giants to TRI had left big shoes to fill. In July 1962 Grace Wyndham Goldie, now Head of Talks and Current Affairs, Television, discussed a number of names with the Director of Television. There was Patrick O'Donovan, and Robert Robinson, and she was also thinking about hiring foreigners: 'It would be valuable to give a greater "one-world" feel to our current affairs programmes by having as some of our regular contributors people who are Canadians, Australians, Indians, French or otherwise.' She was considering V.S. Naipaul, 'a brilliant young Cingalese who speaks excellent English', and also Murray Sayle, 'an Australian writer of some note . . . we have also of course such lesser people under consideration as Brian Redpath and David Dimbleby.'[64]

The foreigner who joined *Panorama* in 1963 was heavily disguised, indeed, more British than the British. 'We called England home,' says Michael Charlton. Like so many educated Australians Charlton spoke, as he still does, like a pre-war British gent. He was, and remains, an unashamed élitist. 'Most of my metaphors are military,' he says: 'the BBC was like the Brigade of Guards or the Parachute Regiment. I was speechless when I was asked to join it.'

Charlton had already had two successful careers in Australia. As a cricket commentator he had come on tour to Britain with the Australian team for the 1956 Test Match series. That same year, as a newsreader, his was the first face to be seen on ABC, Australia's version of the BBC, when its television service began. Later, modelling his programme on what he had seen in telerecordings of *Panorama*, Charlton had become presenter and joint Editor of ABC's current affairs programme *Four Corners*.

Paul Fox, *Panorama* Editor now promoted to head the Television Current Affairs Group, described Charlton as 'the Dimbleby of Australia'. It's a measure of *Panorama*'s prestige that when Fox offered him a reporting job on the programme Charlton was prepared to leave behind everything he'd achieved 'down under' and bring his family to Britain. 'A great Antipodean decision is about to be made!' he wrote to Fox. 'I'm still overawed by *Panorama*, and not sure I'm the man you really want – you're all so bloody good!'[65] 'Now,' says Charlton:

> I was a member of the First Division. *Panorama* was then a reporters' programme. It was meant to be serious, reflective and distinguished; you were given all the resources to do that, so the producers were really ancillary. It was an élite programme and that was the way to do it: I make no apology for that. Today television offers you a Niagara of information but little reflective understanding. The BBC needs to recover some sense of élitism, of being a distinguished caste. I think the reporters exist who could do it. The problem today is mediocrity. I think the country is not content with that. 'The hungry sheep look up and are not fed . . . '

If this sounds mandarin, against the temper of these times, no one should think that Charlton, with his academic bent, did not engage with the real world. A report of his from Vietnam,[66] for example, dealt sharply and directly with what the Americans were doing there. Charlton's film showed Vietnamese villagers being driven from their homes on American orders, and sad civilian casualties of American bombs and guns being fitted with artificial limbs. And he talked to reluctant and unhappy American conscripts: '*What do you think of the war? It stinks.*' This all made the American press furious. Spluttered the *Washington Post*:

> The American war effort in Vietnam was given caustic treatment Monday night by the semi-official British Broadcasting Corporation in an hour-long TV report by the network's leading hatchet man, Michael Charlton. On the basis of this and previous reports from the Far Eastern theater, Charlton would probably qualify as number one man on the list if the United States ever imposed an effective censorship on foreign TV operatives.[67]

There was a protest from Robert Komer, President Johnson's special adviser.[68]

As Charlton still says: 'In Vietnam it was not just a matter of getting some fighting; it was a matter of getting a context, a history of how the Americans came to be there.' This was surely right. Talking recently about why he had so wanted to take the *Panorama* job Charlton said: 'What was fascinating about Europe was that it had a history – as opposed to Australia. That's why I wanted to do it.' Jack Saltman, a producer who often worked with him, regarded Charlton with some awe: 'He was august.' But Charlton's relentless, not to say sometimes tedious, determination to take every story back into history could try his colleagues' patience. For a film about the 'soft underbelly' of NATO in Turkey, Charlton insisted on taking an uncomfortable 12-hour car ride to the Dardanelles, there to deliver a 17-second piece to camera.

Michael Charlton continued that tradition of intelligent, informed reporting from around the world that *Panorama*'s giants had so firmly established. But he was reluctant to look for ways to sell his serious-minded reports in the increasingly clamorous and competitive television bazaar. 'Being in the BBC was a serious activity. We were there to inform and educate. I was incapable of being a barker. Our duty was to interview those who made the decisions at critical moments. Television current affairs is an adjunct to academic history. It's suffused with emotions and other distractions, but serious historians admit its value.'[69] But surely the primary role of current affairs television is to interest people now, not to be the handmaiden of history. And no one who feels that emotions in a television film are 'distractions' is going to make programmes that are popular with a large audience. Charlton is reconciled to that: 'It may be caviar to the general, but *Panorama* should come into its own at great moments, on big occasions.'

The problem is that by then, no one may be watching. With rare exceptions, long films about complex current affairs issues need all the help they can get in terms of presentation and production. Unless you are content with a late night or Sunday lunchtime slot, and the small audiences that go with them, then an illustrated lecture is not enough. If you want to do serious current affairs in peak time then you must try your hardest to find ways to interest potential viewers. In a television review for the *Guardian* in 1971 Peter Fiddick wrote: 'The guy who put it about that there is nothing so dead as yesterday's newspapers could not have seen this night's television.'[70] To be fair, Fiddick was criticising ITV's *World in Action* as well as *Panorama*, but his complaint was that all the serious current affairs he'd been watching that night had left 'scarcely any imprint whatsoever' on his mind; it had all taken far too long for what it had to impart: 'You would have got the same information in newspaper reports taking five or ten minutes to read. And since the tele-visual elements in all these cases added virtually nothing, you would surely be better off doing that in the train in the mornings and spending the evenings at the flicks. The point is that if television wants to succeed in these areas it has to work at it very hard indeed.'

Charlton's time at *Panorama* coincided with a move away from a magazine programme towards long, single-subject films. They gave him scope for interviews with world leaders, shot 'as for live' as a long conversation between two serious people. As Charlton says: 'We were interested in talk and writing rather than film.' But there Charlton does not speak for every *Panorama* reporter. Naturally enough, he wanted to control the shape and intellectual content of his films. But perhaps he did not see, as others did, the absolute necessity of accepting all the help he could get from producers, in order to communicate his ideas effectively.

Today Michael Charlton looks back on that time as 'the end of the primacy of the reporter'. That is probably so, but it was not the end of good current affairs television. Making a serious and effective film of any great length requires not just brains and understanding, but showmanship too: that's why in current affairs television it generally takes two to tango, reporter and producer. Without showmanship, some of *Panorama*'s output in the late 1960s and early 1970s began to grow dull and staid, predictable and unexciting. It might still inform and educate, but how to entertain it sometimes forgot, or simply considered beneath its dignity.

That same day in 1963 that Michael Charlton threw in his lot with *Panorama*,[71] another reporter joined the team. He was not a foreigner, but his background and approach made him far more of a foreign body in the bloodstream of the programme than his Australian colleague.

Michael Barratt was, as he describes himself, 'the hick from the sticks'. Starting as a tea boy on the *Sunday Mail* in Glasgow he had worked on the *Daily Record* and then gone to Africa as Editor of the *Nigerian Citizen*. There he had covered the horrors of tribalism, notably the massacres that signalled the start of the Nigerian civil war. Then, the sensational fall from grace of War minister Jack Profumo brought Barratt to *Panorama*. Working at Bush House for the BBC's Africa Service, taking the milk train up to London from Wolverhampton, Barratt was abruptly ordered back to the Midlands, back to the sticks, to help *Panorama* assess the Profumo scandal's effect on the Tory grass roots. In the Birmingham studio Barratt was told he had a one-minute slot and that Richard Dimbleby would link to him live for his report. There was no Autocue. Within 10 minutes of the programme going off air he got a call from Paul Fox: 'Come and see me.'

Says Barratt: '*Panorama* was a different world for me, a world I never dreamed of. It was the world's best-known programme.' He remembers that his father, as a civil servant, had just achieved an annual salary of £1000. Now his son the television journalist was under contract for £4000 a year.

Barratt's first proper job on *Panorama* was not abroad but on the streets of Notting Hill, just a mile or so from Lime Grove. *Panorama* had done an extremely successful programme on the Rent Act and the slum landlord Peter Rachman. The Director General had ordered an immediate follow-up. For a week Barratt chased after Rachman's 'enforcer' Michael de Freitas, a terroriser from Trinidad, known as Michael X. Barratt's 'piece to camera', shot by cameraman Reg Pope, as he pursued his quarry down the street shouting 'Come back, Mr de Freitas', remains an early classic of the genre.

Asked by Paul Fox what his specialism was, Barratt had replied that he was a specialist in non-specialism. This was his ticket to travel widely at home and abroad. At *Panorama* he felt in exalted company but was shy about joining in *Panorama* social events, hurrying home when his work was done. His next Editor David Wheeler he found intimidating. Four decades later he still remembers his criticisms: 'I suppose that was all right, that trip of yours, but you're banned from using adjectives'; or, in the cutting room, tapping with his silver pencil: 'That doesn't work, does it?'

Barratt's greatest joy lay in doing something different with every assignment – the thrill of covering Eoka terrorism in Cyprus one day and Quebec separatism in Canada the next. He was the classic reporter as fireman – dashing from one story to another, to the detriment of his family life. Like many others he got hopelessly behind with doing his expenses. When he later joined *Nationwide*,[72] he says, the BBC finally admitted defeat and sent him a memo: it had been decided to write off £36,000 in accumulated advances he had never properly accounted for.

Barratt's most memorable story was with Dr Albert Schweitzer deep in the dark heart of Africa. Philosopher, leading exponent of Bach and a medical expert, Schweitzer had pioneered a system of treatment in which patients who came for help to his jungle hospital brought their families with them. It was an exclusive – no other television reporter had interviewed Schweitzer – and it brought 'herograms' from Lime Grove to reporter Barratt, producer Richard Francis, and cameraman Erik Durschmied: 'ECSTATIC PRAISE ALL LEVELS TELEVISION CENTRE SCHWEITZER FILM STOP CONGRATULATIONS REALLY FIRST CLASS STORY WITH SPECIAL PLAUDITS DURSCHMIED PICTURES REGARDS = FOX'.[73]

If Michael Charlton felt the compulsion to explain how and why something had come about (a perfectly proper *Panorama* preoccupation), Michael Barratt concentrated on what was happening here and now. He did not take an intellectual approach to the story but politely and firmly wrenched the guts out of it. It is only to be expected then that he should still think 20 minutes long enough for most stories, and a magazine format of several different and contrasting items the ideal for *Panorama*. He left the programme in 1965, just as it was about to shift dramatically in favour of the single subject. 'I retain a passion for *Panorama*, but I really do feel the TV viewer greatly misses the kind of programme *Panorama* was. So many viewers pine for programmes like *Panorama* with the status it had then. I would love to see it return to the way it was.' That day has not yet come.

Today Barratt is even better remembered for his time presenting *Nationwide*, the popular, early evening current affairs programme, than for his *Panorama* reports. Fifteen years after Barratt left *Panorama* another *Nationwide* presenter joined it: 'I am', says John Stapleton, 'the only *Panorama* reporter to have introduced the Miss UK contest.' He did not much enjoy his brief posting to the flagship: it was a shock after on-the-day journalism:

> Instead of a programme going out that night there was the possibility of it going out in six weeks. In my mind I reckon a week is long enough. I was not ideally suited to the long painstaking enquiry, reflecting on this and that . . . *Panorama* felt it had to have a pompous air. We looked at international and political issues in huge detail but did not kick enough doors down. The programme didn't feel risky enough. It didn't identify enough villains. I was on a different mission. I think the test of a good *Panorama* should be 'is it going to change something?', but *Panorama* was 'holier than thou'.

John Stapleton, used to working on a big, popular multi-item programme, was unhappy on a *Panorama* which seemed to him pompous in tone and over-serious in content. After 18 months he left. But *Panorama* must do more than kick the door down or collar a villain. It has to explain not just what's going on but why; and then look at what to do about it. And that can't be done very often on the day; it's just not *Panorama*.

More foreigners

In May 1967 the BBC Press Office announced: 'NBC Reporter for *Panorama*. Robert MacNeil of the National Broadcasting Company in America is joining *Panorama*. He will be seen in *Panorama* regularly when the new season starts in the Autumn.'

Robert (Robin to his colleagues) MacNeil was no stranger to Britain, though by birth a Canadian. He had been at ITN for its first bulletin in 1955 and later endured what he calls 'the drudgery and the discipline' of Fleet Street as a young news agency reporter. When he joined NBC's London bureau his good looks and easy on-screen authority soon led to his becoming anchor of a national NBC programme. Then in 1966, on election night in America, Paul Fox was in the studio gallery. On the strength of what he saw he offered MacNeil a job. When the young Canadian grew disenchanted with the way the news was being done in America – more attention was being paid to selling the news image, he thought, than to the news itself – he accepted Fox's offer. The BBC paid him £8000, one third of what he had been getting at NBC.

'I loved working for *Panorama* immediately', says MacNeil today in his New York study near Central Park, 'and I was mightily impressed by *Panorama* people. If they weren't smarter than me they were certainly better educated.' In an article for the *Radio Times* he had compared American and British approaches to news and current affairs:

> I don't believe American television is exploiting its journalistic possibilities nearly as fully as the BBC. American TV presents an exceedingly slick and visually exciting nightly summary that in many ways is superior to the bulletins over here. But what is lacking in the United States is the deeper analysis and informed commentary that programmes like *Panorama* and

Twenty-Four Hours provide. There is too often more show-business than journalism in the American product.[74]

MacNeil looked at British institutions and issues with foreign eyes and often saw them more clearly than British reporters might have done. His two reports on mental hospitals and how the 'revolving door' syndrome kept patients coming back time after time are an example. A trilogy of *Panorama* programmes, two in Bradford, one in Pakistan, examined in detail the issues surrounding Asian immigration. And then, from the other side of the Atlantic, MacNeil explained to the British audience what was happening to America as the fighting in Vietnam ground on. When the presidential election primaries began in 1967 – Lyndon Johnson was running against Eugene McCarthy – *Panorama* followed the body of a young US sailor, Ronald James Keller, as it came back home from Vietnam for burial. Keller had left a widow of 17 with a baby 10 months old. MacNeil filmed the funeral in Exeter, New Hampshire. 'It was', he says, 'the furthest I have ever been led into pure advocacy journalism.'

Later MacNeil reported for *Panorama* on President Nixon's first year in office. Flying over on the plane he and his producer Frank Smith were still groping for an idea, a framework within which to tell the story. This was long before the early John Birt era, in which no reporter or producer would have been allowed out of Lime Grove without a clear plan of battle, if not an actual script. Rather than just interview people individually, MacNeil and Smith decided, they would bring them together as the guests of Perle Mesta, the celebrated Washington hostess and the model for the musical *Call Me Madam*. 'It was probably the first time,' says MacNeil, 'that she'd ever had a black man sitting down to dinner. It was Chuck Stone, a journalist with a moderately radical newspaper. He pulled no punches that night, but neither did anyone else.' To round it all off they persuaded Ethel Merman, the original star of *Call Me Madam*, to sing 'The Hostess with the Mostest'.

This shows MacNeil's *Panorama* trying to make the medicine go down in as delightful a way as possible, but he was always clear that the programme was indeed all about making you better – better briefed about the big issues of the time. That is still what he thinks the BBC should be doing with its current affairs programmes, including *Panorama*: 'I believe that increasingly in Britain the public's airways are given over to commercial uses. There should be at least one broadcaster which does not have the same priorities as the commercial broadcasters.'

MacNeil eventually returned to the United States to present *The MacNeil Lehrer Report* on the publicly funded – though poverty-stricken – Public Broadcasting Service, PBS. He remained true to the idea of a serious current affairs programme, even at the expense of a much smaller audience. So what are his criticisms of *60 Minutes*, the hugely successful current affairs programme on American commercial television? MacNeil believes that the basic idea of a reporter-led programme is right. 'You play the stories off their reactions,' he says, 'you get at the reality through them.' Star reporters who have been with the programme for many years have helped *60 Minutes* hold on to the authority that, he thinks, has ebbed away from the evening news programmes in America. But the *60 Minutes* cult of personality can impose straitjackets on its journalism; the reporters get stories tailored to their strengths: 'It is formulaic, like a lot of preformed sandcastles. Reality is being made to fit those formulas because people find it comforting. Too often it can be just good guy versus bad guy. *Panorama* had more freedom, individuality and variety . . . I loved my time with the BBC and *Panorama*; I learned every day there.'

Not afraid of being serious, Robert MacNeil was never pompous either. *Panorama* in the 1960s and early 1970s was much the better for him.

Stars

'He was so beautiful,' sighs former producer Barbara Pegna. Jealous, less good-looking reporters called him 'the poor man's Tony Curtis'. It was a rather unkind remark about a kind man. Richard Kershaw was a Cambridge history graduate who had also studied at the University of Virginia at the same time as Teddy Kennedy. At the Commonwealth Office he'd worked for the Secretary of State, Sir Alec Douglas-Home, afterwards Prime Minister, and later he had been a feature writer at the *Financial Times*. In the early 1960s he reported, mostly from Africa, for both *This Week*, on ITV, and the BBC's *Panorama*. He became Editor of *Africa Confidential*, a private circulation newsletter for those who needed to know more about what was going on in Africa than they would find out from a broadsheet newspaper. But in 1967 Kershaw came to work for *Panorama* on a full-time basis.

The idea, he says, was to make *Panorama* more professional, less chummy. Kershaw was hired as something of an expert on Africa, entitled to do 'declarative reporting', as he calls it, in which he could speak with authority about what he thought was really happening there. While other journalists were being thrown out of South Africa, he and his producer Andy Mulligan managed to get in.[75] 'In those days in *Panorama* you were allowed to build on your expertise. The Editor would ask you, for example, "When should we go back to Israel?"' He remembers his deep indignation when the BBC Director General Charles Curran came down to Lime Grove to watch *Panorama* go out one Monday night, and afterwards gave him 'pointers' to whom he should see and take advice from before he next reported from Nigeria. That seemed to Kershaw to be an attack on his professional competence, and an interference with the journalistic job of going to find out for himself.

As his films frequently demonstrate, Kershaw liked to walk with kings. He was firmly in that *Panorama* tradition of trying to talk to the men at the top. Success at that level was seen as the measure of the programme's clout. '*Panorama* was senior, proconsular,' he says, 'you travelled around with the country's leaders, wherever you were.' But of course formal interviews don't always make for interesting television – as Robin Day was finding out in the *Panorama* studio. Where once the audience had gasped and gaped in admiration as *Panorama* reporters spoke to King Hussein of Jordan or Prime Minister Vorster in South Africa they were now less impressed – unless the interview revealed something new or moved the story on. Perhaps *Panorama* stayed too long in this tradition of talking at length to top people, reluctant to recognise that the world's leaders were unlikely to reveal dramatic policy developments even when so august a programme as *Panorama* sent its correspondents to call.

Julian Pettifer may not have been a giant, but he was certainly a star, probably the last of the star reporters on *Panorama*. Pettifer joined the programme in 1969. Brilliantly he bridged the gap between the old world and the new. Intelligent and charismatic, excellent with words and persuasive in vision he came close to the great reporters of an earlier generation, Ludovic Kennedy and Robert Kee, James Mossman and John

Morgan. But, just as importantly, he was altogether a television professional, as expert as any producer in how to make films in a way that would attract the viewer's attention and hold it.

So if Julian Pettifer was the last of the stars, he was also the first professional television current affairs reporter on *Panorama*, equally interested in the story and in the way it was told.

On leaving Cambridge, Pettifer had joined Southern Television in Southampton. Local television then was a wonderful place to learn the trade. Every day could mean shooting a film report somewhere in the area; bringing it back to base to edit and add a commentary; then perhaps presenting the regional news and doing a studio interview for the local current affairs programme. After four years of that Pettifer came to Lime Grove and the BBC. There he worked first for *Tonight*, the irreverent, cheeky, early evening topical programme, and then for *24 Hours*, the late night show. By the time he joined *Panorama* Pettifer had made countless films, and been named Reporter of the Year by the Guild of Television Directors and Producers. He knew pretty much all that was to be known about how to do television current affairs; and he was very good at it. 'Most of the good television factual series of programmes have been reporter-led,' he says. 'It's all about telling stories, and if you choose your storyteller carefully and he has authority then it must work better. Investigative journalism in particular is better done by people you can see and hear.'

Pettifer gives as an example of how the reporter can help a programme one he made for *Panorama* in Vietnam with producer Jo Menell. 'When Johnny Comes Marching Home' had five separate stories in it: there was the helicopter pilot, the cowboy conscript, the ammunition truck driver, the historian of the infantry division, and the nurse at a field hospital. Of course it could all have been done without a reporter, but, as Pettifer rightly says, his presence helped link the stories together so that they flowed one into another to make a more coherent and effective programme.

Pettifer understood how a reporter can help the viewer really understand what was happening. For example, as any current affairs television team knows, being under fire is a trying experience. Not only is it terrifying, but it is usually impossible to film what's happening in any way that conveys a sense of what it's really like. The cameraman – even if he dares to raise his head – cannot usually see who's doing the shooting or even where the incoming fire is coming from; sitting at home all you are likely to see are some shaky, wildly angled shots of trees, buildings, sky or mud. And no matter how good the sound man may be, by the time the noise of battle comes out of the average TV set the fusillade of automatic fire and the explosions of mortar bombs all round you will sound at best like a couple of champagne corks popping.

This is where the technique the silent cinema discovered, and Hollywood made the most of for its horror movies, comes in useful. If you have a reporter handy you can 'play it on the reverses'. Even if you can't see the cause of the terror, you can show what it's doing to someone there who's experiencing it. By looking at the fear on the reporter's face as he ducks and dives into cover, by hearing the alarm in his voice, the viewer can begin to understand what it's really like to be there. Of this technique Pettifer was a master. No one who saw him in a camera piece while under fire in Saigon during the Tet offensive of 1968 will have had any doubt about just how dangerous the situation was.

On *Panorama* Pettifer, perhaps the first professional current affairs reporter, covered everything – foreign wars like Vietnam, social institutions like the Church of England, great political events like American presidential elections. Julian could be quite superior with his junior colleagues, but he did not forget his early experience in making human interest stories on *Tonight*. 'There are many things that reporters may find banal that people find interesting,' he says, and quotes the ebullient Welshman Donald Baverstock, his boss on that programme: 'Don't underestimate the audience's intelligence, because they're pretty smart, but don't overestimate their knowledge.'

If there was a criticism to be made of this near-perfect reporter it was that he sometimes seemed to share *Panorama*'s increasing complacency, its assumption that a cool, calm look through that Window on the World was still the best way to get at the truth of a story – even when the glass was in need of a good clean. In 1973, in the days when any kind of access to the Soviet Union was a rarity, Pettifer reported from Kiev – in co-operation with the Soviet news agency Novosti. Phillip Whitehead, who had worked on *Panorama* before going off to run the rival *This Week*, was critical:

> Another promised land appeared through the rose-tinted lens of Julian Pettifer and his colleagues from Novosti in Kiev (a *Panorama* Special, BBC1).

Ever since Pettifer first emerged gleaming from the Mediterranean in some long-forgotten *24 Hours* special he has seemed close to the complete film reporter. One watched Kiev therefore with mounting dismay. A month in the Soviet Union, at such a time, thanks to the coincidence of the royal visit would surely not yield a travelogue? But it did . . . Would the team have gone to the third city of the United States and made a film under surveillance, with no interviews, and no mention of Mayor Daley's record, the trial of the Chicago Seven, the blacks, or the impact of national political scandals? They would not . . . Novosti would have been well-satisfied with the product, but why was *Panorama*?[76]

In the *Evening Standard*, Elizabeth Cowley had much the same criticism: 'Julian Pettifer's progress through Kiev for A *Panorama* Special (BBC 1) was competent, beautiful – and so bland that if one didn't know about Solzhenitsyn and company – or the Jewish persecutions – one would pack a bag and be off to sun-dappled Kiev on the holiday-happy river Dnieper in the morning.'[77]

Critics also contrasted Pettifer's *Panorama* style with *World in Action*'s, when both programmes went to Chile following the overthrow of President Allende. *Panorama* had interviewed the generals and their supporters who had taken over the country, *World in Action* concentrated on their victims. In the *Listener*, Stuart Hood thought Pettifer's tone too cool:

The general question posed by the programme was the degree to which television journalists can continue to remain detached in their reporting: at what point can they legitimately allow their feelings about what they discover in the exercise of their professional skills to become apparent? It is clear that the *World in Action* team, which brought back from Chile interviews with the victims of the men whom *Panorama* questioned with its usual polite aloofness, feel that neutrality is not possible in every situation . . . This is one of the reasons why *World in Action* is more interesting and successful than *Panorama*.[78]

The 1960s had come and gone, yet *Panorama* continued on its stately way as if the Beatles, Profumo and *That Was the Week that Was* had never been;

its manners remained polite, its judgements cool; its attitude to those at the top rather as if one member of a gentleman's club - the Garrick perhaps – was talking to another. As Shaun Usher put it in the *Daily Mail*: 'One intends no disrespect – not much, anyway – in claiming that *Panorama* (BBC 1) has a predictable approach. Light without heat, and not too many surprises, has been its life-style, man and boy, these many years.'[79]

Pettifer had become part of a programme that was, if not sleep-walking, then certainly assuming it could take its accustomed stroll on Monday nights for granted. By the mid-1970s he himself began to feel that *Panorama* was wandering rather aimlessly, losing its way. As news programmes developed they had begun to take the wind out of *Panorama*'s sails. It seemed to Pettifer that the flagship was rudderless, without an obvious future: 'It became unclear what we ought to be doing, who we were talking to, what the balance between home and foreign stories should be, and how *Panorama* should change now that the News was improving.' So in 1975 Pettifer moved on, to make programmes about natural history and the environment.

Players join the gentlemen

'I know what he's like, we'll get two good years out of him'. That's how *Panorama* producer Jack Saltman remembers Editor Brian Wenham telling him in 1969 about the new reporter he had just hired. Alan Hart was in India when the call came from Wenham; Hart's response: 'I'd like to come, but I'm sure the BBC won't find me acceptable.' It is true that Hart was not the typical *Panorama* reporter. Where Pettifer, for example, was tall and Oxbridge elegant, blonde and good-looking, the epitome of grace under pressure, just perfect in a punt, Hart was clearly from an altogether heavier sort of mob: bulky, pinkly perspiring, a graduate of life rather than a good university. It was of course for exactly those reasons that he was being hired.

Wenham had seen Alan Hart close-up at ITN. There Hart had demonstrated an ability to go and get the story more often than any other reporter. He had also shown that he could turn any story he did get into the lead. Most memorable had been what he'd done with Biafra in 1967. In Nigeria (the classic British colonial construct) the Ibo, one of three very different ethnic groups, were attempting to establish their independence in the new, breakaway state of Biafra. Other television programmes, including *Panorama*, had covered this faraway dispute perfectly adequately, but when Hart got to work on it he turned it into a blockbuster of a story that made huge headlines and dominated the television news for weeks on end. His reports of starving Biafran babies, and of a people (who fortunately were Christians and spoke good English) asking only for their freedom, galvanised British public opinion – much to the fury of the Labour Government, which wanted the Ibo rebellion crushed in the cause of Nigerian unity and British trade.

When Wenham, who'd been a senior news editor at ITN, got the *Panorama* job he knew Hart would be not just a former ITN colleague he could rely on, but a powerful dose of salts to liven up the existing *Panorama* team. And that's exactly what he was. Naturally enough Alan Hart was, as a result, probably the most unpopular reporter among his colleagues that *Panorama* has ever seen.

Hart made normally urbane and sophisticated people lose their tempers. For a start he was very quick off the mark. On stories that required good coverage rather than extensive research – let's say the catastrophic floods in the newly established state of Bangladesh – Alan was there and back with an impressive programme before the rest of the team had decided they might quite like to do it themselves. His stories were so quickly on the air that *Panorama* successfully competed with news coverage at a time when that was becoming rare. Alan had immense energy and a determination to get the story that sometimes left his colleagues looking flat-footed.

Their toes were trodden on too. The Middle East had been one of Richard Kershaw's areas of expertise; but it was Hart's interest too. Kershaw recalls Egyptian diplomats in London ringing him to ask why Hart was trying to remove his name from a *Panorama* bid to interview their President and substitute his own. Hart firmly denies the story. On this occasion, for the sake of friendship, the author declines to say where he thinks the truth lies.

Alan Hart struck up a close relationship with some important politicians, among them Golda Meir, the Prime Minister of Israel. His success as a reporter, he says, was the way he could get on with people: 'I became, when the camera was off, the human being they could sit down with and bare their souls to. It happened with Golda, it happened with Arafat. Knowing them I learned a lot more.' Wasn't his success really due to his news sense, his instinct for a story? 'I did have a superb instinct, but it was based on that background knowledge. It was nothing to do with ego. I didn't even like being recognised. I was always reporting for my mum in the front room of her council house.'

One of Hart's greatest coups was in 1970. Palestinian terrorists had hijacked planes, which they were holding at Dawson's Field in Jordan. The country erupted; civil war broke out; the entire region was on the edge of catastrophe. As the fighting spread through the Jordanian capital, Amman, television and print journalists were flown up, up and away. Hart's camera team was happy to leave, but, waiting at the airport, Hart persuaded another BBC cameraman there, Bernard Hesketh, to stay on with him, in what was a very dangerous situation. Hart got a message to King Hussein asking for an interview. 'Yes, if I live,' came the answer.

Next day they did it. The tripod had already been shipped, so the camera had to be balanced on a pile of encyclopaedias in the royal palace. It was a powerful interview: 'Did you think you were going to die?' asked Hart. 'If your name's on the bullet you're dead, but my name wasn't on one this time,' replied Hussein, in his stiff-upper-lip, British public school style.

With Hart's BBC team at the interview had been the *Sunday Times* heavy hitter Murray Sayle. To prevent the *Sunday Times* running the story before Monday's *Panorama*, Paul Fox, then Controller of BBC1, dramatically rearranged the Saturday sports programme schedule to show Hart's exclusive interview that evening. This was the sort of exciting journalism that had been part of *Panorama* when Fox was its Editor in the early 1960s; Hart was the man who came closest to reintroducing that sort of 'scoop' to *Panorama*.

But, blazing a trail in the current affairs firmament, Alan Hart was a shooting star, too bright to last long. Following the Six Day War, in which Israel had halted its triumphant advance at the Suez Canal only because that was as far as it wanted to go, it had always seemed that another Middle East war was likely. Hart had been assiduous in courting the principals involved, ready for just that occasion, and whenever he came on a *Panorama* trip to Israel he had been in the habit of sending three dozen red roses to Prime Minister Golda Meir. Her secretary Lou Kaddar, says Hart, told him Golda felt Alan was the only one of all the men around her to treat her like a woman. This excellent relationship had led to a long profile of Meir on *Panorama*, and many interviews – probably too many.

When the Yom Kippur war broke out in 1973 the Israelis were taken by surprise. As Hart arrived in Jerusalem on day 2 the fighting was going badly for them: 'The state of Israel was going down the tube,' he says. Sending his usual huge bouquet to the Prime Minister's office, Alan begged for the crucial interview. Two hours later, he says, Kaddar called: 'Golda thanks you for the flowers; she may or may not be able to see you this evening.' At 10pm Hart was again called to the phone. It was Meir: 'Alan, we are asking Nixon for planes and tanks; we've got to put the pressure on. I'll have to give the first interview to the American networks.' Hart says he told her he quite understood: roses were no match for tanks. But, frustrated at his failure to get the interview he had invested so much in, Hart now let his disappointment cloud his judgement. Other BBC journalists told him they felt that they were being denied access to facility trips with the Israeli armed forces, and they blamed this on the predictable complaints being made by the Israelis of pro-Arab bias in the BBC's World Service radio broadcasts. Fatally for his BBC career, Hart sent a cable to the Director General – which he made public – that seemed to endorse the view that BBC broadcasts were biased.

Hart says that nothing official was ever said to him about his outburst when he returned to London. But it was obvious that his time with *Panorama* was effectively over. In any case he had himself become disenchanted with the programme, at odds with his Editor Frank Smith, whom he felt did not value him as highly as did Brian Wenham, now Head of Television Current Affairs.

Alan Hart left no permanent mark on *Panorama*: he was not a team player. But he had certainly given the programme a blast of oxygen which had made it a more exciting place to work. With Hart there the *Panorama* fire blazed up again. And he'd stayed for five energetic years, more than twice as long as his somewhat cynical patron Brian Wenham had predicted.

chapter seven

⊕ The producers – bag carriers or bosses?

On 18 June 1958 Woodrow Wyatt, now nearing the end of his time with *Panorama*, wrote in a fury to Leonard Miall. His contract, he said, was being 'violated'. Why? Because when he was dispatched on a story he was being made to take a producer with him. Producers in his view were interfering with his right to report things as he saw them. Once 'a story and a theme', he said, had been agreed between him and 'the principal producer'[1] then he was responsible for collecting the material required for the story:

> When the actual filming of a quickly made foreign story is taking place it is essential that only one person should be in charge. That must be the person who has the central theme in his mind. Quick decisions have to be taken and action must be speedy if the material is to be collected. This does not allow for committee-type discussion. The only contribution that can be made in most foreign stories by an employee of the production staff coming with me is to get in the way, slow down the process and make the material worse.

This raised an issue that could not be fudged, with implications for the working relationship of all the reporters and producers who would come after. Miall took a note of the phone call he made in reply to the rebellious Wyatt's protest: 'I said that it must be clearly understood that in the last analysis the BBC's director was in charge and not the contributor, but that in practice a satisfactory result was achieved only if there was a smooth working relationship between the two, just as the best journalism arose from the combination of a good editor and a good reporter.' Miall goes on to record that 'after some discussion, Wyatt agreed to go to the Lebanon with his producer David Wheeler in charge'.[2]

David Wheeler had had a great deal of experience with film. He'd worked as a scriptwriter on *Newsreel* at Alexandra Palace, deciding how to cut the available film footage together to make the best possible story. In 1955 he'd turned down the offer of a job at ITN and chosen instead to come to the new *Panorama*, under Michael Peacock. Later he was to become Editor of the programme himself. 'Woodrow had been going out on his own making stories', he says, 'and this was felt not to be right. A staff man ought to be representing the BBC, so that meant taking a producer. It was a delicate situation because Woodrow resented this as a slight on his capacity, but he probably came to see that two heads were better than one.'

Following the row with Wyatt, his immediate boss Rex Moorfoot, the overall Producer of *Panorama*, sent a memo to Leonard Miall setting out his own reasons for wanting a director/producer to accompany reporters on their travels: 'On my coming to *Panorama* I felt that the general picture quality of foreign stories needed improvement. It was no longer enough to send Woodrow Wyatt to interview the prime minister and leader of the opposition in the capital of some Middle East country. Viewers wanted the fuller context of a situation in terms of people and pictures. A director greatly helps supply this.' Moorfoot had other good reasons for sending staff men with his stroppy correspondents – they could co-ordinate, contribute their own ideas, deal with diplomats, and get some experience of foreign parts themselves so that these egotistical reporters were no longer quite so indispensable: 'Summarising then, the sending of directors on *Panorama*-type stories results in better pictures, improved public relations with fewer messes to clear up, clearer editorial control followed through the subsequent cutting, dubbing and transmission, and it is, lastly, an investment in our own staff with a dwindling responsibility of the Wyatts and their like.'³

Grace Wyndham Goldie insisted that the relationship between these two kinds of television people was a creative one, despite 'the fact that the producer was editorially responsible, within the Corporation, for whatever the speaker said, and yet that the speaker had been chosen for his individuality and the acumen of his views as well as for his expository skills'.⁴ But Wyndham Goldie never had to experience this 'creative partnership' herself in the field.

It was a difficult and sensitive issue. In the Army it is the young, relatively inexperienced and expendable subaltern whose job it is to be first 'over the top', leading the charge. He is supported by some grizzled old sergeant who doesn't have to carry the can when it all goes wrong. But television journalism was developing in a different way. When a *Panorama* team went out it was the older, more experienced contract reporter who led, but the younger staff producer from the BBC who was at least theoretically responsible for whether he was advancing in the right direction and whether the objective they had been given was successfully captured on film. 'Contributors' or 'speakers' like Wyatt and his successors were irked that their freedom to do and say what they wanted in their reports was being constrained; producers were irritated that their reporters were indulging their egos to the detriment of the film, while at the same time getting all the glory if the mission succeeded.

While those early giant reporters were happy, as they stepped magnificently across the world, to have a producer running after them to carry the bags and book the flights, they were not so keen to have them make any contribution to the journalism. To them the ideal relationship between producer and reporter was rather like the partnership between blacks and whites in Southern Rhodesia that Lord Malvern had so notoriously endorsed, the partnership between horse and rider.

Squabbles

Robin Day in particular, though he could be an entertaining companion on the road, was not always an easy reporter to work with. In his view the concept of producer and reporter working together was based upon an out-of-date assumption, that the reporter was a mere performer who needed production.

Robin Day had come from ITN, where his reports, whether for the News or *Roving Report*, were usually brief, and he had normally travelled with only a cameraman and sound recordist, without a producer. When in 1959 he arrived at *Panorama*, he saw no reason to change the method of working which had after all already brought him considerable success. In a chapter in the book he wrote later, headed 'Old Sweats and Young Whipper-snappers', he asked why it was that *Panorama* Editors preferred to send producers along with reporters. What was the aim of 'this cumbersome arrangement'? Was it to keep reporters on the editorial rails or free them from the chores? 'Whatever the aim, the relationship between reporter and producer was friction-fraught . . . far too much time and energy was wasted in disputes between reporter and producer. The tension was destructive, not creative.'[5]

The producer Day had particularly in mind was Jack Saltman. Saltman had been a studio director and producer in Manchester before getting a temporary job as an assistant producer on *Panorama*. Though patronised by the programme's grandees he served his apprenticeship to become a permanent producer on the programme.[6] He recalls a long trip with Robin Day to Africa and the Far East. Day had wanted to be in Australia at Christmas for personal family reasons. The BBC had agreed to pay his fare provided he did a number of reports along the way. Off they set, with Saltman, nominally in charge, in economy, and Day enjoying the first class travel to which his contract entitled him. In South Africa they covered the visit of Britain's Archbishop Ramsey; in Tanzania they filmed the new railway the Chinese were building, and in Zanzibar interviewed the unpredictable Sheik Karume: 'Do you realise you are a total embarrassment to your President Nyerere?' asked Day, as heavily armed men loomed close around them.

And then they arrived in Vietnam. A real row started six days later when Saltman suggested that it was high time they got out of Saigon and tried to capture something of the war on film. Waiting for some interview, Day did not want to do this. 'If you instruct me to I will,' was his stuffy response. Saltman did. As he now recalls it, it was not a happy trip up-country. Jumping from a helicopter Day fell heavily on top of his producer;

grumbling his way through an interview with a village headman he burst out resentfully: 'I shouldn't be interviewing anyone of less than cabinet status'. Back in Saigon, as they walked across the square between the Hotel Caravelle, where they were staying, and the Hotel Continentale, where journalists gathered every evening on the veranda to tell jungle stories over a *citron pressé*, Day would argue not just about the script he was writing but about the need for arguing about arguing. After seven weeks of this Saltman felt somewhat drained; but as he at last waved his reporter off to his Australian holiday he thought they had parted friends. He was surprised to find on his return to London that Day had sent letters of complaint about him to both the Editor of *Panorama* and the Head of Current Affairs. With malicious glee Editor Brian Wenham read Day's tirade about his producer's behaviour aloud to the assembled programme team.

Words and pictures

After that trip, in 1970, Robin Day always remained sceptical about the value of producers. Indeed, he vowed never to go reporting again. 'As things developed, younger producers were not content with the "midwife" role. They wanted to give birth themselves. The trouble with this is you can't have things run by committees. If you recruit strong-minded, experienced television reporters you've got to let them get on with it.'

The real problem for producers was that many reporters of Day's generation could not fully see the importance of the film element in their reports. Particularly in Day's eyes, any film sequences were simply to set the scene for his interviews. From his point of view that is understandable; it was for those interviews, both in his film reports and later and more importantly in the studio, that he is best remembered. Filming was an irritating distraction from his always meticulous preparation for the interview – he would press his producers into endless role-playing as he tried out his questions on them.

But from the point of view of the Window on the World, the filming was absolutely vital. Quite soon in the history of current affairs television, it wasn't good enough simply to be seen standing on a promontory in Malta; the novelty of that began to pall. Now producers were needed to spend time and effort making the most of the locations. If the pictures and 'natural sound' that could catch the character of the place were not interesting, then the viewers would not be there to pay attention when the reporter was ready with his big interview.

Panorama's producers were learning that words and pictures judiciously mixed together could be more effective than either alone. It was not just a matter of shooting film which might or might not be important and then writing commentary to try and cover it. Nor, on the other hand, was it sufficient to write a script and then go and shoot 'wallpaper' pictures that would carry a preordained commentary. Rather, it was a continuing evolutionary process: ideas inspired the filming, and the sound and pictures that resulted led in turn to the right words in the commentary. Without the best ideas there could be no film worth more than the old *Newsreel*. Without the best sound and pictures there could be no report that made the viewing of a film worthwhile.

'Such integration between the visual and the verbal requires respect by the visual men, film editors and the cameramen, for the ideas and the words; and respect by the ideas and words men for the importance of visual communication. The two can complement each other and the result be more effective than either alone.' Unlike some of her successors, Grace Wyndham Goldie had quickly grasped this simple, basic truth about how to make good television current affairs.

But, interviewed on the 25th anniversary of the start of his television career, Robin Day suggested that it was the visual side of television that had made it in the end an enemy of good communication: 'I began increasingly to become aware of the limitations and dangers of television; that it was a medium of shock rather than explanation; that it was a crude medium which strikes at the emotions rather than the intellect. And because of its insatiable appetite for visual action, and for violence very often, it tended to distort and trivialise. In my opinion . . . it has contributed to the spate of unreason and violence and conflict in our society.'[7] This is an indictment of television indeed. Of course it reflects Day's own preoccupation with the studio interview and his reluctance to accept that anything else can be half so enlightening. All the same, it is a charge that deserves an answer.

It is true that television current affairs is not usually best at the delicate, the detailed, and the densely argued. The viewer of a programme can't refer back, can't 'read the page again', can't put the book down in the middle and reflect. In that sense it is 'a crude medium'. It's certainly best at dealing with simple themes, or complex ideas presented in a simple way; and that can go wrong and at worst become a travesty of the truth. But while television can 'distort and trivialise', is written journalism really any different? And while it certainly does have 'an insatiable appetite for visual action' does that necessarily mean violence? Surely television is not very different from the theatre or the cinema: it offers a mixture of words, sounds and pictures to try to tell the truth about life. And when those elements are brought together effectively then they have an impact we need not sniffily deplore but should applaud. Anyone who is tired of 'visual action' should certainly sell his television set. Some reporters do come to believe that, as Noël Coward remarked, 'television is for appearing on, not for watching'. So as *Panorama* films grew longer and more ambitious, sensible reporters and producers worked together, to make sure that all the available ingredients combined to make the best possible programme.

Public servants

But who were the producers? If we know something about the early reporters, what were their producers like?

Well, their backgrounds were often similar. 'With only a few exceptions', says Robert Rowland, 'staff and reporters were ex-public schoolboys, mostly Oxbridge and mainly men.'[8]

Jeremy Murray-Brown was a product of Winchester and New College. He had been hired by Grace Wyndham Goldie in 1955 following an intro-duction from his Oxford tutor Alan Bullock. So far, so traditional. But Murray-Brown – today he teaches documentary film-making at the University of Boston in America – says that the generation Wyndham Goldie was hiring was far from hidebound. Indeed, the reason why so many of her recruits were, like him, so young was that 'she realised she would get nowhere if she relied upon old BBC British types. A new medium was calling for new forms, new ways of doing things. She needed people who had not been tainted by that older tradition. In those early days everything we were doing was new. We went with what worked.'

British missions abroad had not grasped that *Panorama* was determined to look at things in a new way, and didn't feel obliged, like the BBC's World Service, to pay close attention to our Government's view. 'Wherever you went', says Murray-Brown, 'you were liable to be called in by the High Commission and told the Government line. They didn't understand we were different from Bush House.'[9]

So some still thought *Panorama* was just another posting in the Foreign and Commonwealth Office; and that wasn't surprising: 'Like so much in the BBC,' says Robert Rowland, 'it was run (broadly) by the kind of person who, some decades earlier, could have landed up being district commissioner in the British Empire.' But, he says, most *Panorama* people were rather brighter than that. A producer on *Panorama* for many years before he became its Editor in 1971, Rowland had been President of the Oxford Union, and was selected as one of only five general trainees at the BBC out of 2000 applicants that year.

Aged 24, he joined *Panorama* in 1962, at what was perhaps the programme's apogee. Suddenly he found himself working with the most famous men in Britain. 'It was a very heady experience,' he says; 'they were brilliant about sharing their ideas when I asked for their advice.' Of all the stories he did – with John Morgan in Budapest, with James Mossman on Oswald Mosley, with Richard Kershaw in Atlanta following Martin Luther King's assassination – it was one with Richard Dimbleby that he remembers best. In 1965, after a decade of presenting *Panorama*, Dimbleby went back to the site of Belsen concentration camp in Germany. There, 20 years earlier, he had been the first war correspondent to report the enormity of what the Nazis had done to so many innocent human beings.

Rowland remembers Dimbleby flying in to what would be a cold, windy, horrible day's filming. The difficult weather conditions meant that, time and again, sound recordist Robin Green had to ask Dimbleby to repeat his links. Dimbleby wrote nothing down, yet in every retake this supremely professional presenter perfectly expressed his feelings and thoughts on returning to this terrible place of death. Rowland was profoundly moved. That year he got married; by the end of it, Dimbleby would be dead.

In those days, Rowland recalls, there was a real divide between the BBC and ITV, between those who believed in a broadcasting service funded by the Licence Fee, and those prepared to work for a channel supported by advertising: 'At *Panorama* there was a mission not to be commercial ... The internal arguments could be fierce, but the companionship and the sense of doing something worthwhile was central. It was a vibrant team effort, and stands as a monument to an era when what you did mattered more than what you earned, who you were more important than who you knew.'[10]

In his essay 'Panorama in the Sixties'[11] Rowland quotes Alasdair Milne, from the rival BBC Tonight empire, on Panorama – 'rather self-important and faintly tiresome', and agrees there was some justice in that:

> Panorama was a fairly sober beast in the television jungle of the 60's. Metaphorically speaking, we wore suits throughout the period . . . 'Measured judgement' would describe the way many producers and programme editors saw their role. The capacity to surprise, to be original, to break new ground was vital – but all in the context of feeling part of a great institution based on Reithian principles of fairness, tolerance, balance and improvement. Respect was tempered by irreverence.

People like that can still be found on Panorama today.

David Harrison first worked for Panorama in the mid-1960s, when Richard Dimbleby was still its presenter. His early experience had included a stint as manager of a Hong Kong hostess club, Tony's Bamboo Bar. Perhaps it was that which persuaded the BBC to hire him as a news trainee. With fluent French, Harrison was sent to the Paris office, and when Panorama came panting into town he would help set up the filming they wanted. 'These were very distinguished chaps,' he says. 'I tried to make myself indispensable.' Liking what he saw of current affairs he went to work at Lime Grove, first for the late evening 24 Hours programme, and then for Panorama. 'Get your reporter to do interviews standing up when you can,' Robin Day very sensibly told him, 'it makes them shorter and crisper'.

On 24 Hours, as on Panorama in the early 1960s, the norm had been to make several stories in the course of one long trip. This involved sending the undeveloped film material that had been shot back to Lime Grove before moving on to the next location and the next story. As Ludovic Kennedy described it: 'Completing film reports from abroad in those days was something of a hit-or-miss affair. The producer gave the presenter [reporter] a shopping list of everything filmed, the presenter wrote a commentary which he hoped would fit and which he then recorded in some quiet room with the sound man, after which both film and [sound] tapes were taken to the nearest airport and shipped to London; then the *Panorama* film editors would chop and change and piece them together for transmission.'[12]

To able and ambitious producers like Harrison this was a most unsatisfactory way of working. First, it meant giving too much control to the reporter, for inevitably his script would to a large degree determine the structure of the film. Second, it was frustrating not knowing before that script had been written whether 'the snaps had come out'. Had that moody shot at sunset worked, or not? Had the villain really been caught squarely in the frame as the cameraman claimed, or was he unrecognisable? Did the reporter look as hungover and incoherent in his piece to camera as he had seemed, or was it just about acceptable?

But from the mid-1960s onwards, a *Panorama* team, when it set off, whether at home or abroad, usually expected to make only one film; they would return with the rushes and view them in Lime Grove before editing. That offered much more scope for the producer and the reporter to make the most of what had been shot, before the script was written. (In later years this would be derided as 'cutting room journalism'.) And of course the producer could now be quite confident that all the film material had been properly assessed: 'You wouldn't find later that someone had failed to look at roll 3,' says Harrison.

In the television current affairs world, only Charles Wheeler is older than David Harrison, and in their long careers both have contributed greatly to *Panorama*. New arrivals on the programme have sometimes sniggered at Harrison's traditional sports jacket, his conservative shirt and regimental tie, and his tall, spare, military bearing; and one or two have thought his equally upright moral stance, which would never allow him to put out a film he knew to be less than completely honest, equally old-fashioned. But, first as a staff man and latterly as an independent producer, Harrison has made a succession of powerful films which have added greatly to *Panorama*'s reputation for fair and authoritative journalism. 'The White Tribe of Africa',[13] with David Dimbleby as its reporter, or 'Journey into Darkness',[14] about the Rwanda massacres, with Fergal Keane, are two prize-winning examples.

Of course reporters who work with Harrison, a former paratrooper, have to be tough. When transport breaks down in the African bush you will be 'yomping' with your suitcase and half the camera gear on your back; when there's a through-the-night edit you will be begging tearfully for a few minutes' rest as Harrison, dozy with lack of sleep himself, drives the cutting room team on through the small hours. And it doesn't pay to let him get an idea in his head that's wrong. It will be hard to shift. Those idiosyncrasies aside, Harrison is a model producer, as caring for his men under fire as any company commander.

Rough diamonds

It would be wrong to think that it is the reporters on *Panorama* who are always the prima donnas. Producers have their little tantrums too. The author remembers, as a reporter, having to make an emergency stop on the motorway as two highly competitive young producers, Anthony Summers and Tom Bower, threatened to come to blows in the back seat of his car, as they quarrelled at screaming pitch about how best to make some particular *Panorama* programme. Both these fiercely ambitious men went on to fame and fortune far beyond what television was ready or able to offer them. Both now write very large blockbuster biographies about big personalities for very large sums of money. In America, Summers's subjects have included Marilyn Monroe, the FBI's J. Edgar Hoover, former President Richard Nixon, and now Frank Sinatra. In Britain, Bower has dealt damaging blows to the late Robert Maxwell, Mohamed Fayed, Richard Branson and former minister Geoffrey Robinson.

Summers's first encounter with *Panorama* had been as an Oxford undergraduate in the early 1960s, hired by the Editor of ITV's *World in Action* to monitor the rival BBC's flagship programme week by week and give him an instant report on what it had been doing. By 1968 Summers was working for the BBC's nightly *24 Hours* programme. Filming with reporter David Lomax on an Indian reservation in Arizona – it was a story about Navajo land rights – Summers was asked to do a little job for *Panorama*.

The American presidential elections were approaching. Having watched and waited until Eugene McCarthy had shown there was support for a liberal democratic candidate, Robert Kennedy had now decided to claim his birthright and win the nomination for himself. His late intervention meant he might split the Democratic Party, and lead it to defeat. For Kennedy it was a most sensitive topic.

Kennedy had agreed to be interviewed for *Panorama*: *Panorama* rather grandly asked Summers, because he was already there, to do it. 'They treated us in a peremptory way,' Summers recalls: "We are the Upper Sixth and we are asking the Lower Fifth to do it for us."' The interview was set for 30 March, a day Kennedy would be in Flagstaff for a meeting of his Senate Sub-committee on Indian Education. Summers had offered to give him the question areas (supplied by *Panorama*) in advance, but when he arrived Kennedy brushed the offer aside: 'No, no, let's go.' In his usual polite but insistent way Lomax pressed him about what his late intervention in the campaign was doing to the Democrats. 'At that moment – I can still see it,' says Summers, 'Kennedy's face darkened. He glowered, there was a pause, and then he let loose a string of strong expletives, saying we had ambushed him, knowing he would not answer that question.' Summers offered to start again, but Kennedy became even angrier. 'I'm not going to sit here and be insulted,' he shouted, then tore off his lapel microphone and stormed from the room. Summers recalls wondering if Kennedy would behave like that if he ever reached the Oval Office.

There was no interview worth transmitting, but Summers shipped the material they'd shot to London anyway, and called *Panorama*'s Editor David Webster to tell him what had happened. There was some mild harrumphing from Webster – 'what else could be expected from the Fifth Form?' was his tone.

But worse was to come. Back in London, *24 Hours* had prepared a compilation of amusing or telling moments from the campaign – 'Quirks of the Candidates'. The producer had included the material shot by Summers, unaware that, in an effort to set up another interview with Kennedy, *Panorama* had assured his press secretary that the aborted Flagstaff interview would never, ever, be seen. Not surprisingly, when the *24 Hours* film went out the Kennedy camp instantly cancelled the *Panorama* interview. Summers found himself blamed again, particularly when, a few weeks later, on 8 June, Bobby Kennedy was assassinated before *Panorama* had been able to talk him round. 'The manner in which I was made a scapegoat – more than 30 years ago', says Summers, 'is something I have never forgotten; the combination of scorn and malevolence with which I was addressed, not by David Webster, but by another senior *Panorama* person! It was obvious why the people in *Panorama* were trying to hang me for their problem: I was just one of those ruffians from *24 Hours*. If you are from a staider, more lumbering school of journalism altogether, like *Panorama*, then I was a tearaway.'

Certainly at times *Panorama* needed 'tearaways.' In 1973 Egypt amazed the world – and caught the Israelis entirely by surprise – when it launched a successful attack across the Suez Canal into the Sinai peninsula. The Yom Kippur War had begun, and for a time it seemed as if Israel's survival was in doubt.

At Lime Grove, different current affairs programmes pooled their resources and their people. While other teams headed for Tel Aviv, *Panorama*'s Editor Frank Smith ordered Tony Summers and the author to Cairo. Inevitably the airport there was closed; the least worst way in seemed to be by road from Libya. Once in Tripoli Summers cut a comprehensive deal with a likely-looking taxi driver which soon had the Lime Grove contingent speeding day and night across the desert, talking and bribing its way through road blocks over the border into Egypt. Arriving at the Nile Hilton Summers imperiously demanded the biggest available suite, spread money liberally around the hotel lobby and telephone exchange, and immediately had notepaper printed (with the correct red logo) which read 'BBC Cairo Office'. Everything was done on a grand scale so that the Egyptian authorities should think of *Panorama* – rather than any other of the many clamouring television teams straggling in from all over the world – as the people who should get the very limited access that was being granted to anything related to the war.

So, after endless lobbying, it was Summer's *Panorama* team, not – much to its disgust – BBC News, that found itself, accompanied by an Egyptian general, crossing a Bailey bridge over the Suez Canal into Sinai, amid the cheers of a briefly victorious Arab army. Such was the euphoria of the general and the relentless energy of Summers that the team drove on as if heading for Jerusalem. Only a shot from a stationary tank on the horizon brought their advance to a halt. Unwittingly *Panorama* had left the Egyptian forces behind and reached the Israeli front line.

Baling out of their vehicle, the team burrowed as deeply as possible into the sand, as their escorting officer recalled a lecture he had attended while on a course in Britain about the effect that shelling had on soldiers not properly dug in. Summers pocketed (and still possesses) a fragment of the round that had just missed them. Shaken but unhurt the team at first crawled and then trudged the rest of their way back through no man's land. There was another anxious moment when the escort was unable to give the right password in answer to a challenge from an Egyptian forward post.

For that Suez adventure, Summers had been on loan to *Panorama*, but by 1975 the tearaway producer was one of the programme's permanent staff. As his Editor was well aware, he was quite unable to resist a challenge.

The Russian physicist Dr Andrei Sakharov, just awarded the Nobel Peace Prize, was under virtual house arrest in Moscow, unable to go to Oslo to collect his award. 'It's impossible – we'll have to get Summers to do it,' said Peter Pagnamenta, and Summers was given his assignment: go to Russia and somehow get the interview with Sakharov which so far no television programme had been able to do.

Hiring a large fur coat and an 8mm film camera which he could hide in its pockets Summers set off for Moscow with his Russian-speaking research assistant Claire Selerie and reporter Michael Charlton. They had previously been briefed by Mrs Sakharov, who had been allowed out to western Europe for medical treatment. She had drawn them maps and given them contacts. After a series of 'dry runs' to see how the land lay, the *Panorama* team managed to evade the KGB 'watchers' and get in to the apartment block outside Moscow where the great man was being made to live. They found him in a flat that was microscopically small, surrounded by his extended family. In order to shoot the interview at all Summers had to get on a bed in a corner of the one tiny bedroom. Speaking in Russian, Sakharov explained to Charlton what he would have said in his speech in Oslo, if he had been allowed to go there; and, in a few sentences in English, he told the *Panorama* team: 'I am so happy to be able to speak to the world and not be silent.'

Summers now divided up the film they had shot in the hope that at least some of it would reach London. Clare Selerie put her film cassettes right at the bottom of her bag and covered them with paper tissues. Fortunately the tough-looking lady who was searching hand luggage stopped just before she reached the film. With Charlton, Selerie boarded a plane for London without incident.

Dennis Bardens, the first 'Editor of *Panorama*', 1953.

(Courtesy of Dennis Bardens.)

Michael Barsley, Producer of *Panorama*, 1954. (Courtesy of BBC archives.)

Woodrow Wyatt, the first *Panorama* reporter, 1956. (Courtesy of BBC archives.)

The young Charles
Wheeler in Berlin, 1955.

(Courtesy of Fritz Eschen.)

Editor Paul Fox with Richard Dimbleby, 1961. (Courtesy of BBC archives.)

A *Panorama* production meeting at Lime Grove in 1958. Clockwise from top left: Rex Moorfoot, producer; Richard Dimbleby, presenter; Chris Chataway, reporter; John Freeman, interviewer; David Wheeler, producer; Woodrow Wyatt, reporter; Kenneth Lamb, producer; Robert Kee, reporter; Jeremy Murray-Brown, producer; Christopher Burstall, producer and Margaret Douglas, Secretary.

(Courtesy of BBC archives.)

Catherine Dove (later Freeman), the first female *Panorama* producer, 1956.

(Courtesy of the *Daily Express*.)

Producer David Wheeler with Richard Dimbleby, 1958. (Courtesy of Hulton Getty.)

'The Spaghetti Harvest', April Fool's Day 1957. (Courtesy of BBC archives.)

Producer Revel Guest with Prime Minister Harold Macmillan, 1962.
(Courtesy of Reuters.)

Grace Wyndham Goldie, Robin Day and Richard Dimbleby prepare for the General Election, September 1964. (Courtesy of BBC archives.)

Panorama goes to America for the Democratic Convention, 1960. Left to Right: Michael Peacock, Editor, *Panorama*; David Webster, assistant producer, *Panorama*; Leonard Miall, Head of Television Talks; Ludovic Kennedy, reporter, *Panorama*; David Wheeler, producer, *Panorama*; Robin Day, reporter, *Panorama*.

Producer Chris Ralling with reporter James Mossman and friends in Wajir, Northern Kenya, 1963.

(Courtesy of Chris Ralling.)

Joan Marsden and Richard Dimbleby in the *Panorama* studio, April 1964.

(Courtesy of the Daily Mail.)

David Dimbleby inherits his father's job, and his floor manager. Joan Marsden with David Dimbleby, 1974. David took over as *Panorama* presenter twenty-one years to the day since Panorama began, on 11 November 1953.

(Courtesy of BBC archives.)

To make the team less conspicuous Summers had decided to travel alone and take a different route home. It didn't help. Though he had left the camera behind, hidden behind the bath panels in his hotel, airport metal detectors revealed the film cassettes he was carrying in his capacious coat pockets. After a nerve-wracking time persuading security that he was merely a lone tourist, he arrived sweating at the departure gate to see in the distance the airport bus pulling slowly away from the aircraft he should by now have been aboard. Summers made what he describes as 'a controlled fuss'. Those who have seen this phenomenon, felt those pale fanatic eyes fixed upon them, heard the quiet hissing speech that sounds rather like a cobra about to strike or a pressure cooker threatening to explode with very nasty consequences for everyone around – these people know what fear is. Soon another airport coach was taking Summers, all alone, across the tarmac to his plane – pure spy thriller stuff.

But had this Le Carré carry-on been necessary? In Moscow the *Panorama* team had never been quite sure if the KGB was really determined to stop them getting their interview with Sakharov. A minute from a Board of Governors meeting suggests they were not:

> D.G reported that a team from *Panorama*, authorised by him (with some misgivings on grounds of safety) to go and film in the Soviet Union, had returned without incident from Moscow with what could amount to Andrei Sakharov's speech of acceptance of the Nobel Prize for Peace . . . The team had been allowed in on tourist visas, but he had no doubt that the Soviet authorities had known and not tried to prevent the team from carrying out its main purpose.[15]

Sitting in a London restaurant some time after the interview had gone out, researcher Selerie was approached by a fellow diner who introduced himself as being from a Russian trade delegation. 'We knew what you were doing in Moscow,' he said. Summers is not convinced: 'They would have said that, wouldn't they, once we'd actually got the film out?'

Before transmission of the interview there was one more heart-stopping moment for Summers in the Lime Grove cutting room. With huge antici-pation he started to view their material – but the first roll the film editor put on the machine contained nothing but shots of a bare-breasted hula-

hula girl. It turned out that the firm Summers had got his film from had mistakenly given him a cassette of processed material belonging to some tourist customer. Fortunately the rest of the stock was all right, and most of the interview intact – 'shot with some difficulty in Moscow by Tony Summers, an experienced BBC producer but an inexperienced camera-man,'[16] said a *Times* review. But *Panorama*'s viewers would never hear the few words that Sakharov had spoken to them in English; that bit of the interview had been shot on the roll the hula-hula girl had already made her own.

By this stage Summers was thinking about leaving the challenges of tele-vision that he found it so hard not to respond to. A peculiarly hair-raising trip to a Lebanon collapsing in gang warfare convinced him the time had come to make writing his full-time career. So Summers did not long remain on *Panorama*. He did however return later as a freelance to produce 'Who Really Killed Kennedy?',[17] an investigation based on research for a book he had written about the President's assassination.

Producer paranoia

Tom Bower remained on the programme for some time. His difficulty was that few reporters were ever quite able to share his vision of the film they were making together, let alone agree on the best way of doing it. The root of the problem was that Bower was always convinced he could do it all better on his own. So his reporter would often find himself treated with unfriendly contempt: either he was too naïve or stupid to understand the wickedness of which the villains in the film were capable, or he didn't have the guts to tackle them properly. 'No, no, no,' would come the loud, angry, nasal complaint from somewhere behind the wretched reporter as he tried to interview some suspect in a way he thought might ultimately elicit something like the truth. This intervention from the producer did not do much to convince the interviewee that he was facing an effective, let alone a united *Panorama* team. As one of Bower's annual BBC reports puts it: 'Tom is an abrasive man, sometimes charming, highly intelligent, but contemptuous of those who disagree with him. He doesn't suffer fools gladly, and . . . is often unnecessarily abusive about others. This communi-cates itself to his colleagues.'

Sometimes a reporter working with Bower would do his research for an interview, prepare his questions and arrive at the location, only to find that Bower had set off a day early and done the interview himself. So before long Bower often found himself working alone as a combined producer/reporter. Much as this simplified things for him personally, it led to new difficulties.

Even at the lowest estimate of his talents a reporter has some residual value: he is something you can cut to when an interview needs to be edited. A 'noddy', a shot of the reporter apparently listening to the interviewee, is an old-fashioned device used to smooth over what would otherwise be a disturbing jump-cut. With any luck, the viewers won't even notice (some will say they should) that one sentence has been joined to another from much later on in the interview, and that the boring eight minutes of prevarication and repetition in between have just disappeared. But without a reporter Bower had no noddy. As a producer, normally never seen by the *Panorama* audience, he could not himself suddenly appear in vision.

This was even more of a problem for Bower than for other producers. His film interviews – were mostly with dodgy, devious, defensive, equivocating crooks and foreigners. For the truth to emerge they had to be heavily edited if their subjects were to say clearly on the screen what Bower was convinced they had really meant to say in the interview but had been strangely reluctant to admit. Without cutaway shots of the reporter listening, Bower's edited interviewees could sometimes jerk madly around on the screen as if undergoing some form of electrical torture – no doubt very much how they felt under Bower's vigorous questioning. A calmly spoken sentence filmed in a wide shot might suddenly give way to a few angry seconds of extreme close-up from another bit of the interview, before the camera cut back again to a mid-shot for some other soundbite. The effect was sometimes less persuasive than Bower must have hoped.

An interview on film or tape can't be rewritten, compressed or expanded, like one for a newspaper; it can only be a series of extracts cut together. Editing what people have said to you in an interview shows much more clearly on the screen than it does in print.

Bower was often cross and angry; fed up with reporters who didn't agree with his view of what the story was; despairing of camera crews who wanted a lunch break rather than go on doorstepping in the cold for yet another 24-hour day; suspicious of the motivation (and contemptuous about the competence) of Editors who insisted on changes to his films.

In Korea Bower, working with reporter Tom Mangold, was making 'Traffic in Babies', perhaps the first television treatment of how international adoptions were being conducted on a commercial basis. A party of Scandinavian women had flown in collect the children they had contracted to adopt. The children were at one end of the hall, their new mothers, seeing them for the first time, were to come in at the other. Bower had realised that this would be an extraordinary moment that had to be captured, and had briefed his cameraman accordingly. But as this dramatic scene unfolded, and the women rushed to clutch their new children to them, Bower became convinced that these magic moments were not being caught on camera. Furious with rage he grasped his cameraman by the waist (it was the relatively diminutive Max Samett), lifted him off the floor and carried him around the hall like a ventriloquist's dummy, pointing him with his camera at these emotional meetings in the hope of getting exactly what he wanted on film.

In 'Israel's Secret Weapon'[18] Bower doggedly pursued a difficult and dangerous story about Israel's secret nuclear weapons programme – his were the first television pictures of the Israelis' nuclear reactor at Dimona. But Bower's activities soon found him confronting some former members of Israel's secret service, Mossad, now involved in importing nuclear material. Doorstepping one of these tough characters, Bower's cameraman was beaten up, and one or more of his ribs cracked or broken. Badly battered, he was in considerable pain. As one would expect, Bower responded quickly. Persuading the Mossad man that it would be better to talk than be publicly sued for assault Bower propped his cameraman (a wretched freelance, naturally) against a conveniently parked car, and told him to carry on filming.

In spite – he would say because – of this monomania Bower made some important *Panorama*s, most memorably a series of films tracing the survival of former Nazis, their allies and their ideology into the new Germany. 'A Blind Eye to Murder?' in 1978[19] was the first, clearly showing that, contrary to the general assumption, important Nazi war criminals had gone unprosecuted in West Germany, and were still living comfortably, at liberty. The last of the series bluntly accused the German Finance Minister

Franz Josef Strauss – the leader of the Christian Socialist Union – of Nazi connections, of accepting bribes from the American company Lockheed, and of funding his party in Bavaria with corrupt contributions from German businessmen. There was a little visual 'sting', involving a hand taking money, that recurred throughout the film whenever Bower wanted to remind the viewer of his theme of corruption but hadn't actually got anything else with which to illustrate it. Roger Bolton, *Panorama*'s Editor at the time, was uneasy. He now regrets letting the film go out, as he did, without further amendment. Bower does not regret anything. 'I was right,' he insists: 'since then it's been proved that the CSU *was* corrupt, that its finances really were built on bribes.'

Tom Bower briefly became Deputy Editor of *Panorama*. In 1985 he hoped to get the Editor's job but, to his bitter disappointment, lost out to Peter Ibbotson; soon afterwards he left Current Affairs to make documentaries for the BBC and write his books. Today, as a highly successful author, he says – as people who don't become Director General quite often do: 'There are politicians in the BBC and there are programme makers; I was a programme maker.'

Producer as auteur

There were other highly individual producers in *Panorama*'s history who found it rather easier to work with reporters than did Tom Bower. But producers generally were becoming more insistent that they were not there just to illustrate someone else's journalism but to contribute their own. This, after all, was what had happened on *Picture Post*. If it is said that, in print at least, one picture can be worth a thousand words, then some television producers have always felt that it is their pictures that should sometimes take precedence over commentary.

Peter Bate, who came to *Panorama* in 1979 from *Nationwide* and *Tonight*, was an accomplished film-maker. Now that *Panorama* films were running for half or all the 50-minute programme Bate didn't feel he needed reporters on the screen at all: 'I wanted my films to have a certain look about them, and that didn't mean keeping the traditions of previous years. The guide word on *Panorama* was journalism, but I felt we were doing illustrated radio.'

Bate was irritated to find that he wasn't taken as seriously as the reporter, even though, he felt, his contribution was as great. 'I remember David Dimbleby as presenter of *Panorama* introducing a film about dramatic developments in Poland. We'd cut it and put it out the same day. David's introduction went: "Peter Taylor has been in Poland with a film crew." I thought: "Funny, I thought I was there too."' Bate felt that *Panorama*'s style had become formulaic, and that the reporters had become much too pleased with themselves. He had a sense on *Panorama* of 'reporter power' arrogance; 'they felt they were bigger than the programme and bigger than the BBC. They were often just holding up the story, or there in the film because the producer couldn't think of a more televisual way of saying something. The audience didn't know or care about *Panorama* reporters because they were rarely seen, and it was because of this that reporters were too keen to get themselves on the screen.' Peter's solution was to make films with stunning sequences which would tell the story visually, and relegate the reporters to a reduced role as off-screen interviewers and commentators.

Now if this is just a matter of trying harder to find those evocative sequences and using them more effectively; if it's a question of letting pictures and sounds, effectively edited, take a bigger share in telling the story, then that's fine. But to suggest that in a current affairs programme trying to explain complicated ideas or situations you can virtually dispense with the reporter surely can't be right. Too many words and you're giving an arid illustrated lecture; but too few, and all you've got is a montage from an early Russian film, with a strong theme, a big impact and not many ideas – let alone any analysis of them. It's only fair to Bate to say that the film he made with reporter Jeremy Paxman about the mysterious death of 'God's banker' Roberto Calvi was deservedly a major prizewinner, in which reporter and producer worked harmoniously and productively together.[20]

Another *Panorama* producer wrote the reporter out of her script altogether; indeed there wasn't a script – or at least a commentary – at all. What Angela Pope did in 'The Best Days?'[21] was to make an impressionistic, documentary programme about a comprehensive school. The only problem with this fascinating film was that it ran as a *Panorama* programme.

'The Best Days?' caused uproar, with the teachers' unions and many education experts angry at what the film had revealed. But without a reporter, it was very difficult to know what the scenes Angela Pope put before the viewers actually meant.

Six years earlier Pope had been at the centre of another row with the film she and David Dimbleby made about senior Labour figures who had found themselves out of office following their 1970 defeat.[22] In 'Yesterday's Men' Dimbleby's questions to Harold Wilson about how he was earning a living and how much he'd got for his memoirs had outraged the former Prime Minister. Robin Day would never have behaved like that. But it was the precisely the conventional way that Day and *Panorama* tended to deal with important people and important issues that had made Pope want to do things differently. 'One of the things that stimulated our thinking on "Yesterday's Men"', she says shrewdly, 'was that while Robin's questions were often tough, they would never discomfort.' Angela liked to get under the skin of things – and of people.

Pope had learned to make films herself while working for Peter Pagnamenta on *24 Hours*. By 1976, she had become a freelance director producer, and Pagnamenta had become Editor of *Panorama*. He was keen to use her talent to the benefit of his programme.

A fly-on-the-wall film about a comprehensive school was Pope's idea. She had been much taken with a similar film of an American school that she had seen.[23] Pitching her project to Pagnamenta she told him she didn't want to make a typical *Panorama* education story, with some decorous, formal filming over a day or so, with everyone always very aware of the presence of the production team. 'The *Panorama* house style was set in aspic,' she remembers, 'I thought there were other ways to skin the cat.' Instead of teaming up in the usual way with a reporter, she wanted to work on her own, with just a minimum two-man crew of camera and sound. Pagnamenta agreed.

'I very much felt at the time', Pope says, 'that I wanted no more barriers than necessary between what was happening in the school and the viewers. Already the camera lens and me would be quite enough.' Not only would there be no reporter, there would be no commentary either. 'The only question in my mind was: "How can I make this speak to the audience?" I didn't see myself as having a duty to the BBC current affairs tradition. I just wanted to make a truthful film about a school.'

Pope visited a number of comprehensives and settled on Faraday High

School, in Ealing – with the agreement of the local education authority. Later, teachers at the school would take issue with its description in David Dimbleby's studio introduction as 'an ordinary comprehensive school'. Though no one had made anything of it during filming, the school was actually recognised by the Department of Education as being one with 'special difficulties'. But in the programme there was no explanation of what that might mean, and no guidance on what weight should be given to it, because there was no commentary.

After many days when Pope and her minimal camera crew just sat in on lessons observing, doing nothing, so that everyone became used to their presence, she began filming, concentrating on one particular year-group. Shooting on film without lights was difficult. Some teachers refused to be filmed at all. At the request of the Headmaster some footage of the remedial class was not used, after some of the pupils were sent home for unruly behaviour.

As Pope had promised, the finished film was shown to the Head and the local education authority. They approved what she had done. With his agreement, the Head was later quoted by the BBC Press Office as saying: 'It is a true film, it deals with reality, which is conspicuously lacking in everything that is written or said about education.' By Christmas 1976 the film was sitting on the shelf, ready for transmission. And there it stayed. For whatever reason *Panorama* seemed to find it difficult to schedule.

Concerned that the BBC might be getting cold feet, Pope bounced her Editor into naming a transmission date by showing her film to the *Observer*'s Michael Davie. 'I have just seen a television film', he wrote,

> that should have Milton and Dr. Arnold leaping from their graves with horror and reforming zeal. It is a film about what goes on inside classrooms of an ordinary London comprehensive school; and it is sensational. It will fill the whole of *Panorama* on 21st. March. My feeling is that the Great Debate on education initiated by the Prime Minister and the Education Secretary, Mrs. Williams, will be a complete waste of time if it does not take as its starting point the problems revealed by the film.[24]

'The Best Days?' was indeed a sensational film. As Nancy Banks-Smith wrote in the *Guardian*: 'Angela Pope's brilliant impression of a day in the life of a comprehensive school was a crossfire of vivid images.'[25] Said the *Daily Mail*'s Comment column: 'The education debate will never be the same again. Suddenly, exploding into millions of living rooms at supper time last night came sound and vision from the schools' battlefront.'[26] 'At long last perhaps', said a London *Evening News* editorial, 'we can get down to basics.'[27]

The film left viewers reeling with a series of vivid sequences of school life. It revealed for the first time how traditional discipline had entirely disappeared, so that in this comprehensive school at least it now seemed to be the children who decided whether or not they were going to do what the staff wanted. Teachers were seen struggling to establish order, sometimes with little actual teaching done, wheedling and positively begging recalcitrant pupils to attend lessons, while those playing truant were seen smoking.

But was this sensational film, which had so brilliantly got everybody's attention, a proper *Panorama*? If not, was that simply because it was so much livelier than most of them (as it certainly was) or was it because, though it generated plenty of heat,[28] it didn't shine enough light on the subject?

After his preview of the film Michael Davie had written: 'There is no reporter. No one asks questions. No one makes speeches to camera. You get the feeling, therefore, that an exploratory drill has been inserted into the heart of the educational system and come out with a core, which is up to you to analyse.'

Any producer would be proud to be told they'd got to the core, the heart of the matter. But it's the job of current affairs not just to produce a sample of reality but to help viewers in the analysis of what's been dug up. On a sensitive topic Angela Pope had got right under the skin again, but she had not given the viewers much help in understanding the significance of what she had revealed. It was an exposé without an exposition. What it meant was entirely in the eye of the beholder.

Foolishly, and for his newspaper, expensively, Clive James in the *Observer* falsely suggested that Pope had made it up: 'Ms Pope is so carefree about palming off concocted effects as cinéma vérité that you start wondering if she knows the difference between fact and fiction.' That was the wrong charge to make. Pope's pictures and sounds were the truth, but it was simply raw material that needed some minimal amount of analysis and explanation to be really useful. Describing the programme as 'raw meat', the London *Evening Standard* said:

> Newspapers are not entitled to boast in such matters but at least journalists are under some obligation to ascertain each side to a question. This sort of television positively revels in what is termed 'a bias against understanding'.[29] It was in no sense a contribution to the debate which is now rightly under way into the successes and failures of London's comprehensive revolution. Nonetheless, the force of its images will clearly be used as emotive canon fodder by the anti-comprehensive lobby. This would be grossly unfair on comprehensives. There are better arguments which this lobby can deploy, valid research to which they can turn. *Panorama* was not argument. It was merely pictures in an exhibition.

That was the proper charge to make. Had Pope's film produced solid evidence of the state of affairs in an 'ordinary' comprehensive school, or simply impressions, impressions that could be too easily dismissed as misleading, untypical, unfair? Under the headline 'Worrying', in the *Daily Mail*, Shaun Usher made the same point:

> Had Ms. Pope chosen a problem class or a typical one? If so, what about the well-spoken and responsible sixth-formers, glimpsed so briefly? Had they improved because of the school, or despite it? The programme gave no clue, for here was an impressionist portrait, not a chart. As such, it was out place in a programme of *Panorama*'s stature. It simply isn't good enough to tell half the story on a subject as emotive as education, and then try and justify it as 'subjective'.[30]

As the *Daily Telegraph* said: 'With no reporter and no commentary, the programme just stuck its cameras in classrooms and let them roll.'[31]

Without a reporter to share responsibility, Pope took all the flak. She defended herself well, and the BBC (publicly at least) backed her. She successfully sued the *Observer* for the article by Clive James,[32] which had suggested she had been 'purposefully selective in her material, unscrupulous and no respecter of truth', and obtained a proper apology and damages. Later, however, the Broadcasting Complaints Commission partly upheld a complaint of unfair treatment made by 19 members of the National Union of Teachers at Faraday High School. The BCC decided that 'the concentration on inexperienced teachers resulted in an unbalanced picture of the classroom teaching at the school'. Of the smoking incident they said: 'The sequence, short though it was, must, we think, have given the impression to the viewing public, as it did to us, of a smoking session during school hours inside the school buildings and to the extent that this may have conveyed an unjustified impression of lack of control on the part of the teaching staff we hold that the complaint was justified.'[33]

It's always possible to say afterwards how things might have been done better. But if Angela Pope had used a reporter to tell us whether or not the teachers of whom we saw most were generally younger and less experienced than others in the school, had we been told that the pupils who were smoking were doing so not in the school but on a neighbouring estate, then viewers would have been in a better position to draw their own conclusions about what was really going on. Had she put what viewers were seeing and hearing in context, she might not have been criticised by the BCC. And, more importantly, if she had done that, the row that followed her programme might not have allowed the real issues in comprehensive education to be forgotten in arguments about what she had or had not done in filming it.

The conclusion must be that it's really not possible, in a long film in a current affairs programme like *Panorama*, just to 'let the facts speak for themselves': they don't. They need an experienced, authoritative helping hand. They need, at the very least, a commentary written by the producer, but better still by a trusted, in-vision reporter, to set those facts in context. Without that a film may make trouble, but it won't begin to change anything. Pope's film, brilliant though it was, did not discuss the issues raised, did not call to account the education professionals who claimed that comprehensive education was an unqualified success. A reporter might have made the difference.

If *Panorama* Editor Peter Pagnamenta had capitalised on the row and devoted the following week's *Panorama* to a discussion of the issues raised by the programme, then Pope's film would not deserve this criticism. As part one of a two-part programme it could not have been faulted. But standing on its own it did not do enough – indeed, anything

– to put this explosive story in context. That surely is what *Panorama* is supposed to do.

In current affairs, producers cannot usually do it on their own – any more than can reporters.

Beautiful friendships

Christopher Olgiati, like other *Panorama* people Peter Pagnamenta and Peter Ceresole, of Swiss Italian origin, had an ingenious and independent temperament. At the BBC's Bush House his dark, intriguing voice had made him a successful presenter in the Africa Service, while his producer Michael Cockerell was kept off the air by a Head of Service who didn't think he sounded right. But Olgiati had always been interested in film-making, and when he and Cockerell both eventually worked their passage to *Panorama* in the 1970s Olgiati had become a producer, while Cockerell had turned reporter.

Olgiati's speciality was extraordinary investigations presented in the most visually striking way. Though the idea and most of the research were usually his, he found ways of working very productively with reporters – particularly Philip Tibbenham. Tibbenham's polite deadpan interviews and wonderful way with words when it came to the script and its delivery, made the most of Olgiati's film-making skills. And Tibbenham had other talents absolutely necessary on the road: he was good company; a past master at coaxing a sulky film crew into a more co-operative mood, and so experienced a reporter that he could often suggest to the producer a better way to tell the story: 'It was an incomparable relationship; now I'm working on my own in documentaries it's not the same thing at all. Whatever is often said about reporters, how happy I should be if I could have that relationship back again! I miss it,' says Olgiati now. Together Olgiati and Tibbenham made some remarkable films for *Panorama*.

'The Friends Who Put Fire in the Heavens'[34] was the story of a shadowy company called Otrag, with connections to former Nazi rocket scientists, which had taken over an area of Zaire the size of France to develop its own commercial space rocket. Their idea was to sell to Third World leaders like the Shah of Iran their very own 'spy in the sky'. It was an extraordinary and fascinating tale.

Then, long before the feature film based on the same story, came an investigation into the suspicious death of Karen Silkwood,[35] the union official whose protests at dangerous practices in an American nuclear fuel processing plant seemed to have provoked her violent death. Tibbenham proved that reporters have at least some uses by donning an anti-contamination suit (in which he was completely unrecognisable) in order to simulate the way Silkwood's apartment had been swept for radioactive material.

In 'The Islamic Bomb',[36] Olgiati and Tibbenham looked more closely than had been done before at how the Arab world was trying to match Israel with nuclear weapons of its own. And there were other memorable Olgiati films with other reporters, for example 'Vietnam – Children of the Dust',[37] about the fate of mixed race children left behind when their American fathers went home, which he made with Jeremy Paxman.

These days, more than 20 years later, as he fights the hydra-headed commissioning system at the BBC to get a documentary under way, Olgiati looks back fondly to the *Panorama* programme of the early 1980s. '*Panorama* gave you an enormous platform, an exhilarating sense of freedom. What a difference between being able to walk down the corridor to the Editor's office and say: "I want to make a film on this" and within two days actually be making it – what a difference between that and today!'

There's no doubt that for every reporter like Robin Day who pronounced producers useless, or producers like Tom Bower who didn't rate reporters, there were many *Panorama* producers and reporters who much enjoyed operating together as a team. Often far from home, working long hours in unpleasant conditions, under great pressure to produce results, producers and reporters found it very useful and comforting to have someone else with whom to share the problems; with whom to discuss, argue and agree the best way forward over a drink paid for by the licence payer. Their expenses then might read: 'to entertaining Mr. Samizdat Samovar, secret service contact, 257 grotties'.[38]

There had been very successful co-operative pairings in the 1960s and early 1970s: for example between James Mossman and David Webster, John Morgan and Chris Ralling, John Gau and Julian Pettifer, and Frank Smith with Robert MacNeil. But it was with two people who arrived on the programme together in the autumn of 1975 that the idea of reporter and producer working closely together as a team came to fruition.

John Penycate eventually turned reporter, but it was as a producer that he established his reputation for some of the most professionally made programmes ever seen on *Panorama*. Penycate's frequent collaborator was reporter Tom Mangold. The pair were in Beirut in 1975, working for the late evening programme *Midweek*, when they got a call from their Editor Peter Pagnamenta, who had just been told he'd got the *Panorama* Editor's job. He wanted to take some of his own people with him to revitalise the scurvy-ridden crew of Lime Grove's flagship programme as they drifted, becalmed.

Penycate was small, shrewd, satirical, sceptical to the point of cynicism; Mangold was sardonic, scornful, suspicious of everyone and everything to the point of paranoia. They were both intensely competitive, and at times seemed to feel that it was at least as necessary that others should be seen to fail as that they should succeed. Indeed Penycate for many years kept a sign on his desk with precisely that message. Their initial skill was in identifying and selling to their Editors an exciting and important story that would justify time for extensive research and a large budget. In this way they avoided the tedious 'please help me out' quick turnaround stories which are so difficult and exhausting to do and seldom repay the effort with prizes or even thanks. 'John is an invaluable asset to *Panorama*,' ran one of Penycate's annual reports. 'He is a model professional, never at a loss for a story, and someone who settles the vast majority of problems which arise on a project without bothering his Editor . . . Being highly intelligent he can read an Editor's mind very well. I am glad his interests and mine have coincided.'

Both Penycate and Mangold were early sufferers from what Nick Hayes, former *Panorama* producer and later Editor of ITV's rival programme *World in Action*, calls 'Terminal 3-itis'. Though far from painful, this is a highly contagious complaint which forces its victims to fly at once to California and film their story there: 'Here, on the west coast of America, the home of electronic revolution/armaments industry/ethnic powder keg/earthquake/AIDS/severe sunburn we can see what will/might/could happen to us in Britain not many years from now . . . '

During the late 1970s and early 1980s Penycate and Mangold, this secretive *Panorama* pair, made a remarkable contribution to the programme. Their stories were nearly always about things that mattered, though it is true that they were usually the more exciting things: stories about the Cold War; about the drug companies; about penal policy and practice; about the activities and accountability of our shadowy security services.

Both men were excellently organised, with contacts they cultivated and research that was thorough and wide-ranging. It showed in their films. More than that, they understood that no matter how good the story, it had to be sold to the viewer. They were quite prepared to act like the fairground 'barkers' an earlier generation of *Panorama* journalists had disdained to be. And so they were insistent on getting film sequences that gave drama and excitement to the story, interviews that said something really worth hearing, editing that gave their narrative pace, and commentary that kept it coherent. Said Nancy Banks-Smith about 'The Deep Cold War':[39] 'I have not seen a thriller more beautiful or frightful, making all fictional cops and robbers look like Tom and Jerry . . . The producer, John Penycate, has seen Jaws too, for doom music, sounding like a bucket being kicked under water, vibrated every time a Russian sub slipped into the sea. Effective, yes. Superfluous, perhaps. I don't know what it did to the enemy but it shivered my timbers.'[40] Sean Day-Lewis in the *Daily Telegraph* agreed: 'John Penycate's riveting film, "The Deep Cold War", was about the threat of the Soviet submarine fleet, already 320-strong and expanding rapidly; what the reporter Tom Mangold called "the new sinister factor in Nato's war game tactics."' The programme was, he noted, 'effectively photographed, sharply edited, neatly spoken and underlined with an unusually effective sound track.'[41]

In 'The Doomsday Doodlebug'[42] the team assessed the potential of the Cruise missile. 'Tom Mangold asked a manager from the American firm that had developed the weapon what effect one of the things would have on London. Poker-faced the man replied: "It could ruin somebody's entire day."' In the *Daily Mail* reviewer Shaun Usher continued: 'Mangold's restraint in letting fearsome answers stand without comment seemed understandable. It was all being said. He and the producer John Penycate also resisted the obvious temptation to unveil a technological nightmare and leave it at that. Instead, they put the Cruise missile in perspective.'[43]

When you had seen a *Panorama* film made by Penycate and Mangold, you knew it, and were glad. So comprehensive was their film on the links between terrorist groups around the world – 'Terror International'[44] – that the mighty CBS *60 Minutes* bought it for showing in America, in effect admitting that, with all their resources, they could not hope to do the story so well themselves.

In 1978, to celebrate a quarter century of the programme, Mangold and Penycate were rewarded with a *Panorama* special on new weapons that could destroy western defences from space.[45] This, said Charles Murray in the *Daily Express*, was 'one of those marvellous cloak and dagger investigations by ace reporter Tom Mangold and producer John Penycate. It made a great old blockbuster to celebrate yet another BBC anniversary – 25 years of *Panorama*.' On the sixth floor of Television Centre distinguished *Panorama* people from the past groaned as they were forced to sit through the two-part programme – good though it was, of course – before getting a chance to talk about their own triumphs and enjoy the BBC's best hospitality.

John Penycate, like so many producers, grew jealous of reporters and became one himself – most recently for the BBC's *Money Programme*. Tom Mangold still makes films for *Panorama*, though no longer full-time. More than anyone else on the programme he survives as the quintessential *Panorama* reporter.

chapter eight

⊕ Those poor, well-paid presenters

Your name is scribbled on a card stuck in a holder on the door. You had hoped it was well known, at least within the BBC, but it is probably misspelled. Inside, you are shut up in a small windowless room which appears to be made entirely of plastic. Rather like a prison cell, it has little in it that can be removed and used as a weapon, or a means of suicide. Only a bent wire coat hanger or two suggests that the management of this institution does not expect you to kill yourself tonight. There is a couch, a chair, a dressing table and mirror, and your own lavatory and washbasin. There is a phone, which you may sometimes find is barred to outside calls, and a television monitor. This may not have a picture on it but will probably relay snatches of conversation between unseen technicians or unrelated sections of a film soundtrack you have not heard before. You are in a dressing room, alone, preparing to present *Panorama*.

That at least was the experience nearly 20 years ago. But today *Panorama* has no presenter, indeed has not regularly employed one since the mid-1980s. The figure who seemed so absolutely essential to the success of the programme through so many decades has been dispensed with. It is almost as if in the corner of this cell-like dressing room there was all the time an oubliette, a hole in the floor down which *Panorama* presenters have now disappeared forever into oblivion. All the fears and anxieties of the men who have been banged up alone in this little room over the years have been realised; nobody wants them any more.

Of course, as we all know, it wasn't like that to start with. The first *Panorama* back in 1953 depended vitally on its presenter – and paid the price. When poor Pat Murphy made such a mess of things the programme nearly died with him. As it was, the sprightly Max Robertson came to its rescue, for two years holding together with increasing success the anarchic ragbag of items that was then the programme. But in 1955 a new presenter arrived, a man who made the new *Panorama* work, a man against whom all other *Panorama* presenters since have been measured.

Biggest and best

The strange thing is that at first the viewers – or the critics at least – did not think Richard Dimbleby ideal as *Panorama*'s new front man: 'This programme has improved almost out of recognition in its new guise,' wrote Patrick Campbell, 'though Mr. Richard Dimbleby is not the ideal master of ceremonies.'[1] A month later Campbell had decided that Dimbleby was actually making the new programme worse. *Panorama*, he said, 'has borrowed from its compère a new, ponderous and, I fear, slightly stodgy look – as though television's window on the world were covered by a somewhat dirt-encrusted lace curtain. There were times in the past when *Panorama*, though unpredictable, had sparkle. Today it is entirely predictable and entirely dull.'[2] Campbell was something of an eccentric, at least in his own television appearances, but Peter Black – a keen student of the way television was developing – has to be taken more seriously. Early in 1956 he wrote:

> In the shuffle of programmes since the coming of ITV *Panorama* has been given a weekly spot and been considerably reorganised. What was a small mobile adventurous craft has been loaded to the gunwales. There have been some gains . . . But the losses have been severe. Richard Dimbleby, experienced and authoritative broadcaster though he is, is the wrong man to introduce such a programme to the audience it is trying to please. He has

that jolly-uncle manner that you can spot in many of the old hands in the BBC; a suggestion of slightly anxious coaxing which springs from his suspicion that you are not as interested in what he is talking about as he is.

Loaded down with Dimbleby's bulk and weightiness, Black seems to have felt, *Panorama* looked like sinking. As it settled down as a more serious current affairs programme than before, Dimbleby's strengths and weaknesses became more apparent.

Dimbleby didn't use autocue: in those days it was a cumbersome device bolted to the camera on which the script, typed in giant letters on rolls of yellow paper, would scroll down – with the operator hopefully keeping pace with the presenter's delivery. Instead, says Joan Marsden, the studio floor manager with whom Dimbleby always felt most secure and at ease, he would remind himself of what he had to say in his links with notes scribbled on hand or shirt cuff, or on cue cards that Joan had carefully stuck beneath the camera lens. Marsden (she has always been known in the studio since as 'Mother') was a huge help to Dimbleby, and the greatest admirer of his professional skills. In 1965 *Panorama* producer Dick Francis was writing to the studio managers, asking that Joan continue to be assigned to the programme: 'I know that Richard Dimbleby in particular regards her presence in the studio, old hand that he is, as extremely valuable to him every Monday night.'[3] 'Mother' could be rude, but she was wonderful for a *Panorama* presenter to hold on to.

A decade later Marsden was still seeing to it that the show could go on: 'Just a note to record how Joan Marsden rescued *Panorama* last Monday night,' wrote *Panorama*'s editor Peter Pagnamenta to the head of Studio Management. 'This was in connection with the late arrival of two Landrovers, two trailers, two large fish tanks and three 35lb.Trout for *Panorama*, with the obvious handling difficulties. Joan coped with her usual calm and exceptional resourcefulness, and we really appreciated her work.'[4]

These days a digital videotape report can be started instantly, as soon as the presenter stops talking, but then film stories needed eight seconds to get up to speed in the telecine machine. Without a precise script it was difficult for the studio director in the gallery to know when to 'cue telecine' so that the first frame of the actual film report was reached just when it was needed. Richard Dimbleby developed a personal technique of touching his ear to give the watching director the cue to roll the film. Then, on the studio monitor, out of the corner of his eye, Dimbleby would see the leader on the film counting down to zero; in his eyeline beside the camera Marsden as floor manager would be doing the same backwards count, silently, with her fingers. On cue, he would finish speaking just at the right moment for the director to cut to the film report he had been introducing. Only the most confident, the most experienced, the most articulate presenter could be relied on to do that.

As Michael Wall wrote later of Dimbleby in the *Listener*: 'He is a professional; he knows his job in front of the cameras better than any man on either channel; he is competent, solid, and "unflappable". The studio director knows that if there is a hitch he has only to let the camera rest on Dimbleby and the audience and the others in the studio will be put at ease until the trouble is over. His size, his voice, his well-known tones of awe and respect before important personages (will anyone ever forget his interviewing of King Hussein, who was overawed enough to address Dimbleby as "sir"?), his slight pomposity, and above all his essential gentleness provide the perfect and necessary contrast to the bright intense commentators, who like to wear bow ties.'[5]

Catherine Freeman (then Catherine Dove) confirms that Dimbleby was indeed 'a consummate professional', calm and good-tempered. Only once was he cross with her, when, during rehearsal, she cut to a shot of him combing his hair over a bald patch. He was a producer's dream presenter, able to ad lib with easy authority and, in response to the floor manager's signals, effortlessly stretch or contract his studio links as late changes in the running order demanded. And all this was done with a friendly comforting manner that put every viewer at ease.

In 1964, nearly a decade after he had joined the programme, the *Daily Sketch* called Richard Dimbleby 'an institution of the television age, a comfortable, rotund embodiment of security and promise, the Town Crier of the Telly whose very appearance seems to bring assurance that it's 8.25 and all's well. He has become the visible incarnation of something as essentially British as the chimes of Big Ben, warm beer, and the flag on Buckingham Palace.' Vastly experienced, so familiar to the viewers, so solid a centre for the programme, Dimbleby was the perfect foil for the younger *Panorama* people around him who were exploring the new terrain of television journalism. In Jonathan Dimbleby's view, '*Panorama* broke the new ground the more easily because Richard Dimbleby never moved at all.'[6]

But some members of the *Panorama* team at that time see it differently. 'There were no barriers then,' says Charles Wheeler, 'so many things that had never been done before. But Richard was a drag. He tended to soften the edges of what we were doing. He just didn't like the programme being controversial; "I've had letters of complaint from viewers," he would say.' Wheeler recalls urging Michael Peacock to go with him to see Cecil McGivern and try to get Dimbleby removed from the programme, and they did. But McGivern replied that 'without Richard Dimbleby there would be no *Panorama*', and so of course he stayed.

It wasn't that Dimbleby was a right-wing Conservative, but conservative he certainly was. Alone at Lime Grove Studios, says Jonathan, 'he distrusted those who pushed too hard or argued too well; who tumbled governments and destroyed reputations with one *bon mot*. It was a shallow, sharp world which he slightly feared and a little despised.' In turn, of course, he was distrusted by the BBC's young Turks. They saw in *Panorama*, and in Dimbleby, a 'subservient allegiance to the status quo and the establishment; its pontifical airs; its self-imposed isolation from the people; its pervasive middle-class, middle-brow morality. The young *avant garde* . . . chose Dimbleby as their symbol of the Corporation's complacency.'[7]

In 1956, quite soon after Dimbleby took over as *Panorama*'s presenter, he came under attack from Cassandra in the *Daily Mirror*: 'Richard Dimbleby shimmers in his own unction . . . to listen to Mr. Dimbleby describing a royal occasion is like tuning in to an oily burial service.'

And after he was sacked from *Panorama* at a few hours' notice (he'd written an article critical of the monarchy)[8] Malcolm Muggeridge took to disparaging Dimbleby, the great commentator on those royal occasions, as 'gold microphone in waiting'.

Richard Dimbleby was not the man to put pointed or penetrating questions to people in authority. 'What is this IRA?' David remembers his father asking Lord Brookeborough, the Prime Minister of Northern Ireland. It was rather like asking the Pope: 'What is this Communism?' And when Dimbleby was liberated from the studio and flew to Corfu to interview the King and Queen of Greece the results did not impress at least the more radical reviewers:

A filmed interview with the King and Queen of Greece might seem a perfect example of go-getting TV. But Dimbleby turned it into a creaking exercise in the art of curtsying. The real questions were unforgivably shirked. The deference became odious. The facts were submerged by protocol and courtly civility. Here *Panorama*'s style degenerated into mere timidity. And that, I fear will be the final epitaph of a programme which has too eagerly identified reporting with respectability and facts with personality.[9]

But for most of Dimbleby's 11 years on *Panorama* there was still a majority of the programme's audience which shared his decent, deeply conventional assumptions about life. And, at a time when a Third World War still looked more likely than not, Dimbleby's reassuring presence was immensely valuable to the programme. In October 1962, as ships carrying Soviet nuclear missiles were steaming towards Cuba and it seemed that East and West were on collision course, *Panorama* mounted a special programme on the crisis.[10] Paul Fox, at that time Dimbleby's Editor, says:

He was the perfect professional, and he had an understanding with the audience that no other television reporter or presenter has ever had, before or since. And perhaps it's exemplified by the time he did a special programme about Cuba. The night when the Cuban crisis looked at its worst. The Russian ships were on the way. Kennedy hadn't decided what to do. It really looked as though there could be some serious conflict between the Soviet Union and the United States, out in Cuba. And Richard did a special programme. And it was announced and a viewer phoned up and somehow came through to me, and this viewer said to me, 'there's only one thing I want Richard Dimbleby to do. I want him to tell me if it's safe for my daughter to go to school tomorrow.' And that was the trust Richard got with his audience, and the understanding he had achieved.[11]

As Grace Wyndham Goldie later wrote, Richard Dimbleby was 'a kind of living embodiment of stability, a reassuring symbol that somewhere at the heart of disturbance lies a basic kindliness and an enduring common sense'. That was indeed an accurate measure of the man, with all the advantages such a presence gave *Panorama*'s presenter, and all the disadvantages too: so helpful when a difficult or frightening subject like the threat of world war was to be dealt with, so unhelpful when it was high time to question the accepted order.

At Panorama's prow

Presenting *Panorama* has always been a strange and lonely job. As you meditate in your cell-like dressing room there is an ominous knock on the door. Then, escorted by an assistant floor manager, you are led, like a prisoner entering the dock – perhaps even mounting the scaffold – into the studio. It may be small and sweaty, or vast and cold. There you will become the centre of a flurry of impersonal activity as microphones are pinned to your lapels, 'deaf aids' stuffed in your ears, and the transmitters and receivers for these gadgets hitched to the back of your trousers where they will not actually show but will ruin the way your suit looks. The director will speak to you in your ear to make sure you can hear his technical instructions while you are on air. Your Editor, also watching you on the screens in the gallery, will mutter a few words of encouragement or, more likely, reminders of what you should not say or do. You read a few words of your script 'for level', to make sure the technicians can hear you properly. Everyone around you is tense, preoccupied with his own technical concerns. Then the strident voice of the floor manager is heard: 'Two minutes, studio', and the noise begins to subside. The little group of people around you begins to melt away. It's rather as if, having adjusted the noose round your neck, the hangman was stepping back off the trapdoor on which you now stand alone, ready for the drop. You are on your own now.

Checking your script one last time you move to your mark on the floor and wait, as the final countdown begins: 'Five, four, three, two, one,' says the production assistant in the gallery in your ear. Then, from the 'fold back' speaker on the floor, comes the *Panorama* title music, interrupted by another countdown, this time for you alone. 'Coming to you in ten, nine . . . ' and so on from the gallery, while the floor manager counts down the last three seconds silently, waving his fingers at you. Your chest grows tight, your breathing shallow; suddenly, as the floor manager makes you a commanding gesture, the red light on the camera glows, and you are on air, with millions watching; all the work put into that week's programme by so many people now in your hands, for you to make the most of or throw away in some stupid mistake. 'Good evening . . .'

And it is just at that moment of maximum terror, when you are most conscious that everything depends on you and that nobody can help, that you are required to be at your most friendly and relaxed; to project a warm reassuring invitation to viewers to join you for the next 40 or 50 minutes to see something you are sure they will find rewarding.

Says David Dimbleby, Richard's eldest son, who eventually followed his father to become presenter of *Panorama* himself: 'I've always thought presenting was the most difficult thing, the toughest, most difficult thing on television. While it's very difficult to refuse the job of programme presenter if you're offered it, when you are actually doing it you wonder why. All the same, my instincts have been for the drama of presenting things live. Any live performance gets your adrenalin going.'

Presenting is a high-wire act. Every time you appear you risk destroying your reputation. If you make a mess of it the programme will recover; you may not. And yet what is it exactly that you are doing to make this risk worthwhile? Creating that inviting atmosphere that will encourage the viewer to switch on and stay with your show; introducing different reports and linking smoothly from one to another; saying 'good evening' and 'good night' – this is your skill, what you are paid for. It's vital, and yet it seems so nebulous, so utterly insubstantial. Is it really work for a grown man or woman? This is what nags away at the presenter, as it did even at Richard Dimbleby.

David remembers that he was not always very excited watching Richard Dimbleby at work in the *Panorama* studio, and, he says, his father felt the same way; wasn't he being wasted? In 1964[12] for example David was at Lime Grove when for the first time a British Prime Minister came to be interviewed there for *Panorama*. In the programme Sir Alec Douglas-Home is led in to the studio by Dimbleby, every inch the gracious host – but the actual interview was conducted not by Dimbleby but by Grand Inquisitor Robin Day.

In the BBC files there is some evidence that Dimbleby was pushing the different Editors he worked for to give him more to do than simply present other people's reports and interviews. In 1958 Grace Wyndham Goldie wrote to Kenneth Adam, the Controller of Programmes, Television: 'Rex

Moorfoot[13] is aware of Dimbleby's desire to be used more as a personality and less as purely a "linking" man, and has this very much in mind. He says that in the last four editions of *Panorama* Dimbleby has, in fact, had separate stories of his own, including a studio interview with Sir Oliver Franks on unemployment.[14] However large their egos, however important they feel themselves to be, most presenters deep down worry that their jobs are not really serious, their contribution not as important as that of the reporters and producers whose work they introduce.

When a programme like *Panorama* employs a presenter, his position is always self-contradictory. Alone in the studio, with the weight of the programme on his shoulders, he must make it his own show, must convey confidence in its contents. Though he may have less to do with actually producing the programme than almost anyone else there, the presenter must persuade the viewer that at the very least he has orchestrated the contents; that even when he presents reports from others he has a thorough knowledge of what they say and mean; that he is the most important person on that programme.

And yet the presenter is not only a hired hand, like the contract reporters; he actually spends far less of his time on the programme than they do. Richard Dimbleby would sometimes be driven into Lime Grove in his Rolls-Royce on a Friday afternoon for an editorial meeting at which the likely stories for the following Monday's *Panorama* would be discussed. Then, on the Monday morning, he would come in again, be given a running order and start work on his own studio links that he would use to get neatly from one film report or studio item to another. He would record commentaries to film stories that had been made without a reporter. And, unless the programme had organised an outside broadcast for him away from base, that was usually it.

A presenter may sometimes do a bit more than this, looking at a film or tape report to make sure that he gives it the best possible introduction – perhaps while it's still in the final stages of editing. Here he has an important and delicate role, and this is where potential conflict lies.

Unlike the producer and reporter of the film or videotape, who have actually made it; unlike the Editor, who will not only have commissioned it but has by now seen it (probably more than once) in rough cut; the presenter comes to it absolutely fresh. He is in fact the first ordinary viewer.

If he doesn't understand it, if he's bored by it, if he finds it wrong-headed or offensive in some way then so may all the other viewers. He is the canary in the cutting room coal mine, and his initial reactions will be watched with interest. Is he excited by it? Does he fall asleep? What does he think?

But then again, who is this man, who has no personal stake in this report, to start giving his opinion about it? Things are tense enough in the cutting room as the producer and reporter try to satisfy themselves and their Editor. The last thing they want is another voice, another view, on whether they have got it right. So the presenter had best tread carefully here. On the other hand, he is the one who is going to have to introduce this report – make it his own. What happens if it doesn't satisfy him, as to political balance, say, or the tone of its reporter's commentary? How far is he entitled to demand changes to satisfy his own views? Mostly, common sense and pragmatism prevail in this situation: there simply isn't much time to argue, and the Editor's decision – in television as in print – is final. But in 1982 this always potentially explosive issue did indeed blow up: it tore a hole in the *Panorama* flagship's hull, while the presenter, who had lit the fuse, was hoist on his own petard.

When in January 1982 Editor George Carey hired Robert Kee – 20 years after he had reported for the programme – as *Panorama*'s presenter, he told his team it was because Kee had 'instant authority'. Kee had certainly earned it. In scores of current affairs programmes and factual television series for both the BBC and ITV his intelligent, original and lively reporting had produced some brilliant television journalism. 'Merely by his presence', wrote Clive James in the *Observer*, 'Robert Kee confers distinction on *Panorama*.'[15] Now he was to lend that distinction, that authority, to *Panorama*, presenting the programme – as it so happened – in an hour of maximum danger.

In April 1982 Argentina invaded the Falkland Islands in the South Atlantic, territory it had long claimed but which still remained determinedly British. With the support of Parliament, the Prime Minister, Margaret Thatcher, despatched a naval task force ready to recapture it, if the Argentinians should refuse to withdraw. But the Falklands were a long way off. With the British fleet at sea, and a news blackout on its progress complete, there was something of a journalistic vacuum. The Government was determined to keep the country united in support of this dangerous and risky enterprise. *Panorama* thought it right to find out how far it was succeeding.

For Monday 10 May George Carey had commissioned a *Panorama* that would try to do just that.[16] On Sunday, the day before transmission, he and his presenter Robert Kee joined the production team in Lime Grove to look at a rough cut of the film that had been made. It was the typical *Panorama* weekend routine, but this programme clearly had explosive potential. The situation had changed since the programme had been planned. HMS *Sheffield* and the Argentine cruiser *General Belgrano* had both been sunk: here was a report in which various people – some of them Conservative MPs – were asking, however tentatively, whether it was right that British troops were still on the high seas, on their way to war. As a result, there was, says Carey, 'quite a full cutting room'. This was not a film to get wrong.

Christopher Capron, formerly a *Panorama* Editor himself and now the Head of Current Affairs, was there, and so was Alan Protheroe, Assistant to the Director General – 'the DG's flak-catcher general', as he called himself. Arriving at Lime Grove on a similar occasion in his black chauffeur-driven BBC car Protheroe had announced himself as the ADG, only to hear the commissionaire ring through to tell *Panorama* that 'the KGB is here'.

As the film unrolled on the little screen of the Steinbeck editing machine the reporter Michael Cockerell read aloud his draft commentary script. Afterwards Carey asked Kee, along with everybody else, for his reaction. *Panorama*'s presenter clearly didn't like what he'd seen and heard.

Unlike anyone else in the cutting room Kee had fought in the Second World War. A bomber pilot, he had been shot down and had subsequently spent three years in a prisoner of war camp. He was unlikely to feel easy with any programme which could conceivably damage the morale of the British soldiers, sailors and airmen who had already come under enemy fire in the South Atlantic. When he saw the film he was, according to Michael Cockerell, angry. 'He seemed to feel', says Cockerell, 'that this was no time for any expressions of dissent or doubt about Government policy.' Kee thought the film was wrong to pay so much attention to the dissenters; and he had a slightly different criticism too. Later he wrote: 'When I was first shown a rough-cut of this film the previous evening I criticised it severely for identifying in a confusing way *Panorama*'s own view of the Falklands crisis with that of the minority view it was claiming to look at objectively.'[17] As Kee now recalls it, Carey responded: 'I see what you mean, I'll do something about it.' Carey thinks he simply said something to the effect that: 'I'm sure we can sort out the problems.' In all (it was later asserted by the BBC) Carey, after discussion with everyone present, ordered some 38 changes to the film.

On Monday, transmission day, Carey reassured Kee that changes had been made that he thought should satisfy his particular concerns. But Kee did not insist on checking that for himself. 'I blame myself for that,' he now says; 'I made a mistake.' The next time he saw the film was as it went out, as he sat in the studio waiting to interview Cecil Parkinson, the Chairman of the Conservative Party and a member of Mrs Thatcher's war cabinet. Kee said nothing critical of the film on air (though he later said he had considered doing so) and in Hospitality after the programme seemed merely 'subdued'. Cecil Parkinson was 'in good form', says Carey, and made no complaints at all about the programme. However, back at Westminster later that evening, Parkinson rang to warn Carey that a head of steam was building up among Conservative MPs incensed at what they saw as a most disloyal *Panorama*: 'There's a bit of a stink going on down here at the Commons,' said Cecil.

The explosion came the next day. In Parliament, Sally Oppenheim MP described the programme as 'an odious, subversive travesty in which Michael Cockerell and other BBC reporters dishonoured the right of freedom of speech in this country'. Mrs Thatcher said she shared the deep concern which had been expressed. And so, in its own way, did the *Sun*: 'The British Broadcasting Corporation needs a shake-up. Too many of its studios are infested with arrogant little know-alls ready to serve up their loaded version of "truth" to the viewers.' At the end of the week the *Observer* saw it differently: '*Panorama* (BBC1) examined the chances of a diplomatic solution, the voices of Parliamentary dissent, and Argentine reaction to the Task Force. Given the war hysteria in other parts of the media, this was a gratifyingly measured, original and unsensational programme, in the best traditions of the BBC.'[18]

But by then, at a meeting of the Conservative backbench Media Committee[19] Tory MPs had used the BBC's Chairman George Howard and his Director General designate Alasdair Milne for bayonet practice. Said the

Press Association: 'There were no holds barred. MPs' description of the confrontation with Mr. Howard were lurid. "He was absolutely crucified," said one. "He was roasted alive," said another, "there were blood and entrails all over the place."'[20] When Howard spoke about the BBC's role in reporting World War II, Winston Churchill, the wartime leader's grandson, furiously retorted that the BBC had not then 'seen fit to give equal time to the Goebbels propaganda machine'.[21]

As a withering fusillade was now directed at *Panorama*, its man in the front line began to waver. Robert Kee was not enjoying this particular campaign. He felt he'd been unfairly placed in an exposed position by his commanding officer Carey. At the beginning of the Falklands crisis, in one of the first *Panorama* programmes that he presented, Kee had interviewed Lord Carrington, who had resigned as Foreign Secretary as soon as the Argentinians invaded. At the next News and Current Affairs meeting later that week Carey had been much criticised for letting Kee go 'over the top' in some tough questioning. Carey had defended his presenter, saying that in those circumstances no question could be too tough. Kee had told him afterwards: 'You are a marvellous Editor.' Says Carey: 'It was a golden moment.'

Now Kee was again under attack for a *Panorama* he had fronted. This time he felt even more unhappy because he was not responsible for the film report the programme had contained. Asked by many of his friends why he had allowed himself to present it, he wanted to dissociate himself from it. But for *Panorama*'s public face to disown the programme, or any part of it, would clearly be deeply damaging – to *Panorama* and to everyone else who worked on it. At a meeting at Lime Grove Kee told Carey and Christopher Capron that Monday's *Panorama* had been wrong, and that he wanted to make that point in public. Carey told him that if he did so he must not 'impugn the integrity' of the programme. On the Friday, in the time-honoured way, a letter from Kee appeared in *The Times*. In it he thanked the BBC's Chairman and Director General designate for publicly defending the programme and the film report it contained earlier in the week but told them – in effect – that they had been wasting their time, since he could not defend it himself: 'the interests of that truth for which the BBC has always stood' required him to abandon 'programme solidarity'. *Panorama*'s presenter was disowning his colleagues and their 'poor objective journalism'.[22] Today he says: 'I knew that I was breaking my contract when I wrote that letter.'

In his own 'Private and Confidential' account of the affair addressed to Alasdair Milne, the Director General designate, Capron wrote: 'Kee gave me the impression that his letter would be as moderately worded as possible and that, in his view, it would be possible for him to continue to present the programme. I was therefore, all the more dismayed and angry when the resulting letter emerged. It is written in a way that must make it very difficult, if not impossible, for him to continue to present *Panorama*, as he so clearly questions the motives and even truthfulness of his Editor and colleagues.'[23]

Carey now told Kee that while he respected free speech he thought that Kee had 'ditched' the programme and could no longer go on presenting it. As Carey quite reasonably said, he couldn't have a situation where, every week, the papers would be ringing up asking him if the presenter agreed with the reports he was about to introduce.

Curiously, even though he had turned his fire on his own programme, Kee did not immediately resign his commission. But the BBC stood firm on the principle of editorial responsibility. An instruction to the members of the BBC Press Office said: 'We should take every opportunity to stress, in background briefings, the journalistic principle that Editors must edit.'[24]

The BBC told Kee it proposed suspending him for a month, but that scarcely seemed a satisfactory solution. So on 21 May Kee handed in his resignation. It took effect three days later. 'I'm extremely sorry, of course,' said Aubrey Singer, Managing Director of Television, in a statement, 'but he was in breach of his contract and obviously felt that he couldn't restore an effective working relationship with the *Panorama* team.'[25]

Today Robert Kee says he feels that as someone used to making his own programmes, presenting his own conclusions rather than somebody else's, he should never have taken the job of *Panorama* presenter. He had for many years been a highly effective and authoritative reporter, making films that he could stand by. But as a presenter he had been required to lend his 'instant authority' to other people's work, work that he might disagree with. And he had disagreed. There was no shame in that. But it was a pity that such a distinguished television journalist should end up rubbishing the programme he had been given the privilege of presenting. It was because Kee was so good that his defection caused so much pain.

This remains a potential problem for all presenters of any calibre. Only the bland or ignorant don't mind what they introduce. But presenters can't be a sort of second Editor, exercising a veto over what they are introducing. Having made their contribution to the discussion of the programme's contents, presenters must accept the Editor's decision – just like producers and reporters. If they fundamentally disagree they must resign – but preferably without writing to the newspapers to disown their programme while it's under fire.

Paid to be prominent

As the public face of *Panorama* its presenters have normally been paid more than others on the programme. In 1955, when he began, Richard Dimbleby was earning 80 guineas (£84) a show. In April 1958, when the new *Panorama* had proved a success, he told Michael Peacock[26] that he had been offered £10,000 a year for 10 years if he would move to ITV. The following month, perhaps as a result of this broad hint, Kenneth Adam, Controller of Programmes, Television, wrote: 'There seems little doubt that Dimbleby has been underpaid.' So Dimbleby's BBC fees in general went up by a third – on *Panorama* to 100 guineas (£105) a programme. But by 1962 Ludovic Kennedy and Robin Day were getting the same money. In November 1963, with new reporters hired to replace those, like Kennedy, who had defected to the independent Television Reporters International, the weekly wages bill looked like this: Michael Barratt, Michael Charlton and Roderick McFarquar all on £100 each; John Morgan on £115; Day on £142; and Dimbleby on 150 guineas (£157 10s).

Dimbleby, of course, unlike the reporters, only worked for *Panorama* on a part-time basis. But though he was earning (in BBC terms) good money for his *Panorama* work, it was not spectacular. And his position was not necessarily secure. Even contract reporters, if they could adapt to different programme styles, might expect to stay on when a new Editor took over every two years or so. It was more difficult for a *Panorama* presenter. As the most obviously public face of the programme his was the easiest to change in order to signal some new way of doing things. Despite his fame, despite his personal popularity with the public, Dimbleby was not much more secure than any other presenter.

Back in 1957 there had been an early attempt to get rid of him when Charles Wheeler had persuaded Michael Peacock to join him in talking to Cecil McGivern about it. The suggestion had been rejected then, but in 1959, when Peacock returned to the programme, this time with the title of Editor, he tried again – as a confidential memo from Kenneth Adam to Leonard Miall makes clear:

> During conversations with Dimbleby on other matters today, D.D.Tel.B learned from him that there was a thought of dropping him from *Panorama*. This was a shock to D.D.Tel.B., and although I knew that Peacock had it in mind that eventually it might be desired to make a change, I did not know that Dimbleby would get to know. D.D.Tel.B recognises Peacock's anxiety to make changes which will improve *Panorama*, but does not wish these to be made for change's sake. He points out that removing Dimbleby is front page news. In his view Dimbleby is as good as *Panorama* is. There are other and important matters relating to Dimbleby's position in the television world which may make any *Panorama* change of link-man at the moment a matter of concern to the Service as a whole.[27]

So it looks as if it may have been only Richard Dimbleby's importance to BBC television 'as a whole' – particularly as commentator on the big political occasions – that ensured that he kept his job on *Panorama* for the rest of his life.

In 1960 Dimbleby wrote to the BBC explaining why he could not that year be the commentator for the Oxford and Cambridge University Boat Race: 'The trouble is', he said, 'that I am under strict doctors' orders to take a complete rest from work at intervals, whenever I can. They regard this as an absolute "must".'[28] In the years that followed, in great secrecy, he began having treatment for cancer. In those days cancer of any kind was a virtually unmentionable disease, the testicular cancer from which Dimbleby suffered even more so. Despite weekly radiotherapy that left him exhausted Dimbleby continued to preside over *Panorama*. But in 1965, with his health now in serious decline, he was faced with a renewed threat to his job. A new Editor was appointed, hired from the same editorial chair at ITV's *This Week*. His name was Jeremy Isaacs.

Refit

At *This Week* Jeremy Isaacs had run his programme without a presenter, and his plans for *Panorama* left little room for the style of presentation Dimbleby had made his own. 'So you're the young man who's going to get rid of me,' was how Dimbleby ruefully greeted his supposed nemesis when he arrived at Lime Grove. But Isaacs had been told what few others then knew, that Dimbleby was by now seriously ill. Isaacs had been ordered by Paul Fox not to get rid of the man who was now for ever identified in the public mind with *Panorama*. So Dimbleby remained, though he doesn't seem to have been happy with the style his new Editor now wanted him to adopt. 'The new *Panorama* was unveiled with chairman Dimbleby firmly in his old seat', wrote Peter Black, after Isaac's first *Panorama*:

> But for how long? It was plain from the start that this was quite a different Dimbleby. He had speeded up his delivery, the language was more emphatic and at the same time more neutral. For the first time in *Panorama* Richard was the objective introducer. There was no hint of the old proprietorial touch, of the personalised performance - the hands in the jacket pockets, the short smile, the changing intonation – that not only summed up an item but conveyed an opinion . . . I adhere to my view that *Panorama*'s new Editor Jeremy Isaacs will want to imprint his own style on the show. The personality of the chairman will inevitably diminish.[29]

Jeremy Isaacs took over from David Wheeler as Editor of *Panorama* in September 1965. Philip Purser wrote in the *Sunday Telegraph*:

> Must Dimbleby be unseated now that *Panorama* has abandoned its magazine format? After the first edition of the new season I would have said 'yes'. His doom-laden introduction from the studio added nothing to the two reports from India and Pakistan, indeed, emphasising the remoteness of the conflict in space and time . . . But in the second *Panorama* last Monday Dimbleby vindicated himself handsomely. The subject of the Pope's visit to New York had to

be composed from a mixture of live and recently recorded material plus one hark-back to Rome. Combining the functions of reporter and anchor-man he tied everything together impeccably from New York: which still suggests some more mobile role for Richard, making more use of his great gifts and prodigious experience in the field, prising him away from that presidential desk.[30]

That was not to be. Dimbleby's programme from New York was his last for *Panorama*, and he never again set foot in the studios at Lime Grove. At the Programme Review meeting on 27 October 1965 Paul Fox, the Head of the Current Affairs Group, 'reported that Richard Dimbleby was likely to be in hospital for at least two weeks and would require a further period of convalescence. He said there would have to be several replacements for Dimbleby during his absence . . . Members expressed their good wishes to Richard Dimbleby and hoped for his speedy recovery.' But it was soon apparent that this was unlikely. On 5 November the News and Current Affairs meeting was already discussing the preparation of the tributes that should be paid to Dimbleby on his death. On 20 December, standing in for Dimbleby as *Panorama*'s presenter, James Mossman sent him the programme's best wishes. But two days later, just after 9pm, in St Thomas's Hospital in London, Dimbleby died.

Almost at once ITV and then BBC programmes were interrupted to report the news. Within the hour Frank Gillard, the Director of Radio Broadcasting, had said: 'This is news which will bring sorrow to almost every home in England, and the sense of deep personal loss to millions of people in Britain and the world who never had the chance of meeting him, but who nevertheless have long regarded Richard Dimbleby as a close family friend.' Jonathan Dimbleby, in his biography of his father, quotes from a letter sent by a member of the public to the family: 'It is with tears in my eyes that I learn tonight of Richard Dimbleby's death. It is as though a part of England itself had gone.'

For all his services to broadcasting in war and peace Richard Dimbleby had never been offered a knighthood. No one had done more to maintain the monarchy in high public esteem, yet no member of the royal family came to his memorial service.[31] But the public, wiser than their monarch and her ministers, knew his worth. The outside broadcast of the service was watched by five million people in the middle of a Monday afternoon; six and a half million watched a recording of it later that night. Dimbleby's lifelong friend Wynford Vaughan-Thomas, like him a war correspondent and broadcaster, had this to say: 'Ours is a transitory art; our words and pictures make a powerful and immediate impact, and then fade as if they had never been; but Richard brought a sense of permanence to our profession. We knew him as a simple man, a good man, and in the end a very brave man. He gave warmth to the spoken word, friendliness to the formal occasion and dignity to the whole new world of broadcasting.'

In the decade from 1955 to his death Richard Dimbleby had presented a current affairs programme which had become established as the essence of good public service broadcasting; a programme able to inform, educate and entertain a large audience in peak time. Said Robin Day: 'It was Richard's solid presence and personality which won the viewers, kept the viewers, guided the viewers and held the programme together . . . No presenter or anchor man has ever achieved his combination of qualities, his rapport with the viewer, his professional aplomb, his mellifluous speech, his sense of occasion, be it glad or gloomy, or his easy natural authority.'

It had been Dimbleby's immense prestige and popularity which had done so much to make *Panorama* a serious success. Now he was dead. Here lies Caesar: when comes such another?

Robin Day had no doubt about that. According to Joan Marsden, Dimbleby's ultra-loyal floor manager, there was a row when Day tried to sit in the studio chair that Dimbleby had used, which she had wanted preserved for posterity. Day, she says, did not succeed.

Day had made his television name at ITN as a newscaster and inter-viewer. Back in 1956[32] he had famously asked the Prime Minister if he was going to sack his Foreign Secretary Selwyn Lloyd, and Harold Macmillan had given him an answer. A gasp had gone up from every political journalist. Said the *Manchester Guardian*: 'Everybody wants to know what a Prime Minister thinks about his colleagues, and Mr. Day asked the right questions; but Mr. Macmillan is the first holder of his office to have satisfied public curiosity so bluntly. This may be judged a good or bad development according to taste, but it is certainly new.' The following year,[33] after the Suez crisis, he had asked the President of Egypt whether he would now accept the permanent existence of Israel as an independent state. 'Well,' Colonel Nasser replied, 'you are jumping to conclusions.' 'No,' said Day, 'I am asking a question.' That interview too had been rightly remarked as a big step forward for television journalism. As the Lancashire *Evening Post* put it: 'The political significance of what Nasser said is for assessment elsewhere. The fact remains that television again showed itself capable of a tremendous service in bringing world figures into our homes to talk as human beings, and not as the gigantic generalisation of good and evil which they otherwise seem through the mists of propaganda.'[34]

So when Day arrived at *Panorama* in 1959 he might have hoped for a role as studio interviewer, if not presenter-in-waiting. But that was not immediately possible. Like Ludovic Kennedy, Day had stood that year – and lost – in the General Election. He was too closely associated with a particular party[35] to be allowed to do political interviews. So when he joined *Panorama* he had to labour in the field as a reporter for many months before he was regarded as sufficiently fumigated to be allowed inside the *Panorama* studio.

Presenter as interviewer

Once there Robin Day quickly established himself as the best studio interviewer on the *Panorama* team, though his tough questioning gave BBC Governors palpitations: 'The Director General reported a feeling on behalf of some members of the Board that Robin Day's handling of his interview with Mr. Marples in *Panorama* on 2nd. May had erred on the side of discourtesy.'[36]

Rather to Day's dismay politicians soon seemed to become more accountable to him and to *Panorama* than to Parliament: 'The television has really bypassed the House of Commons in its political interview of Ministers, not even excepting the Prime Minister and Leader of the Opposition,' said Sir John Smyth, VC, MP. 'Are we really willing to allow the television interview, viewed admittedly by several million people, to assume greater importance than the proceedings of the House of Commons?' In his book collecting together some of his television interviews[37] Day wrote: 'The attitude of many politicians was one of envy, fear and resentment, summed up by one Sunday tabloid[38] in the question "Who does Robin Day think he is anyway?"' After his interview with Prime Minister Sir Alec Douglas-Home in 1964 a newspaper reported that 'Mr.

Day forgot nothing in his probing for an Achilles heel . . . Sir Alec returned every thrust with ease – not least when Mr. Day raised the issue of amateurish and indecisive leadership.' Day wrote: 'What had happened to our Parliamentary democracy if a Prime Minister was to be judged by his ability in "parrying the thrust" of a TV interviewer? This was a question which worried me deeply, and reinforced my conviction that Parliament should be televised.'[39] Nevertheless, as *The Times* put it: 'Single handed, a week ago, Mr. Robin Day had more scope and time to call the Prime Minister to account on a range of current issues than the Leader of Her Majesty's Opposition.'[40]

So in the early 1960s Robin Day made *Panorama* the principal platform for major political interviews in Britain. He liked doing them because he was in charge. They were his own work, not the work of a committee – though, as we have seen, he was always pressing his colleagues to rehearse him by playing the role of his interviewee. And his public justification for these interviews was this: 'In a TV interview, provided there is time for probing cross-examination, the politician cannot be wholly shielded against the unexpected. The politician's own brain is seen to operate. His (or her) real personality tends to burst out. Truth is liable to rear its lovely head.'[41]

Well yes, up to a point. Talking to Day, or 'Robin', as they began calling him to soften the impact of his questions, senior politicians did reveal something of their personality and policy. Day's rigorous questioning, always most carefully prepared, did require them to give some sort of an answer. But as time went on, the politicians, coached by their media gurus, became more adept at parrying the thrusts of the Grand Inquisitor. The interview sometimes became more a demonstration fencing match than a successful attempt to call the country's leaders to account. Day himself described how a wily politician like 'Rab' Butler would deal with him:

> The more critical the questions, the blander does Mr. Butler become. You bowl what you think is a deadly ball, and 'Rab' will turn it neatly to leg with an answer on these lines: 'I am so glad you asked me about that important problem because it is one of the many matters on which the Government are absolutely determined to press ahead with the urgent measures necessary.' Such an answer, delivered with great emphasis, appears to be that of a

resolute reformer. I do not suggest that this is an unjustified description of Mr. Butler, but when you read his words next day you see that he has not committed himself or anybody else to anything.'

As they became more practised in television interviews the politicians not only avoided making policy on air but managed to obscure what their existing policy was. It was all very well that *Panorama* should have these important people in its studio, but were they actually doing enough to justify their presence there? In 1967, when Day had consolidated his reputation as *the* political interviewer on television, Peter Black wrote a shrewd article following a *Panorama* interview with Foreign Secretary George Brown. It was headlined 'Question: how do you put reality into this ritual?' 'It is true', said Black, 'that the Foreign Secretary spoke about Moscow, de Gaulle, Hongkong, the Middle East, the UN and the third world war. But it was all predictable speculation containing nothing that Day could not have got out of Jim Mossman, or Mossman out of Day. That it was the Foreign Secretary doing it was the only conceivable point of interest. Political interviews of this character will destroy *Panorama* unless it can find a better way to handle them.' Political interviews like George Brown's had become a ritual from which the audience learned nothing: 'I cannot think of a single political situation during the past fifteen years that has been significantly illuminated, let alone changed, by any discussion on television.'[42]

Even Day himself seemed to recognise that just getting very important people to talk to him in the studio might not be enough. To mark the Commonwealth Conference in July 1964 *Panorama* assembled a cast which included the Prime Minister, Sir Alec Douglas-Home, Kenya's Prime Minister (soon to be President) Kenyatta, Prime Minister Keith Holyoake from New Zealand, President Ayub Khan from Pakistan and Dr. Eric Williams, Prime Minister of Trinidad. But, as Day says: 'The televised discussion between the five heads of government was inevitably polite and platitudinous except when Trinidad's Dr. Williams, wearing dark glasses, lived up to his nick-name of "Dr. No"; asked what the Commonwealth meant he said: "In our part of the world it has not meant very much so far. It does not mean anything."' Was that revelation really worth a whole *Panorama*?

In his 1967 article Peter Black identified another reason why these big political interviews were not more revealing. 'If there must be studio interviews, why have them only with journalists whose minds work the same way as their guests? It is like having hotel keepers grilling one another on behalf of the customers.'

The fact was that Robin Day, though a trenchant and fearless interrogator, was a fully paid-up life member of the political world at Westminster; he subscribed to its agenda and ways of working. His questioning might be tough but it was never radical; holding a deep respect for those who had been elected – he had after all tried hard to be one of the elect himself – he was content to deal with the issues the politicians wanted to talk about rather than insist on raising those they didn't.

Early in the new *Panorama* season, in September 1967, Robin Day, Robert MacNeil and James Mossman together questioned the Prime Minister, Harold Wilson.[43] In the *Guardian* Stanley Reynolds reported:

> The highlight of the show was a struggle for precedence between the insistently pugnacious James Mossman and the insistent Robin Day. Day, the chairman, was firmly moving the Prime Minister through the questions on his list; he kept telling Mossman rather wearily 'we must go on, we told the Prime Minister we would talk about this.' But Mossman wanted to continue pressing Mr. Wilson on Vietnam. At one point Day motioned to Mossman with a pencil which Mossman pushed aside. The Prime Minister and *Panorama*'s new Canadian reporter, Robert MacNeil, sat back in obvious amusement.[44]

But while his *Panorama* colleagues might grow impatient with the stately studio minuet with which Day was largely content, BBC management rather liked the way he was on the same wavelength as the politicians he interviewed. In 1969 Mossman was criticised for what the BBC decided was his over-vigorous questioning of some distinguished Commonwealth leaders. A fortnight later he was banished from the studio when the Prime Minister came in to be interviewed, and Day, who had been in the United States to report on President Nixon's inauguration, was recalled to replace him.[45]

Robin Day was essentially a member of the political establishment. This did not mean that he could not ask brilliantly barbed questions of the most important, and self-important politicians. 'How low does your personal rating among your own supporters have to go before you consider yourself a liability to the party you lead?' was the question he famously asked the then leader of the Conservative Party, Ted Heath.[46] No one could do it better than that. But though he was always sharp, Day was still innately respectful of political convention. He was, for example, appalled that *Panorama* people should ever want to talk to members of terrorist organisations, and thought such interviews should be banned by law. He disapproved of *Panorama*'s coverage of the Falklands campaign and its filming of an IRA road block at Carrickmore. He even withdrew from chairing a BBC debate on the future of Northern Ireland (which the Government didn't want) on the grounds that this would mean television usurping the functions of Parliament.

Day was unhappy with the way Hugh Carleton Greene, who became Director General in 1960, had tacitly encouraged a revolt in the BBC that reflected the changes taking place in society. Day deplored what he thought were the excesses of the satire boom and its lampooning of political leaders. While Carleton Greene introduced his fresh air revolution with programmes like *That Was the Week that Was*, 'other BBC people had to soldier-on under the old rules of fairness and accuracy and a reasonable respect to those elected to office. These other BBC people were regarded as fuddy-duddies, while Frost and Company (briefly) were privileged to indulge their snide and mocking pleasure.'[47] Day felt he and *Panorama* were being made to look dull and dusty by these overtly anti-establishment programmes: 'We, in ITN, and in *Panorama*, were not anti-anything. We did not knock for the sake of knocking. We were in the business of straightforward journalism, not showbiz. We were breaking new ground in public service broadcasting. We were out to make topical television relevant, probing and professional. We were not unfair, we were not biased, we were not offensive or smutty.'

And quite right too, in current affairs. But why should Day think that just because *Panorama* had to be fair and impartial, every other kind of programme had to be so too? *Panorama*, after all, was the BBC's main current affairs programme. Of course, carrying that kind of cargo, the flagship had to steer a straight course, recognising its responsibility. Did that really mean that no one else should have any laughs, no one should satirise the serious or send-up the sententious? Of course not.

Robin Day could be pompous and determinedly old fashioned, but he certainly understood *Panorama*'s mission. At Richard Dimbleby's death at the end of 1965 he was the programme's most considerable figure, and he had been on it longer than any other reporter. But his hoped-for inheritance as *Panorama* presenter came at a most awkward moment for him. As he well knew, Jeremy Isaacs, who had only just taken over as editor of *Panorama*, wanted to do away with presenters altogether. Now that Richard Dimbleby had left the scene Isaacs saw no need to hire a replacement, and life for Day became ever more difficult.

To add to his anxieties he had new competition. Ian Trethowan was, like Day himself, essentially a political interviewer and presenter rather than a television reporter. Like Day he had worked at ITN. Later, at the BBC, he had presented the weekly political programme *Gallery*; now he was aiming to take over whatever presenting and political interviewing was still going on *Panorama*.

Former *Panorama* producer Barbara Pegna remembers Editor Isaacs in distraction as Day and Trethowan trumpeted about like two angry elephants, fighting to secure the Dimbleby succession. 'Every week there'd be a furious, bright red-faced Trethowan arguing with Day, with Robin coughing away on his cigar smoke and Jeremy caught in the middle, with these warring old boys fighting and stomping out in a rage.'

Through 1966 *Panorama*'s war of succession continued. Should anyone now take their place permanently at the prow of the great flagship, or should different reporters from time to time stand their watch and introduce the programme? As this internal battle raged the crew's morale fell, and so did the audience. 'What has gone wrong with *Panorama*?' asked the London *Evening News*:

> The BBC's once-proud window on the world has been growing steadily more obscured since the untimely loss of its great anchorman, Richard Dimbleby . . . Mainly through Mr. Dimbleby's death the programme has been losing viewers. I'm told the drop is a million . . . Still to be decided is whether there will be a regular anchorman, like Robin Day, or whether there will be a succession of names – any one of the team of Michael Charlton, John Morgan, Michael Barratt, James Mossman and Ian Trethowan, for instance. The point is that not only the audience but prestige too is dribbling away.

The wind of change is a-blowing, and the old veteran doesn't know which way to bend.[48]

The day that article appeared Paul Fox, the Head of Current Affairs, wrote a private note to John Grist, congratulating the new, albeit caretaker, Editor of *Panorama* on his appointment: 'The anchorman situation is to be discussed between us: the difficulties of one choice over another are pretty clear.'[49] Within a fortnight the decision had finally been made, and a signal to that effect sent to the flagship: Robin Day would be promoted. He had won. Trethowan complained but was told, quite rightly, that Day was a star and he was not. Accepting defeat, Trethowan moved into BBC management and, only 10 years later, in 1977, emerged top of the heap, as Director General. By then Day was long gone from a regular job on *Panorama*.

A prickly presenter

In 1967 Robin Day's appointment as presenter was reluctant, almost grudging. John Grist seemed to regard him more as a liability than an asset. Discussing publicity for *Panorama* in the New Year he wrote to the Chief Press Officer, Television: 'Robin Day will start introducing the programme from 2nd. January. This obviously presents something of a problem in terms of publicity. I am extremely reluctant, for a variety of reasons, to make a great splash, either about Robin or the new format.'[50] This lack of enthusiasm cannot have made Day a happy, confident *Panorama* presenter. And the critics did not feel that the programme was much improved, even after David Webster took over from Grist: '*Panorama* is going off the air for its annual summer siesta,' wrote Milton Shulman later that year, 'and I doubt if it will be much missed. The window on the world has shrunk to a keyhole with limited vision and shallow perspective.'[51] Shulman pointed to the way other, daily, programmes were now chipping away at *Panorama*'s former monopoly, and concluded: 'With David J. Webster as its Editor and Robin Day as its front man, the pre-eminence of *Panorama* as a TV news magazine never returned.'

Though long one of the best-known figures on British television, Day had specifically been told not to think of himself as the new Dimbleby. He was there, as he noted himself, to 'introduce the acts', and do the interviews, not be 'Mr *Panorama*'. There was in general a growing feeling that television people were throwing their weight about, and that it was wrong for any individual to dominate a programme as Dimbleby had done. In the summer of 1968 the BBC Governors issued guidelines[52] reminding the interviewer (somewhat sententiously) that 'undeferential courtesy founded on thorough homework' was the basis on which he should go about his business. He must eschew pomposity, self-righteousness, or condescending omniscience; 'nor must he appear a Grand Inquisitor', though he should of course put 'penetrating and persistent questions'. Well, would you believe it!

On ITV David Frost had been making some remarkable factual television programmes which had often scooped the BBC. Excellent as some of them were they were scorned by the television establishment as being just a promotional vehicle for Frost rather than serious current affairs journalism. In January 1969 the BBC's Director General Hugh Carleton Greene wrote to John Grist, by this time Head of Current Affairs, Television, warning against the 'cult of personality' in current affairs broadcasting.[53]

Perhaps in seeking some sort of efficient but characterless presenter the BBC denied Robin Day the chance to develop that rapport with the *Panorama* audience which Richard Dimbleby had so successfully achieved. *Television Today* did not take kindly to the new anchorman: '*Panorama* has never been the same since the death of Richard Dimbleby. Ever since it has lacked the warm personal presentation that made viewers watch such a programme regularly.'[54]

Pre-eminent as a political interviewer, Day was never a perfect *Panorama* presenter. And if one reason for that was a certain lack of full-hearted support from the BBC, another was his own fault. The trouble was that for Robin everything other than the studio interview he was about to conduct was essentially a tiresome distraction, irrelevant, a waste of time. He had a most infuriating way of turning to the viewers at the end of a film report by one of his able colleagues and saying dismissively 'That was a report by ...'; and then, in his studio interview, ostentatiously refusing to take up any of the points the film had carefully raised. 'You unprofessional sod,' producer Barbara Pegna remembers thinking on one such occasion.

At the beginning of 1968 Dennis Potter fired another broadside: 'Poor old *Panorama* is ailing. This one-time arena for TV heavyweights has dwindled to the level of a croquet match played on a damp lawn between two make-shift teams of distressed gentlefolk . . . Plenty of purple or even ermine memoirs of better days. But an overall mood of soggy boredom, arthritic ponderousness and interminable gum-chomping gossip about the value of the pound.'[55] *Television Today* remarked: '*Panorama* plods on under the taut, nervous presentation of Robin Day, predictable and desperately in need of new television reporters.'[56]

Panorama's timbers were crumbling. Julian Critchley, writing in *The Times*, clearly felt that it was time for a refit: '*Panorama* has become more of an institution than a programme. The shop window of the BBC, it has been running basically unchanged for years . . . it has been a personality programme doing some things, such as the formal interview with leading politicians, extremely well. Even so, its reliance upon the studio discussion, on the satellite and upon its Anchorman, has made it appear old-fashioned.'[57]

As Editor David Webster prepared to leave the bridge, Current Affairs sent out a call for the man they thought could best oversee the refit – and deal with Day. Once more they offered the job of Editor, *Panorama* to the Editor of ITV's *This Week*.

Phillip Whitehead had worked on *Panorama* under Jeremy Isaacs, and when things had all gone so horribly wrong had soon afterwards left the BBC to rejoin Isaacs in ITV. Now his *This Week* programme had just won the Guild of Television Producers' award, and the BBC was asking him to come back to take over their flagship. 'It was', he says, 'rather as if Derby County had won the League, and they were offering me Manchester United.' Yet, to the consternation of John Grist, now Head of Current Affairs, Whitehead insisted on making conditions before he accepted the job.

While he accepted that change would have to be gradual he wanted a commitment that change there would indeed be. In particular he wanted to make sure that he would have backing for reducing the role Robin Day was playing in the programme: 'A programme built around Robin as Presenter, with its Westminster/Garrick Club view of the world, would be less than *Panorama* "the window on the world" ought to be.'

Whitehead liked Day personally, but that wasn't the point: 'He was a fine piece of siege artillery as an interviewer, but he was no more an editorial aide in the turbulent sixties than he was later to be a candidate to be DG.'

Feeling that he wasn't going to get the freedom of action he wanted, and the full backing of the BBC in standing up to Day, Whitehead said 'no thanks' to *Panorama*.

Grist was apoplectic: nobody turned the BBC down when a job like this was offered. He accused Whitehead of running scared, and of exaggerating the real difficulties of dealing with Day. Grist's letter[58] pointed angrily to 'the satisfaction with which you joined in demonstrating with Robin the wide gulf between you. The Editor of *Panorama* must be a big man – he is surrounded by a lot of tough prima donnas and he operates in a very exposed area of public controversy. The Editor has to cope with the people himself – that's what he's paid for. You had the assurance of the support of Charles Curran, Huw Wheldon and myself, amongst others. If that was not sufficient for you, you are quite right in not taking the job. You must have confidence in your own powers to do the rest . . . You have been offered a very rewarding opportunity. You have turned it down. I think in the years ahead you will regret this.'

Late that same night Whitehead replied, in a hand-written letter, fiercely repudiating Grist's suggestions that he had been faint-hearted in refusing the job offer: 'I deeply resent the suggestion that I had no guts for it,' he wrote. Whitehead felt Grist was looking for someone to manage Day rather than make the best programmes: 'The Editor of *Panorama*, you say, has to cope with his tough prima donnas, and "that's what he's paid for." I would suggest that I am now and should have been paid for one thing above all, my judgement about current affairs and the ability to take decisions based on it. If you want a Labour Relations Officer hire one.' Whitehead remained unconvinced that if there had been a showdown on *Panorama* he would have had the necessary backing to do things his way:

> I have no intention of being crucified in the Isaacs manner. Those scars do run deep on all of us, as you said. I wanted to be my own boss, working only to you and the D.G. – that was the quid pro quo for the exposed position, etc. The dense corporate forest in which you move with such skill holds no terrors for me – as a survivor. I'm not that pessimistic about BBC politics! But I wanted to have the best programme going, whatever that cost. That meant a process that, whatever emollient compromises we found, some people would not have liked. At those times I needed a guarantee – yes a guarantee – that was tangible evidence that all the fine phrases couldn't be gone back on.

That guarantee, said Whitehead, had not been forthcoming, and so he was saying no. 'Panorama is too important to be left to administrators. I hope you will now appoint someone who will also address himself to the problems despite the mood of self-congratulation at Lime Grove.'

Grist had left open the possibility that Phillip Whitehead might change his mind, but he did not. So instead the BBC settled on what Whitehead calls 'a more subtle character' prepared to try to work with Day.

Brian Wenham came from ITN where he had been a senior producer. He was used to dealing with difficult front men – like the hard-drinking newscaster Reginald Bosanquet. But, as Day fought for airtime – for interviews, for studio links, for 'good evenings' and 'good nights', he and his new Editor soon fell out.

Reporter Richard Kershaw remembers just such an occasion. Kershaw had returned from the United States with a film report on pollution – an early attempt by Panorama to get to grips with environmental issues. It ended with a sequence of pictures of a polluted river, accompanied by a sad and angry Pete Seeger song. It was a powerful conclusion: it did not need Robin Day popping up to say goodnight before the end titles. But that's what Day thought he was contractually entitled to do.

Kershaw was sitting in the studio with Day during transmission. (This was normal practice. If the film broke in the telecine machine or there was some other technical cock-up then the reporter was there to be interviewed by the presenter to fill the gap.) As the studio gallery began to count down to the end of the programme Day became increasingly agitated. 'What about my "good night"?' he demanded angrily. As the programme came off air without his being allowed to say anything to the viewers, Day exploded with rage and stomped out of the studio to complain.

Instead of an asset, Day began to be seen – not just by Wenham but by many in the Current Affairs group – as a burden on board Panorama: a big gun to be once again wheeled into position when a prime minister had to be engaged in interview, but otherwise altogether too unwieldy for the modern, lively craft Wenham and a newer generation wanted Panorama to be. When Wenham was promoted to Head of Current Affairs Day's berth on Panorama was no longer secure.

'Robin Day is likely to lose his regular spot introducing the Monday night Panorama programme in a massive shake-up at the BBC,' reported the *Daily Express* in late 1971. The significance of the move was disguised as part of a reshuffle of all the current affairs programmes and those who presented them: 'The aim is to destroy the "cult of the personality" which has grown up around the small screen pundits. No longer will a TV front man become identified with a particular programme and make it his own, as has Day with *Panorama* . . . The new policy will help bring fresh faces to the screen.'[59] In January 1972 Richard Last reported in the *Daily Telegraph* that Day had now left *Panorama*, after 12 years and eight editors.[60] The stated intention was to run the programme without a presenter.

Day went off to do other work for the BBC, in television and radio.[61] Over the years he would return from time to time for the big interview, partly because he was still (in his own style) so very good at it, and partly to justify his fees and spread the heavy burden of them between different programmes.

Ousted as *Panorama*'s regular presenter, Day devoted even more energy than he had previously done to seeing that he was paid what he thought was due for the work he was offered. He was a demanding contributor. 'I am returning the contracts enclosed unsigned', began a letter to Artists' Contracts, 'because I consider your Department's handling of this matter to be impolite and improper, and because the fees offered have not been agreed by me.'[62] Day's contention, on the face of it perfectly fair, was that when at short notice a freelance contributor like him accepted and carried out an assignment he should subsequently be offered a fee for it that compared 'fairly and reasonably' with similar work he had done before. Day felt he was being taken advantage of, but there were endless arguments as to what was 'reasonable' which drove both programme and contracts people mad.

In 1976, in exasperation, Wenham, as Head of Current Affairs, wrote to Day offering a fixed sum of £250 for all items he took part in up to 30 minutes in length. Said Wenham, with that dry and biting tone for which he was renowned, 'Perhaps you could address yourself to this simple thought which may well save us much unnecessary fuss.'[63] But Day persisted in haggling. The following year he wrote to Wenham[64] asking for more money on top of an agreed fee of £350 for a by-election programme he had taken part in because it had overrun by 45 minutes. He had rejected the extra £25 offered him as a gesture of goodwill by Contracts. In

September Vin Harrop, Artists' Contracts Manager, finally wrote in a fury to his head of department:

> It seems to me that nobody any more has either the will or the desire to resist Robin Day's often over-excessive fee demands. He is arrogant, rude and offensive to my Assistants in the extreme, something we have had to contend with for a long time, but on occasions recently his insults to staff in this Department have been quite intolerable . . . We would not mind his snipes at us of 'faceless bureaucrats' and 'you do not decide my fees, Current Affairs does that', if we felt that everyone was behind us standing firm on fees that we have assessed in consultation with others and, based on our knowledge and experience, considered reasonable. But reasonable fees mean nothing to Robin Day, he knows what he wants, and more often than not he gets it.[65]

Day had been deeply upset by his removal from *Panorama* – particularly as the presenter's job, supposedly abolished, was before long reinstated. 'The sixties, which were a brilliant decade for me in *Panorama*, had ended in bitter dispute and discontent,' he later wrote.[66] 'Someone called him "a great man manqué"; or at any rate, an outstanding man who had followed the wrong signpost,' said Ivan Rowan, who had talked to Day for the *Sunday Telegraph* as he left *Panorama*.[67] There was something in that. Day, so often more famous and better informed than the politicians he was interviewing, might have made an even greater mark on British life if he had, like so many other of the early *Panorama* people, gone into politics.

In his Westminster flat, next door to the Millbank studios where today's television interviewers daily interrogate the politicians, only a three-minute walk from Parliament itself, Day was, in the last months of his life, a rather sad figure. Agreeing to an interview for this book, Day insisted that the author should first spend some days in his flat looking through the quite extraordinary collection of press cuttings from all over the country that he had commissioned an agency to collect for him from his earliest days in broadcasting. And so, beneath the portrait painted by June Mendoza, in which he wears his famous bow tie in the Garrick Club colours, Day urged the author on through nearly half a century of his professional life.

Surely by any standards it had been a remarkable career? But Day was morose. Reminded of his successes not only on *Panorama*, but on *Question*

Time and *The World at One*; of the honours he had received, not least his knighthood; of his national fame and reputation; of the high regard in which his peers held him;[68] all this seemed not sufficient to satisfy him. He remembered his days on *Panorama* more for what he had not been able to do there than for his undoubted achievements on the programme. As soon as he could, the Grand Inquisitor, who had remorselessly put so many questions himself, would wriggle out of an answer, and play the famous, not to say familiar, video recording of his song and dance routine with Des O'Connor.

It was Robin Day's continuing regret that though he had acquired fame he had never enjoyed power. On *Panorama* he had at least been in control of the interviews he conducted, and he despised those interviewers who were prepared to let Editors tell them, through an earpiece, what to ask next. But he felt that his long experience of news and current affairs journalism at the highest level qualified him for some senior role in broadcasting management, and he was disappointed that he, unlike his old rival Ian Trethowan, had never been offered one.

Sir Robin Day's memorial service was in the Temple church, among the barristers' chambers where his working life had begun, rather than anywhere connected with broadcasting. And Day left clear instructions that his own side of his correspondence with the BBC was to be destroyed.

The hereditary principle

Because his father and the programme were virtually inseparable in the public's mind, David Dimbleby had inevitably been associated with *Panorama* all his life. And indeed, he had first worked at Lime Grove while Richard Dimbleby was still *Panorama*'s presenter. As a reporter David had not immediately struck gold: 'I am sorry to have to tell you', wrote Paul Fox, 'I found your report on Saudi Arabia very disappointing.' Fox didn't like the report's shape or its script. There were phrases in the commentary 'that are not the sort of writing that distinguish a programme'.[69] Unusual praise for a reporter, on the other hand, came from Sylvia Hewitt, the Talks Booking Manager: 'Thank you for sending me in such splendidly clear accounts of your expenses.'[70]

Whatever his professional anxieties (which are probably no different from any other presenter's) David Dimbleby's style has always been cool, calm, unflappable. And he has survived with aplomb the few BBC crises he has been involved in. In 1970 he had been contracted to make a programme for BBC Current Affairs with the working title 'Her Majesty's Opposition'. When in 1971 it finally appeared it was called 'Yesterday's Men', a sharply satirical look at what had happened to the Labour Party's leaders, now out of office and wandering disconsolately in the arid desert of opposition. 'It was', remarked Huw Wheldon, 'as if you had made a programme about doctors with their co-operation, and then called it "Quack, Quack!"'.

There had been a big row, but in 1974 Dimbleby was nonetheless appointed *Panorama*'s presenter. His first programme in this role went out on 11 November, 21 years to the day after *Panorama* began, and only nine years after his father's death. To have so swiftly succeeded his father in this way was a remarkable achievement, and Dimbleby justified the choice. His studio introductions have always been effectively delivered, his interviews politely persistent. And when things go wrong on air he copes as well as any presenter in that dreadful situation can.

On 8 November 1976 Dimbleby had two film reports to deal with. First he introduced a film from Rhodesia: it rolled without any sound. He tried again: the film did not roll at all. Abandoning that report, David introduced the other item, a film on the IMF. This film also failed to roll. David was left to deal with the situation as best he could, facing the nation. As the *Observer*'s television critic Clive James reported it: 'He was bereft of inspiration. His heart ached, and a drowsy numbness pained his sense. Eventually he began to speak, his sentences cast in some spacious epic measure, with heavy sighs marking the caesuras. "We sit in silence. Hmm. Hope you stick with BBC1. Aargh. While we sort this out."'

In the studio gallery director Tom Gutteridge could only watch in horror as his screens went blank. There was nothing he could do. Just as the programme had started an anonymous brown-coated technician had arrived in the gallery, scarcely noticed, to replace a couple of fluorescent strip light tubes that had been giving trouble. In what was no doubt the approved drill he had simply turned off the power to isolate the units. Dimbleby was left gasping as critic Clive James watched in glee: 'As if the sirens were singing in his earpiece, his tongue grew thick and ceased to move. Telephone. "Hello? OK." David wheeled back to camera and said "I'm sorry", but already his voice and image were fading. It was the Rhodesia film, returning as capriciously as it had departed.'

David Dimbleby's great strength is never to have been a prisoner of the BBC, in the power of the Corporation. 'I have never wanted to have both feet in the BBC's camp,' he says. With his family's local newspaper business to run he has always had another job, and an alternative source of income to rely upon.[71] As a result 'I have never felt I *had* to do anything that the BBC asked me to do'.

Dimbleby would return in September 1980 to present *Panorama* again, but in November 1977 the programme's then Editor, Christopher Capron, decided he wanted a presenter who worked full-time on *Panorama*, making programmes as well as presenting. He chose Charles Wheeler, who had worked as co-Producer and reporter when *Panorama* was relaunched in 1955.

Wheeler had been asked to apply for the *Panorama* Editor's job by Brian Wenham in 1971, as Wenham prepared to get rid of Robin Day. Based in America for the BBC, Wheeler had actually come to London for a formal Board. However, the family reasons that had made him want to return to work in Britain disappeared, and he had withdrawn from the competition.

Now that he was *Panorama*'s presenter he did not much enjoy it. He found it awkward introducing films he did not greatly like, and thought the programme had changed for the worse since his earlier experience of it. Then, he felt, it had been a team effort, as producers and reporters strove together to make a coherent programme out of a variety of different items. The *Panorama* of the late 1970s, on the other hand, was essentially one of single-subject programmes made by competing teams whose rivalry was often ruthless. Furthermore, as a television news reporter since his first experience of *Panorama*, Wheeler had been his own producer. For a report of up to, say, 15 minutes, he still thinks that is the best way of doing things. But now on *Panorama* he heard producers talking about 'my film'. This, he felt, was wrong. Reporters still had to lead, as they had in the earlier days of *Panorama*.

Wheeler stuck it for a year, until 1978, when Capron hired a man with little knowledge of television but a wealth of experience in Fleet Street – Fred Emery. Emery had been a foreign correspondent for 20 years and was now political editor of *The Times*. He was astonished to be approached by *Panorama*, but agreed to become presenter while continuing with his day job as a print journalist. The deal was that he would be credited as 'Fred Emery of *The Times*'. This was a mistake. It implied that the programme was in some way dependent on the newspaper, and could not find anyone else to do the work. Television critic David Wheeler, a former Editor of *Panorama* himself, was affronted: 'This edition of *Panorama* was introduced by Fred Emery, billed as "Fred Emery of *The Times*". He spoke his few words to camera quite nicely, but I did not understand why he should be there anyway. Surely, BBC current affairs and *Panorama* have been going long enough to develop their own people? If not, why not? It must be a confession of inadequacy to have to pull in a man from another outfit to front the BBC's main current affairs vehicle.'[72]

As it happened, the long lock-out that stopped publication of *The Times* for a year meant that Emery could work on *Panorama* full-time. To begin with he was quite uncomprehending of why it took so much longer to produce a television report than a newspaper article. 'If anyone had told me it would take six weeks to make a film I would have said they were crackers,' he says. Yet he soon caught the television current affairs contagion. 'Going from daily print journalism – the froth of daily news coverage – to long-form television journalism was wonderful: it was so much more rewarding to do things in depth.' Emery discovered the satisfaction of making a complicated, important story work on the television screen, and he had a boyish enthusiasm which anyone who saw him on film or in the studio enjoyed. But when *The Times* went back to work in 1979 Emery went with it, to become at first assistant to the Editor and then his Deputy.

David Dimbleby returned – but again not for long. In contrast to the situation during his first stint as presenter, single-subject programmes had now come to be the *Panorama* norm. There were fewer studio interviews and discussion programmes too, altogether less for the presenter to do. So, as then Head of Current Affairs Programmes Christopher Capron confirms, Dimbleby simply grew restless and left, to present first *Nationwide* and then the Sunday programme *People and Power*. Now Dimbleby makes occasional appearances on *Panorama* to chair a studio discussion or present a special programme. He remains one of the very best presenters of current affairs programmes on British television.

In 1982 another television journalist who had known the early days of *Panorama* was summoned back to sea as the programme's presenter: Robert Kee. But, as we have seen, he did not last long in his new role before self-destructing. *Panorama's* front-man blew himself out of the water by publicly denouncing his own programme. He left the flagship adrift, without a figurehead and with a nasty hole in its hull, just when it was under heavy fire from the Conservative Government. All hands now rushed loyally to the pumps, and the then Editor George Carey asked one of his reporters, the present author, to take over as presenter while the damage to *Panorama* was assessed and repaired.

You can't turn down an offer of the presenter's job on *Panorama*. It's one of those things – like editing the programme – that anyone who does it is bound to remember as a career high point. Even if there are other mountains to climb later on they sometimes seem like the Cairngorms after Kanchenjunga; you will take them in your stride.

May 1982 was not the easiest easy time to be the figurehead, the front man for *Panorama*; but it was exciting. Amid shot and shell from Tory MPs and ministers playing the patriot in the Falklands conflict, Editor Carey was determined not to be driven off course by what had happened. 'Steady as she goes' was the order, and the ship sailed on. '*Panorama* returns to the subject of the Falkland Islands crisis on Monday May 17,' announced the BBC Press Office firmly. 'Among other things it will look at the progress of the negotiations and present the results of an opinion poll on what people believe to be essential for a satisfactory settlement of the conflict. The poll will also cover people's views on the military options. The programme will be presented by Richard Lindley.'[73] The poll showed that 'an overwhelming majority of the British public give widespread backing to the BBC for its coverage of the Falklands crisis. In an independent survey, out today, 81% of viewers and listeners polled throughout the United Kingdom say the BBC has acted responsibly in its tv and radio coverage. Eight out of ten people also believe that the BBC should continue its traditional policy of reflecting a full range of opinions on its programmes.'[74] This was good news, and seemed to vindicate *Panorama* and other BBC programmes which had not been scared off from examining issues raised by the Falklands crisis.

When his country goes to war a journalist should ask 'Why?', but not

'Where will the troops land?' At that difficult time in 1982 some people couldn't see the difference. 'For another week *Panorama* has taken upon itself the role of chief interrogator of Britain's behaviour,' fumed a reader in the *Daily Telegraph*. 'I felt furious. I am sure many others felt the same to see Mr. Nott, the Defence Secretary, wasting an hour of his precious time listening to, and sometimes being interviewed by, Mr. Richard Lindley in the role of interrogator . . . especially towards the end of the long drawn out *Panorama* programme, he was subjected to disgraceful interrogation about the future of the Falkland Islands, by a man who holds no responsibility whatsoever.'[75]

Well, either you get it or you don't. In one sense the *Daily Telegraph*'s reader was quite right. Unlike John Nott and his Cabinet colleagues *Panorama*'s presenter bore no responsibility for prosecuting the war or re-establishing the peace in the Falklands. But if there is any point at all in a programme like *Panorama* it is exactly at this kind of moment, when the flag-waving is at its most vigorous, the exhortations to shut up and rejoice loudest, that the journalist is required to say: 'Hang on a minute, what's this for exactly, what are we doing, and why?' That's where the journalist's responsibility lies. And that's why John Nott was invited to the *Panorama* studio.

When *Panorama* heard the gunfire in 1982 it didn't disappear over the horizon, any more than it did at the time of Suez in 1956; instead it sailed towards the sound of battle, determined to ask, not about military tactics, but about why the Government was committing our forces to war, and what their objectives were. After the Falklands fighting was over, and British rule restored, the author found it a matter of some satisfaction to present 'The Media War',[76] a *Panorama* about the Government's attempts to manipulate the media during that time. Made by reporter Michael Cockerell and producer Sally Doganis, 'The Media War' won the Royal Television Society's award for best current affairs programme that year.

As presenter during the Falklands crisis the author was, to begin with at least, what the Army calls 'local, acting, unpaid'. In other words, promoted to do a new job, given the rank and the responsibility, but not paid any extra for a role that can be taken away at any time. As it happened, the idea of just being *Panorama*'s presenter was not particularly appealing. Since most programmes by this time were single subject films only a 'good evening', an introduction to the film, and a 'good night' were required. That didn't take all week – even for a slow worker like the author. Without commitments to a job outside television (like David Dimbleby), or to a good deal of work elsewhere in the BBC, a *Panorama* presenter is under-employed. And if, like the author, you are not quite sure that you can, or even want to, go on making a full-time living as a television presenter, then you will not care to commit yourself exclusively to that career path. Former Head of Current Affairs Brian Wenham had always kindly conceded that the author had a 'screen presence', though he thought it a rather chilly one, but other critics were not so generous: '*Panorama* (BBC1) which is now presided over by a man called Richard Lindley, a cross between Barry Norman and Sir Alec Douglas-Home, opened this week with a little survey on the lines of *Weekend World*.'[77] What could be more unkind?

The lure of presenting *Panorama* while continuing to report for it was strong. But for most Editors this is not an attractive proposition. Obviously if your presenter is away making a programme he cannot easily present another one in the studio. He cannot contribute his efforts to putting together a group of guests for a studio discussion or perhaps even be back from some location in time to contribute his opinion, if required, about the film due for transmission. He is in other words, being self-indulgent. The solution found in this case was to add another reporter/presenter to the *Panorama* team.

'Fred Emery of *The Times*' had already shown in the late 1970s what an able performer he was in television too. Now that *The Times*, under the ownership of Rupert Murdoch, was changing direction, Emery was ready to return to Lime Grove full time; and the BBC was keen to have him. So now *Panorama* was presented by either Emery or Lindley.

Two alternating presenters was an attractive idea, but it did not contribute to making *Panorama* pre-eminent among current affairs programmes. Both presenters valued their other role as reporters as highly as they did their presenter job. They were content to be seen as workers in the field who from time to time had a wash and brush up and came into the front parlour to greet the visiting viewers. But in the end presenters have to be special. However much reporters may deride them as overpaid drones, living off other people's labours, they are, or should be, stars, capable of bringing in the punters, adding to the audience. And if there is to be a presenter, there can't really be more than one – it distracts from the magic spell a successful programme must cast.

When *Panorama* moved away from the magazine format to the single subject the need for a presenter to act as link man between one item and another had begun to fall away. Nothing is more infuriating for a reporter and producer than to have the dramatic opening that they have devised for their report ruined by some dull studio introduction – when they could have rolled excitingly into their story straight off the programme titles. That's fair enough. If *Panorama* is to be simply one story then it may be best to find some device other than a presenter to reinforce the programme's identity – the brand. But it's sometimes also said that, even if the shape of the programme were to change, even if there was more than one item, that the temper of the times makes a presenter for *Panorama* inappropriate; that viewers today simply don't want anyone to welcome them to a programme week after week; that the very idea of a presenter is patronising, authoritarian, fundamentally old-fashioned.

That doesn't seem to be the case with other current affairs television programmes such as *Newsnight*, with Jeremy Paxman, or ITV's *Tonight with Trevor McDonald*. There, in different ways, presenters are seen to add value to their programmes: why not on *Panorama*?

Perhaps the presenter works best where he not only links prerecorded stories but follows them up himself in live interviews; or where he handles certain items from start to finish in the studio. On *Panorama* of course this requires a superman or woman: someone who is not merely a good presenter with a popular touch but an authoritative interviewer too. There are not many of these people around, very few purely 'television' people who have built up the authority to take on – let's say – the Prime Minister, and deal with him in a way that is neither bland nor deferential. If they are that good, most such people will already be taken, already *parti pris* in some way, involved in some other enterprise that makes them vulnerable, simply because *Panorama* cannot offer more than one day's work a week.

In the early 1970s, Head of Current Affairs Brian Wenham and Editor Robert Rowland briefly hired Alastair Burnet as their *Panorama* presenter. He was brilliant on every count, as ITN's *News at Ten* had previously discovered. But, as the Editor of the right-leaning *Economist* magazine, he was open to the charge that he was not politically impartial, as a BBC presenter must be seen to be. Burnet became Editor of the *Daily Express* and left *Panorama* before this could become an issue. But David Dimbleby found that his family newspaper business could make life difficult for him at *Panorama*, when his company's confrontation with National Union of Journalists became a matter of public comment.

Finding a presenter for *Panorama* today would not be easy. But if the will were there it could be done.

chapter nine
 # The Editors

Captains courageous, charismatic, crusading, courteous,
cantankerous and chaotic

When Michael Peacock first came to *Panorama* after its major refit in 1955 it was as joint Producer of the programme with Richard Cawston. The idea was that Cawston, who had run the *Newsreel* programme at Alexandra Palace, would be primarily responsible for the film side of things, but just before the new *Panorama* went on air on 19 September he developed tuberculosis and had to withdraw. Peacock, who had turned 25 just five days before, was left to produce the programme on his own.[1]

Earlier that year, on 3 June, Grace Wyndham Goldie, the Assistant Head of Talks, Television, had written to her immediate boss Leonard Miall about the new *Panorama*: 'I will, as agreed, keep a general eye on it. Michael Peacock will be in charge.' But that had been amended so that it read: 'I will, as agreed, be responsible. Michael Peacock will produce.'[2] So although Peacock was expected to produce a good *Panorama* week after week, he had to let Wyndham Goldie make the final decisions. 'I found a reporting relationship with Grace uncomfortable,' he says; 'she was undoubtedly an interventionist.' It can't have been easy.

On 10 January 1956 Wyndham Goldie wrote a rather supercilious note to her protégé about the previous night's programme: 'I thought this a disappointing edition of *Panorama*.' After some detailed criticisms of technical and other faults she concluded: '*Panorama* is such a good programme and has done so well in the past that I am sure we can do better than this. It was not at all a bad programme and had interesting ingredients; but it was disappointing, given the possibilities of the ingredients, compared with what has been done previously and with what we hope and expect the programme to do.'[3] Peacock's angry, resentful reply is scribbled at the bottom of Wyndham Goldie's memo:

> I think that you and H.T. (Tel)[4] underestimate the difficulty of putting out a weekly programme . . . I am doing my best and if that isn't good enough then perhaps someone else had better take over the programme as soon as possible. The only way to run a programme like this is to delegate . . . Of course I accept most of your points about technical faults, but not your judgement that *Panorama* has been so much better in the past. There have been far worse ones since I took over, and if you are referring to the old *Panorama* then you'd better bring back Barsley.[5]

They didn't, and Peacock continued to run *Panorama* through 1956.

Before his team went on its summer holiday he wrote to them about what he wanted in the new season:

> Current Affairs: The increasing importance of Television Current Affairs output (and, therefore, of *Panorama* current affairs coverage) means that more time must be given to the planning and preparation of our material in this field. This is not to say that our efforts in the past have been criticised; in fact, it is generally admitted that we have rung the bell with almost monotonous regularity. However, in the future we must make sure that the chances of error and unbalanced, biased and inaccurate reporting are reduced to the absolute minimum. This will mean more work for many of us.[6]

This was prescient: *Panorama*'s coverage of Suez and Hungary that autumn would establish the programme as pre-eminently the one to turn to on television for reliable, responsible reporting of the big stories round the world. By the time Peacock left the programme in 1958 *Panorama* headed the list of the BBC's top 20 programmes, and was being watched by a quarter of the adult population.[7] Its importance was formally established in 1959, when Peacock, who had been working for Outside Broadcasts, returned. This time, indubitably in command of his ship, he was given the title he deserved: Editor, *Panorama*. 'I got a carpet in the office,' he says.

But while Peacock had been away *Panorama* had lost its unchallenged status as the only BBC programme of its kind. A flotilla of other BBC factual television programmes had put to sea. In particular *Tonight*, a lively and highly manoeuvrable craft, now threatened to leave *Panorama* wallowing in its wake, with its sails flapping. In March 1957 Peacock had written to Leonard Miall:

> As I told you a week or so ago, I am worried about the long-term future of *Panorama*. Next autumn will see the start of *Panorama*'s 3rd year as a weekly programme under its present management (and its fifth year as a series). There is therefore a serious danger that the programme will become stale. In addition to this, we now have a number of competitors within our own ranks: *Tonight, Behind the Headlines, Talk of Many Things, Picture Parade,* etc., which are constantly encroaching upon us both in subject matter and techniques of presentation.[8]

By the autumn of the following year Peacock's more pedestrian successor Rex Moorfoot thought *Panorama* was in serious trouble. He wrote to Miall:

> I am gravely disturbed about the future of *Panorama*. In April D.D.Tel.B.[9] described *Panorama* as: 'Our main programme vehicle for topical affairs, controversial subjects, intelligent comment, etc.' Since then its contents have been narrowed and its style restricted by the introduction of *Tonight, Science is News,* and *Monitor*. The only field left exclusively to *Panorama* is its considered current affairs investigations. Now its work in the last field is being crippled by the sapping of producers' editorial control ... Rather than a slow death I would recommend that *Panorama* in its present form is wound up and its best aspects transferred to alternative programmes.[10]

Moorfoot was under fire, not least from the newspaper critics, who detected a fall-off in *Panorama* under his command. 'What's scared *Panorama*?' was the *Daily Sketch* headline: 'The fifth week of the fifth year of *Panorama* came and went last night without leaving a ripple on the little screens of Britain . . . Less than a year ago its serious tackling of controversial issues made front page news. Today it seems frightened of its responsibilities.'[11] Under the headline '*Panorama* is losing its zest', the London *Evening Standard* was equally critical:

> It is beyond argument that television owes a great debt to *Panorama*. Its creators have evolved a compelling and sophisticated technique that remains a living text book for the whole industry. But *Panorama* bears at present an air of sagging middle age. Its performers have lost their former zest. It could be argued that the general improvement in TV has sharpened the cutting edge of criticism; or that past glories shine out with distorted clarity. But the fact remains that I expect something better from my *Panorama* than we get at present.[12]

It wasn't just the critics but his own producers who had rounded on Moorfoot and what they saw as the poor state of *Panorama*. David Wheeler[13] had worked on the programme since it had set on its new voyage of discovery in 1955 – and he would one day become its Editor. Saying that the programme had reached a crisis, he told Moorfoot: '*Panorama* has, over the last six months, undergone a steady decline in quality. Indeed, much of the content of the programme since our resumption in September has been mediocre.'[14]

The first problem, Wheeler agreed with his Editor, was the growing impact of *Tonight*, which had started in 1956: '*Tonight*, to a great extent, uses the basic techniques of *Panorama*. The "uniqueness" of *Panorama*'s appeal, as the initiator of a new type of journalism, has vanished. No doubt this was inevitable. But the inevitability of a development does not lessen the consequence.' A weekly *Panorama*, Wheeler pointed out, could not match the topicality of a daily show like *Tonight*; and all the lighter items which *Panorama* used to do were now being covered by the more informal *Tonight*.

Bad enough; but Wheeler now identified another 'more serious' reason for the current failings of *Panorama*.

The BBC, not for the last time, was engaged in trying to bridge the gap between News and Current Affairs by bringing them together in a new Directorate. The attempt to dictate from the top who did what, when, and how was, argued Wheeler, stifling producer initiative:

> *Panorama* was at its best when its producers, given, where necessary, general policy clearance on a subject, felt able to go ahead and treat it in a stimulating and controversial way. Management must have sufficient confidence in *Panorama* producers to give them executive responsibility for the programme. If experience shows that its confidence is misplaced then it is the producer who should be changed, not the system. There is no other way of making *Panorama*, once again, a worthwhile hard-hitting programme.

Wheeler gave illustrations of how a distant management was now taking the decisions about what could be done and what couldn't – and taking far too long about it; and, in a passage that could have been written by producers trying to work under John Birt's regime 30 years later, he continued:

> Another time-wasting procedure is the growing insistence on the submission of some sort of written treatments for stories. This is neither possible nor desirable. Producers must have freedom to manoeuvre and 'play their hunches'. The vetoes – and the indecision – have had their effect on the rest of the programme. The production team is disorganised and lacking in drive. One of the Corporation's greatest assets, as I am sure you would agree, is the enthusiasm of its producers. It is increasingly hard to maintain this enthusiasm when one sees a straitjacket being clamped on the programme. The sharpness and edge of *Panorama* have been lost. Originality has been sacrificed to a grey, 'safe' respectability.

But Michael Peacock's second tour of duty in command of *Panorama* seems to have made all shipshape again, and the appointment of Paul Fox as his successor as Editor seems to have raised morale still further. There was at first a certain surprise that the man from *Sportsview* should now be in charge of the most important of the BBC's current affairs programmes. Some reporters were at first rather sniffy about him; but they were soon won over.

Fox had a genius for looking after his reporters and producers while they were out gathering material, and for making the most of it in the programme. He made every contribution by his *Panorama* team seem vital and important. Recognising the quality of the people working for him, he was, and remains, generous in his praise of them:

> I think one of the greatest strengths of *Panorama* was of course its reporting team. We had a magnificent reporting team. I was very fortunate. It was led by Richard Dimbleby, then there was Robin Day, Ludovic Kennedy, Jim Mossman, Michael Charlton, John Morgan, and Robert Kee. Now there wasn't a better reporting team in the world. And they were brave and they worked hard, and they went abroad and they – after all there were a fair number of wars going on – they reported from Algeria, they reported from Vietnam, they reported from the Middle East. It was an outstanding team of reporters and producers and the Editor's job was a simple one: just to combine that together.[15]

Fox underplays his own strengths here; he was a real operator. For instance, while in Moscow to set up live coverage of the 1961 May Day parade, Fox got wind of Yuri Gagarin's epic journey in space as the first man to orbit the earth. With extraordinary energy he was able to organise a special BBC programme, the first of its kind, in which live coverage of Major Gagarin's triumphant reception in the Russian capital was seen by British viewers as it happened.

Fox and his team seem to have asserted their determination not to be told what to do and how to do it simply in the interests of better co-ordination between News and Current Affairs. It helped that Fox understood the BBC system well and had gained the confidence of both Donald Edwards, Editor, News and Current Affairs, and of Director General Hugh Carleton Greene. At a weekly meeting, he says, Carleton Greene tried hard to get better co-operation between News and Current Affairs, and most problems evaporated: 'But, I mean, it would be foolish to say there weren't tensions; of course there were tensions. But I think at times the tensions did help to produce better programmes.'

But pressure on *Panorama* from other current affairs programmes at Lime Grove did not decrease. There were constant clashes because their subject matter, as well as their format, often overlapped. In 1963 Alasdair Milne, Editor of *Tonight*, complained in incoherent irritation to the Assistant Controller, Current Affairs Talks, Television:

> As you know Keith Kyle has been working for us based in Nairobi for some six months. On Tuesday last week, during my absence on holiday Tony Jay quite rightly cabled Kyle to film a story on the R.A.F.'s efforts on the aid the starving people of Kenya [sic]. Kyle despatched his story to us late last week and it was cut and ready for transmission tonight, Monday. On my return today I discover from the Ed. *Panorama* that on Friday morning he despatched Robin Day to Kenya to cover the same story. There was of course no mention of this enterprise on the projected arrangements for *Panorama* nor were we informed during the week that he had this story in mind. Naturally I understand his predicament with only one programme a week; but I would like it put on record that at the cost of several hundreds of pounds, in the present budgetary state of this programme, it is an extremely damaging loss. I have agreed to withhold the story on which there is no doubt we had prior claim.[16]

Later that year Fox, now Head of Public Affairs Programmes, Television, sent an 'urgent' note to Alasdair Milne headed '*Panorama* and *Tonight*': 'I feel it is high time to underline to you the persistent niggling clashes that are re-occurring with such regularity between *Panorama* and *Tonight*.' Fox gave two examples: first, a *Panorama* special on the Buchanan Report (about transport in Britain) had been ruined because *Tonight* had devoted nearly all its programme to the same subject earlier in that evening; and second, *Tonight* had changed its plans about where best to base itself in the States in order to cover the aftermath of President Kennedy's assassination, and had ended up exactly where *Panorama* had already chosen to be: 'I have already warned that the same thing will happen about Kenya. I think it is deliberate. I think it makes the Television service look stupid. And what is the point of the Wednesday meeting of Departmental Heads if this sort of laughable Group-planning and Group-economy cannot be decided upon?'[17]

With *Tonight* first on air early on a Monday evening, a pre-emptive raid on the target before *Panorama* was in position to open fire later in the evening was always a threat to the stately flagship. These clashes set *Panorama* people thinking. How could they better differentiate their programme from other magazine programmes like *Tonight*? Without having to rely on management intervening on their behalf all the time, how could they better armour themselves against competition from within the fleet?

Under attack

In 1961 David Wheeler, by then far the most experienced producer on the programme, had suggested that, under the *Panorama* label, a way should be found to do current affairs in greater depth:

> The field of topical programmes in depth is one in which, it seems to me, we are falling sadly behind the opposition. A recent case in point (but only one of many in the last six months) was last week's Granada programme on France, 'Paris – the Cancer Within'. It had its faults but was streets ahead of anything we have done. Indeed, with rare exceptions, we do not attempt this kind of programme. There are many topics that are worth fuller treatment than they can possibly receive in a magazine. They do not get done because there is no organisation for getting them done nor any one person charged with responsibility for thinking on these lines.

Wheeler suggested that *Panorama*'s reporters would like the idea of a series of in-depth programmes to which they might contribute. 'Television reporters are now full-time professionals, not unseated Members of Parliament, with a "life expectancy" of at least ten years. An occasional opportunity to work on larger projects, would, I know, be both welcome and beneficial to most of them. Members of the *Panorama* production team might also welcome the chance to involve themselves, from time to time, in "depth" treatment of subjects.'[18]

A separate programme didn't happen, but in 1964 producer Richard (Dick) Francis had similar points to make about *Panorama* to Wheeler – who, after a spell away from the programme making documentaries, had now become its Editor. He wrote:

> *Panorama* is losing its status. Faced by increased competition, particularly from News, we pass up many important stories. Thus we no longer provide

the definitive coverage of current affairs, we are no longer indispensable. We should rise above competition, and identify *Panorama* more by its treatment than its placing . . . *Panorama* must increase its impact. We should drop the 'four-story' concept, and plan for a major feature each week, plus 'reports', 'compilations', and short 'colour' and news pieces . . . By planning one main feature for each programme four–five weeks in advance, we could achieve more depth and polish.'[19]

Robin Day had jokingly called Paul Fox, when he was Editor, 'five-item Fox', but now the pressure to move away from the magazine format was really building up. In the spring of 1965, in response to a memo from Fox, as Head of Public Affairs Programmes, Television, Wheeler set out specific proposals for 'The Future of *Panorama*'. On the assumption that *Tonight* should be scrapped he argued for a main news programme at 7pm to replace it, and a daily current affairs programme much later in the evening.

'We then come to the problem of *Panorama*. It would, I am sure, be impossible to maintain it in the format of a topical magazine if anything like the above suggestions were adopted . . . I would suggest a new-model *Panorama* covering not more than two (but usually one) subject a week. I think fifty minutes might be too long – a 50 minute film is not easy to do on a weekly basis, assuming existing budgets and facilities. 40 minutes might be better, or even – if we decide definitely to make it always single subject – half an hour.'

Even if *Tonight* stayed, said Wheeler, *Panorama* should move away from a magazine format to at most three subjects. 'In other words, if *Panorama* is to lose news topicality to a refurbished *Tonight*, then it must be able to offer the higher quality to be derived from committing the bulk of its resources each week to one subject.'[20] Now all was cleared away and ready for an Editor who would change the shape of *Panorama* in a fundamental way. Paul Fox had already spied him sailing in the enemy fleet, in ITV.

A pirate boarding party

Since 1963 Jeremy Isaacs had been very successful running Associated-Rediffusion's *This Week*, the weekly 30-minute current affairs programme that ITV was rightly proud of. Recently it had been outrunning *Panorama*

– in June 1965 for example *This Week* had won a silver medal at the Berlin Television Festival while *Panorama* had not been mentioned. But however successful Isaacs was at ITV it was seen as an extraordinary thing at the time to invite someone from commercial television to take over such a quintessentially BBC programme as *Panorama*. Indeed, Fox's first attempt to get Isaacs appointed failed. At his BBC selection Board Isaacs recalls Grace Wyndham Goldie asking him insultingly if he could be trusted not to take 'freebies' – free flights and accommodation for his reporting teams in return for some favourable mention in the programme. Undeterred, Fox tried again, and the following year, in 1965, Isaacs became Editor of *Panorama*. Isaacs, it was reported at the time,[21] had accepted the job because he liked the prospect of a 50-minute programme, and because he welcomed the idea of hiving off short, topical news stories to the new late night daily programme, *24 Hours*. That would leave *Panorama* free to deal in depth with big subjects.

Isaacs was said to find *Panorama* too posh: 'He is witheringly critical of aspects of the present *Panorama* which he describes as "a class programme, with very little contact with ordinary people". His determination to produce longer items and film reports will have the interesting consequence of considerably lessening the role of the eternal link-man, Mr Richard Dimbleby . . . Whatever happens in the autumn, Isaacs' appointment is sure to produce fireworks.' It did. Isaacs's remarks about the class bias of *Panorama* caused offence in the BBC hierarchy; many certainly saw him as alien, an unwelcome outsider: 'Poor Jeremy arrived at Lime Grove in a blue denim shirt and gave off a terrific feeling of dynamism – Jewish oomph,' says Barbara Pegna, an assistant producer there at the time. 'It was quite odd when this swashbuckling character came to *Panorama*. Quite frankly, he wasn't one of us.' Isaacs makes no complaint of his reception at Lime Grove; indeed, he says he was made welcome.

At *This Week* Isaacs had got rid of his patrician presenter Brian Connell: let into the secret of Richard Dimbleby's cancer, he couldn't do the same with the famous face of *Panorama*. But Isaacs insists today that Dimbleby wasn't really the problem: 'It wasn't just that I didn't want a front-man,' he says, 'it was that I didn't want to be in the studio. It was important to get out into the streets and meet real people.' As it was, Dimbleby would present very few *Panorama* programmes under Isaacs before his cancer finally stopped him working. The first, on the Indo–Pakistan War, was not a great success. '*Panorama* slows down coverage' was the judgement of the *Daily Telegraph*'s critic. There were two elements in the one story, with Leonard Parkin reporting from Pakistan and Michael Charlton from India: 'Neither produced any remarkable action pictures or any new revelations, and both purveyed a good deal of propaganda confirming the immutable attitudes.' Isaacs remembers getting up at 5am on the Tuesday following *Panorama* to get the papers and read this and other not very flattering reviews.

Determined to get him out of Lime Grove, Isaacs sent Dimbleby to New York, to cover the Pope's visit to the United Nations. Jo Menell, who had been filming for *Panorama* in Detroit on some other story, was sent to New York to help produce. He recalls Dimbleby saying to him: 'Your man Isaacs [Menell too had come from ITV] is going to be the ruin of the programme.' 'Richard never came back to Lime Grove again,' says Isaacs. The last programme before Christmas, just before Richard Dimbleby died, was presented by James Mossman. On behalf of *Panorama* and its viewers he bade a touching 'good night' to Dimbleby, who he knew would be watching from his hospital bed.

In January the following year, in the wake of Richard Dimbleby's death, Isaacs put together a remarkable programme on cancer, until then a subject virtually impossible for television to tackle. Assistant producer Barbara Pegna found a former patient, a Mrs Norfolk, ready to describe how she had been successfully operated on for breast cancer; there was a report from the Christie Hospital in Manchester showing a patient with cancer of the larynx undergoing radiotherapy; Sidney Farber from the Children's Cancer Research Fund explained chemotherapy for children with leukaemia; there were contributions from America and Sweden; there was an explanation of the importance of smear tests to forestall cervical cancer; and a GP and patients in a hospital cancer ward talked about how people felt when they were told they had the disease, and the general ignorance there was about it. The programme, introduced by Richard Dimbleby's son David, drew a very large audience of 10½ million viewers, and, according to producer Dick Francis, got a Reaction Index of 84, *Panorama*'s highest ever.

The Cancer programme showed Isaacs beginning to move towards his goal of a single subject programme. Through the spring and summer of 1966 the programmes were divided between those with several stories and those with just one. *Panorama* on 25 April had 'American Heart Operation', 'British Aircraft Workers in Germany' and 'Advice to the Chancellor'; on 9 May 'Homeless Families In Kent', 'Belgium's Language Crisis' and 'Payroll Tax'. But on 6 June there was simply 'Mental Illness', and on 13 June 'Vietnam: people and war'.

Isaacs was determined to get away from the brief, inevitably superficial, extended news report to something altogether more profound. Demanding more resources with which to do it, he wrote to Paul Fox: 'The cancer programme I believe proved up to the hilt the case for solid research on *Panorama*. I would suggest that *Panorama* should acquire at least one or possibly two research assistant posts.'[22] Three months later he was asking for an additional camera crew 'to maintain and increase *Panorama*'s status and authority'.[23] That would have made three crews in all, plus a freelance cameraman[24] who was now under contract. At this stage Isaacs was thinking of a six-week cycle for *Panorama* which would mean aiming at one programme with a 50-minute film, four with a 40-minute film plus a 10-minute interview; and one with a 10-minute film and a 40-minute studio discussion.

But all was not well aboard *Panorama*. Isaacs was finding it desperately difficult dealing with the BBC's bureaucracy. At Rediffusion he had direct access to the top, but at the BBC he had to deal with several hostile baronies who had no love for this ITV interloper. Without a regular presenter or a consistent format *Panorama*'s ratings were slipping. Isaacs agrees that some earlier programmes were 'pretty incompetent', and he had suffered from a succession of technical cock-ups. Now he was asked whether the single-subject idea was really a good one. While Fox thought *Panorama* should always deal with the big news story of the week, Isaacs thought a real film report required a longer time to make and could not normally be done in a hurry. 'You couldn't just grab,' he says, 'you had to think in advance.' As for having to include a hot news story, Isaacs thought that ridiculous when there was in existence *24 Hours*, the nightly current affairs programme, as well as the News.

There was a growing lack of agreement between Isaacs and Fox that would prove fatal. What's more, the idea of a single-subject *Panorama* was provoking the interference of some of those BBC barons hostile to Current Affairs.

In June Aubrey Singer, the Head of Outside Broadcasts, Features and Science, wrote to Paul Fox: 'This change of policy raises certain questions – not the least the question of a clash of subjects caused by an increase of 52 documentaries a year (for that is what many of the new *Panorama*s must be).'[25] Infuriatingly Singer suggested that *Panorama*'s programmes should be individually offered for prior approval to the Controller of BBC1, as were single documentaries. Fox wrote back angrily: 'Relax and stop worrying – you'll get high blood pressure.'[26] After a further heated exchange Michael Peacock, as Controller of BBC1, had to write to Singer: 'Please drop this subject . . . this is none of your business.'[27]

Tempers were beginning to fray. It had been Fox who had persuaded Isaacs to join the BBC, but now, in the summer of 1966, the Head of Current Affairs was under increasing pressure to demonstrate that he'd chosen the right man. Addressing a confidential memo to 'Editor, *Panorama* ONLY', Fox wrote:

> I want to get a couple of things absolutely clear about the new *Panorama* season before we set out on it:
>
> 1. Neither I nor Controller BBC-1 nor others up on the Sixth Floor will be happy with the continuing drop in *Panorama* audiences. They must be improved.
>
> 2. Now that we are embarked on a season of single subjecters, you must be fully aware of what's wanted: it is NOT stockpiled, sociological Documentaries. Mental Health was *Panorama* only because of Mental Health week; Cancer was *Panorama* only because of Richard. We are not in the Documentary business. Particularly with forty minutes, we remain very much in the Current Affairs business.
>
> The new *Panorama*s must remain topical, current; all-embracing *the* topic of the week. It can mean – and will mean – scrapping the prepared programme and starting anew on a fresh programme of urgency. This is a firm directive – laid down by C.BBC-1 – and one I agree with very much.

Finally, Fox was clearly furious about Isaacs's buccaneering editorial style, and the way he was making decisions about *Panorama* programmes involving expensive foreign travel without consulting him first; he wrote rudely: 'We face enough problems without you making things more difficult by ignoring the generally-accepted, fairly lax conventions.'[28]

Isaacs tried to hang on to his concept of dealing with a single subject in depth while reacting, as Fox insisted, to the topic of the week. In the *Sunday Telegraph* Philip Purser singled out a *Panorama* on the seamen's strike: 'The special rushed out on the first day of the strike seems now to be the most encouraging pointer of all to the re-styled *Panorama*. It indicated that the full-scale treatment need not always require patient preparation, need not always stand back from the press of events. Reliance on the news of the day may go, but the news of the day will still be able to assert itself when it's big enough.'[29]

But inside the BBC, as Isaacs tenaciously nailed his single-subject colours to the mast, doubts were being expressed – quite unknown to him – about the course he was plotting. John Grist, Assistant Head of Current Affairs, Television, wrote a private and confidential note to Fox: 'I think it would be sensible if we had a long discussion about the future of *Panorama* with Huw Wheldon, Michael Peacock, yourself, me, Isaacs and Webster, because I am afraid at the moment that there is a danger of tension and misunderstanding in the new season.' Though the single-subject programmes so far had been widely admired, said Grist, *Panorama* audiences had been falling:

> It is quite clear that *Panorama* has now slipped into a different audience bracket. It is running in the 4/6 million area, whereas in 1964 at this time it was running around 5/7 million . . . As I have pointed out before, *Panorama* has tended to lose its identity since the death of Richard Dimbleby. The familiarity of a large-size personality like Dimbleby obviously adds to the loyalty of the audience. We in current affairs know from experience also that it is easier to hold an audience with a magazine-type programme when the focus of interest is constantly changing. The structural problems of creating this same change of interest in a programme devoted to one topic, is much more difficult, and requires very considerable editorial skill. The present Editor has, I think, like many of our younger producers, worked on the theory that a reporter or personality should not come between the audience and the material. This is fine intellectually, but it does, I think, by down-grading the personality of the reporter, weaken the interest of some marginal

viewers. I think the present Editor could do more to think in terms of the personality of the reporter, even though he may find the personalities of some of them unpleasant.[30]

Came August, and Paul Fox sent the text of a brief article to the *Radio Times* to run on the first day of the new series:

Tonight *Panorama* leaves behind its magazine format which dealt with several subjects. Instead, it sets out to become a new programme treating a major single topic each week . . . Why the change? There are several reasons, and the most important is a personal one: *Panorama* without Richard Dimbleby can never be the same again. When the irreplaceable centre-piece of a programme leaves you, them just as in life, you don't look for a replacement: you shape a new programme.[31]

Isaacs submitted a list of future programmes to his bosses: 'Hospitals'; 'Labour'; 'Priests'; 'Poverty and Politics (in Peru)'; 'Gambling and Crime'; 'Fuel Policy'; 'Nasser's Egypt'; 'Halfway for LBJ'; 'Poverty in Britain'; 'China in the World'; 'Fetichism in the BBC';[32] 'The Monarchy'.[33] When some of these ideas had been previously discussed, Michael Peacock, Controller of BBC1, had not been impressed by what looked a rather worthy but unexciting list of topics. He had written to Fox: 'Do we really want a Johnson profile? And will the Peru story be sufficiently relevant, topical and interesting for *Panorama* in the autumn? They aren't even in the Cup!'[34] But Isaacs had sailed unswervingly on.

Walking the plank

It was a doomed voyage. Experience over the seamen's strike had suggested that *Panorama* could chuck a planned programme overboard and successfully substitute one that covered a major topical story. But the seamen's strike had been a domestic issue, with pictures and people readily available. When Hendrik Verwoerd, the Prime Minister of South Africa, was assassinated there was a dilemma. Ready to roll was a carefully crafted *Panorama* on Wales, designed to tie in with the opening of the new Severn Bridge. Long in preparation, it was a thing of beauty, a seamless, lyrical exploration of the contours and character of the principality, professionally produced by Robert Rowland and powerfully reported by Welshman John Morgan. In other words it was hard to cut down to make room for anything else. Though producer Jo Menell did his best in a desperate dash to South Africa, he had no time to get more than 10 or at most 20 minutes' worth of film in the can. Isaacs decided that there was no other material available in London to make up a decent 40-minute *Panorama* on South Africa, and that in any case Verwoerd's assassination was essentially a news event rather than the cue for an in-depth look at South Africa. He therefore gave what Menell had brought back to *24 Hours*, while *Panorama* sailed resolutely on with its long-planned programme on Wales.

In ignoring what was undoubtedly the major international news story of the week, Isaacs was taking *Panorama* into waters previously uncharted. His crew was divided between those who strongly supported him and those who feared that a single subject, particularly one that was not a top story, would bring shipwreck. Robin Day, facing an end to the career he had made for himself as a regular studio political interviewer, redoubled his efforts to get rid of his captain with a personal letter to the Controller of Programmes, Huw Wheldon:

> It may well be a good idea to have a regular weekly documentary programme of the kind Jeremy Isaacs has always preferred, but I believe it is a mistaken and retrograde step to put this in the *Panorama* space under the *Panorama* name. Almost every day some member of the public complains to me about the change to a one-subject *Panorama*. Trite though it may sound, the old-style *Panorama* was, to a great many homes, their window on the world. Recent and typical comments from reasonable viewers to me have been:
>
> 'Quite frankly this has killed the programme.'
>
> 'I always used to know there would be at least one item which I'd be interested in and therefore I watched it all. Now I don't bother if the subject doesn't appeal to me.'
>
> . . . In short I am convinced that one of the BBC's greatest assets is being squandered – namely the prestige and popularity of a programme whose

authority, flexibility and variety commanded immense respect and affection among the public. Of course much of this was due to Richard's unique personality and stature. But is it not an appalling waste to throw away the goodwill and respect which he did so much to build up for the programme? Is this tremendous achievement, in which successive *Panorama* Editors and commentators have played their part, to be thought so ephemeral as to be not worth continuing? As one who has worked for *Panorama* longer than anyone (except Richard himself and David Wheeler) it would be a bitter disappointment to be told that there is no longer a place on BBC-TV for this kind of weekly programme.[35]

Two days later John Grist put his own view in a memo to Paul Fox, blaming Isaacs's character as well as his course for what had gone wrong with *Panorama*:

I think the 40 minute single-topic programme was probably beyond his capacity and organisational powers; faults which could have been overcome if he had been able to delegate. He has personal problems in the sense that it is difficult to have an exchange of ideas without him getting fairly rapidly to screaming pitch. He is, in fact, one of the most able people I have seen working in a cutting room with film. Unfortunately he seems to have few powers of negotiation and persuasion. He has also totally failed in his use of the studio, which leads to fraught situations on Monday night, and also to considerable lack of style in the programme. He has been particularly inept in the mixed studio/film programme on a topical issue.[36]

Today Grist says 'it was hell' putting on a *Panorama* week after week with Isaacs as Editor. Margaret Douglas, secretary to Michael Peacock a decade earlier and now a studio director, had been brought back to stop *Panorama* falling off the air. Grist was appalled at how disorganised Jeremy Isaacs was. Isaacs's method, he says, was to fight everyone. 'He was a good leader but had no idea how to get the staff work done.' And the initial mutual admiration between Fox and Isaacs had disappeared. 'It was going to be a lovely relationship', says Grist, 'and it all went sour.' At the time, Isaacs says today, he did not realise how critical Grist was of his performance as *Panorama*'s Editor.

It seems that by this stage an early replacement for Isaacs had more or less been decided on. Grist's memo to Fox continued:

> The new Editor will have to be able to override the natural problems created in the minds of (a) [David] Webster, who will not get the succession,[37] and (b) all those others on the programme, like [Jo] Menell and [John] Morgan, who are closely associated with Isaacs. The new Editor will have to be somebody who puts their morale up by coming to join them, rather than creating new problems for them in the middle of their season. The new Editor will also have to overcome the lack of authority to which the programme has been condemned in the last few months.

The disappointment at *Panorama*'s performance in its new rig reached the Board of Governors. Exasperatingly for the BBC managers, the Board took the view that *Panorama* should now strive to dig deeper with the single subject and let topicality go hang:

> The Chairman [Lord Normanbrook] recalled that members of the Board had commented on a number of occasions on the new character of *Panorama*. They had said that the single-subject programme seemed often to achieve length rather than depth. It seemed to him possible that the programme was attempting to be too topical. Immediate comment on the news was the appropriate function of *24 Hours*. It might be that *Panorama* should seek greater detachment from the news of the day. More time could then be devoted to the study of a single subject.

This was not what the BBC management wanted to hear, and indeed, despite his pleas, Isaacs had been refused permission to sing his siren song directly to the Governors. Treading warily on a slippery deck, Director General Hugh Carleton Greene said that 'in his view *Panorama* ought to meet both requirements – that of treatment in depth, and of topical presentation.'[38] The minutes suggest that the Director General did not reveal to the Board that the decision had already been taken to relieve Isaacs of his command, but the very next day the *Daily Telegraph* reported that 'Jeremy Isaacs, 34, in charge of the BBC's *Panorama*, is giving up the job at the end

of the year because of a disagreement about the future of the programme'.[39]
On the same day Fox told the Current Affairs meeting:

> It had become clear during the last few weeks that the idea of a single subject
> was not working out; it had been decided that in future the programme
> should establish a new type of magazine reporting, in some ways like the
> *Panorama* of 18 months ago, but containing two or three rather than three
> or four items (although with still a single theme when suitable); the present
> Editor, Jeremy Isaacs, did not wish to do this and still had faith in a single
> subject, at forty minutes; two recent programmes had shown the disad-
> vantage of this length: the Rhodesia programme had been stretched to fill 40
> minutes, while the German programme should have been 25 minutes; on 30
> January the programme would return to a 50 minute length and an 8 o'clock
> placing.[40]

Today Fox says: 'I'd felt Jeremy was absolutely the right guy for *Panorama*.
I just thought we needed someone from somewhere else. He'd been
running a successful programme at *This Week*. But I feel I did Jeremy a bad
turn in bringing him in.'

As Isaacs recalls it, he was not consulted before he was so abruptly
ousted. A man of strong feeling and high emotion, he remembers getting
into a taxi in tears. 'He was', says Jo Menell, 'crestfallen but unrepentant.'

Back in ITV as Associated-Rediffusion's[41] Controller of Features Isaacs
wrote about his experience at *Panorama* in more measured tones. Given
the proliferation of news and current affairs programmes, said Isaacs, 'I
believed *Panorama* should have a sharply defined identity. Its best chance
of that was a specific role. That role, the most important one, telling the
big stories in the solidest possible way. One long look each week at things
that mattered. Some viewers might not be interested, others could
perhaps be wheedled into trying something new. The BBC gave me a
chance, albeit a brief one – ten years for the old *Panorama*, ten weeks for
mine. They didn't like what they saw. I was beginning to. So were the
viewers. The BBC changed its mind. It's their prerogative. I argued, I lost.
A very resistible force met an immovable object . . . "Auntie" is not quite
sure where she is going. She knows where I was headed though: too fast
in a new direction.'[42]

'On one point', says Isaacs today, 'Fox was right and I was wrong; if you were going to do a single subject, it had to be (or at least look like) the main story of the week. But on the central issue I was right, and events have proved me right.' For more than 20 years now *Panorama* has been a single-subject programme. Whether for good or ill, Isaacs's view of what the shape of *Panorama* should be won out.

All at sea

Panorama was now in trouble; up the creek, you might say. The BBC had backed the course Jeremy Isaacs had steered; now it had to find – and justify – another. The first priority was to find a replacement Editor. As a stop-gap John Grist was appointed, while remaining Deputy to Paul Fox in the Current Affairs Group. It was decided that from 30 January 1967 *Panorama* would revert to its old, longer length of 50 minutes, and go out at 8pm on Monday, instead of 40 minutes at 9.05pm.

Said the London *Evening News:* 'Mr. Grist will need lots of luck in his new post. But there are always the boys in the backroom to offer advice. I wish him well.'[43]

With Michael Peacock, the Controller of BBC1, and Paul Fox, Head of Current Affairs, Television, both former highly successful Editors of *Panorama*, no one now taking charge of the programme was going to feel carefree. In a memo addressed 'John Grist ONLY' Fox thanked his Deputy for taking on 'the onerous job of Editor *Panorama*', and set out the marks he was to steer by:

> What is needed in *Panorama* is to restore the authority and identity of the BBC's major Current Affairs programme. In other words: to make it a top programme again. A big audience is essential to *Panorama*'s well-being. The new placing ensures a good inheritance. This means that worthy, though important, subjects must be done not only authoritatively, but attractively. In a magazine programme, designed for a peak family audience, there are ways of sugaring the pill.[44]

It was all very well telling Grist to do important stories in an attractive way that drew big audiences. His immediate concern was to manage the crew so that the best of them did not all jump ship. Soon Grist was writing to Fox:

> The problems are greater than I had imagined. The programme is in a serious state, but it can, and will, be saved. It needs a sense of priority in the Television Service and Current Affairs Group. The recent disturbances and the malice created over a long period will take time to settle. It is reasonable to assume that [Jo] Menell and [Phillip] Whitehead will resign. The fact that the Editor is temporary adds to the feeling of uncertainty. There is obviously a very difficult time ahead for some months, but in the long run the blood-letting may help.[45]

Blood-curdling stuff. Menell and Whitehead did go to join Jeremy Isaacs in ITV, taking with them cameramen and film editors, but full-scale mutiny on the flagship *Panorama* was avoided. Some of those who stayed think Grist, the stop-gap Editor, has been underrated. Says a producer of that time, Paul Hodgson: 'He was civilised; he did not try to control; he was not obsessed with getting power for himself. And he was prepared to take risks with limited resources; he'd send me to France for a week just to see if there was a story for *Panorama*: "Go to de Gaulle's press conferences; let me know if there's anything we should be doing."' By the summer of 1967 Grist had restored morale and brought the programme safely through to the point where command could be given to David Webster (and his experienced deputy Robert Rowland) for the new season.

There were a lot of liquid lunches in 'Slosh' Webster's time as Editor. If he expected his reporters to be prepared to spend the night in a ditch in some faraway place he didn't begrudge them their five-star hotel the next day if they could find one; and on their return home he would debrief them over a couple of bottles of decent wine. Like Fox, whom he greatly admired, he knew how to play to his reporters' strengths: 'I was lucky because I had a star cast; I could send [Michael] Charlton to some earthquake in Iran on a Friday and he'd come out with a magnificent 20-minute story for Monday night that did something that BBC News still wasn't doing. They did not give the flavour that we did . . . We were not going to give up on the world; our job was getting people to watch things they didn't know they were interested in.'

Webster imposed a genial discipline on a *Panorama* that had nearly sunk after Isaacs's departure. 'A *Panorama* to be successful must bear the stamp of a bloody-minded Editor,' he says. 'Get the programme schedule under control, then you can wheel and deal.' And so David Webster did.

In the doldrums

But if *Panorama* was now in safer waters it had paid a price. It was a programme increasingly perceived as no longer making waves, no longer exciting envy and admiration, no longer a model for other current affairs programmes to emulate. As Milton Shulman wrote, in his article 'Keyhole on the World', previously quoted: ' . . . the interesting thing about *Panorama*'s decline is that it has taken place during a period of tumultuous, exciting and awesome news events . . . The last two programmes of its present series demonstrated for me why I no longer consider *Panorama* the compulsive, authoritative programme it once was.' One of these programmes had dealt with the riots in Detroit (it had 'added nothing of significance') and with Cuba ('so uncritical and so bland that it might have been issued by the Cuban Tourist Board . . . This sort of fawning reportage may look nice but non-objectivity is too high a price to pay for this kind of scoop'). The other programme, which had included reports on Britain's hippies, on the Middle East, and on China, 'seemed desultory, unresolved and pinched . . . The one dominating feature of both these editions of *Panorama* was how familiar and stale most of the comments and views were.'[46]

This is a harsh view of a programme that was still acknowledged as the most important current affairs programme on British television. But *Panorama was* getting dull; Shulman was not alone in his criticism: 'Now it is just another current affairs item,' mourned Maurice Wiggin, 'one of many, and not the least boring. Its unique authority has slipped away, its imitators outflanked it. It stands out like a nice old hotel, dignified and rather formal, surrounded by new snazzy motels, snack bars, dives and discothèques, holiday camps and fly-by-night clubs. The staff are first-rate, the guests distinguished, but the food is rather dull.'[47]

But if the menu was generally unexciting, the staff nonetheless from time to time cooked up something thoroughly satisfying. In 1968 there were two fascinating profiles, the first, by James Mossman, of Oswald Mosley, the former British fascist leader, then 72 and arguing that he still had '20 or 30 years left' in which the call for him to lead Britain might still come. Later in the year the new reporter on the *Panorama* team, Robert MacNeil, contributed a portrait of another politician all too sure of himself and his convictions, Enoch Powell. Even if these excellent profiles were unadventurous, to suggest that convivial, pipe-smoking David Webster's *Panorama* never broke new ground would be wrong.

Panorama, like most of the media, had been late to wake up to what was happening in Northern Ireland; too long ignorant and uncaring of the widespread discrimination practised by the Protestant Unionist majority against Roman Catholic republicans; content to accept Stormont's assurance that the Government of Northern Ireland was dealing fairly and effectively with growing nationalist pressure. And the BBC had been ready to accept whatever limits its Northern Ireland Controller, a pillar of the Northern Ireland ascendancy, imposed on television and radio coverage in the province.

Panorama had made an earlier attempt to find out for itself what was happening in Ulster but had had to abort the operation when reporter Leonard Parkin and producer Jo Menell were both seriously injured in a car crash there. But in December 1968 Richard Kershaw and his producer John Reynolds tried again. The first big civil rights march was planned in Armagh – and had been given official permission. The rumour was, however, that the march would be stopped, with violence if necessary, by Ian Paisley's supporters. Though clearly a force to be reckoned with, and for that reason worth talking to, Paisley at that time did not have a political party of his own. There was an unofficial BBC Northern Ireland ban on interviewing him. It was no doubt thought that the sight and sound of Paisley revealing the ugly face of Protestant bigotry would spoil the image of Unionism that the Government of Northern Ireland and the BBC there both preferred the world to see. But *Panorama* was not part of BBC Northern Ireland, nor under the thumb of its Controller, Waldo Maguire, who was furious when he heard that Kershaw had filmed an interview with Paisley for his forthcoming programme.

At Armagh the riot police allowed Paisley's supporters to build barricades across the road and, when the civil rights protesters tried to exercise their legal right to march, barred the way themselves. While Kershaw and his crew were filming, a separate group of police assaulted them, smashing the camera; one of them used his baton on Kershaw. Nevertheless Kershaw managed to retrieve the camera magazine, with the exposed film still intact and, back at his hotel, send a radio report of the incident to London – which was broadcast. Nervously nursing an injured knee, Kershaw was phoned by a furious Maguire: 'I've been researching you. You're a mere contract reporter. If you go on talking like that about your knee you'll never work again.'

But in London it seems that the BBC now saw a chance to cut the Controller, Northern Ireland down to size. Kershaw was told he would be interviewed by William Hardcastle on radio's *The World This Weekend*. Kershaw again explained what had happened at Armagh and how the police had beaten him up – at the same time as an official Northern Ireland Government statement was still denying that anything untoward had occurred.

In a television interview with Kershaw next day John Craig, Minister of Home Affairs and responsible for the police, apologised to him on camera. A formal enquiry was set up, and the police paid compensation for the camera equipment they had so comprehensively smashed, though not for the bruises Kershaw and his crew had suffered.

BBC Northern Ireland had been shown that it could not expect to control absolutely the BBC's reporting there, and certainly not *Panorama*'s. But it was still a powerful fiefdom: there would be another demonstration of that 10 years on, at Carrickmore. Meanwhile, *Panorama* had shown a flash of its old form. Said T.C. Worsley:

> If it's information plus illumination that you're after, you still can't do much better than dear old deathless *Panorama*. It isn't very exciting: it seldom surprises you: it has been going on, just as it now goes on, for as long as one can remember: it misses – who doesn't? – Richard Dimbleby. But it is solid, reliable, and can still bring in a scoop, as it did the other week with its profile of Mr. Enoch Powell. Last week it cleared up for me unemotionally and factually the issues in Northern Ireland. It cut through the confusions with lucid diagrams, presented the case for each side, gave the Reverend Paisley the freedom of the air. In short a first-class

piece of competent, efficient journalism which is really all one should want from it.[48]

But somehow, as Worsley suggests, it doesn't sound very exciting.

'Curiously', says Robert Rowland, 'Jeremy Isaacs's changes (to lengthier, better researched, more considered items) were the beginnings of *Panorama*'s move into a journalistic solemnity which outdid anything undertaken during the Dimbleby years.' Writing on '*Panorama* in the Sixties', Rowland describes the programme he remembers from that decade: 'The programme was not investigative. Jeremy Isaacs' questions "Does it matter?" and "Did we add anything new?" were, I believe, the basis of our journalism. We rarely asked: "Is there anybody out there who doesn't want this told" – except in our probing of the political debate.' But, says Rowland, '*Panorama* certainly mattered, if comment on world affairs and high quality on-the-spot reporting matters. It added something new often by just "being there" and helping the audience to understand what was happening by offering the perspectives of highly experienced and literate reporters.'[49]

The BBC's brilliant but fatally erratic Derrick Amoore saw the same *Panorama* differently: 'Too often, it seems to me, *Panorama* stories, though indisputably the work of civilised and literate men, tell the similarly literate and civilised nothing they didn't know before.' Amoore was never a *Panorama* person, but in 1968, as Assistant to the Head of Current Affairs, Television, he was well placed to evaluate the programme's strengths and weaknesses. For Amoore it wasn't just that *Panorama* didn't do investigations, but that it didn't question underlying assumptions about what was important and what was not:

> It has tended to be, in the best sense, a 'public affairs' programme, concerned essentially with the area where human activity becomes subject to law and institutions. But it has a built-in leaning to interpret this role too narrowly. There is a natural tendency (reflecting both the personal interests of many of the programme-makers and the fact that this kind of story is easier for *Panorama* to do than others) to restrict the programme's concerns to those issues that become explicit, and can be covered through existing representative bodies. It is in this sense that *Panorama* may damagingly be identified

as a 'political' or 'establishment' programme – not because 'it's always got politicians in it'.

As an example Amoore pointed out that while arguments about the justification of sanctions against rebel Rhodesia[50] had been well aired, it had been a newspaper rather than a television programme which had actually thought radically enough to uncover the large scale sanctions busting that was already going on. *Panorama* people needed to start thinking in a new way, said Amoore:

> After a year of essential consolidation and morale-building the prospect of a complacent rut is distinctly possible: it seems to me that we must now undertake to inject into *Panorama* attitudes to countervail the inclination to question the content, but not the <u>usefulness</u>, of official decisions; and to constitute a unit designed to press research to the depth where the programme itself can take factual positions, as distinct from simply acting as a high-powered vehicle for the often mutually exclusive positions of other authorities.[51]

Amoore suggested a special *Panorama* unit to research stories outside the mainstream of conventional thinking, a unit that would develop its own authoritative position rather than simply arbitrate between existing orthodoxies. It did not materialise. Number 10 Downing Street may have a think tank in one form or another but that is not a concept that the BBC's Current Affairs Group has ever felt entirely comfortable with – let alone able to afford. But the idea that *Panorama* should not necessarily accept the usual rules of the game as the right ones, and should instead decide for itself what are the proper subjects for debate, would return a decade later when Roger Bolton, a man from the awkward squad, took over *Panorama*. Meanwhile the emphasis was on livening up a programme thought to have grown stale and predictable. Once again the BBC reached out to ITV for a new Editor.

Lemon juice for the crew

Phillip Whitehead had previously worked as a *Panorama* producer under Jeremy Isaacs, and he followed him back to Associated-Rediffusion when

Isaacs was so abruptly ousted. In 1968 he had been given the Current Affairs Award by the Guild of Television Producers. Now John Grist asked him to return to Lime Grove to take over *Panorama*. But Whitehead held true to the course Isaacs had tried to steer. He wanted editorial freedom with no veto over what he chose to put in the programme; at least a partial return to the single-subject *Panorama*; and no regular presenter – which meant getting rid of Robin Day. It was particularly on this last point, Julian Critchley reported in *The Times*, that negotiations foundered.[52]

Another ITV candidate was more flexible about the format of the *Panorama* he proposed to edit, and less insistent on seeing the back of Robin Day.

Brian Wenham was often abrupt, and sometimes abrasive. He is notoriously (if apocryphally) remembered for his terse response to a reporter who asked if they could have lunch to discuss his job and future prospects. Wenham is said to have replied, in what became known as a Wenogram – short, pithy little notes of praise or blame: 'No lunch, no job, no future.'

Oxbridge bright, but not brittle, Wenham came to Lime Grove from ITN, which the BBC had always acknowledged as the relatively respectable end of ITV. There, with sensitive political antennae, he had helped give weight and authority to energetic but sometimes rather simple-minded news reporting. Now at *Panorama*, where there was already quite enough intelligence and weight, he planned to inject a bit of ITN's much needed get-up-and-go.

Interviewed for the BBC's Oral Archive, not long before his death, at an early age, he told Frank Gillard: 'I think in 1969[53] *Panorama* was still regarded as the jewel, but it was thought by some to be a slightly tarnished jewel.' And he explained the insoluble dilemma that by now all *Panorama* Editors faced:

> You always knew that if you appeared on a particular Monday when there was a massive event going on, and failed to reflect it, you would probably look very odd. Equally, if you appeared on a Monday and tried to reflect a topical event but actually failed to do it adequately, then it would look even odder. So this is a conflict which is built into the nature of all forms of weekly journalism of a general sort. You can escape the problem by saying 'we will

do weekly politics', or 'we will do weekly business' . . . but if the whole world is your oyster, that is just a problem you have to live with.[54]

And now there was competition not just from other programmes but from a new channel, BBC2. As Wenham was piped aboard *Panorama*, a highly popular American series, *Alias Smith and Jones*, (soon known in Lime Grove as ALAS), was scheduled against the programme, doing serious damage to its audience figures. Said Wenham:

> I thought this was rather a poor do and went to David Attenborough, who was then the Director of Programmes, and said: 'Is it actually the situation you wish to achieve, that your flagship programme of journalism week by week is actually being hammered into the ground by this very good but very popular and slightly meretricious import?' and he said: 'Well, actually, that's the way of the world, and the reason we have two channels', which is a view I came to endorse wholeheartedly when I started to run BBC2 myself.

Faced with these challenges, the *Panorama* audience, as Wenham admitted, 'fell significantly during my stewardship'. Gone were the days of eight, nine or even ten million viewers. 'The worst occasion we had was when I sent off Alan Hart, a reporter, to the Middle East to make a profile of Golda Meir which we transmitted in August,[55] which achieved the abysmally low figure of two million, though it was a very good piece.' Said the *Daily Mirror*: 'Brian Wenham, 33, Oxford graduate formerly with ITN, has been producing *Panorama* for a year and reckons it is now in the shape he wishes. "I want to challenge the audience," he says. "We are not here to indulge ourselves, but I like to do things I think are important and should be done, rather than what some people might think a mass audience might want."'[56]

As Editor of *Panorama*, and subsequently as Head of the Current Affairs Group, Wenham was struggling to keep a traditional *Panorama* afloat. Perhaps his most daring innovation was to get *Panorama*'s running time extended from 50 minutes to an hour.[57] 'The extension to a 60-minute programme will enable the reporters further to develop the variety of topics they handle and the techniques they employ, whether film camera, live or studio.'[58] The idea was to have time for big studio debates and for 'the multi-reporter story, covering major topics from different standpoints and different places, to give the fullest possible picture of what is happening'. Under Wenham's successor Robert Rowland,[59] for example, a *Panorama* programme about the world's food shortages included a film report from France in which a housewife went shopping, another report from the vast acres of the US grain belt, studio interviews with experts, and graphic sequences to show how sea currents had failed to deliver what were apparently vital anchovy shoals to the right places around the globe. (The programme[60] was known within *Panorama* as 'The Great Anchovy Disaster'.) Certainly Nancy Banks-Smith didn't think it had worked:

> I watched *Panorama* for the first time in a couple of months and was shocked to see how stale it now seems . . . One gained almost nothing from seeing *Panorama*. Grain hoppers hoppering away add little to my grasp of the world wheat situation. And there was a plethora of graphics: jolly little farmers and comic housewives and funny Frenchmen and big hands putting pennies in piggy banks. And when they say 'There is a big question mark over the Russian harvest' they mean precisely that. There's Russia, with its very own question mark. As one who is 44 today and feels it, I resent being spoken to as if I were four.[61]

But a current affairs programme that demands close attention for a whole hour is never going to succeed with everybody. In peak time on a Monday evening, *Panorama* could not afford to ignore the size of its audience, as ITV's Weekend World[62] – on Sunday morning – did. While there were good and interesting programmes during the early 1970s, too often subjects were covered at too stately a pace, at inordinate length, at a time when the world was speeding up. People were getting impatient. '*Panorama* feeds us the stuffing' was the headline to Mary Malone's View in the *Daily Mirror*:

> *Panorama* reminds me irresistibly of the geese farmers of Strasbourg. Both believe in forced feeding. It's profitable to our Common Market neighbours producing expensive paté but as a TV treatment it chokes us. Just as the geese honk in protest, there's a crashing of gears in homes throughout the nation as viewers leap across to the opposition. So we're into Europe, and last night *Panorama* (BBC-1) was up to its usual game of stuffing it down our throats.

Michael Charlton in a Brussels bar bought Ted Heath a drink and asked him a lot of boring questions.[63]

Other critics too found *Panorama* 'a drag'. Attacking a programme about the British pub, Pearson Phillips in the *Daily Mail* found in it 'nothing humane. Nothing natural. This is one of *Panorama*'s many present problems. It seems incapable of being familiar and unofficial. It stays on the outside of every problem, quoting Lord Soper and the Consumer Council. It misses out what we people in the communications industry call "ordinary people". It is too wordy. It needs a fresh, intelligent influence.'[64]

Through the first half of the 1970s *Panorama* drifted. Its programmes were varied: sometimes interesting, quite often dull; always thoughtful, but frequently boring; about important issues, but self-important too; usually well-made but distinctly slow and old-fashioned. The programme was, if not dead in the water, certainly torpid, causing scarcely a ripple. It had to sharpen up.

When the Annan Report on the Future of Broadcasting appeared in March 1977 it was distinctly critical of Lime Grove: 'The weakest part of the [BBC] output seemed to us to be the current affairs programmes ... ITV current affairs is more adventurous and interesting ... we agreed that some affliction of feebleness had struck the current affairs output ... We think the BBC has yet to recognise how greatly in need current affairs is of revivification.'[65] But Annan was out of date; that 'revivification' was already well under way.

Playing with paper clips

'Now that most people are back, a few points about *Panorama* content, style and logistics for the new season.'[66] It was the autumn of 1975 and Peter Pagnamenta had become Editor of *Panorama*. It was a new departure.

The *Panorama* pendulum had set the programme ticking with a miscellaneous ragbag of items, and then swung towards a magazine format with four or five different reports. Under Jeremy Isaacs the pendulum had briefly swept right to the other end of the format spectrum and the single subject, before swinging back again to a programme that would frequently include more than one story. That had continued under Editors Brian

Wenham, Robert Rowland and Frank Smith, though the single subject had increasingly re-asserted itself, even with the programme running at 60 minutes. A profile of Sir Alec Douglas-Home on his 70th birthday was an example of this spacious, leisurely style.[67] In Peter Pagnamenta's view *Panorama* had become journalistically lazy, not up to speed with other news and current affairs programmes. Now this was to change, to make a much more brisk and bracing *Panorama*.

Still only 33, Pagnamenta had spent three years as producer in the BBC's New York office. There he had seen the start of the weekly CBS programme *60 Minutes*, and been greatly impressed. It was not that Peter wanted *Panorama* to return to the magazine format that *60 Minutes* had adopted. What he did want was to inject much more pace and energy into the programme, to update what he rightly thought was a rather dusty, old-fashioned style of film-making. Certainly that might mean doing more than one item, but they were other ways in which Pagnamenta wanted to change *Panorama* too.

Whether or not he meant the order to be significant Pagnamenta addressed his opening memo first to producers, then to researchers, and only then to reporters. His concept of *Panorama* meant reducing the role that reporters had so far played. With rare exceptions they would never again take the lead as they had done in the past. In Pagnamenta's view reporters slowed things down too much; there was simply no time in the sort of programmes he wanted to make for star reporters to shine. In the Pagnamenta *Panorama* reporters were for doing interviews and writing the script, not really for using their experience and knowledge to address the viewers, nor even for leading them through a story as a trusted guide – though that is what they did on America's *60 Minutes*. Pagnamenta was not really interested in what his reporters thought about the stories he dispatched them on. Their job was to report sharply, simply and effectively on that aspect of a situation Pagnamenta had decided these shorter reports would cover; and producers would be just as much involved in the journalism as they were.

Peter had brought with him to *Panorama* some very lively people – Tom Mangold, John Penycate, Tom Bower, Tony Summers and Clive Syddall among them. Because he was planning to make two films for most programmes he had no real need to get rid of the reporters he found already on *Panorama*, but some of the old guard posed a problem. Richard Kershaw for example had joined the programme at a time when his expertise – particularly on Africa – was valued. But Pagnamenta had no plans for 'whither Zambia?' programmes, nor did he value personality reporters; so Kershaw went. Julian Pettifer, perhaps the last of the stars, took himself off to ITV where the money was better and he would be given all the scope he wanted to use his personality and reputation to make programmes about the environment, a subject about which he cared deeply.

Then there was Michael Charlton. Though Pagnamenta – as another intellectual – admired him, Charlton simply didn't fit the new brisk, brash, zippy style that Pagnamenta – as *Panorama* Editor – wanted. He was evidently unhappy, chivvied along by impatient young producers, and rarely given the chance to show his understanding of the big issues – like the global battle between East and West. When Charlton secured what viewers found a 'memorable' and 'spine-chilling' interview with Alexander Solzhenitsyn he came into his own.[68] No matter that the great Russian exile got it all wrong, foreseeing the crumbling of a demoralised West before an ever mightier Soviet Union, it was still a marvellous interview, worthy of *Panorama* at any time. But such opportunities for Charlton were rare, and he left, to work increasingly on Radio 3, at the highbrow end of the dial. Other reporters, perhaps more adaptable, perhaps less pontifical, perhaps simply excited by the promise of a more lively *Panorama* under Pagnamenta, happily stayed.

'I hope that *Panorama* film stories will meet all, or some of these, criteria,' wrote Pagnamenta to his crew, in that first memo: 'That they advance a story and tell us something new. That they are focused on an aspect, or a leading question, or a person, or an institution, or a group. That they have a narrative device of some kind, rather than a mere "survey" or "sitrep" formula.' There were great strengths in these guidelines. No longer would a team take off for, let's say, Japan, not really knowing what they wanted to do until they got there; no longer, once they arrived, would they try and cover the whole country, its history, its people and its institutions, in a way that would at best be superficial and at worst entirely spurious. Pagnamenta's films – and they were often his ideas – focused the *Panorama* torch in a much narrower beam on smaller subjects, with the aim of bringing out the telling detail. Reviewers soon noticed the difference. Said Shaun Usher:

> It is not a novel discovery – I'll be inventing the wheel, next – but *Panorama* (BBC1) has improved so much recently that it seems a different programme. Admittedly, some of the studio-bound discussions are sterile and predictable as ever, and could have been mounted at any time in the past ten years or so. Filmed reports, which one thinks of as *Panorama* specials, are in a different class. They are sharp without being jazzy or hysterical, and have no trace of the old philosophy of the series, an implicit belief that the audience owed it grave attention, without making much attempt to earn interest.[69]

Usher was talking about one of Pagnamenta's most successful programmes, 'A Traffic in Babies'.[70] The idea had come to Pagnamenta when he happened to see a transnational adoption going on in the lobby of the hotel where he was staying in India. Made by Tom Mangold and Tom Bower, the film showed how childless couples in the West were adopting – often buying – babies in Korea, Thailand and Bangladesh. It was the first time the phenomenon had been reported so graphically. But though Mangold's commentary touched on the general principle of transnational adoption, his focus was on the individual human examples he and Bower had discovered, rather than the issues raised.

That was the disadvantage of the Pagnamenta *Panorama*. In its admirable determination not to get bogged down in dull debate, it sometimes shrank from tackling the underlying issues as just too boring to deal with. When the real question was whether Margaret Thatcher was out to smash the trade unions or do a deal with their leaders, for example, Pagnamenta instead commissioned a piece entitled 'Trade Union Blues', which focused on the comic aspects of a small band of Conservative trade unionists, overwhelmingly outnumbered by their Labour brothers. It was quite entertaining, even revealing (in a small way), but was it really to the point?

Sending his teams into the field Pagnamenta would describe the exact image he wanted them to get into their film – the Cypriot Archbishop Makarios without his familiar tall stovepipe hat on, for example. Tom Mangold rose to this particular challenge with a simple technique –

blackmail. He persuaded Makarios to allow himself to be seen without his hat by suggesting that otherwise *Panorama* would use pictures they had of him smoking. Often Pagnamenta was clearly trying to get *Panorama* people to see beyond the conventional way of doing the story – and attract a new audience in the process. At other times it seemed more of a private joke.

Fiddling obsessively with a paper clip, Pagnamenta communicated his ideas and instructions in language that sometimes seemed delphic, sometimes simply obscure; and, as producer Clive Syddall recalls, he had a way of sowing dissension in *Panorama*'s ranks: 'When [reporter] Mangold and [producer] Penycate were working together in Los Angeles for example, Pagnamenta would phone Penycate and tell him not to let Mangold slouch about on screen, hands on hips. Then he would phone Mangold to tell him to get Penycate to shoot better sequences. Then the two of them would have a go at each other as if they'd thought of these ideas themselves.' Pagnamenta loved to hear the gossip about rows between producers and reporters on the road. And in the cutting room, in the early hours of a Monday morning, with two films to fit into the programme that night, he would happily pit one exhausted production team against the other as they fought to ensure that they got a longer length for their film. This was not always the best way to treat grown-up people.

What *was* good was Peter Pagnamenta's attention to detail, and his unrelenting determination to make the most of the effort his teams put in. He was probably *Panorama*'s best-ever Editor at anticipating events – not the traditional, predictable *Panorama* fare of American Presidential Elections and Commonwealth Conferences, but the things which most people hadn't yet noticed coming up. He would brief his production teams and have them return weeks later with a story ready to broadcast just at the moment the subject swam into public consciousness. As a later *Panorama* Editor, George Carey, puts it: 'You had to distinguish those ships that were just catching a breeze, and those whose sails you were going to have to blow into yourself.' Pagnamenta was very good indeed at spotting those ships that would be gloriously under full sail on the day of transmission.

And when it came to Monday night, Pagnamenta had devised a striking studio set in which the presenter David Dimbleby walked between large colour blow-ups made from a significant frame in the films which he was introducing. Under Pagnamenta *Panorama* had a vigorous and recognisable style again. Audiences went up.

A real gentleman

It was 1979, and *Panorama*'s next Editor had reached the end of his traditional two-year stint. At a rather emotional dinner party Michael Cockerell found himself called on to make an impromptu speech about the departing Christopher Capron. Unfortunately, a typically cynical remark of John Penycate's came into his head. There were just three kinds of Editor, Cockerell remembered Penycate saying: the tough, the weak, and the pathetically grateful. Cockerell suggested that Capron fell into the last category. It was an unfortunate remark which Cockerell immediately regretted, and for which he apologised in a hand-delivered note early next morning. For while there was a touch of truth in what he had said, it was far from being the whole story about the most courteous and well-mannered Editor *Panorama* people have ever had the pleasure of working for.

Christopher Capron was a genuine gent, a landowner with a modest stately home in Northamptonshire – popularly known as Capron Towers. Despite this (for a television journalist) unpromising background he had made a considerable career in the BBC, and had come to *Panorama* after editing *Tonight*. With his baggy sports jacket– surely there was a pheasant in that pocket? – his appearance was that of a country squire just returned from a walk round the estate with his dogs. His personality was good humoured and avuncular, his manner modest. There were those who said he had a great deal to be modest about, but they underrated his shrewdness in managing the people and the politics of *Panorama*. And they had little to complain of, for under Capron's editorship reporters and producers were given all the latitude they needed to make some of the best and most satisfying prize-winning programmes *Panorama* has ever produced. If Peter Pagnamenta had made *Panorama* less pompous, Capron made it thoroughly enjoyable – for viewers and production team alike. As Michael Cockerell was to write in his letter of apologetic explanation: 'The past two years have been marvellous . . . You created the atmosphere that enabled us to create programmes. And you never yourself took any of the credit for it – you were grateful to us.'[71]

'The idea was then', says Capron, 'that you would end up as Editor of *Panorama* as the summit of your career. But it was clear to me when I arrived that the role *Panorama* played was going to become increasingly difficult.' Capron inherited some formidable, battle-scarred reporters and a relatively small production team. He had little flexibility in the kind of programme he could run. He could not, as he had been able to do on a daily programme like *Tonight*, respond quickly to events – throwing out a planned programme in favour of something more topical. The *Panorama* crew was simply not organised like that, ready to muck in and co-operate. 'There was virtually no team spirit on *Panorama* at all,' says Capron, as shocked as if he had found his village cricket team at odds, 'it was mostly a collection of competing egos. There were no volunteers for the fireman's role of helping out in a crisis.'

Though he at first tried to leave a 10-minute slot for a topical interview at the beginning or end of each 50-minute programme, he rapidly came to the conclusion that this was not an attractive format. His decision was to go for good, well-made news feature stories that ran the full length of the programme. So when individual producers or reporters had an idea that sounded interesting Capron was very ready to accept it. He let producer Tom Bower 'do his own thing', as he puts it, making a series of programmes about the way the British authorities as well as the Germans themselves had allowed Nazi war criminals to escape prosecution, and he commissioned Mangold and Penycate to produce some of their best films, on international terrorism and the way the Cold War between East and West was being fought in the air, on land, and at sea. In 'Arming Apartheid' Bill Cran and David Taylor followed the sanctions-busting trail through the West Indies, filming themselves as they debated how best to take the next step in their investigation. In Rhodesia the author and Robin Denselow were given time to camp out with the ruthless 'Fireforce' brigade as it fought 'the terrs' in defence of white supremacy;[72] and the same team reported from Iran as the Shah fell and Ayatollah Khomeini returned.[73] Michael Cockerell and Philip Harding won an Emmy for their absorbing account of how Georgi Markov[74] had been murdered by the Bulgarian secret police on the streets of London with a poisoned bullet fired from an umbrella, and Christopher Olgiati and Phil Tibbenham got a Golden Nymph at Monte Carlo for their investigation of the secretive rocket company Otrag.[75] *Panorama* people were always keen to fly as far away from Lime Grove as possible, but nonetheless at home there were good programmes about violent football fans, nuclear power, and the crisis in Fleet Street.

All this was greatly helped by the relatively generous way *Panorama* was, for a time, being funded. Head of the Current Affairs Group Brian Wenham regarded *Panorama* as a priority. Thanks to some very creative accounting by the group's Organiser Glynne Price money was diverted from other programmes to ensure that the flagship was unusually well found. Says Capron: 'Those were glorious days. We hardly knew what money meant. We were incredibly lucky. We never seriously worried about money at all.' It wasn't that people working on *Panorama* were particularly well paid – they were certainly worse off than those in comparable jobs in ITV. But programme budgets were not a problem. Looking back, producer Christopher Olgiati says that he never found lack of money an obstacle to thorough research if it was really needed. 'I remember having to make half a dozen trips to Germany before I got access to the Otrag story,' he says. 'Nobody then queried what I was doing, or tried to stop me. Editors should hire and fire but they should let people they think are good get on with it.' Capron did, and got some very entertaining programmes as a result.

But there is no denying these programmes were first of all about things that interested *Panorama* reporters and producers, or gave them opportunities to make good-looking, dramatic films. Often from faraway places, telling exciting stories, these programmes were not normally about the bread and butter issues that were central to the lives of the *Panorama* audience. They were what Chris Capron wanted – news feature stories, what you might find in the glossy review section of a Sunday paper or an 'Insight' piece rather than on the news pages. And there was not much sense that *Panorama* had to deal with its traditional political agenda either. While there might be the occasional Robin Day interview – one with Joe Haines, former Prime Minister Harold Wilson's press secretary, provoked a spectacular row because of Day's alleged rudeness – nobody else was much interested in making programmes that explored important aspects of political debate.

In 1979 for example, when the Labour Government's hopes of hanging on to power were rotting away in piles of uncollected refuse, *Panorama* did not delve particularly deeply to explore the 'winter of discontent'. This was the sort of story Capron felt *Panorama* couldn't cover as well as other, newsier, programmes did; so he didn't often do them. Under Capron it could be said that *Panorama* was nearly always entertaining, often fasci-nating, usually informative, but not always important. It was fun to see Peter and Margaret Jay, sometime television professionals, living it up as the British ambassador and his wife in Washington,[76] but was it really worth it?

It was in 1978, while Capron was Editor, that *Panorama* celebrated its 25th birthday. In an otherwise laudatory review of the anniversary programme, a two-parter on 'The War in Space', David Wheeler – a former Editor himself – did not sound too encouraging about the programme's future: 'Last week, *Panorama* was 25, which in television terms is certainly grand-old-manship, if not outright senility,' he wrote. 'It does not have the commanding status of yesteryear. Its reporters are more professional, but less interesting. Yet it would be a bold Controller of Programmes who tried to slay this dragon.'[77]

Capron, the gentleman Editor, had shown that his courteous and accommodating way with *Panorama* and its individual egos could be very successful. He'd achieved what he set out to do. With a team of reporters and producers who were expert at making good-looking films that drew an audience in to watch, listen and learn, *Panorama* was doing well. Yet it wasn't quite clear exactly what the *Panorama* agenda was – or what ground precisely the programme should be covering.

The next Editor would have no doubt about that.

Onward and upward

It is often the people who want to do the right thing and tell the truth who cause themselves and everyone else the most trouble – just like Ibsen's heroes. Under Roger Bolton as Editor the *Panorama* team – and the senior managers who had to support him – sometimes felt that they were taking part in a bloody, never-ending crusade for the truth. There was Bolton, armoured in righteousness, a King Richard the Lionheart, often falling into the clutches of the enemy, a hostage whom a loyal Lime Grove was expected to ransom to allow him to return home in triumph. There were times when the price seemed high, but most of those who worked for Bolton thought it well worthwhile.

Roger Bolton had first arrived at Lime Grove essentially an innocent, untarnished by the world, an acolyte ready to worship at the altar of public service broadcasting. Growing up in an evangelical family he had watched and admired Malcolm Muggeridge, 'St. Mugg', on television, as he followed 'In the Steps of St. Paul'. Later, when he actually worked with the great man, he was deeply shocked to hear Muggeridge compare himself as a broadcaster to a pianist in a brothel. To Bolton, current affairs television was not just a job but a calling. Those who heard that celestial summons took orders in a new secular priesthood in which they swore to do good by telling the truth.

A Liverpool University graduate, Bolton had never sipped the sophisticated, even cynical spirit of Oxbridge, which many in *Panorama*'s team had downed by the pint. He was direct, enthusiastic, friendly, decent; an Editor with whom it was for most people a pleasure to work. His was a simple but burning faith. He was not Bunyan's Mr. Worldly Wiseman; he would simply tell the truth; and the truth would make everyone free. It was inspiring, but it might have been better if (as he himself recognised) instead of joining the BBC directly he had first lived a little in the City of Destruction – or at least joined, say, a large newspaper group. As he later wrote: 'That way I would have had a crash course in the realities of local newspapers, births, deaths, and marriages, and the limitations and frailties of human nature and human organisation. Instead I moved heart and soul into the BBC and found a new religion committed to the unvarnished truth with a dazzling array of opportunities.'[78]

Bolton had worked as a young producer on *Panorama* in the early 1970s. There, as on *Nationwide* and later on *Tonight*, he had certainly not been insulated from life, but his faith remained constant: to work for a BBC funded by the Licence Fee was to shoulder a responsibility for doing the right thing by the people who watched your programmes.

When in 1979 Roger Bolton became Editor of *Panorama*, he was in a position to put his personal credo into practice. It was the year that Margaret Thatcher defeated a worn-out Labour Party, the year in which political consensus was at an end. Bolton was not himself party political, but he was ready to be radical. He thought that *Panorama*, with its ability to look at important issues in some depth, had to have the courage to set its own agenda rather than always follow the Government's; to look again at what had been accepted as immutable truths and accepted policies, and, if necessary, challenge them: 'It seemed to me that the politicians were not tackling the issues. Consensus had broken down, so we had to tackle them. Nobody else was asking the basic questions. You had the thrill of thinking this was fresh territory. Sometimes we were pious and self-righteous, but I thought I had a contract with the public and that that was the most important thing.'

In an interview with Penny Junor, as he took over *Panorama*, Bolton explained his determination to take a harder look at domestic issues, however difficult that might be:

> If you do a programme on Chile and the United States there is no pressure group to create problems and no-one who's going to be a friend of management. On the other hand there are if you do a programme about British nuclear energy, the TUC, the CBI, British Leyland, or Northern Ireland. So although it is going to be more difficult there are domestic affairs which ought to be looked into – and I don't intend to be dissuaded. I think *Panorama* should lead public debate as opposed to reflecting it. This is one of the limitations of television. We look at issues when they become visual. Take Northern Ireland. They shoot someone and we all rush out, but we don't look at the country before there is an incident or discuss the issues and debate alternative policies.'[79]

Carrickmore – the programme that never was

Well, take Northern Ireland. On this subject Roger Bolton had already caused trouble. As Editor of *Tonight* he had broadcast an interview with a spokesman for the INLA, the Irish nationalist group which in March 1979 had murdered Margaret Thatcher's close associate, the MP Airey Neave, with a car bomb at the House of Commons. Though a poll after the programme showed that four out of five viewers thought the interview should have been shown, many politicians felt there was no case for talking to terrorists on BBC television. Some broadcasters of a generation older than Bolton's felt the same way. Robin Day for example was 'appalled . . . sick with revulsion'. Now, only a few months later, as Bolton took over *Panorama*, Northern Ireland was again headline news. The IRA had chosen the previous Bank Holiday Monday to assassinate Earl Mountbatten. One of his young grandsons and a friend of his had also been killed. And at

Warren Point British soldiers had been blown up and killed by another IRA bomb. Bolton's first *Panorama* as Editor[80] was about cross-border security, a quick reaction piece to the IRA's murderous activities.

But in keeping with his desire to look at the issues involved rather than just react to violence, Bolton wanted to do more than simply respond to these events. On 14 September 1979 he wrote to John Gau, the Head of Current Affairs Programmes, Television, formally proposing a 50-minute *Panorama* to be called 'Inside the IRA'. It would be 'an in-depth look at the political and military development of the IRA in the last few years'.

At the time the BBC was involved in always delicate discussions with the Government about the level at which the Licence Fee should be set in the coming years. Bolton was of course aware of the sensitivities surrounding any coverage of Northern Ireland, but, as he later wrote:

> Down in Lime Grove I didn't think these political considerations had much to do with me. That was the job of management. I was a journalist. I proposed, they disposed. I didn't want the independence and initiative of my team to be stifled by self-censorship, and I had an overwhelming, perhaps obsessive belief in the importance of the Northern Ireland question and the special nature of BBC journalism. We were set up independent of commercial and political pressure, to set standards, to tell the truth.[81]

Bolton had some reason to feel that his was also the official BBC view. Following Airey Neave's murder and the *Tonight* interview with the INLA, the Director General, Ian Trethowan, had attended a News and Current Affairs meeting. There he had made a strong statement saying that the BBC must not be intimidated by the politicians. As the minutes put it:

> There might be those, D.G. believed, who would be moved by concern over the BBC's relationship with the Government and such issues as the Licence Fee to ask whether it was worth risking souring relations for sake of such an interview, however justified the BBC believed it to be. That, he considered to be a dangerous, insidious road to take. It would lead to a conscious or unconscious policy of playing safe which after a time would inevitably bring the realisation that the BBC had shed something of crucial importance.[82]

So Roger Bolton could be forgiven for thinking that all he had to worry about was good journalism. But events were to show that when it came to it, fine sentiments like these turned out not to be worth very much.

The proposed *Panorama* programme on the IRA had from the first been encouraged by Richard (Dick) Francis, a former Controller, Northern Ireland himself and then Director of News and Current Affairs, with a seat on the BBC's Board of Management. James Hawthorne, the contemporary BBC Controller, Northern Ireland, was also told about the proposed *Panorama*. The rules laid down that the Director General himself had to give approval if any member of the IRA, an illegal organisation, was to be interviewed; but Bolton repeatedly said he had no plans to do this, although he did intend to include an interview with an IRA defector – an interview which had already been authorised and completed. The programme was given the go-ahead, and *Panorama* producer David Darlow crossed the water to do the necessary research before filming began.

Although this was not revealed at the time, Darlow now says that during several weeks of research he secretly met Gerry Adams, widely believed to be a senior member of the Provisional IRA, as well as a leading figure in Sinn Fein. Adams agreed to be interviewed: the details were to be arranged later. Darlow says he kept his Editor fully informed; Bolton says that while he had certainly told Darlow to make contact with Sinn Fein he was not specifically told about Adams. Though Adams had not been convicted of IRA membership Bolton says he would have felt it necessary to 'refer up' to higher BBC authority any decision to film an interview with him.

Now reporter Jeremy Paxman arrived to join Darlow, and filming soon began. Bolton says his brief to the team was first to collect material which would explain the history of the IRA up to the point where it split and the Provisionals broke away. They would then meet to decide exactly how to proceed. But on 17 October, while Darlow and Paxman were in the Irish Republic filming the historical part of their story, they got a telephone call at their hotel which, far from being unexpected, as the team claimed at the time, was what Darlow now says was a call he had been hoping for. He was told that 'guides' waiting at their hotel would take them somewhere to see something they would want to film.

Darlow says that what he expected they would find at the end of their journey was Gerry Adams ready to be interviewed. Again, contrary to what the team said later, they were not told their destination, nor even whether it would be in Northern Ireland or in the Republic.

With their 'guides' in their car Darlow and Paxman were now told to drive north across the border. Bolton was not informed. Darlow says he was extremely nervous that their passengers – both well-known IRA contacts – would be recognised and that they would all be arrested. They arrived safely in the village of Carrickmore, but what they found there was a disappointment.

Paxman remembers a group of men in balaclavas coming over the hill armed with mostly elderly weaponry – perhaps an Armalite – and stopping cars: 'This is an IRA road-check – can we see your driving licence?' The team made no attempt to interview the gunmen, many of whom, Darlow recalls, looked little more than teenagers. They were not impressive. The BBC team filmed for 10 minutes or so and then left. It was clearly a publicity stunt designed to show that within a few miles of a British military base, and on United Kingdom soil, the Provisional IRA could, at least temporarily, lay down the law. To that extent it might be an element in their film, but Paxman and Darlow agreed it had been a pretty feeble show of force. Whatever Darlow's hopes of a Gerry Adams interview, it had not transpired.

Heading now for Belfast, the *Panorama* team lost their way in an Irish mist and arrived late; but early next morning Darlow telephoned the BBC programme lawyer, Glenn Del Medico, at home, to tell him what had happened. Then he put Bolton in the picture. Darlow was then himself phoned by the security services and asked to explain what his team had been doing in Carrickmore. He described what had happened there. Not unnaturally perhaps, he said nothing, either to the security forces, or to Del Medico, or to Bolton, about the 'minders' who had led them to Carrickmore, or about his disappointed hopes of a film interview with Gerry Adams. A memo written by someone in *Panorama* after the Carrickmore incident, headed 'Filming To Be Done', puts an interview with Adams top of a list of 13 items.[83]

Jeremy Paxman told Robin Walsh the BBC Editor of News in Northern Ireland, about the Carrickmore incident, and John Gau, Head of the Television Current Affairs Group (who happened to be in Belfast on other BBC business), briefly discussed it with the Northern Ireland Head of

Programmes Cecil Taylor. But *Panorama* Editor Bolton did not directly tell James Hawthorne, the Northern Ireland Controller: with considerable justification he believed Hawthorne must now be fully in the picture. But, for some unknown reason, Hawthorne was not properly briefed by his own subordinates. As a result he was mightily embarrassed by being asked about the incident at a dinner in London, eight days after Carrickmore had occurred, by Northern Ireland Office officials.

When, just before a Cabinet meeting on 8 November, Margaret Thatcher heard about Carrickmore she was furious, and at once sent an angry enquiry to the Chairman of the BBC. The Governors, who also happened to be meeting that morning, were stampeded into issuing a statement which referred to 'what would appear to be a clear breach of standing instructions in relation to filming in Ireland by a *Panorama* team'.

The *Daily Telegraph* accused *Panorama* of 'betraying journalism', saying that: 'If there are journalists in the media who positively want to be martyred in what is falsely described as the cause of "editorial freedom" their wish should be promptly granted.'[84] The *Daily Express* Opinion column, headed 'Close to Treason', said: 'It was as if, during the Second World War, a BBC crew had gone to film the Nazis occupying the Channel Islands.'

The Governors refused to blame Dick Francis, Director of News and Current Affairs, for what had happened: 'At worst he had been too nice to too many people,' said the Chairman, Sir Michael Swann, later.[85] But the Governors clearly did think that somebody's head should roll, and be served up on a platter to Mrs Thatcher. A BBC enquiry conducted by the acting Director General[86] Gerard Mansell led first to Bolton's immediate dismissal as Editor, *Panorama*, and then, after an eruption of anger within the BBC at what looked like the decision of a kangaroo court, to his reinstatement. Eventually there was a fudge. It was accepted that Bolton believed he had done enough to keep BBC Northern Ireland in the picture, acting in good faith in accordance with what he thought was precedent. 'It was possible to say some of the NCA [News and Current Affairs] Minutes left room for different interpretations.' Bolton would therefore not lose his job. However, Mansell 'begged Mr. Bolton to raise his sights when dealing with such problems and to remember the wider interests of the BBC. He should not merely rely on the advice and practice of others. Senior Management did not want to put excessive restraints on programme makers but if the BBC was to be put at risk in any way, those at its head must know about it and be in a position to voice their views in good time, in the overall interests of the BBC as a whole.'[87]

The established church saw to it that John Bunyan, the author of *A Pilgrim's Progress*, went to jail for preaching the Gospel truth. Bolton avoided Bunyan's fate, and narrowly escaped a modern-day martyrdom, largely because of the support he received from the BBC's programme makers. Senior Editors viewed with anger the sight of the Governors saddling up a lynching party under Mrs Thatcher's eye. Rounded up by Christopher Capron, Deputy Head of the Television Current Affairs Group, they jointly declared that 'any severe disciplinary action taken against Bolton would be seen in many important circles as stemming from Government pressure. Rightly or wrongly our editorial independence would seem to be compromised.'[88]

BBC journalists were equally quick to rally to Bolton's cause. The Lime Grove chapel of the National Union of Journalists, never much good at getting improved working conditions for its members, was always ready to respond to demands for a stand on principle. Led by the wily political reporter Vincent Hanna – a leading member of the NUJ who brilliantly represented Bolton at his disciplinary hearing – the chapel voted to bring the world to a halt if *Panorama*'s Editor was victimised simply for trying to tell the truth about Northern Ireland.

Bolton's immediate boss John Gau knew that the proposed programme had been properly 'referred up' the BBC management structure through Dick Francis, the Director, News and Current Affairs, and he was quite sure he knew what all the fuss was really about. 'Deep down, the problem was that this was a political hot potato and the BBC had funked it,' he says. When the row blew up 'the assumption was that the politicians were right and our boys were wrong'.

Gau wrote an impassioned note to the Deputy Managing Director, Television, Robin Scott, with a copy to the Chairman, Sir Michael Swann:

> I joined the BBC in the early-60's that was fiercely independent, journalistically courageous and steadfastly loyal to its staff, especially those under fire. The handling of the Carrickmore incident seems to me to call these

virtues into question . . . The worst aspect of the whole affair is its effect on loyal staff doing a difficult job. Nobody likes filming in Northern Ireland. Indeed Current Affairs is unable to get a BBC film crew to go at all.[89] So to be publicly rebuked by one's masters, to see the facts of the case not being reported and then not to be allowed to defend oneself against distortion and slander, has a shattering effect on morale. It is difficult to see how I shall be able to get anyone in future to go to Northern Ireland, when he sees his colleagues stabbed in the back. Finally there is the question of reporting Northern Ireland and its troubles. Whatever else this furore achieves it will effectively silence proper investigation of the IRA. Indeed there are many who feel that is the reason for a great deal of the clamour. But if the journalistic independence of which the BBC has been justly proud is to mean anything it can only be right that a proper account of how a part of the UK has been in a state of near civil war for 10 years be fully recorded . . . I take complete responsibility for everything done by my staff.[90]

Gau was stalwart in Bolton's defence, and not for the last time. Bolton says he could not have had a better boss. But sometimes Gau seems to have felt he was going in to bat for Bolton without getting much credit for it. 'I fought for *Panorama* long and hard but I always got the sense, perhaps it was led by Roger a bit, that I was not regarded as being on their side.' That must have been galling for Gau. Perhaps the problem was that since Bolton was always confident that he was trying to do the right thing he assumed others would always be happy to support him, and that no compromise on his part could be necessary. 'Here I stand, I can do no other,' he seemed to say.

Bolton was not superhuman; he suffered from all the doubts and misgivings, all the worries and concerns, that any Editor with difficult decisions to make must have. But sometimes his stand on principle seemed just a touch sanctimonious, and then it became a burden to his colleagues. Roger Bolton's cross was one a lot of people had to help carry – and they sometimes did themselves an injury in the process. In the row over Carrickmore both Gau and Bolton were prevented from defending their actions publicly; both were officially reprimanded; both subsequently left the BBC before reaching the heights they might have hoped to attain.

So how far was Bolton justified in bringing trouble on himself – and on those who backed him? With the explicit encouragement of Dick Francis he was surely right to commission a programme that would explore the recent history of the IRA. Mrs Thatcher's argument was that this would only give 'the oxygen of publicity' to terrorists – people who by taking up arms in a democratic society had forfeited the right to have their views expressed. In her opinion, such people should be banned from the box.[91] But Bolton, on the contrary, thought he had a duty to tell BBC licence payers what the IRA was about, rather than simply show them pictures of its atrocities. He was challenging the assumption that on this important issue the Government knew best, that we were safe in its hands, that it was not for the BBC to ask any fundamental questions about policy. And he was right. If Bolton had accepted the Government's view on how Northern Ireland should – or should not – be reported it would ultimately have meant that *Panorama* could never tackle anything that the Government considered out of bounds – nuclear matters, or the security services, for instance.

In the case of Northern Ireland it had become obvious to those in the know that a simple military response could not put an end to terrorism – indeed on a visit to Northern Ireland Bolton had himself been told that by senior Army officers. When the Government simply stonewalled, when it tried to prevent the media making the real situation plain to the public, it was doing a disservice to the country. Good journalism made it easier, not harder, for the Government to explore political rather than purely military solutions in Northern Ireland. Programmes like the one Bolton was attempting in 1979; like the one David Webster's team had made in 1968; like the many more that *Panorama* was to make under future Editors – these would help, not hinder, progress on the path to peace.

On this occasion Bolton's programme was aborted. The film shot at Carrickmore was never shown. The Governors insisted that 'the programme on which Editor, *Panorama* was working when the Carrickmore incident took place must be abandoned. This did not rule out starting again from scratch later on. But a line must be drawn under the events of the past weeks and that meant scrapping the work done so far.'[92]

Whether a more careful, considered approach would have helped get the programme on the air after Carrickmore remains doubtful. Would Mrs Thatcher's rage at learning that *Panorama* had filmed IRA gunmen at large in the United Kingdom really have been any the less if Bolton had made absolutely certain that the Controller, Northern Ireland knew about Carrickmore? No. But if he had, BBC management might have been in a stronger position to influence the BBC Governors' response when the Prime Minister angrily asked them about it.

Then it would have been interesting to see whether the BBC lived up to the fine words Director General Ian Trethowan had used earlier in the year about the duty to pursue its journalism whatever the risks of offending Government. The apparent failure of Dick Francis to speak up loudly at the Board of Management in defence of a *Panorama* project he had himself promoted was not a good sign.

Carrickmore occurred while Trethowan was recovering from a heart attack. His Deputy and acting DG Gerard Mansell came from External Services, where internal discipline prevailed, the Foreign Office subsidised the programmes, and rows with Government (except over money) were rare. He was clearly shocked at the way Editors like Roger Bolton did not feel it right to consider the wider consequences to the Corporation of what they decided their programmes should do. Speaking to the Board of Management in the middle of the Carrickmore row:

> Acting D.G. said that the impression which he had derived from his first profound involvement in Home Services (mainly Television) journalism was that there was a widely held belief among editors at a quite senior level that they need be concerned only with pure journalistic criteria. This belief was held to a dangerous degree ... Acting D.G. added that the experience had also shown him that there was an 'us and them' relationship between Editors, on the one hand, and this Board and the Board of Governors on the other. Meetings would have to be held to put an end to it.[93]

And the Governors took the same view: 'Staff working at Lime Grove were under the impression that they had no corporate editorial ties . . . The Board was aware of a frame of mind in the Television Service which rejected or shrugged off criticism, especially when it came from what some senior television people called "the Regent Street branch". This must change.'[94]

Who's in command?

What are BBC Current Affairs Editors? What should they be? Are they independent captains, sailing away in full command of programmes like *Panorama*, people whose only proper function is to inspire and defend good journalism – and whose only responsibility is to tell the licence payer the truth about the world? Or are they managers, officers in a navy where they must be always obedient to command from Broadcasting House, sent to sort out mutiny and ready to go about without demur if ordered to do so for what their bosses perceive to be the greater good of the Corporation?

There will always be a tension here. But the more Editors assert their independence the more careful they must be to take their senior managers into their confidence, or at least to make sure that no one can claim to be in ignorance of the course they have set. Otherwise they will run upon the rocks, and the programmes they have so bravely set out to make will be lost.

Roger Bolton's very first, rushed, *Panorama* programme had been on cross-border security in Ireland: afterwards he'd apologised to Cecil Taylor, the BBC's Head of Programmes in Northern Ireland, for his 'clanger'[95] in not telling him and Controller James Hawthorne about it before he started filming. All the more reason then that when, in the subsequent and much more considered programme on the IRA the Carrickmore incident occurred, Bolton should have made absolutely certain that Hawthorne was fully informed, even though he had good reason to think that he was. But though his subordinates knew about Carrickmore, Hawthorne didn't. A direct call from Bolton to Hawthorne might have helped the BBC present a united front.

But the Governors were more at fault. Panicked by Margaret Thatcher into an over-hasty condemnation of *Panorama* and its Editor they should have shown more confidence in their staff, and investigated before criticising them so publicly. After all, as journalists, *Panorama*'s reporter, producer and Editor had done nothing wrong – as, later, the

Governors tacitly admitted.[96] The *Panorama* programme had not even been made, let alone transmitted. The only failure had been one of internal communications.

Of course the Governors did have to consider the impact of Carrickmore on the BBC as a whole – particularly on a Government about to set the level of the Licence Fee. In the *Daily Telegraph* Sean Day-Lewis wrote:

> Any day now the matter of the licence fee strategy over the next four years will be put before the Cabinet, and it is very much crossed fingers time at Broadcasting House and Television Centre. As the Board of Governors considered the internal report on the Carrickmore affair last week it must have wondered whether any number of crossed fingers were enough. The Prime Minister having demanded that the BBC 'put its house in order', would anything less than an executive head delivered on a silver platter to Downing Street by Chairman Sir Michael Swann himself ensure a favourable decision on the money issue? . . . many within the BBC will blame *Panorama* for its insensitive timing if the Government fails to order a really substantial licence fee increase.[97]

That was the argument the Director General Ian Trethowan had said earlier in the year had to be resisted: that for the sake of buttering up the Government programmes should be forgotten or deferred. But the Governors had seemed to ignore his brave words. Initially at least they lost their nerve. As John Gau says, it was their instincts that were wrong. In their instant announcement that BBC rules appeared to have been broken they seemed more concerned to placate Mrs Thatcher than to support their journalists. That showed that the gulf between journalists and the BBC senior management that they so deplored was at least as much the Governors' fault as it was the fault of the programme makers at Lime Grove.

Over Carrickmore Roger Bolton was essentially right; his critics essentially wrong. But being right is not always a very attractive trait. If you are confident you are right you've got to be tactful about how you handle things, alert to the impact you are likely to have on those who may disagree with you. Because he wanted to address an agenda that was not always the same as theirs Bolton had a somewhat puritanical approach to the politicians, which was bound to irritate. Like Bunyan's Christian fleeing the City of Destruction he wanted to separate himself from those sinners down at Westminster. 'I felt that politicians and journalists have different jobs to do, and while I respected and liked many MPs I tried to keep my distance from them for that reason. Indeed in my somewhat priggish way I was shocked when Robin Day accepted a knighthood from the Government while still an active broadcaster.'[98] As Bolton himself recognised, this attitude could sometimes lead to a sort of moral snootiness in *Panorama*, a holier-than-thou attitude, a belief that *Panorama* was right and everyone else wrong – even the BBC bosses. Says Alan Protheroe, former Assistant Director General: 'I was very much aware that *Panorama*'s attitude was to form a square and fire outwards before anyone had shot at them.'

Self-discipline

Under Roger Bolton *Panorama*'s reporters and producers were given every encouragement to challenge established institutions – in politics, in medicine, in matters of national security – when it seemed necessary. That was right. But sometimes it could have been done with more care and attention to the likely consequences. Sometimes there was rather too much swashbuckling glee in the way *Panorama* people went about exposing traditional ways of doing things as outdated, unfair, and incompetent – heedless of, indeed welcoming, the outrage caused. Back in 1963 Grace Wyndham Goldie had complained after one *Panorama* that sometimes in Current Affairs there was a sense of 'dogs snapping at the heels' of their quarry: 'I think we have to watch this,' she wrote. Wyndham Goldie was talking about interviews – specifically, as it happens, a Robin Day interview – but under Bolton *Panorama* occasionally let a lively questioning spirit become something too brash, lacking in proper consideration of another, usually older, Establishment point of view.

At Broadcasting House the powers that be were irritated by some *Panorama* reporters who they thought were being allowed to get a bit above themselves. 'D.G. felt that *Panorama* had of late become too polemical,' the minutes of a Board of Management meeting noted in late 1979: 'Richard Lindley had been allowed to go overboard[99] about cuts in public expenditure.'[100] The following July reporter Peter Taylor came under fire:

D.P.A. was severely critical of the edition of 7th. July[101] and of the reporter sent to interview the independent presidential candidate Mr. John Anderson. The reporter's stature in his profession bore no relationship to the interviewee in his . . . In general he found *Panorama* more polemical than he would wish it to be. His guess – and it was no more than a guess – was that there was little editorial guidance or control during the time when a reporter was away on his assignment . . . M.D.Tel said that D.P.A.'s guess was probably justified. He told D.G. that he would give some thought to this problem, which stemmed in part from the Editor's conception of his role.'[102]

On the same day 'M.D.Tel', the Managing Director of Television, Alasdair Milne, wrote to John Gau, Head of Current Affairs: 'I get the feeling that, once again, people find *Panorama* too polemical. Is this fair? Predictably people have drawn attention to Peter Taylor's handling of John Anderson, but there is a worrying loss of confidence. I would welcome a word before I go on holiday at the end of the week.'[103]

Michael Cockerell too came in for criticism after his report from China,[104] not so much for polemical reporting as for being too hard on his interviewees. Gau, in a memo to Bolton headed 'Things', wrote:

Great praise all-round for the China epic – Brian [Wenham] thought it was one of the best films on China he had seen. One reservation, quite generally expressed, and that is Mike Cockerell pushing the Chinese spokesman into a corner, rather than letting the viewer make his own judgement on what he was hearing. It is an age-old problem – is the dramatic effect worth the impression of harassment given. I think there has been a tendency in a number of *Panorama* reports (Tobacco was another)[105] to be a little too aggressive in this area. For instance, Mike Cockerell has a tendency to sound carping. If he could temper his just and appropriate criticisms with a bit of compassion and understanding, he would be a great reporter rather than merely a very good one.[106]

Bolton replied: 'I have talked to Mike already about his slight tendency to carp. We agree to the need to modify it.'[107]

As Bolton himself accepts, the sense of camaraderie and loyalty that existed in Lime Grove, in *Panorama* and other programmes, sometimes looked and sounded to outsiders, and not just the politicians, more like smug arrogance. And a programme proud, if necessary, to stand alone against the world – and its own bosses at Broadcasting House – must expect trouble.

Lessons of war

In January 1981 a more cautious post-Carrickmore Roger Bolton wrote to his reporters and production staff to make that point – and to warn them that if they were going to be righteous seekers after truth then they'd better put on the armour that went with it. Headed '*Panorama*'s Bullet Proof Vests', the memo began:

> According to H.C.A.P. Tel. [John Gau] '*Panorama* is having an excellent season. Its investigative reports are among the best it has ever done. They are certainly some of the finest on television today.' His views are shared by many in TV Centre and outside. However, there are some matters of the style and presentation of our films which we ought to examine because ignoring them involves *Panorama* in needless post-transmission arguments and controversy. They are being seized upon by critics who don't like *Panorama* investigating at all – and being used by them to denigrate the whole programme.

Bolton went on to list three areas where he felt *Panorama* was giving unnecessary cause for hostility. First, he said, 'we must guard against allegations of bias and self-righteousness'. Unless the evidence was clearly set out there was a danger that programmes might seem one-sided. And the tone was important: 'We must be careful that our commentaries don't sound snide and don't load the argument . . . facile jibes are counter-productive.' Next, Bolton said, 'there is a bandwagon beginning to roll that calls into question the fairness of our editing . . . inter-cutting interviews sometimes gives an outsider the impression that we are playing fast and loose with an interviewee's answers. I don't think the small increase in impact and pace by such editing is usually worth the frequent accusations of manipulation and distortion that follow. We must be seen to be above suspicion . . . Finally, and most difficult, how much should a production team reveal in advance about the nature and purpose of a film?' Among Bolton's guidelines: don't lie; be fair; tell contributors as much as you can.

In a conclusion that perhaps showed how much he had learned during his time as Editor of *Panorama* Bolton said: 'I want to impress upon you how very important these matters are. The easiest course is to do less controversial or uncomfortable programmes. That I will never do. But we have to take care of ourselves in an inhospitable climate. Some controversies cannot be avoided, but we need the public to support us, and not have their attention diverted, by argument over presentation, from the content of our programmes. In the future we will be required to be (and should be) more accountable.'[108]

So, to paraphrase, show how you arrive at the conclusion of your film and don't sneer at arguments you don't agree with. Don't cut interviewees so tight that there's a risk of misrepresenting them. And tell contributors as much about the programme you want them to take part in as you can. Good advice for every current affairs programme-maker.

Seven years after Carrickmore Bolton was out of the BBC and Editor of *This Week*, *Panorama*'s ITV rival. He didn't know it then, but he was about to face more angry denunciations from Margaret Thatcher's Government of another of his programmes involving the IRA – 'Death on the Rock'.

But, writing in the *New Statesman* to suggest ways to bridge the gulf that still existed between the programme makers of *Panorama* and the BBC Governors, Bolton seemed altogether wiser than the single-minded man he had been when first he became Editor of *Panorama*. In his article he accepted that while the Governors should be more closely related to those who made the programmes, BBC journalists could not afford arrogantly to stand aloof from the consequences of what they did, dismissing the wider repercussions as unimportant or irrelevant.

Calling for a new Board of Governors, with a full-time Chairman, and with the Director General as chief executive, Bolton conceded that BBC journalists had to change too. As one of its duties, he said, 'the Board needs to ensure that the BBC becomes less arrogant, cultivates politicians without toadying to them, acknowledges that public service broadcasting is not the sole prerogative of the Corporation, is open about mistakes, and generally behaves in a more humble fashion.'[109]

An intelligent and enthusiastic seeker after truth, an inspiring leader, and, by the end of his tenure, a wiser BBC journalist, Bolton was a great *Panorama* Editor. But he was never a Corporation man, and perhaps that was why the BBC let him go.

Calculating the course

Peter Ibbotson was a highly organised, tough-minded Editor, wise in the ways of the BBC, deep in understanding of television politics, a master of the machine. A great fan and protégé of Brian Wenham, he shared his mentor's dry, profoundly sceptical, even cynical, approach to life and work in the Corporation.

By 1984 *Panorama*, and BBC Current Affairs in general, were entering on turbulent times. A panic about BBC1 ratings had, earlier in the year, led to one edition of *Panorama* being moved, and another cancelled altogether, in favour of an American drama series, *The Thorn Birds*: 'one of the most paltry, tawdry, imported soap operas that any TV channel has ever had the contempt to inflict on the viewing public' was how Max Hastings described it in the London *Evening Standard*.

At the Edinburgh Television Festival in August, in a debate on public service television, it was pointed out that *Panorama* was again being given the heave-ho, this time in the week of the TUC Conference, by another American mini-series. While Director General Alasdair Milne sat silent in the audience, furiously fuming, *Panorama*'s new Editor Ibbotson made a brave and very public attack on what he said was the growing marginalisation of Current Affairs, and called for a greater commitment to it from BBC bosses. He was supported by Roger Bolton. But Ibbotson believed that *Panorama* could do things to help itself. He had concluded that the programme should on the whole no longer attempt to do more than one subject at a time. In his view that only invited comparison with longer items in the News – and *Panorama* did not have the resources required to do them as well as News.

In the very week he took over *Panorama*, in the autumn of 1983, Peter Ibbotson encountered this problem. Without so much as a by-your-leave to Britain, the United States had launched an invasion to oust a Marxist military regime which had seized control of a former British possession in the Caribbean, the island of Grenada. With Operation Urgent Fury in progress, television crews began converging on the area, fighting for permission to get ashore on Grenada. Should *Panorama* join them? It was a dilemma for Ibbotson and he hesitated, before finally deciding (on Wednesday) to dispatch a team (on Thursday) who were expected to fill half the programme on the following Monday.

With unscrupulous determination producer David Wickham swept aside all opposition and managed to secure three places on the US military transport planes that, on Sunday, flew the hundreds of journalists waiting on Barbados to Grenada. The author took one place, the cameraman another. In response to desperate pleas from BBC News, which had failed to get its own seat, Wickham gave up his own ticket to ride to news reporter Brian Barron, on the clear understanding that *Panorama* would be the first to use whatever material was obtained. Once on Grenada the author made for Government House and interviewed Sir Paul Scoon, the Governor General, who was extremely cross that the Americans had invaded his territory without any request from him. It made a rather good and exclusive story. Brian Barron then did his own interview with Scoon and a camera piece for the News.

Through the night and following Monday morning the *Panorama* team edited their tapes on equipment set up in their hotel room, back in Barbados. As they hacked away, calls began to come in from London demanding that *Panorama* hand over Barron's material so it could run on the early evening News. This would have upstaged *Panorama*, so, to the fury of BBC bosses Alan Protheroe and Tony Crabb in London, the *Panorama* team said 'no'. With their hotel door now bolted and barred against Barron, Wickham and the author were phoned by Ibbotson. 'I have been ordered to tell you', he said, 'that if you do not hand over the tapes you will be fired. But, of course, I haven't been able to get hold of you, have I? So keep the door locked and don't answer the phone.'

At 2pm Wickham took the edited *Panorama* tape to the local TV station where – after some heart-stopping technical hitches – 'the bird flew', and the team's report went by satellite to Television Centre. So *Panorama*'s material ran first – as had been agreed – and Brian Barron, for once, came second, on the *Nine O'clock News*. The following day's newspapers credited *Panorama* with a mini-scoop.

On the team's return to London Wickham was summoned to see the

Head of Current Affairs, Christopher Capron. 'Did you refuse to hand over this tape?' 'Yes.' 'So you did hold it back for *Panorama*?' 'Yes.' 'Well then [opening a bottle of wine] you should consider yourself very severely admonished.'[110]

It was fun to beat News at their own game, but Peter Ibbotson was convinced that this was just not going to work except on rare occasions. *Panorama* was not set up to be a quick reaction show. It would normally do its job best when it dug deeper, and uncovered more, to give the background to the news, rather than the news itself.

That meant longer reports than anything that the News or *Newsnight* might contemplate. But Ibbotson also believed that 50 minutes, since the mid-1970s *Panorama*'s running time, was just too long for an audience to cope with in a world that now ran ever faster. Most subjects, he was convinced, could be covered more sharply – but still comprehensively – in 40 minutes.

Michael Grade had just taken over as Controller of BBC1; his skill was scheduling programmes so as to ensure that they made the maximum impact. Grade had bluntly told Ibbotson that *Panorama* was tired, and that he wanted to take it out of its present slot (where it got in the way of big audience entertainment programmes), and move it after the *Nine O'clock News*. There, Grade thought, *Panorama* might even attract a bigger audience for itself.

Since he didn't think *Panorama* should any longer try to compete with the News, Ibbotson had no objection to his programme running after it. And he was greatly in favour of what he thought might be a better start time than ten minutes past eight o'clock.

And so it was decided. After a short, and essentially cosmetic, consultation with the *Panorama* team, the programme moved to a 40-minute slot after the News, at 9.25pm. It is Alasdair Milne's view that *Panorama*'s decline dates from that moment. As Director General, he says, he warned Grade against the move. But for a time at least, audiences went up considerably.[111]

The best laid plans . . .

Peter Ibbotson was no eager visionary, no dangerous enthusiast like Roger Bolton, but a cool, calculating Editor carefully weighing programme proposals, considering them from every angle for their likely effect inside and outside the BBC. He would always want to know what was around the corner before he took the risk of sending his teams to go and find out. So it was remarkable that under his management a programme was made that caused *Panorama* more trouble than any other, before or since. The programme concerned was 'Maggie's Militant Tendency'.

In the 1983 General Election Thomas Finnegan was the official Conservative candidate for Stockport South. He had, however, twice previously stood (in a different constituency) for the racist, anti-Semitic National Front; so, during this election campaign, Cabinet minister Keith Joseph (who was Jewish), refused to speak for him. Embarrassed and angry, the Conservative Party was forced to disown its own candidate. At Television Centre on the night the announcement was made, *Panorama*'s Fred Emery was presenting *Election News*, with producer James Hogan. Previously Hogan had worked on *Newsnight* and *Panorama* programmes investigating the far-left group Militant and its 'entryist' tactics, in which Trotskyite Militant supporters had secretly worked their way into membership of the Labour Party in an effort to influence its policies. Now, watching the News, it seemed to him as if something similar might be happening with the Conservatives, and that in the Tory tidal wave that followed Margaret Thatcher's triumphant campaign to recover the Falkland Islands some politicians on the unacceptable far right might be swept in to become Conservative Members of Parliament.

That thought had occurred to some Young Conservatives too. Phil Pedley, their Chairman, began an investigation of the subject, an investigation which had the official approval of the Party hierarchy. When Hogan heard this he felt that *Panorama* and the Young Conservatives could work together on the story to their mutual advantage. *Panorama* would get access to research and useful contacts; Pedley would get publicity for the Young Conservative Report when it was published in early 1984. Hogan's proposal for a *Panorama* programme was agreed by Editor Ibbotson.

Ibbotson was looking for distinctive stories; he wanted investigations – not of dodgy double-glazing salesmen but of big mainstream issues that only *Panorama* had the resources and the clout to tackle. 'Maggie's Militant Tendency' looked to be exactly what he was after – if the story stood up – and a conversation with a senior figure at Conservative Central Office convinced him that it did. 'They were concerned about some of the people on the candidates' list,' he says; 'we duly filmed along the lines of the Young Conservative Report.' Michael Cockerell was assigned as *Panorama*'s reporter on the story.

Cockerell had won a Royal Television Society award for his *Panorama* about the Government and the media during the Falklands war, and was making a considerable reputation as *Panorama*'s main political reporter. He had a sharp eye and a sharper tongue for the detail of political life, its insincerities and hypocrisies, but he was no revolutionary, no lefty Luddite of the political system, let alone of the Conservative Party. Indeed, in his private life he had successively married the granddaughter of a Tory Prime Minister and then, as if that wasn't enough, the niece of a Tory Chancellor who was also the sister of a Tory MP. He had even played cricket for the MCC at Lord's.

Cockerell had been the reporter on *Panorama*'s film about Labour's Militants, 'Are There Cuckoos in the Nest?'. Now, as he began research for this new programme, he was, he says, 'deeply sceptical' of the whole thesis that the Conservative Party was being penetrated in any serious way by people from the far right. Nonetheless he had previously made a programme about the National Front and was well aware that the membership of right-wing but still respectable organisations like the Conservative Party's Monday Club might overlap with the membership of others which were not.

As Cockerell and Hogan, along with their researcher Alex Gerlis, delved deeper into the story, the more serious it all began to look to them. And so it did to the Young Conservatives. 'It is our considered opinion', said their Report, 'that a number of Conservative MPs are too closely connected with the extremist co-ordinating groups.'[112]

On 30 January 1984, two days after Phil Pedley presented the Young Conservative Report to the Party, *Panorama* screened its programme. In the studio, to be interviewed after Cockerell's film, was the man who had received the Report, the new Party Chairman, John Selwyn Gummer.

The film was introduced by presenter Fred Emery as 'a major investigation into extreme right-wing links with the Conservative Party' and it was, by its very nature, essentially a matter of establishing guilt by association, setting out to show that some Conservative MPs were much too close for comfort to the far right. To establish the argument that extreme right-wingers were attempting to enter the Conservative Party, Cockerell began with the case of Don Mudie, a man, he said, who had been leader of the paramilitary group Column 88, had spent 30 years in neo-fascist politics in Britain, and still celebrated Hitler's birthday. Mudie was shown listening to Nazi music with a swastika flag behind him.

So far, so fascist. But the point was that the previous year Mudie had stood as an official Conservative candidate in the local elections in Cleveland. Conceding that the problem of attempted entryism was not on the scale it was in the Labour Party, Cockerell nevertheless insisted that Mudie's case was not unique. A secretive group called Tory Action, said Cockerell, held views which exactly echoed those of the National Front. There were other bodies which acted as a bridge between the Tory Party and the extreme right. The film went on to try to expose those connections.

Quoting from its newsletter, Cockerell established that Tory Action was crudely racist in its attitude to blacks and Jews, and he showed that some Tory MPs had at least some association with the organisation: Harvey Proctor for example had attended its parties and sponsored a reception for Tory Action in the Houses of Parliament. But under commentary making those legitimate points the film had used film of Proctor at a quite different political and social occasion in his Billericay constituency. While it made no difference to the issue of the accuracy of the charge against him, it allowed the programme's critics to suggest that *Panorama*'s evidence was not to be believed. Says Cockerell now: 'I was aware in writing the script that I should have been clearer, but there just wasn't room. It very often happens in television that you are saying facts over picture which is not exactly right. We did not use the power of the pictures to mislead anyone; but we should have labelled it better.'

The film went on to link other Conservative MPs with far right organisations like WISE (Welsh, Irish, Scottish, English) and the Focus Policy Group run by the Nazis' historian, David Irving. In 1972, for example, Neil Hamilton had attended a youth leaders' conference of the Italian neo-fascist party MSI. More recently, in Berlin as part of a Parliamentary delegation, Hamilton and his fellow Tory MP Gerald Howarth were said to have goose-stepped in front of their hotel, and Hamilton to have given a mock Nazi salute, to the outrage and embarrassment of some of their colleagues and their German hosts. The film ended with a demand from a local Conservative Party official, the expert on political extremism Professor Paul Wilkinson, that the MPs named by *Panorama* as consorting with the far right should be kicked out of the Party.

In the interview with Fred Emery that followed, Party Chairman John Gummer agreed that there were some people in the Conservative Party whose extreme right-wing views he rejected, but he gave no commitment to expel anyone.

Gummer appeared to feel that he and the Party had got off relatively lightly. In the *Panorama* Green Room after the programme he was relaxed and not at all upset. Indeed, he remarked, perhaps jokingly, to Emery words to the effect that 'if you'd seen the half of what we've got in our files, you would really have had a programme'. But this *Panorama* followed the programme of less than two years before which had revealed some Tory MPs' doubts about the wisdom of reclaiming the Falkland Islands by force.[113] To many in the Tory Parliamentary Party it seemed to be yet another BBC attack on them. As the Conservative 1922 Committee grew restive, Gummer quickly changed his tune and made an official complaint to the BBC.

Alasdair Milne, the Director General, ordered an enquiry, and studied the evidence on which the programme was based for himself. Summoned to a meeting with John Wakeham, the Chief Whip, at 12 Downing Street, Milne rejected the 38 complaints that Wakeham and Gummer had made, but undertook to look into 'further issues'. When a programme is threatened with legal action additional research is often required for the benefit of the court, but 'Maggie's Militant Tendency' was soon dubbed the most thoroughly researched programme *after* transmission that there had ever been. After further enquiry Milne announced that 'it seems to me that the research is rock-solid',[114] and on 23 February the BBC Governors gave unanimous support to the programme.

Meanwhile some of those named in *Panorama* - including Hamilton and Howarth – had issued writs. Their solicitor was Peter Carter-Ruck, whose very name and reputation were enough to inspire fear. He wrote to the BBC: 'This programme for which you carry editorial responsibility, appears to have used every contrivance and deception and the use of disingenuous juxtaposition for the political purpose of making a denigratory attack upon the Conservative Party.'[115]

In March, the *Daily Mail* weighed in with an article written by Robin Oakley[116] headlined 'Lies, damn lies . . . and *Panorama*'. It listed what it called *Panorama*'s 'dirty tricks': 'Serious distortions in a BBC programme which linked the Conservative Party with racism are revealed in an investigation about the methods of *Panorama*, flagship of BBC current affairs television.'[117] There was now once again a serious rift between the Conservative Party and the BBC, and *Panorama* was again the cause.

It had always been clear that this would be a potentially explosive programme. 'They won't say I'm a grey, boring Editor of *Panorama* after this goes out,' Peter Ibbotson had remarked, and early on he had taken the routine precaution of alerting Margaret Douglas, the Director General's Chief Assistant, to this particular *Panorama* programme coming down the track. Before transmission, the film made by Cockerell and Hogan had been carefully examined. Much later, after it was all over (or appeared to be), Tony Crabb, then the Controller, Corporate News Services, was asked to look at how it had all gone so horribly wrong. He wrote a chronology of the progress of the row over 'Maggie's Militant Tendency', beginning just before transmission:

> The sensitivity of the subject is recognised, and it is viewed two days beforehand by the then H.C.A.P. Tel. (Christopher Capron) C.A. to D.G. (Margaret Douglas) and Glenn Del Medico from the BBC Legal Department, together with the programme Editor (Peter Ibbotson). In 3¾ hours of discussion 42 separate legal points are raised, most important being assurances on witnesses to 'goose-stepping incident' in Berlin, and the status of the organisation 'Tory Action'. On advice, the goose-stepping sequence is dropped from start to middle of programme. After a number of other changes, the programme is approved for transmission.[118]

Still a senior programme lawyer for the BBC, Del Medico today recalls that it was only late on the Friday evening before Monday's transmission that he was first told about the programme. That short notice, he says, was quite normal then, but not the right way to go about dealing with contentious issues. 'Watching the film for the first time,' he says, 'I thought it was a really dangerous programme playing with political fire.' Clearly, since it accused various MPs of being racists and, contrary to assurances they had given the

Party, of being members of far-right organisations, it was actionable. Del Medico remembers that, later, Michael Cockerell had seemed positively to relish the prospect of getting a libel writ, but Cockerell denies that. 'Of course I didn't want to go to court,' he says, 'but I thought I'd got the journalism right, and that if the programme was to be subject to legal scrutiny then it would defend itself.'

Del Medico thought that some of those named would sue, but that the way *Panorama* was relying on a Young Conservative Report had been a good idea. 'The general thrust of my reaction was: "Can you prove it?" My mistake was to accept the assurances I was given that the evidence to support the allegations would be forthcoming.' Del Medico now says that when the *Panorama* team, in response to Milne's demand, produced their evidence after the programme, it was not as strong as he had been led to believe. Nonetheless he agrees that he still advised going on. He felt there was a good chance of 'seeing off' Harvey Proctor and a better than evens chance of doing the same with Hamilton and Howarth. '55 to 45,' he told Milne. 'Christ, as tight as that?' was the DG's response.

Though the BBC Governors may not all have been solidly behind him, on this occasion at least Milne had the support of the BBC Chairman. Stuart Young was a Jew; once assured that the programme was soundly based – 'rock solid' – he was keen to see the BBC stand its ground against any racist tendency in the Conservative Party. In fact the Board of Deputies of British Jews now opened its own files on Conservatives it considered anti-Semitic to help *Panorama* support its programme.

Margaret Douglas, as the Director General's Chief Assistant, was one of those who had seen the film before transmission. In it there was a photograph of Neil Hamilton in some student election in which, as the 'Monarchist' candidate, he was posturing in a costume which the commentary described as 'military uniform'. In his statement for the court case Hamilton said: 'The event was theatrical and was loosely based on the Nuremberg Rallies . . . I was dressed in an ice-cream vendor's jacket.' 'Surely they're only joking?' Del Medico remembers Douglas asking about the sequence. 'We should have paid her more attention,' he now says.

Looking back on it, other people working on *Panorama* at the time say they also felt the programme had made too much of arguably unimportant elements – like the behaviour of some of those who had been in the delegation to Berlin. 'I was shocked when I saw it,' says Philip Harding, then the programme's Deputy Editor. 'I thought they'd mixed up some nasty high jinks with a serious story, and this was overhyped.' Others thought the programme felt too flimsy altogether: 'It was a house of cards,' says one.

Douglas believes she was naïve during that viewing session. Nowadays, she says, people would take more care to get affidavits from the people they interviewed on a story like this. As it was, over the months that followed many of the people from whom the programme team had obtained information fell away. As Peter Carter-Ruck himself says, his firm interviewed no fewer than 60 witnesses, and it later transpired that Conservative Central Office had spoken to several of the BBC's witnesses about their statements. After these conversations some of them decided that they would not after all be willing to repeat in court what they had previously said to the BBC.

Negotiations between the BBC and the MPs who had issued writs dragged on. As well as the formal exchanges between Del Medico and Carter-Ruck, other lines of communication were opened. Fred Emery, the *Panorama* presenter, had an excellent contact at the top of the Conservative Party; Hamilton and Howarth developed a 'back channel' with Alan Protheroe.

As Assistant to the Director General Protheroe was officially in charge of BBC journalism, responsible for its professional standards. But, brushing aside his own codes of practice, he was secretly 'wired' when he set off for his clandestine meetings with Hamilton and Howarth at the Institute of Directors. At Protheroe's request, a radio producer friend of his fitted him out with a small Nagra tape recorder concealed inside his jacket. To start it recording Protheroe had to reach inside as if to scratch his chest. This he managed to do successfully. But during the meeting a repetitive, clicking sort of noise made itself heard: the tape had run out and was revolving uselessly, flapping as it did so. Explaining that this was the sound made by some new kind of pager, Protheroe made his excuses. In the lavatory he managed to switch off the recorder before returning to complete the conversation. Hamilton says he was quite unaware that he was being secretly recorded.

But these meetings went nowhere. BBC management still believed the *Panorama* film had got it essentially right, and – to the last – expected to settle the case out of court. Importantly, the Corporation had got the Gatling gun of money to fight with, while the MPs had not. But that changed when the right-wing multimillionaire James Goldsmith – no friend to the BBC – offered to guarantee counsel's fees with a loan if the MPs still wanted to go to court. They did. So on 13 October 1986 the trial began.

Panorama had done its best to put the charges it was making to the MPs it had named in the programme. Some, like Hamilton, had persistently ducked and dived to avoid having to answer. As the statement made by Christine Hamilton puts it: 'Neil and I had devised a method for making sure that the *Panorama* personnel would not be in a position to say that Neil had refused to speak. This was by denying them an opportunity to speak to him, but I gave them every opportunity to tell me what they wanted.' Hamilton had been unwilling to face *Panorama*'s questions, but he now gave an impressive performance in court as the little man, cruelly libelled by a mighty BBC, his career as a newly elected MP now in jeopardy. 'Neil Hamilton', wrote Carter-Ruck, 'proved to be an excellent witness, forthright, clear, precise, sincere and entirely truthful.'

By 1986 Norman Tebbit had become Chairman of the Conservative Party. Today, as Lord Tebbit, he confirms that in the run-up to the trial he was receiving information about the BBC's legal strategy from a source inside the Corporation. 'The Governors', he says, 'had been assured by the Director General that the BBC's defence was sound. But my source said that the Governors had not been told that their legal advice was not quite so encouraging; it was more on the lines of "on a good day, with a fair wind, and the right judge they had a good prospect of success".' Tebbit now says he suggested to Marmaduke (now Lord) Hussey, the newly appointed BBC Chairman, that the Governors should demand to see the legal advice that had been given to the BBC.

In his memoirs[119] Hussey says he did speak to the BBC's barrister Charles Gray, as the case began: 'I asked Mr. Grey [sic] what our chances were of winning it. "Very unlikely."' 'This is inaccurate,' says Gray – now Sir Charles Gray, a High Court judge. 'Though the BBC's defence was not without difficulty, my junior and I both thought the case was winnable.'

In his opening address Hamilton's and Howarth's barrister Richard Hartley said the BBC *Panorama* team 'had used methods of which Hitler's propaganda minister, Dr Goebbels, would have been proud', and the effect of the first few days of court proceedings on the BBC Governors had been devastating. Before the court had a chance to hear *Panorama*'s defence Hussey ordered Gray to 'settle this case this afternoon for whatever you can manage'.[120] Says Gray: 'I remember being surprised that the Governors should be so naïve and react in such a panicky way to the opening speeches. Our advice was that this was the worst possible time to put out feelers for a settlement.'

And so it proved. At 6.30pm on Thursday 16 October a miserable *Panorama* team – Editor Ibbotson, reporter Cockerell, producer Hogan and presenter Emery – were summoned to Room 222 at Broadcasting House. There they were told by Protheroe that the BBC was abandoning them; that if they chose to fight on at their own risk and expense it would be in the light of the BBC's decision to settle, which would certainly undermine their position. The BBC lawyer Glenn Del Medico, who was also present, was as aghast as the *Panorama* team that the case which former Chairman Stuart Young and the Governors had supported so stoutly was now being so suddenly dropped. It was, he said, 'quite astounding and wholly unacceptable . . . Tebbit has got us now.' If there were any moves to fire the *Panorama* people concerned, said Del Medico, then an industrial tribunal might be the place to ensure that the issues were fully aired.

That weekend the newspaper headlines read: 'BBC libel cave-in'; 'MPs win Hitler libel battle.' By Tuesday the BBC had agreed to pay each MP £20,000, apologise unreservedly, and pay their legal costs and expenses amounting to £240,000.[121] It was an extraordinary humiliation for *Panorama*, and a public vindication of the MPs.

Today, Hogan, Cockerell and Ibbotson still insist that just as it was right to investigate and expose the left-wing militants who had infiltrated the Labour Party, so it was right to investigate and expose far-right sympathisers in the Tory ranks. Neil Hamilton, now no longer an MP, says he finds it hard to understand how the *Panorama* team can still feel 'Maggie's Militant Tendency' was justified.

Phil Pedley, the Young Conservative Chairman, who had featured so importantly in the *Panorama* film, had also been sued by Hamilton and Howarth. But he did not accept defeat, as the BBC did, and the two MPs dropped their libel case against him. 'Tebbit didn't tell us to settle,' says Hamilton; 'there was just no point in going on with Pedley: he wouldn't have been able to pay our costs.' As it was, they were ordered to pay some of his. But that was no comfort to *Panorama*.

In retrospect 'Maggie's Militant Tendency' was the beginning of the end of *Panorama*'s power – its power to do what its Editor wanted. Its pride was humbled by the court case and the verdict against it. Partly because of that debacle, the Director General was soon to lose his job. A new Chairman had been appointed - told to get BBC journalists under control. And, shortly afterwards, John Birt arrived to do the business.

Once that had happened *Panorama* would never again have an Editor able, like some buccaneering Errol Flynn, to set sail on a course he alone had chosen, out of all control. In future, Editors would be 'cabined, cribbed, confined' by new procedures – 'process', John Birt called it – and by the consciousness that they had better not make waves without prior approval from the top.

As with the *Titanic* struck by an iceberg, the scale of the damage that 'Maggie's Militant Tendency' had done to *Panorama* was not at first obvious. The engines still worked; the ship sailed on. It was not apparent to the crew for some time that, back at the Admiralty, in Broadcasting House, decisions were being taken which would shortly affect all aboard the flagship, with the reporters most in danger.

Targeting reporters

He had been publicly supportive of 'Maggie's Militant Tendency', but on 27 March 1984 Director General Alasdair Milne had tossed a damaging letter bomb on to the Lime Grove desk of Chris Capron, Head of Current Affairs Programmes. It was headed 'A Certain Unease About Lime Grove.' 'What troubles me', wrote Milne, ' . . . is who is actually producing these programmes. It seems to me that *Panorama* in particular is run by the reporters, and I think it is high time that the editor and the production team reverse the balance. I would like an assurance from you, therefore, that I am either wrong, or that some urgent action will be taken to put things in their proper perspective.'[122] Alarmed, Capron replied:

I assure you that you are absolutely wrong in your suspicion that reporters are running *Panorama* or any other Lime Grove programme. The only partial exception to this is Esther Rantzen who is billed, paid and contracted to be Producer as well as presenter of *That's Life*. Nonetheless it is the Editor, Gordon Watts, and not Esther, who runs the programme and is answerable to me for it. What is undoubtedly true of *Panorama* is that with its present brief (set out clearly in the post-Oakley Court paper to the Governors and never questioned since) to be primarily a reporting programme it now has some of our most experienced reporters. With the longer lead time available for the production of most reports for *Panorama* than for most other Current Affairs programmes, clearly the reporters' input into their preparation, content and eventual shape is greater than elsewhere. So it ought to be and were it not so I would speedily remove (indeed have done so) the reporter in question from the programme. But that is quite different from allowing them to run the programme. They don't, as any fly on the wall of Smith's Yard cutting rooms on almost any Sunday would readily confirm to you.[123]

Obviously badly cut up by Milne's little bombshell Capron continued in a wounded tone: 'It was disconcerting to receive a memo from you headed "A Certain Unease About Lime Grove" because I like to think that the last two years have constituted one of the most successful periods this Department has ever enjoyed. Our programmes have won (see attached) far more awards than in any comparable period.'

Squally clouds were now thickening on the horizon. The halcyon days of fine sailing weather were coming to an end. To be thoroughly anachronistic, had Bette Davis been aboard she would have warned the crew to 'fasten your seat belts; it's going to be a bumpy night'.[124]

All at sea

Between the broadcast of 'Maggie's Militant Tendency' and the court case about it two and a half years later, a new captain had come aboard *Panorama*. 'Without a doubt', says Paul Woolwich, 'he was the best Editor of his generation.'

David Dickinson was certainly smart, with a D.Phil from Yale to prove it; and there was no doubt that he had an instinctive flair for what would make a good, intelligent *Panorama*. But Dickinson was also mercurial and sometimes distracted – 'Peter the Pan', as one of his senior producers dubbed him. He was not always there when the team had need of him. His was not a reassuringly steady presence on board.

As a highly successful Editor of *Newsnight*, Dickinson had not been at all sure that he wanted to run the venerable *Panorama*. The flagship's creaking timbers, he felt, were always in need of attention: 'Over the course of its life it gets more and more weighed down by its history, encrusted by barnacles on its bottom. It has constantly to be reinvented, and that's even harder to do now than it was in the eighties. *Panorama* is the most difficult programme to do. If you had, say, five shots in your locker for a magazine programme like *Newsnight* it was OK as long as three of them worked. In each *Panorama* you had just one shot – it was hit or miss.' It was impossible, Dickinson says, to do 40 consecutive winners in the *Panorama* season. 'It can't be done, any more than it can be done on a newspaper. And because it was so high-profile you felt you were laying yourself and your team on the line every Monday. The pressure was enormous.'

Dickinson did not always show grace under that pressure, telling a group of the more elderly reporters at a *Panorama* party that he was out to cut them down to size. Today he puts it more soberly: 'People don't watch *Panorama* for the reporters. They're watching the brand, not the reporters' brand. The visibility of reporters goes in and out of fashion in current affairs. Reporters have to have credibility, but there was too much of the old guard on *Panorama*. A lot of people on the show had been there too long. If you wanted to make the programme fresher you needed to get new blood.'

Dickinson clearly regarded some of the reporters who had been working on the programme for some time as 'the barnacles' on the bottom of the *Panorama* boat which needed scraping off as soon as possible. In a memo addressed to the Head of Current Affairs, Peter Pagnamenta, Dickinson said: 'I would like, as you know, to be shot of three of the more senior reporters.' After explaining what was wrong with them – 'in danger of becoming wet . . . reluctant to spell out his story in plain language' – he added: 'The only definite replacement I would put my name down for at the moment would be John Ware, the fellow from *World in Action*, who will be coming to see you soon.'[125] Whatever the worth of his judgements about his existing reporters, one of Dickinson's real contributions to *Panorama* was to get Ware to join the team. Today, 15 years later, Ware is certainly himself now one of the 'old guard', but there are few who would say that he has been on *Panorama* too long.

With Dickinson as Editor *Panorama* made some good programmes. There was an excellent report from South Africa, made under difficult conditions by producer Mike Dutfield. 'Comrades' examined the intolerable pressures building up in the black townships and the way young militants were imposing savage 'people's court' justice on blacks who co-operated in any way with the whites who were oppressing them. 'It sounded', said Richard Last, 'grimly reminiscent of the French Terror; the feeling that a dam must soon burst was overwhelming.'[126]

Dickinson's own favourite was 'The Siege of Paris', a dramatic examination of what was behind a spate of terrorist bombings in France. Some found it too dramatic, too full of impressionistic reconstructions and music, 'this merger of commonplace images with menacing effects', as Robin Buss described it in the *Times Educational Supplement*. 'Heavy on drama and short on analysis, it amounted to no more than a cheap political thriller,' he concluded loftily. Others felt that reporter Gavin Hewitt and producer Chris Oxley had used these thriller techniques in a highly effective way to explain a complicated story of how the French Government, though talking tough, was actually doing deals with terrorists to buy them off.

But somehow, with a flicker of lightning on the horizon, *Panorama* seemed unsure of itself and where it was going. What would the future hold? Was that thunder they heard? Was there a real storm on the way? As Editor, Dickinson did not always seem to giving the programme his full attention. Some of *Panorama*'s best producers, such as Oxley and Dutfield, left. And then something unprecedented happened: a *Panorama* programme was not ready in time and, at the very last minute, was dropped.

Losing its bearings

Reporter Michael Cockerell and producer Jana Bennett had been in America investigating what they called 'The Private Wars of Colonel North', the illegal American arming of the Nicaraguan Contra rebels, and the arms-for-hostages deals with Iran. Because so much of the library videotape footage was recorded on the American NTSC rather than the European PAL technical system it seemed to make sense to edit the programme in the United States. But a snowstorm on the east coast delayed the team's flight from Costa Rica to New York, and the edit got under way very late, not till the middle of the week before Monday's transmission.

David Dickinson flew to America to be ready to approve a programme that was obviously only going to be completed at the last minute. But once there he concluded that it wasn't going to work; editing was going too slowly. On Friday, Dickinson phoned his senior *Panorama* colleagues Paul Woolwich and Deputy Editor Michael Hogan and told them he had decided that they would have to bring everything back to London if they were to get the programme on air. At least at Lime Grove they could call on more than one cutting room. Woolwich and Hogan tried to dissuade him, but they were unsuccessful.

The flight back to London lost not only precious hours' editing time, but the whole momentum of the edit. Day and night that weekend three Lime Grove cutting rooms were now at work on this complicated film. On the afternoon of Monday 2 February they began dubbing to a script that was still being polished as they went along. As transmission time drew closer Dickinson went over to Television Centre, where the programme would be transmitted, while Hogan stayed behind in Lime Grove to oversee the final dub. According to Hogan, Cockerell and Bennett the film was finished in time for transmission. 'There was a physical product,' recalls Hogan. 'There wasn't time for it to be reviewed, but I would have run it.'

Dickinson does not agree that the film was ready. Dramatically – bravely, perhaps – he decided to run a standby programme, an old *Panorama*, instead. In the Lime Grove Club Hogan, Bennett and Cockerell ordered a morose drink. There was 'a sense of loss'.

This unprecedented failure to get a heavily advertised programme on air came at a time of turmoil in the BBC. Alasdair Milne, the Director General, had been abruptly sacked by the new Chairman, Marmaduke Hussey, on 29 January 1987. 'Milne quits BBC in crisis of confidence' was *The Times*'s headline next day. Now, just four days later, *Panorama* had failed to get its act together.

At the weekly Programme Review Peter Pagnamenta, Head of Current Affairs Programmes, Television, admitted that 'never before had *Panorama* failed to have the programme ready for transmission . . . M.D.Tel [Bill Cotton] noted there had been fifty calls to [the] duty office suspecting government intervention. Against the background of the events of the previous days it had looked as if the place was falling apart.'[127] By the time the Board of Management considered the matter Cotton had clearly decided where the blame should fall: 'The programme team had returned to London from the United States on the morning of transmission day with material recorded to different technical standards and had underestimated the work that needed to be done to put the programme together. M.D.Tel said the team had not told anyone of their difficulties until a very late hour. Replying to M.D.X.B.[Managing Director External Broadcasting] he said there had indeed been an editorial decision to assemble the programme on return to London but the team had not appreciated the problems this raised.'[128] This exonerated Editor David Dickinson, but was unfair to Cockerell and Bennett. No wonder these Minutes are always marked 'CONFIDENTIAL'.

Three weeks later on 23 February, the 'Irangate' programme finally went out to general applause. Later it won the Golden Nymph award at Monte Carlo as the year's best current affairs television programme. But its failure to 'make the gate', to get on air first time round, seemed specially significant. As the Managing Director, Television had suggested, it made things look 'as if the place was falling apart', and *Panorama* with it. Under Dickinson *Panorama* was showing physical signs of cracking up. As John Birt began to get a grip of BBC journalism and Dickinson prepared to step down as *Panorama*'s Editor the flagship was losing way, its crew at a loss as to what they would now be required to do.

'Something is rotten in the state of *Panorama*,' said the London *Evening Standard* in the summer of 1987. 'No one knows for sure if it has failed, as reported, to produce material for its first two programmes in September, or whether there is simply some deliberate reshuffling going on which has put the programme back a week or two. Whatever; there is deep pessimism about the quality of the forthcoming series.'[129] That deep pessimism was understandable. Year Zero was now at hand.

Led by John Birt, the black-Armani-suited revolutionaries from London Weekend Television were moving in to occupy the seats of power at Broadcasting House and Lime Grove, ready to impose on a demoralised

Current Affairs their own theories of how television journalism should be done. It would be some time before *Panorama* people started enjoying life again.

That difficult period deserves a later chapter of its own.

chapter ten

⊕ The Panorama style

The women

Panorama had been given the go-ahead by a woman, Mary Adams, Head of Talks, Television. Under another, Grace Wyndham Goldie, the programme had become important. But for all that, *Panorama* remained for the most part a deeply male preserve in which masculine beasts of the jungle prowled and postured while a few self-effacing female secretaries and willing researchers indulged their roars and growls.

This is not of course surprising. Women with the education, experience and powerful ambition of a Woodrow Wyatt or Robin Day were then scarce in any field, and just as rare in journalism or the new world of television broadcasting. But in any case there seems to have been precious little effort made to find them. In the early *Panorama* days the programme gave the established author Marghanita Laski a spot as one of the programme's regular arts critics, but not until 1958, three years after *Panorama* turned to current affairs, was there any serious attempt to find a woman reporter. Then, in the course of an interview with the London *Evening News*, the programme's Producer, Rex Moorfoot, revealed that he was looking for one. '*Panorama* has job for a woman' ran the headline. Moorfoot explained that in a few weeks' time he would once again be holding regular auditions for reporters of both sexes: 'They are tele-recorded and we look at them again. They have to be held on Mondays as that is our studio day. The trouble is of course that TV commentators are few and far between. But we have found two in this way who are first class – Robert Kee and James Morris. We are looking for a woman commentator, but so far have failed to find one. We are conscious of women's appeal in the programme, and we are sometimes criticised – for example last Monday we didn't have a single woman's face in the programme.'[1]

The wonderful irony here of course was that, without knowing it, Moorfoot had already found his woman. As a man, James Morris made a number of reports for *Panorama*, most notably from Japan and from Venice, the city he was to write so brilliantly about. But, then, after leaving the programme to become a full-time writer, James Morris changed his sexual orientation to become Jan, a woman. If only he'd stayed, *Panorama* would have had the woman reporter it did not acquire until decades later.

As it was, Moorfoot's efforts to find a woman reporter were only partially successful. Following the *Evening News* article plenty wrote in, but mostly their experience and talents didn't seem quite right. 'I hear you are about to audition for a team of women interviewers for *Panorama*,' wrote the theatrical agent Moss Murray, suggesting an actress called Anthea Sherwood. Another actress, Maureen Prior, wrote to Richard Dimbleby: 'I do know there is a strong feeling of antagonism to women interviewers and even more to actresses becoming same.' Secretaries applied, and men proposed their wives; about his, Edward Joffe wrote: 'She is a competent actress and a talented coloratura soprano who sings pop with equal verve. In addition she plays the piano, the accordion and the Univox. She was also a runner well-up in the Miss South Africa competition in 1956.'[2] Clearly Mr Joffe hadn't been watching recent *Panorama*s much. It was difficult to see how his wife's musical talents could have been successfully deployed while she reported on current affairs from Suez or Siam.

One woman did get through – through sheer persistence, it seems from the *Panorama* files – and because she was already a broadcaster. Nan Winton had worked with Peter Haigh, a pre-*Panorama* television person-ality, on *Information Desk*, a viewers' questions programme, and had met Leonard Miall while acting as BBC hostess at the Radio Show. He suggested she wrote to Moorfoot, but nothing came of it until she put up some stories herself – the declining quality of bread, and the resistance to new fashions in the north of the country – which she was commissioned to do. These reports led to others – on mental illness, on health foods, on cosmetics for men – but it was not long before, in June 1960, Winton got a job as a BBC newscaster that took her away from *Panorama*.

This is always a temptation for women in television. Newscasting has its own hazards and difficulties. But it is on the whole nice work if you can get it; better paid than reporting, a job with regular hours that allows you to plan your life; an assignment where you don't get all horridly hot and sweaty in some foreign part. Most men don't get offered this studio-based job until they've seen some service and look a little travel-worn. Television managers – and, it seems, the public – like their women newscasters with the bloom of youth and innocence still on them. Who can blame women for seizing an offer to stop reporting the world and start reading other people's reports about it instead?

Like women reporters, women producers were rare on *Panorama*, but not quite so unusual. Catherine Freeman came first. In 1954, following a six-month television producers' training course, Catherine Dove – as she was then – was seconded to Talks, Television. There she worked on programmes connected with the arts. Until then, she says, she had been rather dilettantish in her approach to life; everything was 'rather interesting, rather amusing'. It was really a continuation of the Oxford undergraduate existence that she had only just left behind. But now she began to take life more seriously. Wyndham Goldie, on the prowl for television talent, had recruited her for the 1955 General Election results programme, where she worked with Michael Peacock, shortly to take over *Panorama* as its new Producer. Freeman decided that she wanted to get into the studio and become a director. And she did – for *Panorama*.

It was all very new, she recalls; television was just beginning to move out of the very genteel into something altogether more vital. By and large Freeman produced the arts items for a programme that was still not wholly dedicated to current affairs. In September she invited Sandy Wilson, the author of *The Boy Friend*, to take part in the first of the new *Panorama*s; in December she was organising a five-minute 'Theatre Flash' from *The Remarkable Mr. Pennypacker* at the New Theatre, and planning to bring ballet dancers into the studio for a 25th birthday tribute to Sadlers' Wells.

The following year Freeman was producer on a Spanish expedition that caused nervousness at Lime Grove. The idea was to do a nice little feature on the sherry festival in Jerez, to take advantage of the fact that Richard Dimbleby was already going to report from Gibraltar, not far away. The attraction of the scheme was that the Spanish sherry producers – mindful of their market in Britain – were ready to pay for the *Panorama* crew's flights. In June Peacock had been congratulated by the Talks Organiser on his 'careful budgeting' – but the poor but high-minded BBC knew that this Spanish freebie was too dodgy a deal. Instead, a formula was devised which looked more defensible – though it came to much the same thing. *Panorama* would pay the fares but the crew's expenses in Jerez would be picked up by the sherry houses. Wyndham Goldie cautiously agreed: 'provided (a) the team sent was a highly responsible one [and] (b) there were no strings attached, i.e. no advertising in return for the hospitality.'[3] Obviously Freeman was regarded as being 'highly responsible'. When the item eventually ran in *Panorama* – men trod the grapes and explained the production process – Dimbleby's script ran: 'Let's go away from the garden of the consulate here and out on to a vineyard a few kilometres outside Jerez where they've just begun to pick the grapes from this year's harvest. (ACTUALITY – guitar music.) Perhaps the best-known families in the world of sherry are those of Sandeman and Williams & Humbert and Gonzalez Byass and Domecq. But there are many other firms.'

As the producer, Freeman had enjoyed the trip – but for one incident. Her crew, Peter Hamilton and Robin Green, had warned her that she should beware the Spanish men, however gallantly they might be behaving towards her during filming. She had scorned their warnings as chauvinist xenophobia – and was furious to find herself fiercely fighting off some unwelcome attention from the mayor of Jerez at the door of her hotel room that night, just as the crew had predicted.

Freeman produced some remarkable *Panorama* stories – including the notorious interview with Brendan Behan, the natural childbirth item that caused so much offence, and what was probably the first *Panorama* report about assaults on children; but her real passion remained the arts: her proudest moment was luring the poet T.S. Eliot into the Lime Grove studio. But the arts and feature items were being squeezed out of the new *Panorama*. When Cecil Madden, Assistant to the Controller of

Programmes, Television, tried to get Peacock to take an excerpt from *The Good Woman of Setzuan*, with Peggy Ashcroft, *Panorama*'s producer wrote back: 'No, I do not want to restart "Theatre Flashes" in *Panorama*.'[4] That was the end of them.

So as *Panorama* became increasingly devoted to current affairs Catherine Freeman was, by the end of 1957, ready to move on. She'd been encouraged by Wyndham Goldie to think she would be in charge of a new arts series, which she had herself suggested. But it was not to be. Instead of Freeman, it was her presenter, the charismatic and ambitious Huw Wheldon, who stepped in to take control of *Monitor*.

By 1958 *Panorama*'s first woman producer had left the BBC altogether, later to make a most distinguished career for herself in ITV.

It was Peacock, on his second time around at *Panorama*, who recruited the next *Panorama* woman producer, Revel Guest, in 1960. Guest was writing a column about the United States for the Westminster Press when she met Peacock and Miall at the Democratic Convention in Los Angeles, and accepted their invitation to join the programme. She was 31, and would work on *Panorama*, initially as a researcher, for the next seven or eight years.

Guest remembers that, to begin with, lots of what she thought good ideas were turned down. It took her a good six months to understand what *Panorama* wanted. It was a tough place where nobody felt the need to be nice about the efforts of others. Guest had strong views and spoke her mind. 'That's what they liked,' she says, 'they suffered me, rather.' And she discovered that Wyndham Goldie too responded well to people who wouldn't let themselves be frightened of her. *Panorama*, she found, was 'unutterably exhausting; the pressure you were under was huge. There was always money available for programmes if you needed it, but you had to fight for it. Access in those days was unbelievable. For example, when I was doing a profile of 'Rab' Butler [the Conservative cabinet minister and presumptive Party leader] he rang me up himself. The power one had was ridiculous.'

Guest was an unusual *Panorama* producer; not just a woman but one with strong Conservative views. But though she put herself forward – unsuccessfully – 26 times as a prospective parliamentary candidate, she maintains that this had no effect on how she was treated as a *Panorama* person. 'No interviewee ever queried what I was doing or what my political views were. *Panorama* was a very unusual group of people – we were seen to be responsible people. Party politics were not important. What we were doing was righting wrongs.' Guest felt that *Panorama* in the early 1960s had the clout to make things happen: 'At *Panorama* in my tiny way I did make things change.' She recalls a story about sick children that helped make it easier for mothers to stay with them in hospital, and a report on Liverpool docks that led to changes in the dockers' casual labour system. She always felt free, she says, to do and say what she liked as long as she got it right: 'There might be room for a bad story, but not for inaccuracy.' At the time, *Panorama* was always in the paper the day after transmission: 'You'd better be bloody right,' said Peacock.

On *Panorama* Revel Guest remembers traditional documentary film-making techniques being swept aside by the brisk new challenge of current affairs. 'Those were the days when you couldn't see anyone inside anywhere until you had seen them outside. You had to do all the intervening shots to get them from the exterior location to the interior one.'

Until then virtually everything had been shot with the camera rooted to the spot on a tripod – quite unnecessary with the new and lighter 16mm cameras that had by now arrived to replace the massive 35mm Mitchells. Looking at hand-held material of James Baldwin that Revel's American cameraman Albie Maysles had shot in Harlem, in New York, Editor Paul Fox was taken aback at the way it moved freely around its subject, with wobbles along the way. Yet soon they'd be doing the same thing in Britain, taking the camera off the tripod to run after a villain in the Rachman film that Guest made with Michael Barratt.

After her experience on *Panorama*, Revel Guest was one of the first to set up an independent production company to make programmes for television – and with her company Transatlantic Films she's still doing it. 'As *Panorama* people', she says, 'we were very lucky. We had the resources, we had the money and we had the power. I think we were sometimes resented by others in the BBC: we were a privileged lot.'

When Barbara Pegna found her way on to *Panorama* there was no researcher on the programme at all. So she seized the role for herself: 'I was an intellectual lightweight. Everyone assumed I had been to university, though I had not. But I was almost the only girl around; I was married; it was simply divine.' Pegna was clearly star-struck by *Panorama*'s reporters: Richard Kershaw, 'like an out-of-control Labrador; *so* beautiful'; John Morgan, 'a sort of chain-smoking Dylan Thomas, with a shock of woolly hair and bitten-down nails, who liked a couple of jars in the BBC Club'; Michael Charlton, 'intense and amusing, with an acerbic Australian wit'; and Jim Mossman, 'the most professional and amazing bloke I met; a wonderful conversationalist who had the most marvellous taste and fell agonisingly in love with a most unsuitable man.' For Barbara Pegna, *Panorama* in the 1960s was 'the most exciting place in the world. What a heady atmosphere!'

Working with *Panorama*'s distinguished reporters kept Pegna happily excited. Camera crews she found a different matter. Only Nat Crosby, as she remembers it, treated her kindly; the others resented her attempts to produce and direct. Pegna found she most enjoyed working in the cutting room, putting together stories sent back by the reporters in the field. In 1966 she was in charge of *Panorama*'s Review of the Year – fighting over every story against the lethargy of the BBC Film Library at Ealing. As she wrote in exasperated tones to the Assistant Head of the Current Affairs Group: 'It was only with the greatest difficulty that we finally obtained film we knew existed. We waited for over a month for two vital stories from Ireland despite the fact that we phoned the department every day to chase it.'[5]

The practical problems of getting the BBC bureaucracy to respond as quickly as a current affairs programme required did not spoil the excitement of working on *Panorama*. Yet Pegna felt the exhilaration of still being at the forefront of television journalism could not long continue: 'We felt we were the cat's whiskers; it was like being members of a smart club. But that wasn't going to last, because other members were being admitted.' The future looked more ordinary, and so, Pegna thinks, it has proved: 'We were doing ground-breaking stuff; there is no ground to be broken now.' Pegna was talking about *Panorama*s that tackled new subjects in new ways. But she and the few women before her were also busy breaking though that glass ceiling that had prevented many of them from being promoted to positions of influence and authority in the *Panorama* crew. Soon the women positively swarmed aboard the flagship.

In the 1970s a girl with a stutter could be seen restlessly roaming the little *Panorama* offices or sitting in a corner on the floor nervously chewing a strand of her straight blonde hair. At programme meetings a loud, intellectually self-confident, even arrogant little burst of words would tail off into a self-conscious silence. This was Anne Tyerman. As *Panorama* Editor, Brian Wenham had told her he did not believe in having women on the programme, but he sensibly hired her nonetheless. He and succeeding Editors exploited her ruthlessly. Though Tyerman was only paid as a researcher she was frequently dispatched, often to America, which she grew to know very well, to set up the story before producer and reporter deigned to follow. Often given a very wide brief indeed, she was frequently, in effect, deciding the content of the programme herself.

Tyerman grew expert and highly professional at making films for television current affairs. There were few drawbacks to letting her loose abroad, but when she was sent to set up a story in Australia, with vast distances to be covered, it did not prove cost-effective; since she was too nervous to learn to drive, her taxi bill in the course of her research deeply dented the budget. But her fast, clear brain and organisational powers were the basis for many a film that won plaudits for its male reporter and producer, and she was quite happy about that. Says Anne Tyerman today:

> At Lime Grove people were not cynical about the job they were doing. They were often horrible to each other, but they believed in the project. It was consciously and happily élitist. We had a good life and socialised together – there was no sense of resentment. I travelled the world; it was a privilege to do that. I thought the programme was influential and that I was there to try and change people's lives. This was a really important thing to do, a huge responsibility to the public. Nothing has happened to me to make me change that view. I didn't want to leave *Panorama* – even though that was the only way to get promoted in Lime Grove.

At the end of the 1970s Tyerman followed Editor Peter Pagnamenta to Thames Television to work on *Panorama*'s rival programme *This Week*. When she later returned to the BBC[6] she thought things had changed:

> Then you felt that *Panorama* had power and status, that the BBC had confidence in you. Now all you're conscious of is people trying to rein you in, to control you; you feel like a cog in a machine. Reporters on *Panorama* then

were chosen for much more than just being identikit reporters: they were stars. Why should people want to come and work in *Panorama* now? There are focus groups; you're hemmed in. The BBC is so cautious now. I think you could still get stars to come and work for the programme if only you gave them the back-up. Everyone on the programme then had weaknesses, but they had huge strengths too. *Panorama* stands for television journalism at its best. At its best means being educated, informed and entertained.

Even in her earliest incarnation on *Panorama*, as a producer, Margaret Jay was something of a grande dame, a woman of substance whose words and actions carried weight. Tall, elegant and tough, she says she never felt the victim of discrimination on *Panorama* – and one can believe it. Married to the economics journalist Peter Jay, and the daughter of Labour Chancellor – later Prime Minister – Jim Callaghan, Jay was both highly intelligent and extremely able. She had developed her film-making skills in further education programmes, and by the time she arrived on *Panorama* she was not disposed to suffer fools lightly – if indeed she had ever done so. She had an enviable ability to make Editors see things her way, and was able to move with equal ease and good humour in the company of a Henry Kissinger or a recalcitrant camera crew. After a spell outside television, when her husband became British Ambassador in Washington, Jay returned to *Panorama* as a reporter. There, in the early 1980s, she specialised in programmes about women, children, and sex, reporting with great intelligence and authority – just occasionally too much authority – on surrogacy, child abuse, and AIDS.

Later, of course, television lost Margaret Jay to the Lords, where she became Leader of the House and a member of Tony Blair's Cabinet. Presiding as she did without sentimentality (or indeed any discernible sentiment) over the dismantling of an institution that had stood for a thousand years, it is not surprising that she doesn't see why *Panorama* should necessarily survive beyond 50. There's no reason, she says, for *Panorama* to go on just because it's always been there. Of course she's right about that. And even if she isn't, who would dare argue with Baroness Jay?

She might or might not have liked them, but Grace Wyndham Goldie would have been proud of Jay and Tyerman – and of another in this group of highly effective women, Sally Doganis. They were all adept at getting the best out of the self-regarding and sometimes self-indulgent men on the programme, and bringing a sense of proportion into *Panorama*'s internal politics.

Doganis joined the programme as a producer after learning to make current affairs films on *Newsnight*. 'I was a real Lime Grove girl,' she says. 'At that time *Panorama* was the culmination of your career – you'd made it when you joined. You went from the nursery slopes of *Nationwide* and other programmes and it was a real accolade when you finally got to *Panorama*.'

But when she arrived, in 1982, Sally Doganis found an enormous arrogance among people who had been on the programme a long time. 'They thought they knew what the programme needed, but changing public opinion was passing them by. Nobody bothered about viewing figures; people were making programmes for their mates. For a television programme to be out of touch with public opinion is madness . . . It's just not kept up with the times.'

When she joined,' says Doganis, 'the atmosphere on *Panorama* was really very odd. Everyone outside the two people actually working on a particular programme was an enemy. You could never say to anyone: "How's it going?" It was like schoolchildren writing with their arms over their work on their desks to stop other people seeing what they were doing.' And the men were still very dominant. 'It was the most horrendously male set-up, absolutely ghastly. Jane Drabble[7] warned me about it as soon as I got there. One reporter didn't deign to speak to me for a year. Everything went on behind closed doors. I became quite aggressive as a defence. I was extra second class because I had children. To begin with I had a nine-month contract because of the kids' school holidays, though eventually I went on staff. There were the "real men", firefighters who went to war like Mike Dutfield, David Lomax and Jeremy Paxman. And then there were people like me who only did domestic things like child abuse, caesarean sections, the pill. But it was the domestic stories that got better audiences and were more important.'

Well, yes and no.

No doubt *Panorama* men, like so many irresponsible Peter Pans, sometimes flew away through the window on the world to revel in fights with the pirates that had no real relevance to their audience. But life isn't all about gynaecology or sex-related issues either. Women producers rightly put a stop to the boys playing soldiers all the time, but sometimes they in turn seemed to be playing the caring gentler sex roles too insis-tently. Perhaps, too, women producers contributed to a growing tendency on *Panorama* to focus on the interesting and entertaining surroundings to a story rather than the story itself – what a later Editor, Tim Gardam, calls 'Vanity Fair television'. So, for example, in 1982, 'The Media War'[8] was a prize-winning exploration of the way the Government had dealt with the media during the Falklands campaign rather than a hard story about whether the fighting had been worthwhile (though that programme did come later). And even though it was undoubtedly fascinating to see revealed the image-building and media manipulation that was such a feature of Margaret Thatcher's 1983 General Election campaign, was it really quite so significant an issue as 'The Marketing of Margaret'[9] made it seem?

But the contribution women have made to *Panorama* since they were allowed aboard has been essential to keeping it afloat at all. Most women are simply better organised than men, because they have competing pri-orities. They cannot afford to be obsessed with one subject to the exclusion of all else. On *Panorama* that didn't mean that women producers were any less focused on the story than the men – rather the reverse; but it did mean that when the filming was done for the day the conversation might be about other things; and that when the team was in the cutting room work would be organised so that everyone got at least a few hours' sleep. And contrary to what some mean-spirited colleagues have said, the author, as a reporter, did not like working with women producers because they could be more easily bullied. That suggestion would have made the women laugh, pityingly.

Since the days of Tyerman, Jay, and Doganis there have been many other effective women producers and reporters on *Panorama*. To mention some to the exclusion of others is unfair, but it must be done.

She was young, and never had the good manners to wait for senior figures on *Panorama* to speak before she gave her own opinion, loudly; she was relatively inexperienced, yet still routinely insisted that she was not being listened to with sufficient attention. Small, irrepressible, Lorraine Heggessey was no intellectual, but she had great intelligence and a no-nonsense ability to get quickly to the heart of the matter that irritated and impressed her colleagues in equal measure. She was not to be denied.

Where other producers would sympathise with and cover up for their reporters' shortcomings Heggessey would waste no time in exposing her working partners' flaws. She was damned if she was going to carry anyone – particularly a male reporter. But, full of energy, breezy and self-confident Lorraine Heggessey soon became popular. You could not help but like and admire her. And, though the reporters might never have guessed it from her manner, she admired most of them: 'A lot of the reporters were good,' she says, 'they went out and immediately got stuck in. They were the best in the business, and once you were in a working relationship they were prepared to listen.' But Heggessey found the atmosphere could be patronising too. She resented being sent out to film sequences for some other producer without being properly briefed: 'You can hardly tell the people you're filming that you don't know why you're doing it.'

Nobody patronised Heggessey for long. When Fred Emery went to look at the Falkland Islands after the war with Argentina – the first television reporter to do so – the Ministry of Defence tried to stop Heggessey going as his producer. The lavatory aboard the Hercules aircraft she'd have to fly in was extremely crude, said the MoD, and only a flimsy curtain pinned together would protect her modesty. This feeble objection Heggessey soon swept scornfully aside.

In 1985 Editor Peter Ibbotson commissioned producer Heggessey, with the author as reporter, to attempt a rather risky project. The idea was to get into the USSR – the Cold War had yet to thaw – and interview the wretched band of Jewish dissidents suffering increasing harassment and worse for their crime of wanting to emigrate to Israel. This was not going to be an enterprise that the Soviet Union would welcome; it would have to be carried out in great secrecy, rather in the way that, 10 years earlier, *Panorama* had gone to Moscow to get an interview with Andrei Sakharov.

Having identified, with the help of Jewish exile groups, those dissidents in Moscow and Leningrad who somehow had to be reached, Heggessey and the author decided that their best, indeed their only, hope of getting to them would be to go with Intourist on a package holiday. They bought an amateur video camera in London's Tottenham Court Road and practised using it. To carry conviction with their fellow tourists they thought it best to travel as an engaged couple, and share a hotel room. To preserve the *Panorama* decencies the author supervised Heggessey's purchase of an all-enveloping, passion-killing Victorian style nightgown from Laura Ashley. She didn't like it.

By day, led by their Intourist guide, the author and Heggessey joined the rest of the party as they toured the sights of Moscow – brandishing their video camera ostentatiously to get everybody used to seeing what was still a relatively rare tourist accessory. To her reporter's irritation Heggessey turned out to be by far the better cameraman; all his shots of Red Square consisted of his own furry winter boots walking along. When he thought the camera was off it was on – and vice versa.

That was the tourist alibi. As soon as the bus had returned the tour group to the hotel Heggessey and the author would leave again, as if eager for more sightseeing on their own, and make their way as best they could via Moscow's metro (and occasionally a taxi) to seek out the dissidents whom they had come to interview. Struggling to read the names of stations and streets written in Cyrillic script – or peering with a pen-torch to find the right flat number on some sprawling housing estate – the *Panorama* pair would eventually find their way up dark staircases and along corridors to an address they had been given in London. There they would knock, never knowing who or what they would find within. Some interviewees had been warned they might be visited and were prepared; others were at first suspicious, surprised, then deeply moved that anyone from the West should have come to ask them about their plight. Most of these people had reason to think their flats were bugged, so to establish the team's bona fides communication was at first by writing on a child's 'magic slate'. When their interviews began, these people, trying so hard to express themselves adequately in English, compelled pity and admiration for their stoic bravery under almost intolerable pressures. As Mary Kenny put it in her review of the programme[10] that resulted:

> Scores of Jews are in labour camps or prisons – just for practising Judaism or applying for visas. Bravely, wives and mothers in Moscow spoke to the camera of their hopes for the freedom of their husbands and sons. Their capacity for sacrifice is extraordinary . . . all the darkness of oppression cannot extinguish the faith and the integrity of these indomitable people – and the *Panorama* team are to be admired for their brave achievement in bringing these voices to us.[11]

The interview over, Heggessey and the author would leave their courageous interviewees alone again, hoping that the concierge who guarded the hallway to every block of flats had made no urgent report to the authorities of two foreign-looking people who had spent a suspiciously long time with the Jewish dissident.

Leading this double life was exhausting, and nerve-wracking too. Says Heggessey: 'It was a great risk to take. If we'd been rumbled we might even have gone to some gulag.' But instead of that, Heggessey was called on to make what was, for this feisty feminist, a greater sacrifice. On the slow overnight train to Leningrad the author dozed alone in a top bunk, struck down by 'flu. But he had been recognised as a television journalist. To preserve the cover story that they were just holidaying together, the producer was forced to tell her inquisitive fellow tourists that she was just a girl from the office having an illicit fling with a mighty *Panorama* reporter. Heggessey, who liked to be acknowledged as producer-in-charge, was not best pleased.

Heggessey didn't stay long on *Panorama*, but indignantly denies that she was using it just as a springboard to the top. 'I thought I had the best job in British television,' she says. 'I left the BBC only because they were trying to take me off *Panorama* and promote me to a different job on other shows. I went to [ITV's] *This Week* where I could go on being a current affairs producer. In a way I was refusing to be pushed up the promotion ladder.'

But today Heggessey is back at the BBC – and she has yielded to pressure to become upwardly mobile. As Controller of BBC1 (the first woman to hold that job) she now has a major voice in deciding what happens to *Panorama*. *Panorama* people hope Heggessey fights as hard for the programme now as she fought in her days as a *Panorama* producer.

Upper and lower decks

These days a *Panorama* programme will normally be all pre-recorded on to videotape, transmitted late on a Sunday night. It's pointless for the whole *Panorama* team to be at the BBC at that hour – they can watch it at home like everybody else. But when *Panorama* had a presenter and did interviews it had a studio, and its programmes were transmitted live at a reasonable time in the evening. On Monday nights there was a sense of occasion as

Panorama people: clockwise from top left: Alan Hart, reporter, 1970; Richard Kershaw, reporter, 1969; Robin Day, presenter 1967; John Morgan, reporter, 1961.

(All courtesy of BBC archives.)

Jeremy Isaacs, *Panorama* Editor, 1966. (Courtesy of BBC archives.)

The *Panorama* studio gallery in 1967, from left to right: Tommy Dawson, technical manager; Richard Pigg, vision mixer; Margaret Douglas, director; John Grist, Editor; Angela Goble, production assistant. (Courtesy of BBC archives.)

Reporter Michael Charlton in the suitably grand surroundings of Versailles with French Foreign Minister Maurice Schumann, 1972.

(Courtesy of BBC archives.)

Film editor Ian Calloway in the cutting room with reporter Michael Cockerell, 1976. (Courtesy of Peter Pagnamenta.)

BBC cameraman 'Butch' Calderwood in Vietnam, 1966. (Courtesy of Butch Calderwood.)

Freelance cameraman Erik Durschmied, the battle of Dak To, Vietnam, 1967. (Courtesy of Erik Durschmied.)

Julian Pettifer reports from Vietnam, 1966. (Courtesy of Butch Calderwood.)

A close shave for the author, at 'Fireforce' camp, Southern Rhodesia, 1978.

(Courtesy of Robin Denselow.)

Reporter Tom Mangold teams up with producer John Penycate, 1976.

Michael Cockerell, reporter and Tom Bower, producer 1976.

Princess Diana during her interview
with Martin Bashir, 1995.

(Courtesy of BBC archives.)

Reporter Peter Taylor in Northern Ireland, 2000. (Courtesy of Marcus Robinson.)

Jane Corbin reports the Foot and Mouth epidemic in Britain, 2001.

Reporter John Ware in Omagh, 2001. (Courtesy of BBC archives.)

those of the programme team who were not away making a film would gather (with any programme guests) in Hospitality to watch their colleagues' efforts and to praise or condemn (often both – one in public, the other in private) as they saw fit. Hospitality was of course known as 'Hostility'.

As Francesca Kirby-Green (first a film editor, then a producer) remembers it, there was a sort of class structure operating in the three Lime Grove Hospitality rooms that *Panorama* booked for Monday evening:

> S9 was panelled, posh and set aside for the programme's guests – Government ministers and so on. S10 was almost as posh and was used mostly by the production people; it was also the room where the booze was set out. And then there was S11, for the lower orders like secretaries and film editors. It was not such a bad deal, because that was where the food was. I do remember times when Robin Day used to come and sit with us. I wonder if he preferred our company or just hated theirs. We never dared ask him. He just sat near the connecting doors in silence.

Panorama has always been an edgy sort of place to work in. Great things are expected of its team and the pressure to get results leads to anxiety, and sometimes a paranoid fear that colleagues, as well as events, are conspiring against you. Reporter/producer teams feel themselves pitted against other people on the programme as they struggle to bring the story they've been commissioned to do to the screen, and *Panorama* Editors have always found it hard to make people discuss their ideas freely in programme meetings – they are more likely to ask for a quiet word with the Editor afterwards.

In the beginning that rather private way of working was encouraged by the offices in which *Panorama* was housed. The programme inhabited two little Edwardian houses, next to the rambling old studios in Lime Grove. People would hide away in separate rooms where they could research a story in privacy, and keep their contacts secret. 'It was all very cellular, like a beehive,' says Margaret Douglas, the programme's first secretary, and later its studio director. 'The bitchiness was acute, but almost redeemed by the humour.'

The houses had been solidly built but were now nearing the end of their life. In January 1981 press officer Bob Dulson reported that, in an answer to the *Daily Mail*, 'he had confirmed that part of the ceiling had fallen on to the desk at which *Panorama* producer Philip Harding was working. He heard the ceiling crack and managed to move out of the way, so it missed him. He was covered with dust, but the only damage was a dented film can. The Editor of *Panorama* said: "*Panorama* is not collapsing."' In the 1980s the programme moved into a new office of aluminium and glass, all on one level, at the bottom of what had once been the gardens belonging to the houses; but there was still a series of rooms, in each of which a small team might plot or plan. Today, in the anonymity of White City, *Panorama* people are at desks spread across a large open plan office which houses other programmes too. No doubt it is more efficient and paranoia less pervasive, but though people are together in one room they sometimes seem to be further apart – sitting in silence at their individual desks, communicating with each other by email.

Cutting room tales

'Cutting room journalism' would be the sneer tossed at *Panorama* when John Birt's Khmer Rouge took over Lime Grove, the worst insult they could think of. But criticism of that kind can only come from people who don't understand what a television current affairs film is and how it is made; indeed, don't really believe there is such a thing.

In the late 1980s producer Sarah Manwaring-White remembers being asked which was more important, the words or the pictures. It was a terrible question, a test of adherence to the new orthodoxy, rather like being asked by a sixteenth-century church investigator whether or not you believed in transubstantiation. The wrong answer would reveal you as not of the true faith – it might send you to the stake. But, of course, as Manwaring-White tried to point out, words and pictures are equally important to any current affairs programme which, like *Panorama*, wants to talk about important things to a big audience. To do that successfully a film has to be alive, a living being that interests you as another human being might, not just an assembly of shots, a dead thing in a bottle of formalin used to illustrate some dreary lecture.

John Birt's disciples seem to have viewed *Panorama*'s cutting room, full of bits of film or tapes, as positively dangerous and scary, a sort of

Frankenstein's laboratory where crazed people with no judgement madly sewed together ill-assorted body parts that they had haphazardly scavenged, to create some terrifying monster over which they had no real control. But that's not how *Panorama* films were made. It's true that the cutting room did occasionally resemble an operating theatre in which desperate doctors fought against all the odds to save the life of a pretty feeble patient that didn't really deserve to survive. But mostly it was more like a delivery room, where the child conceived and brought to term by a *Panorama* couple, a producer and reporter, would now be safely delivered into the world – or, if things went wrong in there, stillborn. What happened in the cutting room could breathe life into a film, or leave it limp and inert.

Today, *Panorama* is recorded in the camera as a digital signal. Dumped in a computer, picture and sound then become a series of files that can be edited more or less like any other electronic data. But until the mid-1980s the film editors really were cutters, snipping their way through twenty or thirty 400-foot cans of 16mm film containing all the many different shots that the team had brought, or sent back, to Lime Grove.

Unlike the news, *Panorama* shot 'separate system' – just like a feature film. Each shot that was supposed to have sound with it would – in theory at least – start with a picture of the clapperboard (the 'slate'), with a number on it which would later enable the film editor to synchronise the picture with the sound, which was separately recorded on quarter-inch tape and then transferred to 16mm magnetic film. It could be a hazardous business 'putting a board on' in the middle of a riot, but it would save an awful lot of time that would otherwise have to be spent trying to match sound to picture in the cutting room.

A film was edited 'double headed', with separate sound and picture rolls that could be run backwards and forwards together. 'We cut films on vile Acmade film editing machines in those days', says Francesca Kirby-Green. 'The take-up spools did their best to snap the film, the lock-up system between sound and picture was totally variable, and worst of all, we could not really see what we were doing.' In the 1950s, 1960s and early 1970s stories were shot on negative stock and a 'slash print' made which could be used for editing. Then, right at the end of the process, probably late on a Sunday night, the finished picture – now in a pretty battered state after endless recutting – would be sent off to the laboratory where the original negative would be cut to match the 'cutting copy'. Next day a shiny new print of the film would arrive back at the BBC. Later[12] it got more difficult for the film editors as, to save money, *Panorama* abandoned negative for positive stock ('reversal'); what went through the camera gate was the same film that was edited and later transmitted. It had to be handled with the greatest care.

The film editors in charge of this process were remarkable: precision engineers who did not normally make mistakes even when working under extreme pressure, and at the same time sympathetic and creative people who could quickly see what *Panorama* producers wanted, and make it happen. It is not surprising that film editors like John Gau and Kirby-Green went on to become producers themselves.

Nearly everyone's favourite film editor on *Panorama* for many years was Ian Calloway. Calloway loved his job so much that he devised a cunning way of keeping it. As Kirby-Green recalls it:

> When I signed on as Ian's assistant I had to agree to stand by 'the line'. The line was that editing on *Panorama* was the pits – unspeakable hours, dreadfully difficult people to work with, an absolute living nightmare. In fact when I arrived I found a very happy team. The truth of the matter was that Ian Calloway was devoted to *Panorama* and simply could not bear the thought of being moved off it. He was hugely respected and I doubt very much that *Panorama* would ever have wanted him moved. I guess he was terrified that the apparatchiks in Film Department's front office would have sought his move for reasons of their own. Hence the need to make sure that any potential recruits were put off by stories of how terrible it all was on *Panorama*. So when I 'sold' my job in turn to my great friend and fellow film editor Philip Crump he looked at me with disbelief: 'You hate it, it's awful,' he said. 'Listen,' I said, 'if you sign on then you have to sign on to the secret and you have to promise and complain long and hard about the ghastly working conditions, just like I've done.' Crump did.

Whatever they may have said to the Film Department to which they technically belonged, film editors rarely complained to *Panorama* people. Through long, long hours, by day and by night, in the little rabbit-hutch rooms they inhabited in the nooks and crannies of Lime Grove, they would patiently try to make the material they had been given do what the producer expected of it; lengthening or shortening shots here, changing the order of them there. And, in the early hours, when faith in the film grew dim, and exhaustion threatened to extinguish judgement, it was often cutters like Calloway who would rally the team and suggest that they would yet come through this ordeal with a film of which they could all be proud – and why didn't the producer go home and get a few hours' sleep while he just made a few changes they had agreed on?

Film editors often wore white gloves so as not to get thumbprints all over the film they were handling; and no matter what the pressure of time they worked in a calm, orderly way as they built up the finished film, shot by shot. Cameramen, the people who got the raw material in the first place, were by and large a different breed. Their position was an awkward one.

Cameramen were probably the people who mattered most in the entire operation: without their pictures there could be no *Panorama*. But at the same time they were useless unless producer and reporter got them to the right place at the right time. Even then their situation was difficult. The story might demand that they operate in appalling conditions, with not enough light, not enough time, on the move, and in a tropical downpour or desert sandstorm. Their journalistic instincts – not to mention their producers' urgent demands – drove them to 'turn over'; their desire to shoot good quality material, carefully framed and properly lit, sometimes deterred them. BBC cameramen who worked for *Panorama* might also be trying to build a reputation for their work and impress people in the Drama department, where pictures that looked good were essential. Shaky, out of focus shots in a current affairs film wouldn't help them there, even if they had caught some moment of significant action which thrilled *Panorama*. So to get cameramen sufficiently involved in the story to risk their reputations in difficult situations was an important part of a *Panorama* producer's job.

'*Panorama* producers provide the events and you do the best you can with them,' says cameraman Alan Stevens. Stevens remembers being hired as a trainee in 1962 by Grace Wyndham Goldie because of his enthusiasm for the stories. But he was disappointed to find that in those early days *Panorama* producers, like reporters, were very much journalists first and directors second. On programmes like *Tonight* and *24 Hours*, he discovered, cameramen were part of the team, and really valued for the contribution they were making. But on *Panorama* producers were not really interested in the pictures; they didn't know what they wanted from the cameramen. It was the access to the great, and the interviews that followed, that mattered most to them. Only after that was done would they turn to the cameraman for 'wallpaper' shots that would be enough to carry some commentary. It was not until *Panorama* films grew longer that cameramen – along with the producers – came into their own. Then it became more of a two-way street, with directors helping cameramen to get to the heart of the story, and cameramen making producers think harder about how to illustrate it.

Shot and shell

'Aren't you frightened? isn't it dangerous?' people often ask about reporting from trouble spots abroad. Yes and no. Experience suggests that more television journalists are seriously hurt in car crashes or laid low by nasty foreign infections than are wounded or killed in fighting. That said, it has got more dangerous – and today's journalists more daring. In Afghanistan, in the first months after the terrorist attack on the World Trade Centre, more reporters from the West lost their lives than did military men. Year after year now the media awards for Amnesty International and the Rory Peck Trust pay tribute to journalists who are willingly putting themselves in harm's way. Now that cameras of broadcast quality are so small and light, video journalists are often working alone, without the comforting knowledge that there's someone else in the team who will come to their aid if it all goes wrong. And if they are freelances, trying to do what the established broadcasters don't dare, then they will be taking more risks, pushing their luck without any back-up from the American networks or the great big BBC.

Panorama's heyday in the 1960s came at a time when a British crew from the BBC would be welcome round the world; a time when a white skin and Western ways were still some protection from harm in a faraway and savage land. Living in the best local hotel they could find (though it wasn't often anything as pleasant as the American Colony in Jerusalem, or the Mandarin in Hong Kong) the team would sally out early to get as close to the action as possible before retreating at the end of an often frightening and certainly exhausting day to a shower and a decent meal.

Occasionally – in Cambodia for example – journalist colleagues who were there at breakfast might not be there at dinner, gone missing, never to return. Sometimes a trip up-country – in Vietnam particularly – could turn into something very nasty, with the team under fire, and in real danger. But by and large *Panorama* people did not get hurt, though they sometimes got very frightened.

David Lomax recalls one such occasion. In southern Lebanon with Mike Dutfield in 1982, with a lot of shelling going on around them, the crew found themselves with sniper fire cracking overhead: 'It was probably the Druze shooting, but we didn't stand up to find out: we dived into a ditch. The funny thing was that as I pressed myself into the ground, under fire, I actually went to sleep.' This is a phenomenon other reporters have experienced in life-threatening situations where, for the moment, there is absolutely nothing you can do. On this occasion Lomax was unhurt, but his sound recordist, Malcolm Bartram, got a bullet in his foot. Rescued by a Red Cross jeep, Bartram was taken to hospital in Sidon before being flown back to Britain, where he made a full recovery.

Panorama's producers and reporters, supposedly the brains of the operation, who know what's what, and where's safe, owe a great debt to camera crews who let themselves be put in jeopardy for the sake of the story.

Neville Calderwood, better known as 'Butch', had grown up in a Sydney suburb in Australia. From an early age he was in love with the movies. In 1953, the year that *Panorama* began, he'd reached London and joined the BBC as a probationary trainee technical assistant. Two years later he watched the News read for the first time by a newscaster in vision. 'Gradually', says Calderwood, 'the Corporation settled over me.' By 1955 he was working for *Panorama* as an assistant to cameramen such as 'Tubby' Englander. Later, as a cameraman himself, he filmed everywhere for *Panorama*: there was Malcolm X in New York's Harlem with Jim Mossman; the doomed American war in Vietnam with Julian Pettifer; the aftermath of the Biafran revolt in Nigeria with Richard Kershaw; Rose Kennedy in a rare interview at Hyannisport with Robert MacNeil; and, with Tom Mangold, PLO recruits in Syria as they practised their techniques of international terrorism.

Twenty years after he'd started at the BBC Calderwood had seen and filmed everything. Nothing could any longer surprise or amaze him. Often he seemed fed up, sourly cynical about *Panorama*'s predictability, sometimes insisting that he was more interested in a good restaurant than a good story.[13] Yet when, through the lens of his camera, he saw something significant begin to happen he would not let it go, notwithstanding the poor light conditions or the dangers and difficulties under which he was operating. And when the situation got nasty, he was a good, brave person to be with.

In 1975, Calderwood, with his assistant, and his soundman Freddie Downton arrived in Angola, with the author as reporter and a youthful Robin Denselow as producer. It was a confused situation which *Panorama* was confidently about to explain to British viewers. Following their revolution at home, the Portuguese, who had ruled this west African colony, were pulling out, and three different indigenous groups (backed of course by different Western commercial and political interests) were vying to take over a vast country with equally vast reserves of oil and diamonds. The *Panorama* team arrived in the capital, Luanda, to find the airport a struggling mass of people desperate to get out before the glorious Independence day arrived, and all-out war engulfed them.

Luanda was under the control of the Communist MPLA, the Popular Movement for the Liberation of Angola, not particularly friendly to a British television team. Denselow had, however, managed to get some press passes which had allowed *Panorama* to film military training in the local bullring. On the day the team was due to fly out Denselow and the author decided to use those passes again, to try to find out just how close to Luanda the battle lines were now drawn. Says Calderwood: 'We drove about 15kms. to the outskirts of town, and showed our passes upside down, which is what we always did in Africa, just to see if the officials could read. They waved us on, so we jauntily worked away, filming the last few minutes of our story.'[14]

Panorama had got right up to the front line. But on the way back the MPLA caught up with the team – literally. The abandoned car which *Panorama* had 'liberated' in Luanda just wouldn't accelerate fast enough to escape the military vehicle behind it. The team was arrested and taken by soldiers to what turned out to be the old English primary school, now a makeshift and very frightening detention centre. At the entrance, the first sight was of an elderly Portuguese man with blood streaming down his face being slapped about by the military; then the team was thrown into a small classroom packed with other people. As Calderwood says, 'It was completely terrifying. Fifty people were crowded into that room – Portuguese, black Angolans, two Congolese pilots who had landed their plane by mistake, an American girl [she was the widow of an Angolan who had died fighting on the wrong side], and two Brazilians who insisted they were tourists and had been picked up as they arrived at their hotel. Some of them had been locked up for 47 days.' Wretched producer Denselow was taken away for questioning; it could have been worse: 'I was the only one to be interrogated and it was more like a gentle bullying session than a search for information. I was told I worked for Scotland Yard and when I protested I was told I also worked for the CIA.'

Life in the classroom was deeply depressing. At first the team slept on the floor, then, as others were taken away by the soldiers, on the little school desks. As Denselow remembers it: 'The lights were on day and night, clothes got dirtier and dirtier, and the sanitation – designed for infants – was unpleasantly ineffective.' Talking was forbidden; there was absolutely nothing to do. Sitting in the classroom for hour after hour, the main sensations were boredom, discomfort and growing anxiety. Peering out through the wooden slats the team could see the airport and the last refugee flights leaving for Portugal, as well as the Red Cross planes flying in, ignorant of the prison at the end of their runway.

There was food, but not really of *Panorama* standard. Says Calderwood: 'For lunch we had the same kerosene drum full of macaroni and sardines that we'd had the night before, now gone cold, the oil from the sardines congealed around the sticky pasta. For dinner we ate the same; that night, and the next and the next.'

'We won't be here for long, they'll find us,' Denselow would whisper encouragingly: but it was difficult to remain optimistic. Even when the *Panorama* team's disappearance was noted, where would anyone start looking for it? How would they ever find us in a country collapsing into chaos? How long would we be held? What would happen to us? Not surprisingly, the young assistant cameraman was fearful and angry: 'When we are shot tomorrow', he muttered to poor Denselow, 'I want it to be your last thought that this is your fault.'

Downton, the sound man, found his own coping strategy. As a little joke,

Freddie, the least aristocratic of men, had long called himself Sir Frederick Downton when on BBC business. On flights and at hotels around the world he and the rest of *Panorama* had often benefited from this little deception. Now he discovered a new way to make life more tolerable for us all. 'I remember', says Calderwood, 'Sir Fred found half a red plastic comb on the floor with TAP [the Portuguese national airline] printed on it. Slowly he picked it up and walked from one person to the next, carefully combing their hair. It was eerie to watch. He didn't speak, but just kept combing, and I remember thinking I had never seen Robin Denselow's hair so neat. This act, simplicity itself, comforted those who thought there was none to be had.'

The team had grown used to those heart-stopping moments when the guards burst in to the schoolroom with much shouting and screaming and waving of guns and dragged someone away. After four days it was *Panorama*'s turn. Outside it was dark. As the team was hustled out they saw that their car was still there. Not knowing whether they were to be shot or set free, they begged for a chance to recover their equipment, and managed to retrieve the cans of film they had stuffed behind the seats during their failed dash for freedom. Taken to their hotel in silence – they didn't dare to speak – the team were released without warning into the custody of a mysterious man sent by the British embassy. They took a shower, grabbed their gear and checked out more quickly than any crew ever has before. Then, lying on the floor of a car, hidden under a blanket, they were driven out to the airport, through the barrier and on to the tarmac. A plane had been held for *Panorama*; its engines were revving, its cargo doors still open. Throwing their baggage and camera gear into the hold the team ran up the steps. 'I think I'll come with you,' said the mysterious man from the embassy; and he did.

'I sat on the soft airline seat, magnificently plump under my bum, the wonderful throb of the engines vibrating through my body,' says Calderwood, 'and felt the inexpressible sensation of rushing down a runway. As soon as the plane levelled out, the hostesses converged ready to spoil and cosset a poor television crew who had been in the wars. "Please, you must try some of our macaroni," one said. I turned green and declined. It took 12 years for me to look at it again.'

Back in London, via Lisbon, the team was able to thank all the *Panorama* people, particularly Editor Peter Pagnamenta and his Deputy David Harrison, whose efforts had got us home. And we had to thank the Foreign Office too, which had firmly told their man in Luanda to find and rescue us.

That deeply experienced producer and reporter John Penycate remarks sardonically: 'Bitter experience teaches that our embassies on the ground are desperate for your help but can't help you.' That is indeed often the case. This time Her Majesty's representatives proved him wrong, and we were deeply grateful.

Irregular forces

Butch Calderwood was on the BBC's staff. But there were other cameramen who were freelance, hired on contract and guaranteed a minimum of so much a year to work for *Panorama*. They were often resented by BBC camera teams, ostensibly on the ground that they were 'one-man bands', not always working with a properly qualified sound recordist. The real reason was that the best freelances were often harder-working, braver, and more creative than some of the more pedestrian crews provided by the BBC Film Department in Ealing.

On 6 December 1966, *Panorama*'s fragmentary records reveal, Ernie Christie was guaranteed £7000 a year, to include his camera gear and a soundman. Christie was a South African stills photographer who'd turned himself into a brilliant television cameraman. As *Time* journalist Peter Hawthorne, Christie's frequent collaborator, recalls:

> In the early days of the Congo story he was at a roadblock manned by Indian UN soldiers who opened fire on a Volkswagen that was driven through without stopping. Christie captured the entire sequence on film – the vehicle driving past, the bullets punching through the car, the terrified Belgian driver scrambling out, his wife dead in the passenger seat, their Alsatian dog wounded, howling and limping away. It was all over in seconds but that was all Ernie needed. The film clip became a classic of TV news coverage and Christie got an international award for it.

Like a well-trained soldier, Christie was always alert and ready for action, always prepared to catch the telling moment on film. He'd grown up in an orphanage, done a bit of boxing, and was extremely tough. All dressed up and ready for a night on the town he was, with his crinkly smile, a little bit like Clark Gable's Rhett Butler.

It was frankly difficult working with Christie in black Africa because of the rank racial prejudice he had absorbed with his poor white Afrikaner upbringing, but as long as he kept quiet and didn't start a fight he was a superb cameraman. He got in close, with the zoom lens of his Arriflex camera set at a wide angle, so that the action unfolding before him lost none of its drama; and his pictures were always intelligently as well as elegantly framed to focus on what was really significant about the sequence he was shooting.

Christie would often try to persuade *Panorama* that it would be best if he and a reporter used his own small aeroplane to get about the vast distances of the African continent. Whether it was the cheapest or quickest way to go was doubtful, but it was certainly the most exciting. Producer David Harrison remembers flying with Christie over the sea off the Tanzanian coast, hopelessly lost, with the fuel running perilously low and no land in sight. Making an approach to Lusaka with reporter Richard Kershaw, after interviewing Zambia's President Kaunda upcountry, Christie actually did run out of fuel – 8000 feet up and 11 miles short of the runway. They crash-landed in a maize field.

Sadly, Christie ended his life in a melodramatic moment of suicidal madness, flying his plane into an apartment building, killing an elderly couple who lived there. The man who died turned out to be the picture editor who had given Christie his first job.

On 30 December 1958 footage was dispatched to the BBC containing a truly remarkable story. A young Austrian who had been working for the Canadian Broadcasting Corporation as a cameraman had scooped the world. In Cuba, he had managed to reach the revolutionary rebel leader Fidel Castro in the Sierra Maestre, and interview him on film just as he was ready to begin his victorious march on Havana. This journalistic coup made Erik Durschmied a cameraman–journalist everyone wanted to hire, and in 1960, while covering the bitter colonial war in Algeria, he got an invitation to come and talk to *Panorama*: 'A London taxi brought me to a crumbling building site which turned out to be the famous Lime Grove Studios,' he later wrote. 'Was this the mighty BBC? The Editor was closeted in a tiny room with a barred window. He was a large man for such a small office. His name was Paul Fox.'[15]

Hired by Fox, Durschmied shot some of *Panorama*'s most telling reports, in the 1960s most often with Jim Mossman. On the road in later years, with indifferent manners, and grumbling rudely that *Panorama* reporters weren't what they used to be, Durschmied was not always the dinner companion of choice. Sometimes one had to remind oneself that this was probably the best current affairs cameraman a *Panorama* reporter could ever hope to work with, particularly in difficult, dangerous situations. In Vietnam, in Cambodia, in the Middle East; in the midst of riot, war and terrorist attack; no one was better. Reporters, producers and interviewees alike might sometimes find his manner disconcerting, even downright offensive, but whatever he lacked in politeness he more than made up for with his camerawork. And the nastier the situation became, the nicer and happier Durschmied was.

chapter eleven

⊕ # Coping with complaint

'I was sorry to read your criticism of our *Panorama* programme last Monday . . . ' So began many a letter to a viewer from the Editor of *Panorama*, or his subordinate reporters and producers. It is inevitable that if you impose a Licence Fee on viewers, demanding money with menaces, then those viewers will feel free to complain. And many of them do. The trouble started at once, and it has to be said that after its very first outing *Panorama* responded with arrogance and disdain to a perfectly reasonable complaint.

Appearing in the first-ever *Panorama* programme on 11 November 1953 was George Dawson, who was making a great deal of money as a fish importer. Dawson was being interviewed by the luckless Pat Murphy as a 'personality', a card, in a way that completely ignored the fact that he was widely seen to be allied with Iceland in a bitter dispute with Britain's fishing industry. *Panorama* didn't bother with any of this tedious background, and when the complaints poured in they were treated with lofty disdain. 'Dear Mr. Sprott,' wrote Cyril Jackson, the Television Talks Organiser, to the managing director of a frozen fish company, 'We certainly did not invite him [Dawson] in order that he could put one side of the question. If we had wished to devote a programme to the Icelandic fishing ban we should naturally have had speakers on both sides who would have discussed the case in detail.' But to another complaint Jackson had a rather different answer: 'I do not see how, at the moment, we could arrange a serious programme on the subject, since that would automatically involve a statement of the Icelandic viewpoint and would mean that we should be commenting on a matter which is still under consideration by the Governments concerned.'

So it's perfectly all right to have a 'personality' known for his support of one side of an argument in the studio without putting the other side in some way; there's no need to give any background for the interview; and anyway, *Panorama* can't deal with the issue in any real and impartial way because it's still being discussed by the Governments concerned. Arrogant nonsense, that no one from *Panorama* would nowadays dare to write in answer to a complaint. But the way *Panorama* has dealt with complaints has never been consistent. And sometimes it has been a matter of estimating the power of the complainant to do damage rather than considering whether or not the complaint is just.

It is always going to be easier to rebuff complainants who do not have the public strongly on their side. And for many decades *Panorama* itself felt that in a punch-up with almost anyone it would always win the popular vote. The way it dealt with another bit of the Establishment, which had been losing support at a faster rate than the BBC, was an illustration of its confidence – some would (and did) say arrogance.

Confronting the Establishment

On 24 May 1971 *Panorama* turned its gaze on the Church of England in a programme which sketched a bleak picture of what was happening to the country's established church, especially in the inner city. It looked in particular at the diocese of Southwark, and produced what a statement from Church House later complained was 'a caricature of the Church of England . . . The film suffered from a lack of objectivity in that the great bulk of the scenes showed either failure or, in contrast, some rather avant-garde experiments. Almost no attempts were made to show successful parishes.'[1] Part of the problem was that, in the film, a bishop from another diocese, Leicester, had talked about 'defeatism and disillusion' in Southwark. This had clearly enraged Southwark's bishop, Dr Mervyn Stockwood. But rather than the Bishop of Leicester, it was *Panorama* and the BBC that became the focus of his wrath.

Over a period of months Stockwood pursued Director General Charles Curran and his Director of Public Affairs Kenneth Lamb about allegations made in the programme that the Church had neglected the care of residents in a church-run hostel in his diocese. He told the diocesan synod: 'Mr. Lamb excelled himself by one of the most foolish and pompous demands that any man could have made of a bishop. "Unless and until" I proved to him that the statement [in the programme] was in fact false, he would neither withdraw or apologise.' The BBC had responded in the grand manner: 'The Corporation takes grave exception to the nature and content of the Bishop's attack on certain of its officials and programme-makers . . . and rejects his allegations of "incompetence", "misbehaviour" and "arrogance".'[2]

Stockwood got no satisfaction from the BBC. An invitation to discuss the specific *Panorama* on *Talkback* was withdrawn when it became plain that the Bishop would use the occasion to mount a comprehensive attack on the Corporation in general. Barred from the BBC, Stockwood took his complaint to the papers. In a *News of the World* article he called for radical action against the power of the BBC:

> The sooner it is cut down to size and made to realise it is the servant and not the boss of the nation, the better. Broadcasting House is not the Kremlin, and the British public not a collection of brainless puppets. It is high time that the Chairman of this dictatorial body, Dr. Charles Hill, the former Radio Doctor, realised that instead of prescribing medicine he and his top-brass colleagues might be wise to *take* some . . . And let us hope that the Government will establish a body similar to the Press Council to which complaints can go for impartial investigation.[3]

Though he seems to have lost this encounter, Stockwood was shrewd. He must have realised, from his own bruising experience, that the BBC was unlikely to yield to a lobby it perceived to be weaker than itself. But what if there were some independent body to which complaint could be made?

This was an idea which was already being canvassed. In a leader entitled 'Missing watchdog', the *Sunday Telegraph* had noted that 'the Conservative Party's broadcasting committee is now to press for an independent Broadcasting Council, and the case for such a public watchdog is strong . . . Although the Government has turned down the idea in the past, it merits a fresh and careful study now.'[4]

Court of Appeal

The time did come when *Panorama* found itself in front of the Broadcasting Complaints Commission – the body which was eventually set up – having to justify what it had done. On many occasions *Panorama* found the Commission less sympathetic than BBC bosses might have been.

At the end of 1993 the BCC announced that the most complained-about programme of the year had been *Panorama*. The edition that had drawn the most fire was 'Babies on Benefit.'[5]

'Michelle and Noddy made my blood boil', wrote TV critic Pam Francis in *Today* about two of the young people featured in the programme. The film dealt primarily with life on the St. Mellon's estate in Cardiff, where half the families were headed by single parents. It examined the way young women seemed to be having babies without getting married as their best route to a council flat and state benefits. John Redwood, the Tories' right-wing Secretary of State for Wales, had deplored what he found on a visit. *Panorama* reporter Margaret Gilmore and producer Barbara Want went to the estate in question to investigate.

The fastest-growing group of single parents in Britain was indeed made up of never-married young women. Many of them, particularly in areas where there was high unemployment, regarded the men around as a useless lot, more of a hindrance than a help in achieving a decent standard of living for themselves and their children. When they decided to have babies on benefit they were not being 'feckless' but – given the options open to them – entirely sensible. Why marry an unemployed, dead-beat dad when you were financially better off without him? On the other hand, was it right that the taxpayer should be funding this lifestyle of being supported by the state, of having babies on benefit? Would cutting benefits to these unmarried mums bring about a change in their behaviour that might be better for them, their children and the rest of us? The programme appeared just as the Conservative Party was getting under way with its ill-starred 'Back to Basics' campaign, and lent support to a right-wing radical agenda that outraged all those on the liberal left. It was a good and important story.

Though the individual young women interviewed in the film had not complained about their treatment by the *Panorama* team,[6] Sue Slipman, Director of the National Council for One Parent Families, did. She took her case to the Broadcasting Complaints Commission, which, against the advice of its staff, decided to hear it. The BCC's job was to deal with individual complaints from anyone 'directly affected' by a programme. Slipman persuaded the Commissioners that that meant her and her pressure group, the NCOPF. The BCC upheld her complaint, saying that 'Babies on Benefit' had been 'unfair and unjust'.

For the first time since the Commission had come into existence the BBC now challenged its ruling. Not only, it said, had the Commission got its judgement wrong, but in dealing with editorial questions – whether the programme was fair, rather than complaints from individuals – the Commission was exceeding its powers. If its judgement were allowed to stand it would encourage every pressure group in the land to make a complaint about any programme whose message it regarded as hostile to its cause. Said Caroline Thomson, the BBC's Head of Corporate Affairs: 'The BCC are very confused about what they take to be a "direct interest". They are interpreting it too widely, and straying into territory about whether programmes are impartial or biased, when they should be examining whether individuals have been fairly treated.'[7]

The BBC conceded one mistake in the programme: figures suggesting that American research showed that cutting benefits dramatically reduced the number of single women who continued to have children should have been clearly labelled 'provisional'; otherwise the Corporation utterly rejected a judgement that it believed had come about simply because the BCC had buckled under pressure from an effective and politically correct lobby group.

The BBC took the BCC to a judicial review, and won. The court held that the BCC had indeed exceeded its powers in hearing the complaint brought by the National Council for One Parent Families. Giving his decision, Mr Justice Brook said that if programme makers handling controversial issues 'are constrained to take into account not only issues of fairness and justice to individual people or organisations but issues of fairness and justice to a large, amorphous population of people perhaps numbered in hundreds of thousands, then it is apparent that the public interest is likely to suffer if they feel constrained to play safe.'[8] Slipman's complaint on behalf of all the single mothers her Council sought to represent should not have been heard by the BCC.

It was a victory for *Panorama*, but one achieved on rather narrow, legal grounds. After all, why shouldn't bodies representing vulnerable groups – or powerful ones come to that – bring complaints against *Panorama* or other programmes if they feel them to have been partial and unfair? Why should *Panorama* feel 'constrained to play safe' if pressure groups do have recourse to some body independent of the BBC? Doesn't the programme in any case have a general duty to be fair? Why should it be frightened of a challenge on that ground from anyone?

Of course dealing with complaints is irritating and time-consuming for the programme makers; it would be a pity if the BBC's Licence Fee income was all going on defending programmes rather than making them, rather as so much of our taxes seems to be spent by the police and social services on investigating what they did wrong last time. But a resolute Regulator ready to reject outright complaints that are obviously political, partisan or petty should not be something that *Panorama* or any other programme should shrink from. If a programme is biased or unfair, then establishing that should not depend on individuals being brave and determined enough to make a formal complaint about their own treatment. It should be open to anyone or any organisation to do so – just as long as the body that hears the complaints is not simply a collection of well-meaning amateurs, as the BCC often showed itself to be – and has the confidence of both broadcasters and the public.

Its defeat in the row over *Panorama*'s 'Babies on Benefit' was virtually the end of the Broadcasting Complaints Commission. Under the 1996 Broadcasting Act the BCC was amalgamated with the Broadcasting Standards Council to become the Broadcasting Standards Commission. Now, following yet more legislation, the BSC's role in dealing with complaints is being taken over by Ofcom. But Ofcom will still only entertain complaints about BBC programmes by individuals who are 'directly affected.' General complaints that *Panorama* programmes are biased or unfair will still be dealt with by the BBC – the people who brought you the programme in the first place. Whether, or how far, an external Regulator like Ofcom should take over the functions of the BBC Governors in this area is a hotly-argued subject beyond the scope of this book; but surely *Panorama*, whenever its programmes are accused of bias or unfairness, should not be afraid of facing an independent arbitrator.

chapter twelve
⊕ # Pressure tests

'Don't call me unless the Queen Mother dies,' said Tony Hall, Managing Director, BBC News. It was the summer of 1996, and Hall was off on holiday, leaving his Deputy Richard Ayre, until recently Controller of Editorial Policy, in charge of the BBC's news and current affairs programmes.

With an election coming up and the end of a long period of Conservative rule looking more than likely, *Panorama* was preparing a programme on the way political parties – particularly the new Labour Party – were being presented to the public. 'One day', says Richard Ayre, 'I took a call from Peter Mandelson.[1] It went something like this:

> I understand that *Panorama* is out to 'get' New Labour. Don't believe that anything happens in your studios that I don't know about: you have to stop this programme. Labour will be the next Government. The BBC expects the Licence Fee to be renewed. If this programme goes out in the form it is at present then the BBC can kiss goodbye to an increase. And don't think for a moment that other people at the top of the BBC won't know it's you if this programme does go out.

Ayre says he did not tell *Panorama* about this call. Work on the programme about New Labour[2] continued unaffected.

A television current affairs programme is rather like champagne: it needs to be kept under pressure if it's to be any good. A *Panorama* without pressure constantly applied is liable to be flat when you open it. But it's how you deal with that pressure that's important. Do you let it blast the cork into unplanned orbit and see the champagne pour out messily all over the floor, or do you manage things so that the cork comes out gently, and allows a nice bubbly brew to fill the glass? What happens when *Panorama* feels the pressure? How have its bosses performed when they've come under fire, and what has happened when it's those very bosses who have been the ones to apply the pressure?

External forces

In 1973 a *Panorama* report on the Shah of Iran provoked a major row. The programme[3] had suggested that Iran was using its oil wealth to buy far more military equipment than it reasonably required to defend itself. The Shah was furious, and the BBC's resident correspondent in Tehran, John Bierman, who had had nothing to do with the *Panorama* report, was summarily kicked out. Because a great deal of the new weaponry – Chieftain tanks, for example – was coming from Britain, the British Government was as angry as the Shah.

At a meeting of the Board of Governors the Director General, Charles Curran, described the programme as 'excellent in almost every respect', but the programme caused a good deal of trouble for the Foreign Office, and for the BBC. A new Governor, Sir Denis Greenhill, had until that year been Permanent Under-Secretary at the Foreign and Commonwealth Office: 'When the Chairman asked Sir Denis Greenhill whether he considered the programme had done lasting harm Sir Denis said that he thought it had.'[4]

Greenhill's views seem to have had their effect. On 29 November the Governors changed the minute of their previous meeting. To the passage that read 'the Chairman recalled that the Governors who had seen the programme had considered it to be good with only one or two slight blemishes' was added 'delete "with only one or two slight blemishes" and insert "though marred by some unwise editorialising in a few places"'.[5]

Whether or not he himself agreed with these changes, the Director General had earlier written to *The Times* to defend the programme and try to answer the complaints being made by the Iranian ambassador. His letter continued:

> I can only account for the difference of view between the Ambassador and the BBC by suggesting that there is a second question to be considered. It is this. Should programmes be prepared in order to please those on whom they are reporting, or in order to illuminate the situation for those to whom they are addressed? I realise that this may state the problem too sharply but the question is nonetheless a reality. The traditions of free journalism in this country would undoubtedly place the emphasis on the second objective, if for no other reason than that it is the more conducive to credibility. It is hardly possible to enlighten without questioning, and in a penetrating way. *Panorama*'s reporter did just this.'[6]

This was very gratifying to the *Panorama* team – who of course were told nothing of the Governors' reservations. Even better was the reaction of Brian Wenham, the laconic Head of Television's Current Affairs Group when the author, who was the reporter concerned, expressed regret at the trouble the programme had caused. 'I shouldn't worry', said Wenham; 'I pay you to go and make up your mind.'

What reporter could ask for anything more? But that bond of trust between *Panorama* people and their managers has, in more recent years, not been as strong as it once was.

It was much later, in December 1987: the Shah's appetite for Western weaponry had long ago failed to save him from overthrow and death in exile, and *Panorama*'s presenter Fred Emery was talking to a different and much nicer Shah – Samir Shah, newly appointed by John Birt as Head of Weekly Current Affairs Television. A *Panorama* team had been sent to the Philippines to report on the progress of the 'People's Revolution' there.

Shah told Emery that he was worried. Before they left, the reporter and producer team had discussed with him the story they were going on and what they thought their film would say. But, Shah agonised, suppose the reporter returned from Manila saying that, after investigation on the ground, the story was different? How could Shah be sure that the reporter was right? How could he be confident his report was accurate and unbiased? Emery's reply was blunt: if you can't trust the people who make your programmes, get ones you can.

Samir Shah's question showed the gulf that had opened up between programme makers and their managers since John Birt had arrived, a chasm of no confidence. With that sort of situation it didn't seem very likely that the people who made the programmes would always be able to count on backing when pressure was applied. And so it sometimes proved.

As Grace Wyndham Goldie noted, the more people watched television, the more people wanted to control it. As soon as *Panorama* had proved itself the 'important' programme she had wanted it to be, it came under greater pressure from both inside and outside the BBC. A letter in the files from then co-Producer Charles Wheeler gives the flavour of the relationship between the Government and *Panorama* journalists in early 1957. Not long after the Suez fiasco *Panorama* wanted to interview Captain Fell, a British naval officer in charge of salvaging sunken ships that were still blocking the Canal. A list of questions had had to be prepared and given to the Admiralty. Too hot for the sea lords to handle, the questions had been passed on to 10 Downing St, which had objected to one of them; it was about whether completing the operation on time depended on continued Egyptian co-operation. The issue seems to have gone right to the top: 'Finally the Admiralty phoned to say that the question had been put to the Prime Minister', wrote Wheeler in a confidential note to Leonard Miall; ' . . . the Prime Minister had decided that so long as Captain Fell said: "I may say so, but this is really a political question", the question could stand.'[7] Yes, Prime Minister.

Sometimes the BBC seemed to put itself voluntarily under unnecessary pressure: 'We should keep in touch with the Foreign Office before sending anyone abroad,' wrote the Assistant Head of Talks, Television in 1958.[8] Four years later the channel Controllers' meeting noted complaints by the Colonial Office that it had not been informed in advance of *Panorama*'s intention to send a reporting team to Aden. Said the minutes: 'Board of Management had come to the conclusion that, in future, all staff proceeding overseas on other than trivial or routine assignments should first inform the appropriate Government department – not in order that they should be in any way muzzled but rather with a view to acquiring useful background information and assistance.'[9] Of course. But after

Ludovic Kennedy and his producer Norman Swallow had filmed in Aden, the Governor, Sir Charles Johnston, demanded that their interviews with Arab nationalists be removed from the film. Shamefully, they were. Kennedy cabled Miall in furious complaint at the way the BBC had given in to Colonial Office rule.[10]

A Corporation which had only just freed itself from the shackles of the '14-day rule' could sometimes seem indecently eager to enter Government service as its television propaganda arm. When the Ministry of Defence proposed a programme to boost recruitment to the armed forces, Kenneth Adam, the Controller of Programmes, wrote: 'Mr. Grisewood[11] has asked me to let you know that the Television Service is anxious to help in the Ministry's recruiting campaign.' The proposed programme would have the Minister answering a pre-arranged question about new weapons. He would then go into a pre-recorded commentary (presumably beginning 'I'm glad you asked me that') over pictures. This scenario had actually been suggested by BBC producer Kenneth Lamb. It was soon apparent that the Minister, Duncan Sandys, wanted to take over the programme completely and treat it as he would a ministerial broadcast. As Head of Talks, Television, Miall had to try and claw back at least some control. 'I explained that our object was to promote recruiting,' he told his colleagues, 'but that editorial control must lie with the BBC and that the script would have to be written in the BBC, not in the MOD.'[12]

Pressure from the BBC's own advisory bodies has often proved particularly difficult to resist. Distinguished experts recruited by the BBC to advise on its programmes are given to understand that their opinions are valued; frequently they are miffed when their expertise is ignored by the actual programme makers. In 1963 Walter James, long-serving Editor of the *Times Educational Supplement* and a member of the BBC's General Advisory Council, had written to the BBC Chairman Sir Arthur Fforde following a programme dealing with educational issues. He had made – according to Kenneth Adam, now the Director of Television – 'outrageous accusations of left-wing bias'. And he had gone on to suggest that 'experienced people' should in future stand over a producer and see to 'the balance of the programme's content'.

Wyndham Goldie, now the Head of Talks, wrote an informal background note to Adam. While she defended her producers against charges of

bias and ignorance she conceded that there might be gaps in their experience of life which might lead to problems:

> Producers are chosen because they can be objective and wish to be objective:
> able to resist the innumerable pressures which are brought to bear on them
> by interested parties. Their weakness often is, not that they are irresponsible
> or 'sour', but that so many of them are crusaders at heart. They want to do
> good within the terms of their knowledge and experience. But few of them
> have had the responsibility of executive action in the world of economic and
> political affairs.'

To try to remedy this lack of experience, Wyndham Goldie said, she was in
the process of establishing informal groups of advisers in home affairs and
economics to supplement the guest luncheons she was already holding.
'These contacts are valuable educationally for producers, and also set up a
group of people whom the producers know and who are normally only too
delighted to be called upon either for advice or actually to appear on
programmes.'[13]

But as to the suggestion that any 'expert' should in some way be put in
authority over programme makers, to tell them what was right and wrong,
Wyndham Goldie was uncompromising. In a more formal note to Adam
she wrote: 'I am sure you will agree that Mr. James's suggestion that there
should be "a man behind the throne", either governing or being an equality
with each producer who handles controversial subjects, is both an imprac-
ticable and a dangerous idea.' It would have been 'extremely dangerous' for
any one expert with one opinion to have been in charge of the programme,
for example, which dealt with the Robbins Report on Higher Education.
One view was not enough. 'It is for the producer to get advice from all
kinds of sources, many of them violently opposed, as to who is the best
exponent of a particular attitude and to see that each of these is given an
opportunity, whether through an interview or discussion or any other
suitable means of presentation, of putting these views forward . . . I cannot
believe that Mr. James's suggestion of a single "expert" adviser who knows
the subject would help us in any way.'[14]

The suggestion that a single expert, even one as eminent as James,
should sit in judgement on producers who were duty bound to explore and

assess a wide range of views was finally rejected – courteously but firmly – by the Chairman himself: 'This we feel to be a dangerous thing to try,' James was told.

But the belief that there is somewhere some expert who can ensure that a *Panorama* programme gets it right is one held not just outside the BBC. As part of his effort to improve the standard of BBC journalism John Birt appointed senior 'specialist' reporters and encouraged *Panorama* to use them. His belief was that these people, experts in their field, would make better programmes than *Panorama*'s ordinary reporters. So for example Polly Toynbee, Social Affairs Editor, might come and do a *Panorama* about how Britain was going to look after the growing number of elderly people,[15] or how the Social Fund was failing the poorest people who most needed help.

The idea has real attractions. Specialists know the background to the story; they won't make silly mistakes, or waste time getting up to speed on the City, or Northern Ireland. But 'experts' are people who, over time, have come to a particular view of their specialism that they are likely to defend. That's not necessarily the best way to start out when making a *Panorama* programme. The reporter who knows that he doesn't know too much may be just as well placed to find out the truth as one who feels he knows it all. It can often be better for a generalist to seek out the views of a variety of experts rather than let an expert 'specialist correspondent' make the programme.

What has frequently concerned *Panorama*'s programme makers is that powerful establishment lobby groups often apply pressure not directly to them or to their Editor, but to the Director General or Chairman. The danger of such pressure is that it may remain hidden, leaving the programme makers in ignorance that their ultimate bosses have been 'got at', that undertakings, apologies or concessions may have been made without their knowledge. Those at the top of organisations such as the BBC often like to think of their decision to keep confidential the exchanges they have had with important pressure groups as sparing the programme makers unnecessary worry. But these programme makers would rather know about the representations being made, have a chance to contribute to an answer, and see how their bosses finally respond to the pressure that has been applied.

In the summer of 1979 the nuclear industry was incandescent – near meltdown – over a *Panorama* programme[16] which had dared question the rationale behind the Government's apparent determination to build many more nuclear power stations. *Panorama* had shown that the industry wanted to press ahead with a vastly expensive programme without having more than the faintest idea or concern about what the real cost of electricity from these nuclear power stations would be. The 'nuclear knights' were outraged by *Panorama*'s criticism, and at once began a discreet lobby of the BBC's Director General. By the autumn, Lord 'Toby' Aldington, Chairman of the National Nuclear Corporation, was writing to Sir Ian Trethowan: 'Dear Ian, Thank you very much for an excellent lunch at the Connaught Grill and for a most enjoyable meeting. Let me say how much I enjoy these talks . . . '[17]

Trethowan gave a commitment that the BBC would return to the subject with 'a major programme on the nuclear options in the not too distant future'. At the end of the following month, Dick Francis, Director, News and Current Affairs, wrote to Aldington, eagerly taking up his suggestion for 'one or two of our senior editorial figures to talk with some of your people in the N.N.C.'.[18] A delightful dinner party duly took place on 5 December at which, very politely, the nuclear lobby leaned on the BBC men to persuade them to provide another opportunity for the industry to put its case on television. The *Panorama* people who had made the original programme were neither informed of these developments nor consulted about the discussion programme which resulted.

After 'The Nuclear Power Debate'[19] Audience Research reported that: 'Although most were agreed that the topic of nuclear power was well worthy of debate, they were often less satisfied with the outcome. They thought many important questions had been evaded, particularly regarding those concerning nuclear waste, and generally felt they had heard little that had not already been said before.'[20] Robin Day had chaired the studio debate with his usual fairness, but a letter in the *Radio Times*[21] asked: 'Who planned the programme? The government? Was it a party political broadcast in disguise?' A note from the programme's producer Victor Marmion insisted that 'the government did not plan the programme, we planned it'. But he was only half right. The Government wasn't directly responsible for the programme – but nor was the BBC. The fact is that it wouldn't have happened at all if it hadn't been for the pressure privately applied by the nuclear lobby.

The different ways in which the BBC reacts to Establishment pressure can be seen in the way it handled the row over two separate items in the *Panorama* of 16 July 1962. Following Harold Macmillan's 'night of the long knives', on 13 July, when the Prime Minister had summarily sacked one third of his Cabinet, Robert Kee had interviewed Lord Lambton and Randolph Churchill, who was, as so often, drunk. It was a rowdy, entertaining discussion in which Churchill had applauded Macmillan on the dubious grounds that, whatever his political failings, he had at least shown himself to be a good butcher.

The following morning Hugh Carleton Greene, the Director General, found on his desk a letter from the Conservative Party grandee and former power broker the Right Honourable the Viscount Davidson, GCVO, CH, CB: 'Dear Mr. Greene, If I may put it bluntly, there was a disgraceful section of *Panorama* last night, which was an insult to the British public . . . and to the reputation of the BBC, which you hold in your hand. Those responsible for asking Randolph Churchill and Lambton to appear on the programme should bury their heads in their hands.'[22]

Asked for an explanation of what had happened, Grace Wyndham Goldie (who had not seen the programme go out) tried – rather incoherently, it must be said – to defend the choice of Lambton and Churchill: 'Everybody has said that as far as making good television was concerned, this was undoubtable [sic], [however] it does seem to have been below the standard of comment which the occasion warranted.' But Carleton Greene quickly decided that he was going to put his hands up: on this issue the Corporation would surrender unconditionally. The following day he replied to Davidson: 'I agree with every word you say. This was an appalling error for which I offer no excuse whatever. I can assure you that many people are burying their heads in their hands.' Carleton Greene then sent Davidson's letter and his reply to Wyndham Goldie, saying:

> I regard this as one of the most inexcusable errors ever committed by supposedly responsible people in all my experience of broadcasting. Anyone with any political sense could, and should, have foreseen what happened. The harm done to the reputation of the BBC would have been considerable

at any time. That this howler should have been perpetrated at this time of all times passes my comprehension. I shall have to give serious consideration to ways and means of tightening up the supervision of all political output in the Television Service.[23]

Carleton Greene grovelled over the political part of this *Panorama*, but the BBC took a firmer line when pressure came to bear on the other offending item in the programme. This was a report about the Thalidomide scandal, in which babies with very severe physical deformities had been born to some of the mothers who had taken the drug while pregnant. This time it was not the Director General but the Chairman who had his lapels seized by an influential complainant, Lord Ferrier, in a message telephoned to the BBC: 'So astonished by yesterday's *Panorama* programme that feel bound to let you know my misgiving and my sincere hope that you will call producer to your study . . . The drug item appeared to me personally to be sensationalism of the meanest type. Did it occur to your people that a number of expectant parents may have been agonised afresh by BBC emphasis on this tragedy. Why not have waited until the last affected baby has been born – say end of August.' And then came the explanation of why Lord Ferrier was interested in the story: for personal reasons, but perhaps more importantly, because he was a leading member of the mighty drugs industry: 'Although I am Chairman of an important British pharmaceutical group I am not personally connected with the manufacture or marketing of Thalidomide, but two of my daughters are pregnant.'[24] The next day he wrote again: 'I do hope I haven't been importunate in worrying you, but I am indeed peculiarly situated in being a leader in a small way in the Pharmaceutical Industry, of which I am intensely proud, and being also a proud grandfather, actual and expectant.'[25]

In this case the BBC found it easier to resist the pressure to apologise and back away from an important story. Asked for his comment, Kenneth Lamb, Chief Assistant (Current Affairs) Talks, Television, wrote:

> I personally discussed very carefully the treatment of this item with Norman Swallow, who was in charge of it. We took particular pains to ensure that nothing should be said about the grim plight of these expectant mothers beyond what was necessary to establish the starting point of a more general

enquiry. What the public wants to know, and this is an anxiety that has been very widely reflected in the Press and in Parliament, is how such a tragedy could have happened, and what steps are being taken to avoid its recurrence. I believe we would have been failing in our duty if we had not mounted such an enquiry. I am satisfied that it was treated responsibly and correctly.[26]

Harman Grisewood, Chief Assistant to the Director General, advised that Ferrier should be told to stop trying to pressure *Panorama*: 'I think we should disagree with Lord Ferrier's suggestion that the right approach for us was to leave the subject "almost entirely alone". Now having read the script, I think our item was sensible and appropriate. I suggest you or the Chairman should write, shortly, to say that you have read the script and do not agree that the item was sensational or irresponsible . . . In our view, this is by no means a case of least said soonest mended.'[27]

So here a voice from a powerful lobby was being told to pipe down. In this case public interest in the Thalidomide story was even more powerful than the drugs industry's interest in seeing it hushed up. So the BBC, on behalf of *Panorama*, felt it possible to shrug off the pressure. Perhaps the story also suggests that complaints from senior politicians, who ultimately control the BBC's income, are understandably taken rather more seriously than are most others. But some special interests carry real clout – or at least did once.

In 1979 *Panorama* made a programme about the tendency of government in Britain to keep secret what would in the United States be a matter of public knowledge.[28] Among the illustrations chosen was the way the safety record of a particular car make and model could be easily discovered in America but not in Britain, where an owner might never learn how widespread was some serious defect that the manufacturers and government knew all about. *Panorama* discovered that in the US there had been a great many replacements of faulty wiring in British Leyland's TR7 sports cars. There had also been more recalls of BL cars than those of any other manufacturer.

'Do You Want to Know a Secret?' was well received and it was decided to repeat it during *Panorama*'s summer break. British Leyland had not challenged the facts *Panorama* had reported, but complained they had not been offered a chance to have their say. So now they were – in an interview with a BL executive specially shot and slotted into the original programme. But that wasn't enough for the Chairman of BL; he wanted still more, and wrote to the Governors to say so. As the Board of Governors' minutes put it: 'Sir Michael Edwardes had disowned the judgement of his own subordinates.'[29]

Did the BBC politely tell Edwardes what to do? It did not. Instead, the acting Director General, Gerard Mansell, simply dropped the *Panorama* programme altogether – without revealing the pressure he had been under from BL. 'On balance', his public statement said, ' . . . we were not sufficiently satisfied with the absolute fairness of one part of the original programme or of the success of efforts to put that right in the proposed repeat programme. That was our decision alone and no question of censorship or gagging arises.'[30] That was not the view of others inside and outside the BBC, who saw Mansell's decision as weakness in the face of a powerful interest. The Head of Current Affairs, Television, Chris Capron, protested that the BBC was seen to be bowing to the wishes of a big institution in a way it would never do for individuals.

But the BBC was shortly to face a lobby more powerful still than the motor manufacturers – the doctors.

A medical case history

In the early summer of 1980 *Panorama* began work on a most unusual story, nothing less than a matter of life and death. It would lead to a trial of strength between the programme and one of Britain's most powerful interest groups, and severely test the BBC's ability to maintain editorial control over what it broadcast. It could also be argued – and it was – that scores, perhaps even hundreds, of people in Britain died sooner than they would otherwise have done as a result of the programme.

Small and quietly spoken, Anne Moir was unusual among *Panorama* producers at that time. Not only was she the only woman (Margaret Jay had gone off to the United States with her husband, the new British Ambassador) she was by education a scientist. Most other reporters and producers were the proud products of a liberal arts education who, when it came to figures, had the greatest difficulty in adding up their expenses. Moir, by contrast, had an Oxford doctorate in human genetics. It wasn't the heroic side of medicine, of course, but her scientific background was invaluable when it came to dealing with the doctors: she knew what they were like.

Earlier that year Moir had produced a *Panorama* programme about the development of transplant surgery in Britain.[31] Kidney transplants were by then well established, liver and heart transplants still relatively rare. Moir's programme, with Michael Cockerell as its reporter, had featured the pioneering work in this country of Professor Magdi Yacoub. With her camera team Moir had followed a heart that had been taken from an accident victim in the Netherlands and then flown to Britain, where Yacoub and his team at Harefield Hospital transplanted it into a patient in desperate need. It was a strong, feel-good story with a powerful message: our doctors are among the best of the modern medical miracle workers.

It was after that programme, in one of the medical journals she trawled for possible stories, that Moir came across an item that intrigued her. 'Americans question the British way of death,' it said. The piece drew attention to a problem exposed to scrutiny by the growing number of transplant operations. At what point was it permissible to take an organ from a donor? When was it exactly that the donor was dead? The more Moir thought about it, the more important an issue it seemed. If people were having vital organs removed for the benefit of somebody else then it was obviously essential that they should be dead first. Yet how could this be if their organs were still 'alive'?

In the *Lancet* Anne found a letter from two doctors at a transplant centre (Papworth Hospital in Cambridge), who were concerned about the 'ethics of removing a beating heart'.[32] It appeared that organs were being taken from donors on the basis of 'brain death', and that this relatively new way of diagnosing death was now being questioned. Dr David Wainwright Evans and his colleague Claude Lum were worried that while the transplant donors might well be dying, they might not yet be dead – might indeed even be conscious. If there was anything in this, it was dramatic, and important too. Surely British doctors, in order to save some lives, couldn't be taking the risk of ending other lives prematurely, could they?

Panorama Editor Roger Bolton was interested; he told Moir to do more research on the idea, with the author. In 1980 it was still possible for a reporter and producer to be allowed weeks and even months to research a particularly complicated story before filming began.

At that time relations between the medical profession and television were, to say the least, uneasy. Earlier television series like *Your Life in Their Hands* had treated doctors as gods, incapable of error. When a patient in one of the programmes in that series had died after surgery the episode had not been shown so as not to spoil the doctors' perfect image. But it was no longer like that. Television journalism (particularly on *Panorama* with Bolton as Editor) was taking itself rather seriously, asserting a right and a responsibility to question established authority and received wisdom. Increasingly now the medical profession found itself challenged by what one medical man described as 'pipsqueak reporters'. For doctors, being interviewed was a discomforting experience in role reversal. They found themselves in the same position as a patient, being asked to tell their story to somebody else without having control over how it would be used. They didn't like that at all.

A *Tonight* programme on how to deal with cancer patients, a *Horizon* on the risks of ante-natal investigations, a *Panorama* on ECT – all had upset a profession that felt it had the exclusive right to decide how these issues should be dealt with on television, if at all. Some doctors were all for restricting or withdrawing co-operation. In 1978 John Garfield, a consultant neurosurgeon, wrote in a 'Personal View' for the *British Medical Journal*: 'It is difficult today to talk of dignity in medicine without being accused of secretiveness in a pejorative sense, and of bolstering the mystique of the calling. I believe our patients still look for that dignity which is so difficult to define, but which is so rapidly lost as soon as the doctor faces the television camera, the cunning interviewer, and the dextrous producer.'[33] Whether cunning and dextrous or not, the author and Anne Moir, as experienced television journalists, recognised the medical minefield into which they were stepping.

Despite an enormous research effort, there had been little apparent advance in recent years in the doctors' ability to cure some major diseases – like cancer – or make a dramatic difference to a patient's quality of life. Organ transplantation was a major exception, a huge, popular success story, taking people who would soon die or live out a pretty miserable existence and making them fit for life again. Doctors of many different disciplines now had a big stake in a new field where they could be seen to produce results, transforming very sick patients into people with a good quality of life.

When closely examined the statistics showed that a good many transplants didn't work for long, but there was every hope the record would improve with experience and the development of new drugs to combat organ rejection. And most important of all, the general public were right behind the transplant programme. Many parents whose child had been fatally injured in some road accident drew comfort from the thought that out of a tragic death something could be saved, that organs taken from the dead could make it possible for others to live. People who read accounts of these events were often moved to carry donor cards, which carried a picture of popular television presenter Anna Ford and the words 'I want someone to live after my death'. But as Moir and the author were discovering, there lay the problem. What did 'after my death' really mean?

Through the late 1960s and 1970s doctors in the United States and Britain had established the concept of brain death. If the patient's brain was dead then 'there is no possible chance of recovery',[34] even though breathing, and therefore the heartbeat and circulation, were still being maintained by a machine. Doctors developed diagnostic criteria, simple bedside tests, that would help them decide when a respirator could safely be switched off.

The British version of the tests, said the medical Royal Colleges, 'are accepted as being sufficient to distinguish between those patients who retain the functional capacity to have a chance of even partial recovery and those where no such possibility exists'.[35] That seemed to say that doctors could tell whether patients with damaged brains had any chance of recovery. It did not say that the criteria could distinguish between the living and the dead. But that was what the transplant business needed. Clearly surgeons should not take organs from those who were dying: only those who were dead.

Three years later, in a Memorandum,[36] the Royal Colleges added the necessary clincher: 'The identification of brain death means that the patient is dead, whether or not the function of some organs, such as a heart beat, is still maintained by artificial means.' Now doctors could certify death in patients they believed to be dead even if to a layman they still looked as if they were alive.

In theory, the needs of transplantation had nothing to do with this new way of diagnosing death, but reports in the medical journals suggested the opposite. In March 1980 the *Lancet* had published 'A Brain Death Protocol' by John Searle and Charles Collins from the Intensive Therapy Unit at the Royal Devon and Exeter Hospital. Describing one case they wrote: 'It was necessary to confirm the diagnosis of brain death as quickly as possible if the kidneys were to be obtained in a reasonable condition.'[37]

With that sort of pressure for transplant organs, the criteria for brain death had to be foolproof. Once the diagnosis was made, a patient who had a moment before been alive was now officially dead. In an instant, a patient had become a corpse, a dead body from which the organs could immediately be removed.

What many grieving relatives of a dead organ donor didn't quite grasp was that the body of their loved one was now often subject to more energetic 'treatment' than it had been while alive. The respirator was kept going, and new drugs administered, all to keep the 'corpse', and its organs, in the best possible condition. The transplant team was assembled, the chosen recipient made ready, and the relevant organ removed from the donor. As the author later put it, rather brutally, in his script: 'If he wasn't dead when he was wheeled into the theatre, he certainly is now.'[38]

For weeks Moir and the author pored over medical papers on brain death and talked to doctors in Britain, Europe and America who had been involved in this new diagnosis of death. In Liverpool transplant surgeon Robert Sells agreed that it was right for *Panorama* to explore the 'ground rules' of transplantation. He would let them film the diagnosis of brain death, followed by the process of organ donation in his operating theatre.

At an early stage the team realised that to question the 'ground rules' might deter some donors or worry some of their relatives, and so damage the transplant programme. Was that an acceptable risk? The team were encouraged to discover that in Denmark, where the criteria for brain death included more stringent tests than anywhere else,[39] the proportion of people willing to become donors in the event of their death was the highest in the world. If *Panorama* did expose weaknesses in the British way of brain death perhaps it would help bring about changes to the rules which would ultimately increase the number of potential donors.

The question was this: were the British brain death criteria, these simple bedside tests of the brain stem functions, entirely adequate for the diagnosis of death, or was a further test of some different kind needed to give assurance that the whole brain was dead – a test, for example, like the electroencephalograph, the EEG?

The British Code[40] said: 'Confirmatory Investigations. It is now widely accepted that electro-encephalography is not necessary for the diagnosis of brain death.' But that was not true. In America, after studying evidence about the use of the EEG in 3000 cases, a committee from Harvard Medical School had concluded: 'It is thus evident that electro-encephalography can have great usefulness, not only of a confirmatory kind, but also of primary value, if dependably obtained.'[41]

What it came down to was that British doctors were asserting that when they applied the simple British criteria to a patient – without any confirmatory test – they would never make a mistake. Britain's leading expert on brain death was Professor Bryan Jennett. With some reluctance he agreed to an interview with *Panorama*:

> *Lindley*: Are you saying, using our criteria, that we're never going to remove the organs from a transplant donor before he's dead?
>
> *Jennett*: That is my belief.
>
> *Lindley*: No question in your mind? No possibility of error?
>
> *Jennett*: If I thought there was I wouldn't be doing it.
>
> *Lindley*: Hundred per cent accurate?
>
> *Jennett*: That's right.

So Professor Jennett was confident that in this matter of life and death neither he nor any other British doctor diagnosing brain death would ever make a mistake – and he needed no confirmatory test to be sure.

The problem with a diagnosis of brain death is that, by its very nature, it is self-fulfilling, a death sentence. If a doctor decides you are dead he will switch off your respirator as soon as possible and – if you are a transplant donor – some vital organ will be removed. Either way your blood will shortly cease to circulate. You will soon be incontrovertibly dead. So

Panorama was unlikely to find anyone who had survived a British diagnosis of brain death. But in the United States *Panorama* did find a number of interesting cases where an additional test had picked up people who – judged by the clinical criteria alone – appeared to be dead.

Dave Churchill was unconscious after an accident at sea in Alaska. To help them get a breathing tube down his throat hospital doctors had given him a muscle-relaxing drug. Normally the effect of the drug lasts only for a few minutes; in Churchill's case it persisted for hours. Carrying out the clinical tests for brain death, his doctor thought he was dealing with a man whose brain was completely destroyed. But though he couldn't respond in any way, Churchill was conscious all the time: 'I could look right at the doctor and hear him howling at me and I could see him looking in my eye and I could hear him howling at the other doctors to do these other things that he wanted done. And there was no way I could respond at all, no way at all. There was no way I could move anything. I couldn't move my lips, I couldn't move my eyes, I couldn't move my hands, there was no way in the world I could move anything.'[42] The doctor prepared to switch off Churchill's respirator, but before he did so he gave him an EEG examination. It revealed brain activity that clearly showed that Churchill was very much alive. He made a full recovery.

After the programme the doctors who had drawn up the British brain death Code argued that none of the cases *Panorama* produced would ever have been declared dead by the British criteria – let alone become an organ donor. They would have been ruled out – because they had taken drugs, for example, or because it wasn't clear from their injuries exactly why they were unconscious. But in the United States a study of brain death had shown that making these 'exclusions' accurately was more easily said than done. Over a period of two years, observers in nine different medical centres had watched what happened to 503 cases admitted to hospital unconscious and unable to breathe without help. The results showed that doctors were in some cases diagnosing brain death completely unaware that these patients had taken drugs. They couldn't always be sure they knew the patient's medical 'history'. And the study further revealed that patients who were completely unresponsive to the clinical tests – to all appearances dead – for as long as 30 hours might still survive.

The authors of the British brain death Code now realised that *Panorama* was about to challenge the procedures they had worked out, procedures that had been endorsed by the top medical authorities in the land, the Royal Colleges. As the transmission date approached, they sent messages of concern and protest to the BBC. Leading transplant surgeons phoned and wrote to Director General Sir Ian Trethowan, pointing to the danger *Panorama* might pose to the transplant programme. The pressure was increasing. According to John Gau, then Head of Current Affairs, Television, Trethowan told him: 'This is serious, I think you should pull the programme.' Gau resisted: 'You pull it if you want to, I think it's a perfectly good show.'

Before transmission the programme was shown to Professor Ian McColl of Guy's Hospital, the BBC's medical adviser. In a note to Roger Bolton and Anne Moir, the author wrote: 'McColl had no medical points to make and said afterwards that he thought the medical profession would have been better advised to include another test in the British brain death criteria – even if only for the greater reassurance of the public.'

On Monday 13 October, in its usual BBC1 slot in those days of 8.10pm, *Panorama* went on air, introduced by David Dimbleby. 'The cases we show in the film', he said, 'are from the United States, and not all were potential transplant donors. But they do suggest that British methods of defining death may need re-examining.'

In the studio gallery the author, Moir and Bolton watched as the film unrolled. They thought they'd got it right, but would the viewers agree? When the regular research report for week 42 arrived it seemed to say they had. With an audience of six million, 'Transplants - Are the Donors Really Dead?' had been beaten by Shirley Bassey on BBC2, but those who had watched *Panorama* were glad they had. It 'was considered an excellent programme by reporting viewers', with a Reaction Index of 81, 'a very good figure', compared with a *Panorama* average of 74 for the year so far. 'Richard Lindley was thought to have done an excellent job of reporting the facts concerning the subject. His questioning of the various participants in the programme was considered searching, but always firm and polite. It was also agreed that he raised many points which those at home would have wanted to raise themselves had they been in a position to do so. A few thought him biased against the British doctors and surgeons but, for the majority, he had handled a controversial subject with skill, clarity and the minimum amount of bias.'

As to viewers' opinions of the people appearing in the film, the research said: 'The British participants did come in for a good deal of criticism. They were thought by many to have been complacent, arrogant and irritating, and indeed frightened and appalled some respondents.'[43] The TV critics were also kind about the programme. According to the *Daily Telegraph*, for example, it 'was a hard-hitting, thoroughly researched, totally convincing piece of investigation which only the very insensitive or the very confident could laugh off'.[44]

Viewers' letters seemed fairly evenly divided in praise or blame, but it was a different matter with the doctors. A few of their letters were encouraging, but far more were angry and contemptuous: 'By one sheer act of lunacy, complete bias, and total disregard for fact and balanced reporting, you have thrown the transplant programme into confusion which it certainly does not deserve. I hope you are happy when some of my patients will die in end-stage renal failure, as a direct result of your folly.'

Five days after transmission a *British Medical Journal* editorial entitled 'An Appalling *Panorama*' called the programme 'a disgrace'.[45] Professor Roy Calne, the eminent transplant surgeon at Addenbrooke's Hospital in Cambridge, wrote to *The Times*: 'The potential of television to manipulate and distort according to the wishes of the producer is enormous . . . The results of this biased prosecution of British transplantation practice will be distressing, and its perpetration was a wicked act.'[46]

One of the programme's fiercest and most knowledgeable critics was Dr Christopher Pallis, from London's Hammersmith Hospital. But even he conceded that: 'All said, there *is* an element of doubt about the diagnosis of brain-stem death . . . the problem lies in the inescapable fact that "codes" have to be implemented by physicians, and that all human beings are fallible.'[47] This was precisely the point the *Panorama* programme had made: that the British tests were not foolproof, and that therefore, in the context of transplant surgery, a further objective test of some kind, over and above the clinical criteria, was necessary.

In the *New Scientist* Donald Gould wrote:

> Predictably, *Panorama*'s assiduously researched and soberly presented programme on the diagnosis of death has produced loud wailing noises of outrage, sadness and despair from some of the surgical moguls involved in

the transplant game, and some of their supporters in the medical trade . . .
Perhaps the *Panorama* team has rocked the transplant boat a little. But if so,
so be it. It is not 'irresponsible' to raise questions which interfere with the
smooth running of established practices, even when those practices are, on
the face of it, solely directed toward the common good. People who arch
their backs and spit like a frightened cat in the face of criticism probably have
something to be frightened at.[48]

This was music to *Panorama*'s ears, but the generally hostile tone of the
medical press, a tone soon adopted by newspapers with no particular
fondness for television, was having a deafening effect. The programme had
shot its single bolt some weeks before, but the big guns of the medical
establishment continued to fire salvo after salvo in a counter-barrage. And
they were hitting the media target. On 24 November Moir sent a memo to
the author and Bolton summing up the situation as she saw it: 'We seem to
have lost the propaganda war. The gradual drip, drip of the "might is right"
lobby seems to be convincing quite a number of people in the press that we
got it wrong. The programme did not get the arguments wrong, and indeed
this is clearly illustrated by the fact that, since the programme, the debate
has been raging in the learned medical journals on the medical issues.' As
that debate raged on, the question of a second programme was mooted.
But what kind of a programme should it be?

What the medical profession proposed was a programme in which half
the time would simply be handed over to their nominees. 'This period of
half of the programme time will have no interruptions from the chairman
or any other participant in the programme in or out of the studio and will
not be subject to editorial control.' On 19 November, after a meeting with
Professor James Robson, the Secretary of the Medical Royal Colleges, John
Gau wrote what he hoped would be a conciliatory letter: 'I understand your
and your colleagues' mistrust of *Panorama* though naturally you would not
expect me to agree with you – and I do not. But given your misgivings, we
have obviously thought hard about what we can do to allay them. The
problem is how we accommodate them while, at the same time preserving
our own editorial independence and our faith with other contributors to
the programme, as well as the viewing public'.

The Royal Colleges didn't budge. So now the BBC made further concessions. The author and Dimbleby would not appear in the proposed programme; it would be edited not by Bolton but by Chris Capron, the Deputy Head of Current Affairs; and it would not be transmitted in the *Panorama* slot.

It was a climb-down, but the BBC had at least held fast to its determination not to hand over control of half the programme to the medical profession. The deal was this: in a special 90-minute programme the doctors would be given an independent producer and camera team to make a 15-minute film of their own in any way they liked, while another team (with producer Moir) would make a 10-minute film restating the doubts previously aired in the first *Panorama*. A highly structured studio discussion would follow, chaired by Ludovic Kennedy, between doctors of opposing views.

'The Brain Death Debate' was broadcast on BBC1 at 10.20pm on 19 February 1981. A measure of public interest in the issue was that at midnight four million people were still viewing. One of the doctors raising doubts about the British criteria said that he personally knew of two patients diagnosed dead by the British criteria who were not merely still alive at the time but had actually survived. Later, when he could not produce the evidence, he had to retract, and the BBC carried his retraction. But he still maintained his insistence that an EEG examination was necessary to confirm a diagnosis of brain death.

The *Panorama* team felt their original programme had been vindicated. A review of 'The Brian Death Debate' by Chris Dunkley in the *Financial Times* was headed 'Cheers by the Dozen'. Congratulating the BBC on 'keeping its head under fire from the doctors', Dunkley was critical of the team put up by the medical Royal Colleges who had complained about the first programme:

> What the complainants cannot have foreseen, or they would never have taken part, was that their opponents would marshal their facts better, make a better film of their case, put up a four-man team for the studio debate that was more impressive for being drawn not just from Britain but from Scandinavia and North America, and argue their case more persuasively with – the real clincher for those of us watching who were not medically trained – much less arrogance.[49]

On 25 February, after 'The Brain Death Debate', the author wrote to John Gau to say he thought the decision to keep him out of it had been justified by the results. The programme had put the argument back among the doctors; it was clearly seen to be a real issue among them rather than a mere journalistic invention. He continued:

> I think the problem remains however that the BBC was in effect being defended by proxy. What would have happened if the [*Panorama*] team of doctors had been no good in discussion, or had indeed refused to appear at all? Is the test of a current affairs programme's soundness to be whether the cast can be reassembled in the studio and win a debate? Is that possible in most cases? Do let's have more debates on important issues like last Thursday's. At the same time, and quite distinctly, we need a forum in which programmes and their production teams can be held accountable. Must we let our critics win propaganda battles in the press when we could offer them the opportunity to make their points on television?

Although it's made a few experiments since (with *Biteback* for example) the BBC still has no regular television programme of this kind, in which aggrieved parties or viewers can challenge reporters and producers, and hold them to account. Over on Channel 4 Bolton, *Panorama*'s Editor at the time of the brain death programme, has presented *Right to Reply*, but now, although the programme still seemed full of life, it's been switched off.

Having the first public discussion of the British brain death criteria was, as one of the most senior doctors to criticise the first programme privately admitted to the *Panorama* team, a useful contribution to public knowledge. Against that was the programme's deterrent effect on transplant operations. But that was brief. Referring to the original *Panorama* as a 'farrago of inaccuracy' a contributor to the *British Medical Journal* recently asserted that afterwards 'organ donation was reduced for a decade'. Apologising in its issue of 30 November 2002 for these 'two serious errors', the *BMJ* accepted that 'neither of these statements is true'. On the contrary, 'the figures for organ donation in the United Kingdom in fact showed a continued increase over the 1980s'.

The medical Royal Colleges did not abandon their definition of brain death, nor add new tests to what was necessary for its diagnosis. But in

August 1981 they did announce significant changes in the way the diagnosis should be made. From now on it could only be arrived at by two senior doctors, and both of them would have to be expert in this field; and even when the tests confirmed that the patient's brain was dead they would have to be repeated to make doubly sure. Those changes have not been sufficient to produce the number of donors required.

Round the world argument about how to diagnose brain death continues. In the United States a neurologist who searched the medical literature found reports of 175 patients who, he concluded, were dead by the light of the British tests but had survived on respirators for at least one week. Twenty of them went on for more than two months and seven for at least six months.[50] Were they all dead, when they met the British brain death criteria – dead enough perhaps to be organ donors – or were they still in the process of dying? In July 2002 the Department of Health issued a consultation report, in which it asked whether the defintion of death should now be reconsidered.

The pressure from within – in the commodore's cabin

'Tom, you are a reporter who stands across his stories.' Whatever that meant exactly, it was clearly intended as high praise, and it came from the very top of the BBC. In 1980 Director General Ian Trethowan had, most unusually, summoned *Panorama* reporter Tom Mangold to a private meeting to discuss two films Mangold was planning to make on Britain's security services, MI5 and MI6. The idea was to look both at the services' apparent lack of accountability and at allegations that they were acting illegally, to the detriment of entirely innocent and law-abiding people.

According to Mangold, Trethowan wanted him to drop his investigations but, realising the programmes had now gone too far to stop, he offered: 'Give me the script; I'll take it to Curzon Street[51] and then you'll know it's the truth.' According to Mangold, Trethowan wanted him not to mention this conversation to Roger Bolton, 'that little Marxist shit', as Mangold recalls the cool and sophisticated Trethowan calling *Panorama*'s Editor. Mangold of course did brief Bolton and the Head of Current Affairs John Gau on what had gone on in the DG's office.

The programmes were made,[52] but Trethowan put obstacles in *Panorama*'s way designed to restrict its ability to cover the story properly.

MI5 and MI6 had already refused all co-operation; Trethowan now forbade the team to interview past members of the security services – and then demanded that various sequences and allegations in the films should be removed on the grounds that there was no interviewee to back them up. In his memoirs Trethowan later wrote: 'A body such as the BBC should not get involved in such matters unless it can do so with real authority, and it was hard to see how this could be achieved in the face of the hostility of virtually all those involved, past and present.'[53]

On this occasion the pressure on *Panorama* was at least as great from inside the Corporation as from any outside agency. But *Panorama* had seen nothing yet. In the spring of 1987 John Birt joined the BBC as Deputy Director General. 'My main task', he says, 'was to take over the journalism.'

Drumhead court martial

In Phnom Penh, after the Khmer Rouge Marxists had taken over Cambodia, the paper currency that had been of value under the old regime blew about the streets for years to come, now quite worthless, unregarded. That was how Lime Grove journalism suddenly seemed to be when John Birt arrived at the BBC. Even the dark suits that Birt and his lieutenants favoured looked rather like the black pyjama outfits that Pol Pot's Cambodian guerrillas wore as they came padding quietly down the road in their disciplined way.

Attending a meeting with *Panorama* people Birt was asked what he admired about Lime Grove's recent output. 'Nothing,' was the bleak reply. It was clear that Birt had been given a mandate for change and intended to exercise it. As Ron Neil, soon to be appointed Birt's deputy, remembers, Birt was a man with a presence: when he arrived in a room you knew he was there.

Now that this large, moon-faced, smiling, quietly spoken man had taken control, many a *Panorama* person would disappear, and those who remained would be subjected to a rigorous course of re-education which, for a long time, left its mark on them, and on the programme.

Many BBC journalists soon came to feel that Birt's prime objective was to prevent them causing trouble. 'His interventions', says Peter Horrocks, a *Panorama* Editor under Birt, 'were to do with stopping and controlling, rather than applauding. His personality and character were a large part of that.'

John Birt was heading a new Directorate which for the first time brought

News and Current Affairs fully together. His first priority was to get a grip of News, which was thought to be slight and superficial, and then of Current Affairs at Lime Grove, seen for some time now by the Governors as 'cowboy country', and out of control. But today Lord Birt says he regarded his mission then not as one of repression but of liberation: 'I think the BBC's journalism had been under-attended to by the BBC . . . there was a strong sense the journalism was not punching its weight in the BBC . . . The key issue in Current Affairs was how could you make sure that Current Affairs as a whole was more engaged in the national debate, asking bigger questions, getting to grips with issues?' But how far was all this really about imposing discipline on *Panorama*? Birt says:

> I thought it was too story-based as a programme and wasn't as ready as I thought it should be to engage the big issues of the day. I think they were all more important ideas than the sense that *Panorama* was 'out of control', but it is true that, when I arrived at the BBC, quite a lot of people told me that it was . . . The sort of consensus amongst the people that I sort of quickly formed a bond with, the people that were going to be the future managers and so on . . . the consensus is that the programme needed to assert the importance of the Editor; that the reporters had become too powerful in the mix . . . we were in a position where the reporters, more than the producers, more than the Editor, were determining the programmes; there was a lot of stuff done at the last minute; there was insufficient editorial control of the programming as it came into transmission . . . and the importance of 'Maggie's Militant Tendency' in this (which happened before I arrived on the scene) was very much in people's minds; it was very much seen as a process failure . . . it had all been rather last-minute, the lawyers had come in too late, there wasn't proper scrutiny, nobody had said: 'If we have to face a legal action how can we make sure that we're able to defend it?'

So how important was sorting out a *Panorama* seen to be 'out of control'? 'Was it high up on the agenda? No. Was it part of the agenda? Yes.'

Birt's arrival sent *Panorama*'s reporters and producers hurrying to the cuttings files to look up a most interesting series of articles Birt had written more than a decade before, in 1975. 'There is a bias in television journalism. It is not against any particular party or point of view – it is a bias against understanding,' Birt had said. Too often, he had argued, television journalists were picking at some sore on the body politic but failing to relate it to the underlying cause of the problem, the bigger picture. 'For example, making a film about homeless people is not an adequate way of approaching the problems created by our housing shortage . . . There is a danger that the pressure brought to bear on politicians by the incoherent highlighting of societies' sores by television will lead politicians . . . to deal with the symptoms of crisis rather than to take a longer time to search out fundamental causes and to deal with them.' This seems a good point well made. A programme like Panorama cannot just emote: a strong human story on its own is not current affairs.

But Birt wasn't finished. In a second and third article he was joined by Peter Jay, then his presenter on the Weekend World programme at London Weekend Television. Television journalism, they now said, was 'a misbegotten child of two ill-assorted parents, neither of which is well adapted to the needs of news analysis. One parent is the newspaper office, typically the local paper's newsroom. The other is the film business, more specifically the documentary film.' So television reporters (the poor bastard children of these two traditions) were likely to be either ignorant and ill-educated, or interested only in making exciting documentary films. They were not only asking the wrong questions, they were selfishly choosing the easy options too: 'The reporter recognises that "concerned" interviews with victims of the system and "grabbing" interviews with the guilty landlord or council official are more likely to establish him as a "personality" interviewer than some painstaking and abstract analysis of housing economics which is outside his experience and capabilities.'[54] How Panorama reporters hung their heads in shame as they read these words! All the time, it seemed, they had been too ignorant to understand the story they were doing. Worse, they had been trying to make television interesting, not to get the viewers viewing, but just to boost their media careers.

Birt's programme at London Weekend Television of course was not like this at all. Certainly Weekend World could never be accused of preferring a human interest story to an 'abstract analysis'. The dreary truth was that Weekend World was essentially an illustrated lecture, as tedious as it was sometimes tendentious; a thesis rather than an exploration of real life; an arid analytical exposition of an issue in which inconveniently contradictory opinions, feelings or emotions often found no place at all. *Panorama* people often came across expert interviewees who complained of how *Weekend World* producers had only wanted to hear evidence to support the thesis they had already decided was the right one – something that fitted the script that had already been written. As Charles Leadbetter put it in the *New Statesman*: 'When I worked as a researcher on *Weekend World* in the mid-1980's we routinely cajoled pundits into saying word for word what our editors demanded they say for the sake of keeping the story-line tidy. Inconvenient facts were often left to one side; we were often dull.'[55]

Michael Tracey, writing about the first 10 years of *Weekend World*, suggests that, as a lively young programme maker at Granada, Birt had become very conscious of major gaps in his knowledge of the world and deeply impressed with those whose analysis seemed to make sense of it. *Weekend World* reflected his conclusion that the best way to make a current affairs television programme was to write it all down first: 'The key thing was that it was office work. If you spent time in the office with bright people who understood a story you could write it out, using language as your tool, into a clear exposition of something or other, and that ought to happen before you filmed.'[56]

Says Tracey: 'Birt had a mathematical and engineering disposition which led him to think in terms of the "structure" of political and economic movements; of the relationships between the parts, and of how the thing worked. He had a mechanistic view which he felt, or assumed, would enable him to offer the "truth" of any given political situation.' *Weekend World*'s approach often led to an analysis which might be thorough but was often bloodless. But Birt preferred his method to the *Panorama* way – going out on the ground and then trying to make sense of the real life one found there, even if it wasn't the whole picture. 'Partial truths', said Birt, 'are lies.'

Because *Weekend World* was so 'prescriptive', relying so heavily on its own, office-bound, examination of an issue, it was often deadly dull. But that didn't matter. Around lunchtime on Sundays there was not much of an audience anyway. All *Weekend World* had to do was get a good quote from the long ministerial interview which typically followed the film so that the political reporters sitting over their Sunday lunch at home had something to write about for Monday's papers. So *Weekend World* got a mention in the press, and LWT could demonstrate to the Independent Broadcasting

Authority a commitment to serious current affairs. It didn't much matter that nobody else was very shaken or stirred.

Panorama, of course, in peak time on a weekday evening, saw its public service responsibility rather differently; it thought its job was to deal as best it could with important topics in a way that would attract a large audience. And while there certainly were occasions when the real life captured on film or tape had not been put in sufficient context, *Panorama*'s reporters and presenters greatly resented the suggestion that they had no real interest in making sense of what they had seen through their window on the world.

Back in 1975 the BBC Chairman of the time, Sir Michael Swann, was so impressed by what Birt and Jay had to say in their articles that he wanted them to come over from LWT at once to reform the BBC's news and current affairs along the lines they proposed. Charles Curran, the Director General, scuppered his plans, but 12 years later Birt finally got his chance to come aboard and deal with the BBC's journalism in the way that he wanted. 'Too many BBC programmes looked like they were made on the road,' he told the author, 'and when you people came back to the cutting room and started working on the story and started to appreciate where the logic was taking them . . . they were doing intellectual work in the cutting room and then discovering that they hadn't asked the right questions on the road . . . The programmes tended to not have, so to speak, a beginning, a middle and an end; they didn't tie up all the ends neatly.'

Today Birt insists that he was not out to crush the film-making skills to be found on *Panorama* and other Lime Grove programmes, but to use them to better effect: 'I definitely admired the film-making tradition; I'd been a film-maker at Granada, I'd been part of that tradition even more than I was a journalist. I'd admired the craft of people at the BBC and it was better than the craft of many of the people working in ITV. I wanted to align that craft with a more rigorous and disciplined and analytical approach to the journalism. That was the ambition.'

But that was not the experience.

Keelhauling

On 9 June 1987, even before he had decided on the detailed changes he would make to the structure of BBC journalism, John Birt wrote to Peter

Pagnamenta, still Head of the Television Current Affairs Group: 'I would like us to consider a script of the proposed *Panorama* programme on MI5 and to take legal advice before any filming is planned.'[57]

Earlier in the year reporters John Ware and Tom Mangold had both suggested a *Panorama* programme about the former MI5 officer Peter Wright. In his forthcoming book *Spycatcher*, being published in Australia, where he was then living, Wright alleged that a group within MI5 had plotted against former Labour Prime Minister Harold Wilson to bring him down. The present Prime Minister, Margaret Thatcher, had denied that such a plot had existed and was trying in every way possible to prevent publication of Wright's book. As Mangold noted in a memo to *Panorama*'s Deputy Editor Mike Hogan: 'This story is made for *Panorama*.'[58] In the event it was Ware who was assigned to the story, not least because he had previously interviewed Wright and, in the face of considerable competition, would have a good chance of getting him again. The idea was to have a programme ready by mid-July, when it was thought the British Government might lose its battle to prevent publication of *Spycatcher* in Britain.

Desperate to get interviews with Wright's former MI5 colleagues 'in the can' before the security services put a stop to them, Ware and his producer David Wickham had arranged to talk to Alec McDonald, living in retirement in France. Now, as a result of Birt's instruction that there could be no filming before a script had been written and discussed, they had to cancel it – Ware told McDonald that his pregnant wife had suddenly developed high blood pressure.

Protesting that it was far too early to write a script, since research was incomplete, Ware nevertheless produced a 6000-word memo giving a good idea of his current state of knowledge and what the film's contents were likely to be. But it wasn't enough: Birt still insisted on a script. So, quite absurdly, when so much about the film was still pure conjecture, Ware, Wickham, *Panorama* Editor David Dickinson, legal adviser Glenn Del Medico, Head of Current Affairs Peter Pagnamenta and his assistant Peter Kenyatta all met to concoct a 'Script for Birt', as this highly artificial document was called.

Alan Protheroe, Assistant to the Director General, now agreed that the interview with McDonald could go ahead. Mrs Ware's blood pressure returned to normal and the interview was rescheduled. But yet again it had to be cancelled (Mrs Ware's blood pressure suddenly shot up again) when Birt once more intervened. The team was told that now he wanted a detailed memo listing questions and answers for the McDonald interview, before it would be authorised. Only after this was submitted was Birt's approval finally obtained. The interview was at last filmed in France on 2 July, in the nick of time. Just five days later McDonald received a letter from MI5 addressed 'Dear Pensioner', warning him not to speak to *Panorama*.[59]

It was now made plain to the *Panorama* team that they could not interview anyone else on this story, including Wright himself, without John Birt's express permission. In a private and confidential memo addressed to Tony Hall, Editor, News and Current Affairs Television, John Ware expressed his exasperation:

> I am in no doubt whatsoever that we were under instructions that no further filming could take place without John Birt's approval and until a script was supplied. That is quite impossible on a fairly fast changing story of this kind, particularly if we were to have had any chance of delivering a topical programme for the end of this run. Being a graduate of commercial television (Granada, *World in Action*) I am only too aware (not least because of the expense of ACTT crews)[60] of the need to start shooting with a clear focus. But, a story of this complexity soon becomes a moveable feast made more so by the almost weekly changing legal picture. And I'm sure I don't need to remind anyone that certain film opportunities have to be taken while they can. The Wright story was one of the more important domestic issues of this year and it is now in danger of passing us by. Since we all spoke fully and frankly in Lime Grove on Monday night, I must tell you that, whatever the causes, the BBC's response to this story so far has been, for me, a deeply demoralising experience. The important question is: Can we salvage anything – and where do we go from here?[61]

The answer at first appeared to be 'nowhere'. Birt, it seemed, had entirely stifled what would have been a good *Panorama* story. In response to an anguished memo that Ware had delivered to the Deputy Director General by courier Birt replied: 'I am unclear why you have written to me direct, and indeed why the points in your notes are being raised at all: a research trip to Australia is a matter for your Editor, not for me . . . Whether we make a film depends on our having a story to tell which is interesting, which is in the public interest and which is legally solid . . . Until there is a worthwhile story we can stand up, I see no point in interviewing Wright on film.'[62] A well-informed article in the *Spectator* suggested that the new Deputy Director General had either been 'nobbled' by the Government, or, more likely, that Birt was 'simply unwilling to support potentially controversial programmes'.[63] Birt retorted that while difficulties did exist over the proposed *Panorama* on the Wright allegations, 'these difficulties did not arise from sensitivity over the allegations as such. The problem was that I hold to the idea that lengthy current affairs films should proceed after a period of research has revealed the outline and direction of a story and the means by which it can be told. I resist the idea of film expeditions which record their research and return to the cutting room – many tens of thousands of pounds later – to see if a coherent and useful story can be constructed from the footage. Quite often it cannot.'[64]

This was disingenuous. Ware had already provided an immense amount of detail about what it was planned to include in the programme – the questions it would ask, the people it would try to interview, the pictures it expected to get. All the research that could be done before going to talk to Wright had now been done. Was Birt really suggesting that Ware and his producer should go to Australia, ask Wright what he would be prepared to say, return to London, write their script in still more detail, get it approved, then return to Australia to shoot the actual interview?

The fact was that Birt's refusal to trust the *Panorama* team to make sensible judgements in a constantly changing situation denied them the chance to make the programme they had originally planned for the summer of 1987. It seemed all over. The programme had been stopped. Producer David Wickham left *Panorama* in disgust. And then, in October, John Ware got another memo from Birt. At a dinner at his old Oxford college, Birt said, he'd met a former colleague of Wright's who might prove a useful source. Birt seemed to be signalling that the planned *Panorama* was on again. It was. Ware was at last given the go-ahead to go and interview Wright. And later, when Wright's lawyer tried to prevent some of the interview being used, a bold Birt ignored the BBC's legal advice and decided to take the risk of transmitting it.

Cynics suggest that it was only when Birt knew that Wright would come out of his interview badly and not seriously damage the Government case that he gave *Panorama* permission to go ahead. But at the time he gave Ware the encouragement to pick up the pieces and start again he couldn't be sure that Wright would retract some of the claims he had originally made in his book – as the old spy eventually did. More likely, as Ware himself now believes: 'His intervention was motivated by a desire to get control of a potentially highly controversial project at the start of his BBC career, not because he had been 'nobbled' by the Establishment.' Nonetheless, what had happened showed Birt as Deputy Director General not just calling BBC journalists to heel, but exercising control over an individual *Panorama* programme in a way that had not been done before. For *Panorama*'s other reporters and producers – and for their Editor – it was not a good augury.

In December 1987 a memo from Tim Gardam, *Panorama*'s new, Birt-appointed Editor, seems to show him concerned to get permission from the top before finally commissioning the 'Spycatcher' programme. Headed 'Wright – Private and Confidential', the memo is addressed to Margaret Douglas, Chief Political Adviser, and requests advice on how to get the film into production:

> I enclose John Ware's highly theoretical treatment/outline of a film on Peter Wright and the allegations of a plot against Harold Wilson . . . I would very much like advice on how to go ahead. There is little doubt that this film could become a cause celèbre in the BBC's reputation to maintain independent journalism [sic]. I am anxious that it is made as I think it is a good story. If it is not made I am anxious that it becomes the victim of the government's draconian legal measures, not of BBC apparent censorship . . . At the moment, I haven't shown this to anyone. I will be terribly grateful for your honest verdict on it as a dispassionate reader, and also on your advice on what to do.

Gardam believes he was worried about what would happen if legal rulings prevented transmission, rather than whether the programme could be made at all. To his credit he was trying to get a programme he knew Birt was nervous about into production. Throughout the 'Spycatcher' saga Ware insists that he always thought Gardam extremely supportive. But to find a *Panorama* Editor apparently accepting that he may be told he cannot commission a programme is unusual.

Sometimes armed with a clipboard and stopwatch, like a time-and-motion man in a shirt factory, Birt spent his first few weeks at the BBC observing its journalistic activities. Then, at the beginning of July 1987, he took senior News and Current Affairs staff down to the Woodlands Park Hotel near Leatherhead for a four-day seminar, to give them his verdict and set the scene for the major reorganisation he was planning. 'He was not complimentary, to put it mildly; he took people's breath away,' says Ron Neil, who was one of the few to know by this time that his mortgage was safe. To Peter Pagnamenta Birt seemed something of a Martian, as if he hadn't really seen very much of what programmes like *Panorama* had actually been doing. But Birt was now the sole arbiter of what good current affairs should be. He did not take kindly to Pagnamenta's defence of BBC Current Affairs in general, and *Panorama* in particular. Walking in the hotel grounds with Neil, between painful conference sessions, Pagnamenta gloomily enquired: 'Is my number up?' In less than a fortnight he would find out.

It was a ghastly few days, which ended with Birt requiring each of the company assembled at dinner to tell a joke. It was generally agreed that the whole session had been about whether or not they agreed with Birt. While they did not mind being told what to do, they did object to being told what to think.[65]

Back in London, Pagnamenta learned from a newspaper reporter that he had been sacked. When he eventually managed to see Birt he was told he should 'return to programme-making'. He did, making a new career as series editor in the Documentary Department. In his place as Head of the BBC's weekly Current Affairs television journalism, which included *Panorama*, came Samir Shah. Grace Wyndham Goldie he was not.

Shaping up

It must have been very difficult for a relatively inexperienced producer from a relatively small ITV company to impose John Birt's way of doing television journalism on *Panorama*'s tough old hacks, who'd been used to having their own way. The Director General, Michael Checkland, had apparently told Birt he had to move fast: 'We've got to get on with it and force it through. You're going to have immense problems with some of the established reporters who aren't going to like some of the things we're suggesting, but you've got to have the courage to do it.'[66] The level of anger at the changes Birt proposed became apparent at a meeting he addressed in the cavernous, gloomy surroundings of Studio D at Lime Grove. Flanked by his newly appointed Deputy Ron Neil, and Television News boss Tony Hall with his Current Affairs Deputy Samir Shah, Birt began to feel the effects of the waves of hostility that rolled towards him. 'Lime Grove was used to rough treatment,' says Neil; 'Birt was not. It's the only time I ever remember him breaking into a sweat.'

'I wasn't a shrinking violet,' Birt now insists, 'I was used to opposition, I was used to people expressing themselves forcefully, so I don't believe that I was shaken. Did I expect it to be as ferocious as it was? No.' Far from being under orders to cut Current Affairs down to size, says Birt, he hadn't really been given any guidance at all, and was therefore surprised at his hostile reception:

> The truth of the matter is that I was underprepared for the ferocity of what happened, and one of the things you discovered about the BBC, you know, which I suppose is amusing in retrospect but wasn't at the time, was actually not that people marked your card but [that] they didn't, and you would walk into the lions' den or you would do something, and afterwards you'd say to key people at the centre, 'well, you know, that was a surprise', and it would be perfectly clear from their reaction that they weren't in the least bit surprised; they expected that to happen; and you'd think: 'Why didn't you tell me?'

Says Neil: 'He had expected people to be grateful for his analysis of what he saw as the problems. They were not, and he was shocked. It confirmed him in his view that here in Lime Grove was a powerful culture that was arrogant. He felt Lime Grove journalists had got locked into the hippie sixties and had simply not recognised Thatcher's Britain, stakeholder Britain, and the way people were using their money to assert themselves as individuals. Lime Grove, Birt became convinced, had its own agenda which didn't recognise the new public agenda. There was insularity.'

Birt nerved himself to visit the wild, uncontrollable beasts of *Panorama* in their own Lime Grove lair. Says reporter Gavin Hewitt:

> It was clear at that meeting that fundamental change was about to take place. Anyone there knew that he or she was going to be in for a very difficult time.

Birt was big, earnest; he crouched forward, looking down a lot. He clearly found it difficult to communicate what was on his mind. More than once Birt was challenged to say exactly what was wrong with the programme; how was the journalism to be improved, he was asked several times. When people went on asking supplementary questions – as is the way with Panorama – Birt seemed to regard that as hostility. There was no warmth on either side of the discussion. [Panorama Editor] Tim Gardam sat there ashen-faced. The meeting made things worse.

Listening to Birt, Panorama's journalists felt very low. They realised that their previous contributions to the programme were now to be regarded as worthless. Birt, they felt, had come close to 'libelling the past'. Previously they had at least been respected when they disagreed with senior management. But now it was clear that there was to be no room for disagreement – there had to be consensual behaviour: sign up or ship out.

Some weren't given much chance to show whether they would sail under these new colours or not. Birt confided to one of his senior colleagues that he wanted to get rid of Michael Cockerell, the reporter on 'Maggie's Militant Tendency'. He did. In February 1988 Cockerell announced that he was 'going freelance' and disappeared from BBC Current Affairs television. 'I found, to my surprise,' he says, 'that there was a world outside Panorama.' Cockerell has subsequently built a considerable reputation as the author of a series of definitive television portraits of leading politicians, made for the BBC's Political Documentaries department.

Birt had seen 'Maggie's Militant Tendency' – the devastating outcome of the case had come only the year before – as a 'process failure'. The BBC's lawyers, he rightly said, felt that reporters regarded them as enemies, and as a result were bringing them in to vet a film for potential legal problems only just ahead of transmission, at much too late a stage. At Granada and London Weekend Television, Birt claimed, the system he had developed allowed people to make programmes that were difficult, without dire consequences:

> I *wanted* to do investigative programmes. A lot of people thought because I wanted to put all these systems in place that was a sign I didn't want to make them. I definitely wanted to make them, and John Ware and Peter Taylor and

everybody – they all did these things – I wanted those programmes to be made. I had to manage in an environment where we had to make sure they were made and they were legally secure and we could carry them through ... The BBC had come close to having a nervous breakdown in the mid-eighties, you know, the Governors and the management were at war ... The BBC had been through this horrendous experience, there were a lot of people gunning for the BBC; I was determined to get it right; I wanted to do difficult things, but I wanted to get it right.

Birt was adamant that he did not want decisions being made about difficult programmes when the transmission date was looming, and people had their backs against the wall. So no longer would such programmes be referred up only when the Editor of *Panorama* thought it necessary. Now Editors would be required to keep senior managers informed about what was happening from a project's earliest stages, and programmes would normally have to be completed a week before transmission to allow Birt or his deputies to make any changes they decided were necessary.

At Lime Grove – itself now under sentence of death as a production centre – newly appointed *Panorama* Editor Gardam was struggling, short-tempered with strain and exhaustion, to do Birt's bidding while at the same time getting half-decent programmes out of *Panorama*'s demoralised and mutinous crew. 'Get me a studio,' he would scream histrionically in the cutting room, in despair at making some *Panorama* film fit to pass the Birtian criteria for transmission, and suggesting that the only solution was a studio discussion instead.

Morale on the programme fell. To *Panorama* people poor Gardam too often looked as if he were a collaborator with enemy forces in occupied country. With some justification, he saw himself as standing up for his team and taking care of individuals as resolutely as he could, trying to moderate the rigour and inflexibility of the new systems Birt was imposing. It was an unenviable position to be in, and Gardam deserved more sympathy than he probably got at the time for trying so hard to steer a sensible course in such terrible weather. He says:

> *Panorama* was in a mess, falling apart; it's difficult to remember now how crumbling it all was before Birt arrived ... When he appointed me in April

1987 I began what was for some months the most miserable time of my life . . . I didn't realise how important *Panorama* was. And it was everything that Maggie Thatcher hated. Basically Birt was brought in to clear up the BBC for Duke Hussey. I was appointed to run *Panorama* because Birt couldn't find anyone from outside the BBC to come and do it.

Gardam's job was made even more difficult because his immediate boss Samir Shah – 'A nice man, not a thug,' says Gardam – had nothing much else to do except get *Panorama* 'right', so in effect there were two Editors of the programme.

Shipping out

Some senior *Panorama* people found it all too much to take. Paul Woolwich was a vastly experienced Lime Grove producer. Like many other people on *Panorama* he'd been through a lot for BBC Current Affairs – mustard-gassed in Iraq, imprisoned in Iran, shot at in Beirut. He had done it because he had believed in what he and his colleagues were doing: 'I had felt so proud to be in the BBC.' No more. Programmes now were made on paper, the script written before filming, screeds of theoretical sequences and interviews sent across to Samir Shah for his perusal, sent back, cut up and – quite literally – stuck together in a new order. When the script was finally approved the team would go out and shoot as if painting by numbers, sticking as closely as possible to the approved text, not easily allowing what they found in real life to alter what had been agreed. When the film was ready for viewing Shah would sit there in the cutting room poring over the script, listening to the words but scarcely looking at the screen at all. Sometimes he didn't even see the film before insisting on script alterations. In Woolwich's view that was no way to make a programme that was likely to interest the viewers – but then that was not high on the new list of priorities; if the audience had not mattered at *Weekend World*, why should it at *Panorama*?

Woolwich's breaking point came when, with reporter Robin Denselow, he was commissioned to make a *Panorama* on fraud in the EU – the exploitation of the Common Agricultural Policy, about which Margaret Thatcher had been noisily and rightly complaining.[67] The CAP is a notoriously difficult subject to explain, so, to illustrate what was happening, Woolwich and Denselow researched and filmed some specific examples of fraud – for example: cross-border smuggling between North and South in Ireland; how the Mafia was claiming subsidies for non-existent Italian orange juice and olive oil; and the way German manufacturers were being subsidised for selling substandard meat to Africa. They began their film with lively scenes they'd managed to shoot as EC inspectors arrived to expose fraud in an olive orchard in Italy – exactly the sort of attention-getter, the hook, that any experienced filmmaker knew was tremendously helpful, if not essential, in getting viewers involved in a complicated story. But this did not meet with Shah's approval. Instead of starting with an explanation of the CAP and the corruption that was endemic in its structure, instead of continuing with an analysis of the causes of that corruption, Woolwich and Denselow had jumped straight into a way of dealing with the problem. They had clearly been distracted by exciting things happening on the ground. 'This is the last time *Panorama* will do a story in that way at any time again,' Woolwich was told. Shah says he has since learned that there is more than one way to tell a story.

But this was to be the pattern. No interesting human scene, no unexpected development would now be allowed to precede or interrupt the cool, logical progression of the pre-planned story. When Peter Taylor had the Commander-in-Chief, Land Forces in Northern Ireland telling him that Britain had lost the military war against the IRA he used this dramatic statement as a pre-title. Shah insisted it be buried in the body of the film. 'In the seventies and eighties', says Woolwich, '*Panorama* was interesting; that's why Birt was brought in to sort it out. John Birt came in to stop it being controversial.'

Woolwich was now Deputy to Tim Gardam as Editor of *Panorama*, but he had no stomach for the job. He found it difficult to tell people to follow the new rules: 'I was being paid to ask people to do things that I didn't believe in myself.' He had been on the BBC's staff for 13 years, but he nonetheless decided he would have to leave. 'I was chucking in a career, but I could not have gone on like Tim.'[68] Others left too – or were pushed. Though they were never told so, reporters Fred Emery, Tom Mangold and the author were living on borrowed time, marked down to be moved off *Panorama* as soon as opportunity arose. In the author's case that came quite quickly.

At the end of 1987 producer Tim Copestake and the author were dispatched to India. Their commission was to make a portrait of Rajiv Gandhi, India's youthful and modern-minded Prime Minister, as he struggled to get a grip of the country's many intractable problems in the wake of his mother Indira Gandhi's assassination. As with all far-flung foreign stories it was not really possible to write the script in advance in the new way because a good deal of the research could only be carried out on the ground, in another continent. But Copestake had done all he could to set out the likely contents of the programme, and they had been approved.

To fit in with the dates offered by the Indians for filming opportunities with the Prime Minister, the *Panorama* team had to spend Christmas in India. To raise morale Copestake entertainingly arranged a somewhat surreal Christmas lunch, hung about with decorations he had brought from Britain, at a remote guest house high in the Himalayas; bemused but tolerant Indian staff looked on as the homesick *Panorama* team celebrated Christmas as so many British before them must have tried to do in the days of the Raj.

After some days' research in New Delhi, filming began. There were scenes at the Golden Temple in Punjab with armed and militant Sikhs calling for independence; other sequences illustrated the new industrial technology Rajiv Gandhi hoped would pull India out of the political morass in which it seemed bogged down, the great gulf that still remained to be bridged between very rich and very poor, allegations of corruption in the Bofors Guns affair, and the risk Gandhi had taken in sending Indian troops to confront the Tamil rebellion in Sri Lanka.[69] Finally there was an interview with Gandhi himself: 'Perhaps the most important challenge is to change the attitude in the mind of the average Indian – bring them into the 20th century, get them ready for the 21st,' was the essence of what the young Prime Minister had to say.

Back in Britain the film was put together and then, with relatively few changes, approved by Gardam and Shah. Its conclusion was that Gandhi, a Cambridge graduate with an Italian wife, a former airline pilot more at home in English than any Indian language, was in danger of being too much of a westerner for India's liking, and was not himself in sympathy with the country he had found himself unexpectedly thrust into leading. The modern man was finding it difficult to make an impact on a nation with entrenched traditions and practices. The draft billing for the programme put it like this: 'As an airline pilot Rajiv Gandhi would press a button, pull a lever and get results. Now as Prime Minister of India he's discovering that the world's largest democracy doesn't respond so readily. Ruefully he tells *Panorama*'s Richard Lindley: "There's a bit of slack in the controls."'

In January 1988 the film was transmitted as planned,[70] and later that week the BBC's Programme Review Board, chaired by the Managing Director, Television, had kind words for it: 'David Hargreaves [Head of Continuing Education, Television] praised a fine and penetrating *Panorama* on Rajiv Gandhi. He was not surprised that the Indian High Commission were critical. Controller BBC 2 [Alan Yentob] said it was a lucid film which also looked very good.'

The Indians had indeed been critical of the film. As the BBC's experts in External Broadcasting at Bush House told the team, that was to be expected. It was nothing new, indeed almost traditional, for Indian politicians to demand that their Government denounce any criticism of India by the British media as disgraceful interference in the country's affairs by its former colonial masters.[71] Allegations were made that the *Panorama* team had broken an undertaking to the High Commission that Rajiv Gandhi's interview would be run in one complete unedited chunk, but that was quite untrue. At a Lime Grove meeting before the film had got off the ground it had been made absolutely clear to the High Commission that while the Prime Minister would be given 'the last word' in the programme his interview would be used in sections so that he would be seen to respond to each of the major points in the film as they were made.

Given that BBC management had approved the film before transmission, and that some of the most senior BBC people, meeting in the formal Programme Review, had praised it afterwards, the team rather assumed, as they came under attack, that they would find the Corporation supportive. They were wrong.

John Birt replied to the Indian High Commission's complaint with an apology: 'I am sorry this was a programme with which I could not be more satisfied.' This was not good news for the author and Copestake. But they were now alarmed to hear that Birt was going further, ordering the BBC's greatly respected India correspondent Mark Tully to send him his own critique of the *Panorama* programme. Birt was clearly amassing evidence for some purpose. Tully protested, saying that he was not 'Editor, India', and it was not his job to criticise the work of his colleagues. He was nevertheless ordered to comply with the Deputy Director General's command.[72]

A resident correspondent is always in a difficult position when a visiting team makes a film on his patch which subsequently causes trouble. Tully had done his best to help the author and Copestake but he had not much liked the programme they had produced about the country he was so fond of, a country where, for many years, he had made his home. In his assessment of the programme for Birt (he made a point of sending a copy to the *Panorama* team) Tully said that while he would not quarrel with its overall conclusion he felt that the problems facing Gandhi were presented too starkly, and that the 'cast list' of Gandhi's supporters was not strong enough.

But Tully was grappling with another problem related to the programme: a scheduled visit to India by the new BBC Chairman, a visit which was now in jeopardy. Says Tully: 'Duke Hussey had been due to meet Rajiv Gandhi; following the *Panorama* film the Indians said he would not be welcome in India at all. After I had talked to them they agreed that if Hussey would criticise the *Panorama* programme and apologise for it then he could still make his visit to India, though he would not be allowed to see Rajiv.' According to Tully, that is what happened. Hussey told him: 'This is the sort of programme I've come here [to the BBC] to see is not made again.' BBC Current Affairs was 'wild . . . not properly under control . . . needing to be disciplined.' Tully formed the view that 'the Chairman was not unhappy that this particular programme could be used as a stick with which to beat *Panorama*'.

The apologies made to the Indians by the Deputy Director General and the Chairman of the BBC left the way open for others to make theirs. Hot on Hussey's heels a British Foreign Office minister arrived in Delhi. 'It was a thoroughly bad programme and I am sorry it went out as it did,' Lord Glenarthur obligingly told his Indian hosts. 'Your Government were absolutely right to complain to the BBC. And I am glad that their management has responded to your concern. Programmes like this one undermine the efforts of all of us who are working to promote better relations between us.' Reporting Glenarthur's remarks, the *Guardian*'s Derek Brown noted: 'The touchiness of the Indian Government is matched by nervousness in London that the apparently trivial dispute could divert valuable trade – notably a potential multimillion pound order for British Aerospace Hawk trainers.'[73]

In an editorial two days later, headed 'Grovel, grovel', the *Guardian* said it had 'thought *Panorama* a little sour. But the reporting was sharp and valid in its own terms. Mr. Birt's private views would be better kept that way. Mr. Hussey's olive branches would be best stuffed up his jumper. For the end result is a Foreign Office minister bowing and scraping round New Delhi, apologising for an independent story which ought to have been told; and which, as Messrs Birt and Hussey should now say crisply, is none of his jolly business.'[74]

Tim Gardam and Samir Shah were now summoned to a meeting with John Birt and his senior managers. There they were subjected to four hours of gruelling examination designed to make them admit the appalling blunder they had made in approving this particular *Panorama* for transmission. According to Gardam, Birt was surprised to find that the author was still reporting for *Panorama*. That was soon remedied when he was told he would now be working on a Sunday lunchtime programme; he left the BBC shortly afterwards.[75] Copestake too soon decided he would prefer to leave *Panorama* and make television documentaries for BBC Bristol.

Says Tony Hall, at that time the Editor of News and Current Affairs Television: 'The place needed sorting out, we all felt we should have movement on the programme; you've got to have movement, you've got to have change.' Hall denies there was a 'hit-list', but 'yes, we did feel we should move certain people on'.

There were a few old hacks still to go. Soon Tom Mangold was ousted. While making what turned out to be a prizewinning *Panorama* programme in Wales[76] Mangold was recalled to London by his Editor. Mangold vividly recalls sitting in Mark Thompson's glass-walled office, on display to the rest of the *Panorama* team, as he was told his contract would not be renewed. Fred Emery too was 'let go'.

Naval discipline

As John Birt, through his appointees, got a grip on *Panorama*, a suffocating blanket of fear wrapped itself around the programme team. It led to self-censorship. Birt had complained that the BBC's journalism was not punching its weight, and to help it do so had brought in Ian Hargreaves, formerly features editor of the *Financial Times*, to take charge of it. But by the summer of 1988 *Panorama* journalists were demoralised. They had seen what happened to reporters and producers whose films failed to satisfy the new regime; they became cautious, no longer confident that Editors could protect their backs if they undertook difficult or sensitive missions.

Eamonn Mathews was a bright young producer who had already had one bruising experience on the new *Panorama*. Briefed to make a programme about the rise of house prices[77] Mathews and reporter Robin Denselow had come back with an interesting film about mortgage fraud in an overheated housing market. 'This film is going to cost me my job,' Editor Tim Gardam remarked gloomily as the opening credits rolled. Mathews was shocked that Gardam thought he would be blamed for putting out an excellent programme simply because it did not meet the original brief: he was concerned about the pressures he could see being applied to his Editor. 'What seemed to matter now was not whether you had made a good film, but whether you had obeyed John Birt's orders.'

When, in March 1988, SAS soldiers shot dead three IRA suspects in Gibraltar Mathews and Tom Mangold had urged Gardam to do the story. Gardam had turned the idea down. After the extraordinary difficulties he'd encountered getting another film about Northern Ireland finally approved – it had only recently been transmitted – he'd been heard to say that he never wanted to do a film about the province again. It was left to Roger Bolton and his rival team over at ITV's *This Week* to get out of the trenches and do what became an enormously successful programme – *Death on the Rock*,[78] which left *Panorama* and the BBC looking flat-footed.

Now, as the end of the inquest on the shootings in Gibraltar approached, Mathews and Mangold again proposed a programme on the SAS and its alleged 'shoot to kill' policy. Gardam commissioned them to produce their programme in just three weeks. This contradicted everything that John Birt had said was the proper way to go about *Panorama* film-making – on an extremely sensitive topic. 'Why are we doing this in three weeks,' Mathews remembers asking, 'have we got backing on this? Otherwise it's going to be my blood on the floor and I don't want that.' He was reassured by Gardam that the proposal had been properly 'referred up' and approved, which, so far as Gardam was concerned, was indeed the case.

The film Mangold and Mathews made looked at the accountability – or lack of it – of the security forces in Northern Ireland when they killed people they believed to be engaged in terrorist activity – as had happened in Gibraltar. 'A pattern emerged,' says Mathews: 'people would be shot on their way to arms dumps or whatever. If the SAS were involved they would always give evidence afterwards anonymously. This was the pattern: compare it with Gibraltar.' The programme pointed out that because of the rules covering inquests in Northern Ireland, there was no longer a forum there in which a controversial death could be properly discussed or anyone held responsible. People learned less about what had happened when these killings took place in Northern Ireland than they did when they had happened in Gibraltar.

Even though they pitched straight in, it was hard to assemble the material in time. Mangold and Mathews were sometimes sleeping only two or three hours a night; Mathews was unhappy at working under such pressure but proud that as they neared the end they had got it all together. It was the Wednesday before the following Monday's planned transmission date[79] when the alarm first sounded. 'Birt wants a script,' said Gardam. So, while they were still editing, still unsure of exactly how their material would best go together, Mangold had to break off to write what Mathews calls a 'fantasy' script, since at this stage it would clearly bear little relation to what finally went out. While Mangold hammered away at his typewriter, Gardam fed his words into the computer that was, in 1988, still a new and unfamiliar feature of the *Panorama* office.

Then the viewings began. Ron Neil, the Director of News and Current Affairs, appeared. 'I want you to remove all footage of funerals,' he said. Mathews was beginning to get angry, his memories of interference for the wrong reasons revived. But, as ordered, he took out the film of IRA funerals and replaced it with stills. Then for the first time word came down that the film might not run at all on the following Monday as planned. There would be weekend viewings by senior editorial figures to decide.

Unknown to Mathews, a tussle at the top had begun in which *Panorama* would suffer for reasons that had little to do with this particular programme. Gardam had kept his bosses in the picture, but Neil, at the top of the News and Current Affairs Directorate, had failed to keep Birt fully informed that a highly sensitive *Panorama* programme was speeding towards them. When at last Neil nerved himself to tell him, Birt was furious. He was now in a position where the Governors might think him derelict at not keeping them informed about a potentially troublesome *Panorama* from Northern Ireland.

Birt agrees that he was 'profoundly irritated' to find that the programme had not gone through the due process, and was inclined to delay it. Conscious of the bad publicity that would inevitably result from pulling the programme at the last minute, a desperate Neil begged Birt to delay any decision on whether the film should go out until he had seen it himself. Grudgingly Birt agreed, and asked the Director General Michael Checkland to see it with him. Checkland normally left all the journalistic issues to his Deputy Director; Birt's explanation for involving him now was that at this stage he expected the film to be transmitted and wanted to be able to tell the BBC Governors that both he and Checkland had seen and approved it.

Late on the Friday night Ron Neil and Ian Hargreaves, Controller of News and Current Affairs, viewed the film together and made changes. They agreed that it was now good enough to show Birt, and Neil called him to say so (he was given a further angry ticking off for speaking to the Deputy Director General in the hearing of the programme team). The next day the BBC's most senior people gathered in a Lime Grove cutting room to watch the programme as it then stood. Birt and Checkland were there, along with others including Neil, Hargreaves, Shah, and Gardam. 'It's my least favourite thing', says Birt, 'to be confronted with such a programme which we were watching, on a Saturday, as I recall, against a transmission the following Monday.' They watched the film in silence, Birt, Hargreaves remembers, nervous but steely in his gold-framed spectacles. Then they trooped into Shah's office to discuss it. Mathews was not invited. 'Good', he thought, certain that if he had been there he would have fallen asleep from exhaustion.

In the discussion which followed the viewing Birt asked Hargreaves what he thought. Hargreaves recalls saying that, while the film was not a perfect accomplishment, it was certainly transmittable; it was an edition of *Panorama* that they should be pleased to broadcast. While the manner in which the story was told might have been improved, it was not 'reckless'.

And the programme was 'timely'. But Birt disagreed. He thought the film 'unready'; it could not be transmitted. In an angry exchange Gardam argued that Birt seemed to be saying that there was only one way to make a film – his way - and that if that was so there wasn't much point in his continuing as Editor of *Panorama*.

Birt and Checkland now prepared a statement for the press, while the others fumed and refused to put their names to it. So the statement read: 'The Director General and Deputy Director General saw the *Panorama* programme on the SAS. They are happy with the themes the programme addresses, but they feel more work is needed to prepare it for transmission. The BBC plans to transmit the programme in the coming weeks.'[80]

'I thought Birt's was completely the wrong judgement', says Ian Hargreaves. 'It was not going to be a much better film in two or three weeks' time; postponing it would suggest that we were just a bunch of nancies. We were being pushed into a decision which had no substantive basis. I thought that Birt did not understand the elementary principle of timing in journalism. Timing is of the essence.'

At lunchtime, says Mathews, word came down to the production team that their film was being postponed: 'Later, Ron [Neil] came over in order to explain, but in the end he didn't. He was sheepish. It was as though we had suffered a bereavement – everyone was being very nice to us.' Later Mathews was infuriated to hear from Fleet Street journalists that BBC press officers were suggesting his film had been pulled because he hadn't got it ready in time. 'That's when the scales fell from my eyes,' he says. 'I'd always regarded journalism as a great adventure where Editors stood by you if you got the truth; Tim Gardam did, but it turned out that all the people in the editorial chain of command were powerless; we were being manipulated by forces we didn't understand. TV producers were ten a penny. If it didn't suit you – tough. From that time on I never, ever had full confidence in the BBC to deal with a story on its merits.'

It was unfortunate that just at this moment *Panorama* should be advertising for new producers 'with a track record in tough, authoritative journalism'. Says Mathews:

> Right to my final days on *Panorama* I would say to new arrivals: 'Have you got your wits about you? Have you got it in writing?' You were working in the

Kremlin. That feeling filtered through to a lot of people. You had to make sure on *Panorama* that a lot of people had dipped their hands in blood before you dared start out on a programme. If you are going to fix bayonets and charge you've got to be absolutely certain that the generals are with you. If they're not, then the next time they ask you to go you say 'why?' Of course it was Birt's prerogative to pull the SAS programme. But he didn't explain, or say anything. I felt like cannon-fodder.

The SAS film was replaced by a bought-in programme from Australian television.

Subsequently the *Panorama* team went to Broadcasting House for a round-the-table meeting with Birt, who asked for a number of minor changes to their film, changes that could have been made within a matter of hours. Says Mathews: 'I thought: "Is that all? Why didn't we make those changes at the time?" The programme was finally transmitted 99 per cent the same as before. Games were being played with us, for whatever reason. This did not fit my idea of how journalists should operate. There was no attempt to make the film work in time for transmission.'

Public criticism was inevitable and predictable. The National Union of Journalists condemned Birt for causing 'unnecessary damage to public confidence in the BBC,'[81] while *Private Eye* posed the question: 'What happens between 1 October, when the programme was shelved, and 17 October, when it will at last appear? ANSWER: The Tory Party Conference.'[82] The same suspicion occurred to the *Observer*'s television reviewer John Naughton: 'Was it pure coincidence then that it was pulled until the Tory Party Conference was safely out of the way?'[83]

No doubt, in the light of the row over Thames Television's *Death on the Rock*, Birt was alert to the political impact of a programme which questioned the actions and accountability of the SAS in relation to the IRA. And he would have been right to be wary: after all, *Death on the Rock* fuelled the fire in Margaret Thatcher to recast the ITV system in a way that led to the disappearance of Thames Television as a broadcaster. ITV has not made many programmes like *Death on the Rock* since then. So, though John Birt denies it, political nervousness may have been a factor. But what really seems to have decided him to overrule all his appointees, all the people he had hand-picked to carry out his bidding, and to bump this *Panorama* from its slot, was simply irritation; irritation that the systems he had imposed to prevent this sort of last-minute problem occurring had not worked, that his orders as to how things were to be done had not been obeyed.

Birt does not accept this interpretation of his otherwise inexplicable decision, but most of his senior colleagues do. Birt wanted to teach them – starting with Ron Neil, his Director of News and Current Affairs – a lesson, to show them that he would insist on the discipline he regarded as necessary to current affairs programme making. No matter the damage to the BBC's reputation, and the blow to the morale of *Panorama*'s staff; the important thing was to demonstrate that unless programmes were made strictly according to the system Birt had devised they would not get on the air as planned.

It's hard to say whether that is a better or worse reason for pulling a *Panorama* programme than any other. But it was, without a doubt, Birt's own decision. And so was the spiking of Supergun.

The gun that didn't fire

At the beginning of 1991, with Mark Thompson as Editor of *Panorama*, war in the Gulf looked ever more likely. The BBC braced itself for the usual problems of reporting a conflict in which British lives would be at risk. Criticism came even before the fighting had begun: 'Dozens of viewers have complained to the BBC about the "peacenik" tone of last night's *Panorama*,'[84] said the London *Evening Standard* in January. Defending the programme in the same article, John Birt asserted the BBC's determination to keep the public informed: 'The BBC's Deputy Director-General John Birt warned that viewers and listeners will want the truth about events in any war. This would be subject only to considerations about the safety of British troops on the ground, he stressed.' Excellent stuff: well done, John! But it didn't turn out quite like that.

Ever since Tim Gardam persuaded her to leave ITN for *Panorama* in 1987 Jane Corbin had shown herself a good current affairs reporter with excellent sources. She had already reported the story of the 'Supergun' that Saddam Hussein was trying to build in Iraq – apparently with the help of British manufacturers and the knowledge of Britain's Department of Trade and Industry. Now she showed Editor Thompson satellite pictures she had obtained with the co-ordinates pinpointing the exact position where Supergun was being constructed in a mountainous area of Iraq. Corbin had also secured an exclusive interview with Christopher Cowley, a vital member of the gun's design team.

The programme was scheduled for 7 January, one week before the UN Security Council ultimatum to Iraq ran out, and was clearly a major scoop. But then Birt pulled the programme.

Until this point Corbin had had no problems with Birt and the way he wanted *Panorama*s made: 'He had respect for journalism, he recognised good journalism,' she says, but on this issue she came close to resigning. The programme was only postponed, she was told, not cancelled; but when it still didn't run, Christopher Cowley not unreasonably decided to talk to ITV instead. Corbin's feelings when she saw a rather scrappy version of the story she had uncovered run not on *Panorama* but on the rival programme *This Week* may be imagined.

The rest of the *Panorama* team was also outraged. In a confidential memo 33 reporters and producers wrote to Birt asking for an explanation of his decision:

> We have been told by Mark Thompson that your criterion was 'the public mood', that you feel the BBC should not get out of step with the public mood, and that the Supergun film would have run contrary to the public mood had it been transmitted earlier – even a week earlier. Only a month ago guidelines were issued for BBC journalists covering the Gulf war. They have been discussed thoroughly throughout News and Current Affairs and all of us have been working to them. This criterion of 'the public mood' is neither mentioned nor hinted at anywhere in the guidelines, which we were led to believe were comprehensive and exhaustive. Should we now assume that we are all bound by this new criterion which has not been published or defined or discussed? . . . What worries us is that the new requirement that the BBC heeds the public mood can conflict with our responsibility to report impartially at this particularly difficult time. As you wrote in the foreword to the guidelines: our prime responsibility is to provide 'accurate, careful and trustworthy reporting and analysis. Subject only to considerations about the safety of our troops on the ground, our audience will want the truth about

events; and they will expect to hear a range of views about government action and policies.'[85]

England expects

In his interview with the former Director General at the House of Lords where he now sits as Lord Birt of Liverpool, the author asked for an explanation of what seems an extraordinary own goal. Rather than give viewers the information they had a right to expect, did he instead act to protect the institution of the BBC against Government critics? Birt insisted:

> I was only ever interested in good journalism, I promise you my conscience is 100 per cent clear . . . no programme was ever rolled on for any calculation – you seem to have a thing about 'institutional reasons' – never, no, never. That isn't, that's not how I behave, nothing was ever, no decision was ever made because of institutional reasons . . . The only programme I ever delayed – and I'm not ashamed of having delayed it – was the Supergun, and I did it – none of my colleagues wanted to delay it, I was the one who wanted to delay it and I delayed it for only one reason, and that is, I was extremely concerned that the BBC should maintain the trust of the British people at a time of war.

Interestingly Birt revealed that: 'We knew the Gulf War was coming up, we went back; the advantage was, if you remember, we knew the Gulf War was coming over a very long period of time. We went back and did a huge amount of work on the Falklands War; we had lots of time to think through the issues about how the BBC behaves at a time of war, what are the sensitivities – of which there are many.'

So was it being reminded of the political row over *Panorama*'s Falklands programme that most worried Birt? His concern over Supergun was quite different, he insisted:

> It was a good programme, it was about an important subject, there was no difficulty at all in normal times in putting that programme on air. It was my judgement and my judgement alone that when British forces were about to go to war and there might have been major loss of life, that was not the right

moment to put on a programme of that kind. Now I don't expect everyone to agree with that decision but it was absolutely my decision and my decision alone. It was a matter of taste.

'I thought John just misread it,' says David Jordan, *Panorama*'s Deputy Editor at the time. 'This was pre-declaration of the Gulf War; the idea that this programme would undermine the morale of the nation on the brink of war was ridiculous. It was a fantastic piece of journalism which turned out to be uncannily accurate. When they found the Supergun it was pointing where we said it was and of the dimensions we said, and so on and so on.'

The story of Supergun didn't threaten the 'the safety of British troops on the ground', the only reason John Birt had originally given for pulling a programme. The gun was, after all, aimed at Israel. Nor was the threat to military morale: it was to the BBC. The real danger was that the Conservative Government would react furiously to a story which suggested it had knowingly allowed British companies to help arm Iraq, and that *Panorama* and the Corporation would come under fire just as they had when the programme had broadcast interviews questioning Government policy on the Falklands nearly a decade before.

Lamely, *Panorama*'s Supergun film limped out on 18 February, more than a month after it had been ready to fire. There were no complaints of inaccuracy or bias. If Jane Corbin's programme really was a threat to our soldiers' safety, or even civilian morale, why did it run then, when the first British Tornado had been lost, captured pilots had been paraded on Iraqi television and the land war was about to begin? Surely the real reason was that by now the Supergun story was fully in the public domain; now that ITV had already broadcast it, *Panorama* and the BBC were not so likely to get the blame for causing the Government embarrassment.

Second-guessing the captain

Sometimes John Birt didn't have to take the difficult decisions on *Panorama* and other programmes himself. Colleagues have noted that, as is often the way with men at the top, he would indicate what he wanted done, and at the same time make it clear that others should be seen to decide. But such was the god-fearing state of mind of his subordinates that he often needed to do nothing at all. What Michael Grade has famously called the BBC's 'pre-emptive cringe' took effect without his help or insistence. 'Sliding into Slump' was the saddest illustration of a *Panorama* prostrate for fear of causing political offence.

To this day Samir Shah, then the Deputy Editor of News and Current Affairs, Television (the initials gave him the delightful title DENCAT) insists that it was his decision alone to postpone this programme. How far he was reading Birt's mind aright is not clear.

In early 1992 David Jordan was on the *Panorama* bridge as acting Editor, while the flagship wallowed in the waves. Mark Thompson had gone; his successor had not yet been appointed. So it was Jordan who, as the General Election approached, commissioned a programme on the Conservatives' economic record. His chosen producer was Gerry Baker, his reporter none other than the BBC's economics Editor Peter Jay. Jay of course had helped Birt write his articles back in the mid-1970s about how television journalism should be done, and had coined the famous phrase 'Mission to Explain'. Jay was now the very archetype of 'specialist' that Birt wanted to see appearing more on *Panorama* – not some ignorant generalist like most *Panorama* reporters but an expert who understood what his interviewees were talking about better than they did themselves. This was clearly going to be a magisterial programme that would be unassailable in its authority.

No doubt because of his reputation and contacts Jay secured something of a scoop for this *Panorama* – an interview in which the former Tory Chancellor Nigel Lawson conceded that decisions he had made had led to the British economy booming out of control, and that as a result the ensuing recession had lasted longer than would otherwise have been the case. In other words the Conservatives could hardly claim to have created an economic miracle if they did not also take some responsibility for the recession that had followed. But, as an economics expert, Jay was himself sceptical of any government's ability to exercise control over the economy. His planned programme was certainly no swingeing indictment of the Conservatives – it seemed likely to be more soporific than savage.

Filming went ahead to include other distinguished figures, including former Labour Chancellor Denis Healey, and Sir Alan Walters, Margaret Thatcher's former economic adviser. The programme was intended for transmission on the eve of the Budget,[86] in the run-up to the General Election. And for once there seemed to be no problem about those old-fashioned *Panorama* people who would be bound to get it all wrong. Why, everyone connected with the programme, Jordan, Jay, Baker and Shah were all ex-LWT, *Weekend World* graduates. Surely there could be no problem here? Plain sailing then for this *Panorama* at least.

The programme had been given the go-ahead on the basis of a 10-page pre-shooting script that Jay had written on 25 February, to which Shah had raised no objection. In the middle of the week before transmission Jordan talked Shah through the film that had been made on that basis. According to Jordan, Shah was jittery; Birt had been complaining about the previous week's *Panorama*,[87] which had dealt with the future of the coal industry in the aftermath of the long and bitter miners' strike. Jane Corbin had described the defeated miners at the Maerdy pit in the Rhondda returning to work with their 'heads held high'. This had been seen as unnecessarily emotive language, liable to inflame relations with a Conservative Government still celebrating victory over Arthur Scargill. Shah agrees that Birt had complained about the coal programme, so that he was 'on red alert'.

Jay's explanation for what happened next is simple: 'John Birt had hauled Samir Shah over the coals pretty severely for a one-sided programme lacking in coherence and rigour. Samir reacted by pulling the next thing that passed across his desk.' Shah vigorously denies this explanation.

On Friday afternoon Jordan watched a fine-cut, 'nearly finished' version of 'Sliding into Slump', quite satisfied as to the way it was coming together. But then Shah called him in to say he was very unhappy with the script – which, typically, was all he had seen: it wasn't 'balanced' enough. Jordan thinks that Shah simply felt the film was going to be anti-Tory. Shah's contention was – and is – that Jay had analysed the history of the economic problem Britain now faced (in the correct Birtian way) but that the author of the 'Mission to Explain' had not gone on to set out the options as to what should be done about it.[88] Jordan says that while *Weekend World* had always tried to drive towards a conclusion in a current affairs programme, Shah now seemed to be wanting 'on the one hand and on the other'. Whatever his reasons, Shah demanded major changes to the film, involving new sequences and interviews. Alternatively, he enquired, could the film be truncated, and a studio discussion added? Jordan demurred. Shah did not ask Jay to amend his script; indeed, he did not speak to him at all. Instead, at eight o'clock that Friday evening, without ever actually watching the film, Shah decided that it could not run on the following Monday.

Over the weekend he had another meeting with Jordan and producer Baker. Naturally enough the conversation grew acrimonious. Shah used words to the effect that 'I can't have *Panorama* putting out a programme on the eve of the General Election saying the Conservatives have fouled up the economy'. He says that he continued: 'without saying how the different parties would now clear it up.'

Today Shah still insists that when he made the decision to drop the film it was for editorial, not political, reasons. 'I got no calls from John Birt,' he says, 'either of concern or support. But I should have involved others in a collegiate decision.' Jordan is certain that Shah would never have decided to pull the programme without at least informing his immediate boss Tony Hall. 'I never believed it was Samir's own decision; he's a sensible and clever enough man to know that if you're going to do something like that in the BBC you always cover your back, you refer up.' However Hall confirms that the decision to drop the programme was made by Shah alone. Weekly Current Affairs, he says, was essentially Shah's area of responsibility; and when he was told by Shah what he had done, he simply backed his decision.

Peter Jay was furious that his programme had been dropped, and even angrier when he got a letter from Shah that seemed to blame *Panorama*'s acting Editor Jordan for his failure to speak to Jay: 'I hope by now you will have heard from David Jordan about the events of Friday March 6th,' wrote Shah. 'I was guided by the advice of the Editor of the programme and not by any desire to behave improperly towards you. I accept that I should not have been so guided and should have anyway discussed matters with you directly. I offer my sincere apologies.'[89] Jay replied, vigorously repudiating Shah's explanation of events and accusing him of spreading 'in staff briefings and in unattributable comments to the press ever new and different versions, all untrue, of what you had done and why you had done it, all with the apparent purpose of shifting blame on to other shoulders, mainly those of your subordinates.' Jay ended his angry reply with a challenge: 'You say that you and you alone took this decision. Very well, take responsibility for it. State publicly that you made a grave error of judgement, which had damaged the BBC and your colleagues. And then take appropriate personal action. I shall then be happy to accept your apology and to acknowledge that you are a better man than I had thought.'[90]

Shah did not take up the challenge, but he soon realised that he had woefully underestimated the chorus of disapproval, the howls of derision, that would greet his decision to drop 'Sliding into Slump'. At the very moment that Hall, at Television Centre, was introducing the line-up of BBC journalists who would cover the forthcoming General Election their union was denouncing Shah's decision as 'craven'.

Jay still thinks Shah acted as he did simply to try and make himself look tough – to Birt above, and to *Panorama* programme makers below him. Most others saw Shah differently, as a relatively junior BBC manager terrified of giving politicians in power any excuse to take offence and complain. 'The BBC has got to be very careful indeed over the next eight to ten weeks,' Tory Home Secretary Kenneth Baker had said as the Election approached; wasn't what had now happened a demonstration that his menacing message had had its effect? 'Bullied, Beaten, Cowed' was the *Daily Mirror*'s perhaps predictable headline over an article by its political editor. The decision to pull the programme, said Alastair Campbell, was a triumph for the Tories: 'A triumph all the sweeter because there is no evidence that they exerted any direct political influence on this decision. This time it was simply a case of the BBC running scared.'[91]

In the *Observer* John Naughton acidly remarked that 'Mr. Birt's commitment to analytical journalism does not extend to annoying the Government or its back-bench hyenas, though it does, of course, permit courageous exposés of Labour-supporting gargoyles like Robert Maxwell. BBC sources insist that the pulling of *Panorama* was not the result of political pressure but an internal decision, as if that somehow made it better.'[92]

Former *Panorama* people who had been cast adrift or forced to walk the plank now had their revenge – more in sorrow than in anger, of course. 'All in all,' wrote Roger Bolton about 'Sliding into Slump', 'massive effort and no little money had been spent. And then, suddenly, all that work was thrown away. Why? There is only one explanation, and that a sad one. The intimidation from all the political parties has worked. Ironically, as far as I am aware, none of the political parties had complained about this programme. Perhaps they no longer need to do so. Self-censorship will suffice. The instinct for institutional survival has overcome the obligations of broadcast journalism. The threats of the Home Secretary have not been in vain.'[93] In reply Shah remains insistent that it was the programme's failure to explore the options following its analysis of the problem which made him pull it, rather than any political motive.

'Sliding into Slump' was finally broadcast two months later – at 11.30pm on a Bank Holiday Monday,[94] after the General Election was safely over. Naturally enough its audience was fairly derisory – 1.5 million viewers. Jay had argued to Birt that the journalistically 'right' moment had passed and that there was no point now in putting the programme out. Birt had insisted that it must be broadcast, saying that otherwise the row over it would fester for ever.

It was an episode that had done damage both to *Panorama* and the BBC. Said television reviewer Paul Gent in the *Daily Telegraph*: 'It's hard not to feel sorry for the BBC – under attack from all sides, morale low, its Charter coming up for renewal, umpteen taskforces investigating its workings – but it is often its worst enemy. Who else but the BBC could make a fine programme, make the right decision about when to broadcast it, and still end up with egg on its face?'[95]

Exactly when *Panorama* could expect support from Birt and when it could not, when it would be encouraged to punch its weight and when it would be made to pull its punches, was becoming clearer. Once he had got *Panorama* under control Birt was a resolute defender of its journalism – except at times that could be described as politically sensitive.

The other Iron Lady

In July 1989 *Panorama* had been strongly backed by John Birt when it took on the second most formidable lady in the Conservative Party, Dame Shirley Porter, the leader of Westminster City Council in London. The programme alleged that Porter and some of her close colleagues had systematically directed the council's housing policy so as to gerrymander local elections. Rich and arrogant, Porter continued to deny *Panorama* the interview it had asked for while at the same time threatening dire consequences if the programme went ahead. On this story Birt stood firmly behind the *Panorama* team. Reporter John Ware recalls being at a meeting with Birt when Porter tried to get through on the telephone, once more demanding that the programme be delayed. Birt said 'no'; she had had every chance to give an interview, now her time had run out.

Ware was impressed with Birt's resolute response, and his way of dealing with programmes in general: 'Never once did I feel he was trying water anything down,' he says. 'Often he made sensible script suggestions, improving scripts. He was a strong editorial figure, real Editor material. He knew the way the world worked. He was a more considerable person than people gave him credit for being.'

In 1989 the Porter programme was broadcast as planned. It led directly to the District Auditor's enquiry into Westminster City Council and his decision in January 1994 that he was minded to surcharge Porter and her colleagues £21 million. By now Ware and his producer Mark Killick had unearthed new evidence of even more widespread gerrymandering in Westminster than had so far been revealed. They were given the go-ahead to make another programme to be transmitted on 25 April, 10 days before the local elections. But, as the date approached, the BBC, and Birt, seemed to grow increasingly nervous. Legal advice had confirmed that Section 30 of the Local Government Finance Act of 1982 made it a criminal offence to disclose information about anyone or anything obtained by the District Auditor – as the programme intended to do. *Panorama* produced 200 newspaper cuttings to show how routinely that section was breached. Ware and his Editor[96] argued that no one would take the BBC to court over this: there would be overwhelming support for what it was doing. In any case there was a public interest defence at law – as counsel had agreed.

But Birt hesitated. On 21 April he insisted that further legal advice be obtained before transmission. Says Ware:

> There was certainly an honestly held view by some in the BBC hierarchy who thought that disclosing evidence of the scale of corruption in the Tory flagship council so close to an election was fundamentally unfair, and in breach of the BBC's Charter obligation to be impartial. I thought the

opposite, that it was our duty as a public service broadcaster to put this evidence before the citizens of Westminster so that it could inform their choice. However, instead of the BBC stating their view openly and honestly, they erected a legal smoke-screen. This was to the effect that the programme could not be cleared in time by the lawyers and therefore had to run *after* the election.

A BBC press release denied that the film had ever been scheduled for 25 April.

As Ware points out, all this was going on at a time when once again the BBC's entire future was in the balance following the hostility of the Thatcher years. Would its Charter be renewed on the same basis in the forthcoming White Paper? Where would the Licence Fee be set? As *The Times* reported on 26 April: 'John Major and senior ministers meet today to discuss the future of the BBC amid the dispute over the transmission of a *Panorama* programme alleging large-scale corruption in a Tory Council.' It must have been a difficult moment for Birt. Once again, like so many of his predecessors, the Director General had to consider the effect on the credibility of *Panorama* (and ultimately the reputation of the BBC) of delaying or cancelling a well-timed programme against the damage it might do the Corporation if it went out as planned.

In the event the second Dame Shirley Porter programme was postponed until after the local elections.[97] Two months later, in July 1994, the long-awaited White Paper renewed the BBC Charter for another 10 years and confirmed that the Licence Fee would be inflation-proofed until the year 2001. That was a triumph for which Birt could take considerable credit. But *Panorama*'s reputation had suffered.

After a difficult and hard-fought engagement some landlubbers will see only that the fleet now sails serenely on, whereas others will be quick to spy that damage has been done: damage to its reputation for valour in general perhaps, and damage to individual vessels like the flagship *Panorama*. As one critic, Stuart Weir, puts it, 'the war has been lost as well as won.' As Weir concedes, the BBC was often bold under Birt, 'so why has the BBC frequently abandoned the Captain Courageous mode throughout this period too? The answer seems to be, timing. It is when content and context combine to make political trouble that its nerve fails. *Panorama* can make contentious programmes, but cannot expect to show them at sensitive times.'[98]

That seems a just comment. John Birt had tried to sell the imposition of new controls on programme making on the basis that they would help BBC journalism become more, not less effective. Right at the start, over the 'Spycatcher' film, he had been calling for scripts, for detailed accounts of what interviewees would be asked, and what they would say in return. And when he wasn't satisfied he stopped the project in its tracks. Only when he was convinced that the programme was under his control did he permit Panorama to proceed with it.

For those who worked on carefully planned, lengthily researched programmes, those who were always prepared to get prior approval for what they were doing, those who remembered to keep their bosses informed every step of the way, then John Birt's controlling tendencies were not necessarily an insuperable hindrance. Reporters such as Ware and Peter Taylor found that if they won Birt's confidence they could indeed find him a force working with them to make a programme more powerful. 'After a rocky start I came to view him as a strength,' says Ware. But woe betide those pressed into fast turnrounds, or situations where the story could not be carefully worked out before shooting began. There Birt's determination to impose his idea of discipline on Panorama could be damaging – to morale, and to the programmes. Such were the pluses and minuses of the mechanism designed by this former student of engineering.

And when it came to those issues where politics were involved then Birt could not be relied on to steer towards the sound of gunfire. Too many programmes were postponed or emasculated, with the result that Panorama's reputation suffered direct hits. 'There was no doubt in my mind', says Gavin Hewitt, 'that the BBC was extremely anxious about offending the Establishment of the time . . . the Tory Party then was still immensely powerful. So the big arguments were over programmes that involved the Conservatives: could we be robust when we went to the heart of the Conservative Establishment?'

Hewitt is a tough, but thoughtful reporter who has worked in both news and current affairs, and for the Canadian Broadcasting Corporation as well as the BBC. In 1990 he started out with producer Mark Killick on a Panorama programme about Conservative Party funding. They had discovered that it was not local constituency garden parties that were filling the Party coffers but very large donations – many from abroad – made by individuals who had done well during the Thatcher years. Documenting this sensitive subject was difficult. Birt took a close interest in the progress of the programme, insisting for example that one particular interview with a rather dodgy witness be removed completely.[99] 'Birt was arguing for "context", and also "a mature way of looking at the world, treating serious people seriously"', says Hewitt. 'There was no doubt in my mind that the BBC was extremely anxious about offending the Establishment of the time.'

'Who Pays for the Party?'[100] was due for transmission just before the Conservative Party Conference. Says Hewitt: 'The low point for me came when, in the final days of making the programme, a fax came from Blackpool [where BBC bigwigs were attending the Labour Party Conference] telling me what my opening camera piece should say. It was the most convoluted statement I have ever tried to deliver. I was very uncomfortable with it and so was Mark Killick.' And the television reviewers picked that up when the film went out. The *Independent* said:

> *Panorama*'s (BBC1) report on the financing of the Conservative Party, timed with nervous bravado for the eve of the party conference, relied heavily on graphics and charts to back up its figures, but the one statistic you wanted to see was missing; what exact percentage of Gavin Hewitt's excruciatingly cautious script consisted of qualifying statements or assurances that he wasn't, of course, talking here, heaven forbid, about actual, you know, corruption. 'The question is', as he said at one point, 'whether ministers could be seen to have been put into a position where they are facing a conflict of interest.' By my reckoning that puts the ministers at least three steps away from any problem and if they're that far away, why should the viewer be worrying? Still, with Woodrow Wyatt ready to pop the programme on to the impartiality scales[101], you could understand the strained posture from which most of the narration was delivered; bent over backwards.[102]

Hewitt agreed with this criticism. He felt mortified that he had bowed to pressure to use language so opaque that it had quite pulled the programme's punch: 'It seemed to dilute the thesis of our story. It looked on the screen as if we had lost our courage. I resigned.'

Tony Hall, Editor, News and Current Affairs, Television, arranged a meeting with Hewitt in a London hotel to persuade him not to jump ship. Hewitt says:

> I told him we had become frightened of our own shadows, that we were putting in so much 'context' that we were losing sight of the story we were trying to tell. You can provide so much context that in the end people don't know what you're talking about any more. Managers didn't seem to realise there was a danger that 'contextualising' was ruining the credibility of BBC journalism. The danger was that in being fair we would end up looking foolish. There was a difference between not sensationalising and not being clear. I think Tony Hall accepted that. I got assurances from him that being mature and balanced didn't mean that in the end the viewer would be left uncertain what the charge was that we were making.

Hewitt withdrew his resignation.

It's easy to be bold and resolute when those you may offend are unpopular or powerless; much harder when they are in a position to make life difficult for you. Directors General have a right to expect that when *Panorama* makes a programme that is likely to upset the Government of the day – or even the politicians who may be in government tomorrow – it should, so far as possible, get it right, and be able to defend it. *Panorama* people have a right to expect that when they do their job properly BBC bosses will back them up. The only justification for imposing new controls and disciplines on *Panorama* was to make the programmes more effective. While you can't make good programmes if the Corporation is collapsing around you, there's no point in having the institution at all if *Panorama* can't try to tell the truth about important issues in a timely way. That is the essence of public service broadcasting, part of what the viewers are paying for in the Licence Fee. There were times in the Birt era when, for other than good journalistic reasons, *Panorama* was prevented from doing its duty.

Albatross time

In the spring of 1992 David Jordan was running *Panorama* on a temporary basis, pending the appointment of a new Editor. Gloom was pervasive.

As Steve Clarke had written in *The Times* at the end of January, 'Fear and loathing stalk *Panorama* . . . With falling ratings and an unsettled staff, can the BBC's current affairs flagship avoid going under?'[103] It seemed as if *Panorama* was blighted, an albatross around its neck, with nothing captain or crew could do to lift its fortunes. By mid-March the tide in *Panorama*'s affairs seemed at an even lower ebb. 'New Editor hits morale at *Panorama*' was the headline above an article by the *Guardian*'s Georgina Henry. In the wake of the debacle over 'Sliding into Slump' came even gloomier news: a most unwelcome new captain was taking command. '*Panorama* journalists, already angry over the cancellation of Monday's broadcast on the recession, yesterday claimed to be shattered by the appointment of a new editor whom they see as unsympathetic to the programme's traditions.'[104]

On 11 March Samir Shah had had a two-hour meeting with the *Panorama* team during which he had attempted, without success, to persuade them that his decision not to transmit the 'Sliding into Slump' programme had been justified. At the end of the session he announced that the next Editor of *Panorama* would be Glenwyn Benson, currently the Editor of the Sunday political discussion programme *On the Record*. As *Television Week* reported, the announcement was greeted with a stony silence; it was not what *Panorama* people wanted to hear.

Glenwyn Benson didn't actually land on the deck with a puff of green smoke and a cackle, but to *Panorama*'s dispirited crew it was rather as if the Wicked Witch of the West[105] had flown in on her broomstick to cause them even more trouble. The issue was not that Benson would be *Panorama*'s first woman Editor: the team had no objection at all to that. The problem was a different one. Benson was the quintessential Birtist, the first who had actually served under him at London Weekend Television (where she had risen to be Deputy Editor of *Weekend World*) to take command of *Panorama*. Now at last it seemed John Birt had his own trusted lieutenant in charge of the most important ship in his Current Affairs fleet.

Later that year Benson seemed to confirm every fear that she would be quite happy with a *Panorama* that looked like *Weekend World* – and was watched by a similarly tiny audience. In an article that compared ITV's *World in Action* under Dianne Nelmes with *Panorama* under Glenwyn Benson Michael Leapman reported Benson as saying: 'It wouldn't matter if only five people watched, it's a symbol to the country that the BBC considers the subject we're covering is important.'[106] Benson hurried to correct the impression she had given that to her the number of *Panorama* viewers was of no account. 'Of course I want large audiences for our programmes. What *Panorama* will not do is narrow the range and scope of its subject matter to "pull in the crowds".'[107]

Too late: whatever Benson's explanation, the impression remained that she regarded the size of *Panorama*'s audience as unimportant and viewed efforts to increase it with positive distaste. Among the *Panorama* team her position was widely ridiculed as 'the drive for five'.

And then Benson suddenly threw off her black hat and cloak and revealed herself as Glinda the Good Witch. With a wave of her wand the sun began to shine and *Panorama*'s Munchkins sang and danced again. Of course the transformation wasn't quite that clear-cut. Benson, some of her producers remember, would still sit in the cutting room listening intently to the logic of the commentary while averting her gaze from the screen. If the Birtists had accused the old *Panorama* gang of never letting the facts stand in the way of a good story, so they were never going to let what the viewer was going to see – no matter how interesting – spoil a good script. But by June 1993 Benson had clearly decided that *Panorama* was meant to be different from what she admits was the 'austere' *Weekend World*. She set out her new faith in a long memo to the new Controller of BBC1, Alan Yentob, who was fed up with what he saw as *Panorama*'s unexciting content and low audience ratings.

First she reminded him (tactfully) that *Panorama* was a totem for the BBC – a programme he could not (at this particular moment anyway) kick out of peak time even if he wanted to: 'The BBC's response to the Green Paper cites *Panorama* in defining the Corporation itself: "The BBC's primary task in serving its audience is to ensure a higher quality, richer diversity and broader choice of programmes – particularly in peak times – than is available elsewhere . . . Programmes like *Casualty*, *Only Fools and Horses* . . . which regularly attract very large audiences, are . . . no more important than *Panorama*, *Omnibus*, *Screen Two* . . . which attract smaller but substantial audiences, and meet important public needs." In other words', wrote Benson quite correctly, 'the BBC uses *Panorama* and its position in the peak time schedule to justify the licence fee. The Corporation nails its colours to the mast of serious current affairs at least on this one occasion per week bang in the middle of the schedule, as proof of its commitment to provide something different – a public service.'[108] But for too long, Benson continued, there had been a polarised debate between the Controller of BBC1, who wanted programmes that would bring in a big audience, and the News and Current Affairs Directorate, which wanted *Panorama* to analyse the great issues behind the news. This was wrong – too simple a division. '*Panorama* should be able to mix and synthesise all of the following strands: Central and distinctive vein – domestic stories that are original, provocative insights about Britain today; Long investigations; and Big news – response to the really big news stories which galvanise the nation.'

Benson pointed out that (contrary to popular belief) the *Panorama* audience was, at around four million, much the same as it had been in 1975; but it was getting older. Only 22 per cent of *Panorama* viewers were now under 35 as compared with 40 per cent for Channel 4's *Cutting Edge*. And *Panorama* had an image problem. It was thought of as remote and patronising – though the research said that when non-viewers were shown the programmes, they liked them.

Benson's main recommendations were to stop *Panorama* talking down to people and (in Birt-speak) 'strengthen the synthesis of programme mix', with more original domestic stories, which might bring in new viewers.

Benson's readiness to have *Panorama* deal with subjects ordinary people felt relevant to their lives was quickly apparent. '*Panorama*,' said Russell Twisk in the *Observer*, 'now enjoying a new lease of life after a dreadful spell, showed how victim stories should be handled in a compelling account about "Judy", the Scottish rape victim, who spoke out so bravely about her experience at a Tory conference in May.'[109] And as *Panorama* approached its 40th anniversary Jane Thynne in the *Daily Telegraph* gave the programme a 'Birthday Rave':

> Enjoy programmes about sex and violence? Then *Panorama*'s the show for you. The Beeb's veteran current-affairs flagship is shortly to celebrate its 40th birthday and, like many 40 year olds, seems to be indulging in a wild fling – in this case making programmes that win high ratings. Recently, 'Vigilantes', fronted by rising star Peter Godwin, netted nearly six million viewers, the highest figure for 18 months. Following recent *Panorama*s dealing with rape and whether you can catch AIDS from your dentist, the show seems to be

entering a whole new populist phase. With a forthcoming edition asking whether John Major is the right man for the job, it also appears to be regaining its political nerve.'[110]

Glenwyn Benson rediscovered old *Panorama* ways of explaining complicated stories – commissioning an independent production which took the parents of Tim Parry, 'An Ordinary Boy'[111] killed by an IRA bomb in Warrington, to meet the people whom they wanted to talk to in Northern Ireland's warring communities. By September that year, under the headline '*Panorama* goes populist' Richard Brooks was writing:

> I don't know if John Birt has been watching *Panorama* recently. If not, he might be in for a shock. The long-running BBC current affairs programme has become rather populist and full of human interest stories . . . While Benson accepts that *Panorama* has changed somewhat, she denies any pressure from senior colleagues. 'The change has come not from above, but from *Panorama* journalists themselves. We feel we should concentrate on stories, which are not just big news stories, but go on around people and trouble them. *Panorama* must speak to people directly about the kind of society they live in.'[112]

It was as if Birt no longer ruled, or had sent secret word to Benson that he'd been wrong all the time. *Panorama* changed tack so abruptly that it was in danger of capsizing. In a highly emotional programme[113] about the horrors of war in Bosnia Martin Bell made an impassioned appeal for the West to get further involved: 'To intervene will cost lives,' he said; 'not to intervene will cost more. It is fundamentally a matter of whether we care.' Bell was attacked by Simon Jenkins in *The Times*[114] for indulging in the pornography of violence and of grief, and for showing a bias against understanding – in other words of having an emotional spasm without sufficiently analysing what we should do about the barbarism on western Europe's border. When Benson wrote in response she seemed almost to repudiate – at least on this occasion – the 'Mission to Explain':

> The BBC regularly explores the issues, and *Panorama* has explored them too and will undoubtedly do so again. But the saturation coverage of the diplomatic and military details can induce a quite different kind of bias

against understanding – a sense of helplessness and boredom among the public. Martin Bell's programme corrected that by reclaiming viewers' attention so dramatically to the subject. It is a legitimate function of current affairs to enable people to connect via the camera with what is really happening.[115]

'Only connect.' Well, it's a great start if you can get viewers to think and feel what it must be like in some terrible situation far from their own experience. But in current affairs, in *Panorama*, it isn't enough to leave it there. The whole point of *Panorama* is to dig deeper than that, not just to emote. The only justification programmes like *Panorama* have to use horrific pictures like Bell's is that it helps them explain the situation and what might be done about it – otherwise it is just exploitation of the emotions, self-indulgent journalism.

Under Benson, then, *Panorama* began to emerge from a long night of gloom into a more colourful world where a variety of stories – some obviously popular, some less so – made the programme once again an interesting watch. There was 'The Case of India One',[116] the inside story of corruption in the Metropolitan Police, and 'The Manager',[117] which asked some sharp questions about Terry Venables's business activities at Tottenham Hotspur football club. And then there were stories that made no concessions to popular taste but were simply good television journalism.

'BBC1's *Panorama* has opened its season with a string of hits,' wrote that shrewd commentator Brenda Maddox in the autumn of 1993. She singled out for special praise a truly remarkable programme which followed the secret negotiations which, in the Oslo Accords, brought new hope to the Middle East. Made by reporter Jane Corbin and producer Clive Edwards, this *Panorama* was watched by a small audience of only 2.6 million, but it rightly won the Royal Television Society's top prize. 'Thank heaven', wrote Maddox, 'for *Panorama*'s dazzling programme 'The Norway Channel',[118] on how Norway actually brought together the Israelis and the PLO. That superb international scoop will go a long way to counterbalance the suspicion that *Panorama* is choosing populist domestic subjects in order to fight against an increasingly tabloid ITV . . . *Panorama*'s recovery of its lost voice has been a cause of widespread pleasure for those who admire the BBC's journalistic flagship.'[119]

By November, flagship *Panorama* (now berthed in a new BBC port next to Television Centre) could celebrate its 40th birthday with pride rather than paranoia. The average audience that autumn had been nearly 5.5 million, compared with 3.6 million for the same period the year before. 'There is no big birthday bash', wrote Andrew Cuff, 'and they are not hanging out the bunting at the programme's functional offices at White City, west London. But there is quiet satisfaction about *Panorama*'s resurgence of self-confidence.'[120]

Benson had revived *Panorama*; light had broken in on the prison hulk. When she took over, Benson had been surprised to discover that Tom Mangold was no longer on the programme. At once she had recalled him from the gulag of exile, his skills again recognised and rewarded. *Panorama* was no longer required to be dull but was once again free to try and make interesting programmes.

Belatedly the Birtists had realised that to satisfy a large audience in peak time – and to bring in younger viewers – *Panorama* had to do what it had done in the pre-Birt past: make good, interesting films. When Benson was promoted she was replaced as Editor, *Panorama* by someone not from News and Current Affairs but from Documentaries.

Swashbuckler

Steve Hewlett had made his BBC reputation on documentary series like *Inside Story*, where the film and the tale it told was of the essence. 'Narrative is the thing. *Panorama*s had always felt to me like stopping and starting again all the time,' says Hewlett. When he arrived at *Panorama* he found the crew, newly freed from their Birtist chains, still locked into old ways of thinking, still worshipping what he calls 'the supremacy of the script':

> A team would ask me: 'When are we going have a script conference?' This always seemed to mean that reporters ended up writing a new 'piece to camera' at the end of that process and doing it up against some anonymous brick wall. There was nothing organic about that: I came from a background where the script was the last thing, not the first. People at *Panorama* were absolutely focused on what they were saying, not on what we were hearing;

it was about identifying arguments, ticking boxes. It was 'a bias against communication'.

So much for John Birt's 'bias against understanding.'

Hewlett was interested in making good films, but not just for the sake of it. In fact his BBC career proper had begun on *Panorama* in the early 1980s, when good films on worthwhile subjects went hand in hand. A former student organiser, Hewlett was teaching at Manchester Polytechnic when he started selling local stories to *Nationwide* at £10 a time. When the author and *Panorama* producer Alan Scales, after several days research, had failed to find the owners of a hazardous waste plant in the Manchester area they called Hewlett for help. Sitting next to him when he took the call was a former *Morning Star* journalist who had the right number in his address book. 'I didn't call back at once,' says Hewlett, 'I didn't want those *Panorama* idiots to know how easy it had been.' When he did, he asked if the programme had got any more chores like that for him to do. On visits to Lime Grove Hewlett initially found *Panorama* an unfriendly place full of public schoolboys, most of whom, he says, eyed him with suspicion and didn't speak to him. Some of them later felt rather silly when he arrived back as their Editor.

A three-month contract with the BBC which followed his bit of research for *Panorama* was not renewed when it was discovered Hewlett had once been a member of the Communist Party of Great Britain. However, the BBC's arcane vetting system was shortly to be exposed, ridiculed and radically reformed; Hewlett reckons that his later BBC career may even have benefited from the BBC's desperate desire to demonstrate that he was no longer regarded as a security risk.

Hewlett went to work for an independent production company before returning to the BBC. There he took the documentary route, making several tough programmes about Northern Ireland, but watching from afar in relative safety as Current Affairs was ground down under John Birt. '*Panorama*', he says, 'was driving towards boring.' Now he was back to run the programme he had started out on.

The subject matter came first – a more 'accessible' agenda. 'In Documentaries', says Hewlett, 'if my reaction was "I wouldn't watch it" then I wouldn't commission it. Now I was going to do that in Current Affairs.

But there had been a problem on *Panorama*: if they did do a popular story then their journalistic standards went out of the window. I was quite clear I wasn't going to let that happen.' Hewlett shrewdly made *Panorama*'s agenda as popular as he could – the National Lottery, for example – and found popular ways to tell less popular stories: Bosnia, with the focus on the charismatic British commander General Rose, or Rwanda, seen through the moist eyes of reporter Fergal Keane. But it was an old-fashioned interview with a major public figure rather than a well-told film story which ensured that Hewlett's time as *Panorama*'s Editor will be remembered. It was a programme seen by more viewers than any other *Panorama* – before or since. It was of course Martin Bashir's interview with Diana, Princess of Wales.

Royal salute – medals and muttering

Martin Bashir had not been a reporter on *Panorama* long, but two programmes he had made on Terry Venables, the football manager and businessman, had attracted a good deal of attention, as well as writs. In 1995, with Prince Charles and his wife Diana leading separate lives, Bashir had begun investigating the future of the royal marriage. He had become interested in the allegations of 'dirty tricks' by the security services affecting members of the Royal Family.[121] In the course of his research Bashir had met Diana's brother, Earl Spencer, who was himself concerned about security issues and helpful to Bashir in his enquiries. But progress was slow. Sensing the possibility of a sensational scoop, Editor Steve Hewlett urged Bashir to try and get an interview with Diana.

A *Panorama* person of the time remembers Bashir as a reporter in need of a producer. 'Martin, Essex is above Sussex' was the sort of thing he had to be told. But once he had been given the scent Bashir was wonderful. Crucially, he had an extraordinary ability to get on terms with people. 'If Martin can get into a room with them he can persuade anyone at all to give him an interview.'

After a series of meetings with Diana, Bashir told Hewlett that the interview was 'maybe'. Hewlett told Tim Gardam, now the boss of Weekly Television Current Affairs Programmes. Then Bashir came back with the news that it was definitely on. An interview like this would have impli-cations far beyond News and Current Affairs, so Richard Ayre, the BBC's Controller of Editorial Policy, was brought in. Jim Moir, the BBC's official royal liaison man, was kept out. And so was the man who was supposedly the most important of all – the BBC Chairman, Marmaduke Hussey. To have let him into the secret would have put him in a difficult position: his wife was Lady Susan Hussey, lady-in-waiting to the Queen. But the Director General was told. 'When we briefed John Birt', says Richard Ayre, 'he was delighted, amazed, astonished; he couldn't believe it was close to happening. But he immediately saw the Hussey problem; he told us he would not tell the Chairman; Birt was, after all, Editor-in-Chief. It was my impression that Diana felt that she would be physically prevented from doing the interview if Duke Hussey knew about it, because he would tell the Palace.' Only half-jokingly, Ayre said to Tony Hall, the Director of News and Current Affairs, who was now also in the picture: 'This could bring down the BBC, or the monarchy, or both.'

When Diana at last said 'yes' to an interview Hewlett brought a *Panorama* producer into the secret – Mike Robinson.[122] As the small BBC team met secretly to plan the interview they considered whether Bashir should ask the Princess about her relationship with the rugby player Will Carling. Says Hewlett: 'Were we really going to spend the whole interview talking about her boyfriends? We made the decision "Enough boyfriends – Ed.", so that's why it wasn't in the interview.' Diana did not ask for questions in advance, but knew exactly what ground the interview would cover.

On the evening of Saturday 5 November Bashir, Robinson and cameraman Tony Poole drove surreptitiously to Diana's home in Kensington Palace to tape this extraordinary interview. Because it was the weekend, with most of her staff given time off, Diana was able to keep her aides in ignorance of the explosion she and *Panorama* were about to detonate. Hewlett, at a Guy Fawkes Night bonfire party, was in an agony of anxious expectation. As the evening wore on with no news he tried phoning the team, but their mobiles were switched off. Finally, towards midnight, Robinson called to tell Hewlett: 'I think you've got a film.'

The following week Hewlett, Ayre, Hall, Richard Peel (Controller of Communications, News) and Gardam assembled at a secret hideaway, the Grand Hotel in Eastbourne, to see what they'd got. Appropriately enough, the editing equipment had been installed in a room right across the corridor from the Windsor suite.

'There's that terrible sensation', says Hewlett, 'when you think: "There'll be nothing in it."' But of course there was. Bashir and his team had got not just an interview but a brilliant one. 'We started taking notes in the usual way as the tape started. Then, as story after story came out, we all gradually stopped writing.' 'I've never been so overwhelmed in my life,' says Hall: 'here was a Royal talking like a real human being with all the traumas of a real person's life. I was bowled over by the frankness of it. It was certainly the biggest story I've ever known.' At the end of the tape there was silence. Hewlett remembers Gardam saying: 'He'll never be able to marry Camilla now.' After the viewing Hall and Ayre went for a cliff-top walk. What would the consequences of this unprecedented interview be? Whatever happened, it was going to be a huge story.

There was not much editing to be done. The famous 'three in the marriage' line was moved so that it fitted better with other answers about the royal marriage. Later, Birt saw the interview and took out one particular exchange that he felt was unnecessarily hurtful to the young princes, Diana and Charles's children.

The Princess, says Hewlett, had made it clear to the team that she wanted to tell the Queen what she had done herself – it was the only stipulation she made. Early on the day it had been agreed the BBC would reveal to the world that it had the interview, Diana told Bashir she had now broken the news to the Palace. Shortly afterwards Michael Stevenson, the BBC Secretary, telephoned Chairman Marmaduke Hussey. By this time relations between Hussey and Birt had already soured. This was the final rupture.

'It was an appalling business,' says a senior BBC manager, 'it brought into focus every faultline we had in the BBC.' While of course the Director General was in charge of the BBC's journalism, the Chairman would, in the normal course of events, have expected to be told about an interview as momentous as this. On hearing the news, says Stevenson, Hussey was 'calm, grave, thoughtful. It was only later that I picked up how very angry he was.' The story was released to the press before the phone conversation with Hussey was over. He was not to be given the chance to intervene to stop the interview being broadcast.

A pained note came from the Palace to Birt. The BBC's announcement of the interview, wrote Sir Robert Fellowes, the Queen's private secretary, 'came as a considerable surprise to us, even though we had been told, in the barest of tones, by the Princess of Wales that morning that she had conducted an interview with *Panorama*. We have always valued our relationship with the BBC, though we have never been foolish enough to take it for granted. In order to make sure that this relationship remains in a healthy state in the future, might it not be worthwhile for you and I and, perhaps, one or two others from each side, to meet to discuss the question of whether or not fresh ground rules need to be agreed, to both our benefits, for the future?'[123]

At the BBC elation was mingled with anxiety. Who could say what would happen as a result of this extraordinary scoop? Tim Gardam, according to Tim Suter, the Managing Editor of Weekly Programmes, 'was showing the usual high Anglican agony he often displayed. The more important it got, the more sure Tim was that everyone around him would fail.' Anne Sloman, then Gardam's Deputy, agrees: 'On the day of transmission he was in a terrible panic,' she says: 'something was going to go wrong; we were all going to get sacked.' 'Let's just enjoy it,' she says she urged Tim, before going off to a cutting room guarded by security men to choose sections of the interview for BBC Radio. Gardam dismisses these criticisms as absurd. This was one BBC production that had gone perfectly; excited he grants he may have been: that he was anguished and anxious he indignantly denies.

There was endless speculation about the contents of the interview, but no leaks. When it was broadcast, on 20 November 1995, Bashir's scoop gave *Panorama* its highest-ever audience: 22.8 million viewers watched in fascination, transfixed by a brilliant performance by the Princess of Wales in which what she had to say did considerable damage to the reputation of Prince Charles, the heir to the throne, and to the rest of the House of Windsor. The BBC was relieved to find the politicians not inclined to find fault with the Corporation for broadcasting such royal vitriol. Michael Hastings, from the BBC Public Affairs department, had a meeting with two MPs from the Conservative whips' office, Michael Bates and Roger Knapman, and reported to his boss Colin Browne: 'Both Bates and Knapman saw no substantial issue of concern for the BBC in this – in their own words, it was blatantly obvious that Diana emerges as the villain and not the BBC.'[124]

It was all a great triumph for *Panorama*. Bashir was a hero, and some of his glory rubbed off on the rest of the team; morale on the programme improved still further. But following the sweet smell of success came a sour aftertaste which threatened to spoil everybody's Christmas.

Shortly after the programme was transmitted *Panorama* reporter Tom Mangold got a call from producer Mark Killick. 'He was', remembers Mangold, 'distraught and very anxious. He asked for my help in dealing with something he had discovered.' Killick told Mangold that he had himself received a worried phone call from Matthew Wiessler, *Panorama*'s graphics artist. Wiessler was concerned about an incident that had occurred before the Diana interview had taken place. Late one evening Bashir had asked him to use his computer wizardry to create what were to look like photocopies of two bank statements. It was, Bashir had told him, a top priority job, and Wiessler had worked through the night to finish it before a BBC driver arrived to take the results directly to Bashir at London's Heathrow Airport. Based on the information Bashir had given Wiessler, the 'bank statements' showed payments to Earl Spencer's former head of security by a newspaper group and by another company, one which had featured in one of the *Panorama* programmes Killick and Bashir had made about Terry Venables.

That Venables programme had contained a graphic which, while it accurately showed the information contained in an original document, was not an actual copy of it. Venables was in the process of suing the BBC: what effect would the 'bank statements' made up for the Diana programme have on the Venables litigation? Killick told Mangold: 'I'm scared it looks like *Panorama* is tricking the Princess; I'm scared it's leaking; and I'm scared I know about it. If we are fabricating these documents, what's that going to do with our case with Venables?'

Mangold thought they should bring in Harry Dean, a former Deputy Editor of *Panorama* now working for BBC Current Affairs in Manchester. Together they asked Bashir for an explanation, but he refused to discuss the issue, saying that if his programme was to be queried in any way it should be through the Editor. So together Killick, Mangold and Dean rather reluctantly went to see Steve Hewlett. Faced with what they thought might be a serious threat to *Panorama*'s reputation, they felt they had no choice.

Told the story, Hewlett was angry – not best pleased (to put it mildly) that his prize programme should now have a shadow cast over it: 'I don't see why it's any of your f......g business,' he said. The three *Panorama* men left feeling that they'd done what they had to do. But Dean was called back by Hewlett for another chat, in which the Editor suggested that Killick was simply jealous of Bashir, angry and resentful that he had not been working with him on the Diana story to share the glory. Subsequently Hewlett spoke to Bashir and Wiessler, but took no further action.

In *Panorama* and in Current Affairs generally the euphoria that followed the Diana programme lingered on until the last day before everyone went off for the Christmas holiday. But that morning Matt Wiessler, the graphics artist who had been instructed by Bashir to create the 'bank statements', came to see Tim Suter: he was alarmed that his original computer graphics disc with the 'bank statements' on it had gone mysteriously missing from his London flat. Now for the first time Current Affairs management heard Wiessler's story. Suddenly they felt that the year might end with press coverage suggesting that the Diana interview had been obtained by underhand means. Hewlett, who had until now kept Wiessler's story to himself, was summoned by an anxious Gardam.

Hewlett said he would provide proof that there was nothing wrong with the interview. Sure enough, says Suter, a hand-written note from Diana soon arrived by courier. It said, in so many words: 'This is to confirm that I gave you the interview freely and was not influenced by any documents.' There was a general sigh of relief. 'We could all now relax for Christmas,' says Suter. 'We had had a scare but had got through it.'

But they hadn't. Next March the story surfaced again. *Panorama* people were receiving calls from the press: what was all this about faked documents? As Mangold later put it: 'The toothpaste was now out of the tube.'

On 7 April 1996 the *Mail on Sunday* carried a full account of the manufactured 'bank statements'. At the BBC's White City building Anne Sloman, now acting Head of Weekly Current Affairs, conducted an investigation, and Suter had a long session with Bashir. Martin told him, he says, that he had had the documents made up for the earlier story he was working on about members of the Royal Family and their security. Bashir insisted that the documents had never been used; but, according to Suter, Bashir did agree that Earl Spencer had recommended to the Princess that she should meet him.

Together Sloman and Tony Hall summoned Bashir to an interrogation at Broadcasting House. He sat at one end of a long table while they quizzed him from the other. According to Sloman, Bashir was 'penitent'; but he still could not properly explain exactly why he had arranged to have the fake 'bank statements' made up. 'It was a silly thing to do,' says Sloman. 'It didn't get him the interview; why he did it, God only knows.'

Bashir steadfastly denied that the graphics he had commissioned ever played any part in obtaining his interview, and a BBC press statement backed him up: 'The BBC has been able, independently,[125] to verify that these documents were put to no use which had any bearing, direct or indirect, on the *Panorama* interview with the Princess of Wales.'[126] But if that was the case, what exactly had they been intended for? The press release did not say.

Perhaps anxious above all that nothing should cloud the lustre of the Diana interview, the BBC's anger seemed directed not so much at Bashir for creating the problem, but at *Panorama*, suspected of making it public. On 8 April the *Daily Mail* asked: 'Could a BBC rival be out to get Bashir?', and that became the theme of BBC briefings. Sloman was convinced that the story had been leaked by Bashir's 'jealous colleagues', and *Panorama* people were directly told by press officer Alison Jackson that this would be the BBC line. 'They seemed to think they had a God-given right to leak to the press,' says Sloman. Regarded as 'a nest of vipers', *Panorama*'s journalists not unnaturally felt they were the victims of a witch hunt: 'It's like the Spanish Inquisition here,' said one. 'Everybody's paranoid; everybody's unhappy.'

Hall told Suter to find out exactly where the leaks were coming from, and Suter began rounding up what the BBC considered to be the likely suspects. At the very moment he was interviewing Killick, the BBC Press Office received a call from the *Sunday Times* asking for confirmation that Killick had been called in. From that Suter deduced that there certainly were leaks from inside the programme. But, as Sloman and Hall had to admit in a 90-minute meeting with John Birt, they could not discover who – if indeed it was anyone on *Panorama* – was responsible for making the story of the faked documents public.

It was hard to see how any *Panorama* person could benefit from making a fuss about the 'bank statements' – particularly when it only drew further attention to another programme in which a document had been 'created'. The BBC Press Service statement of 13 April had continued: 'It has been suggested further that there is a link between these two unbroadcast documents and a copy of a document used in the second of two *Panorama* investigations into Terry Venables. This document is the subject of a legal action being brought by Mr Venables against the BBC, but the BBC is confident of its veracity.'

Reading that paragraph, you might think that the 'copy of a document' used in the Venables programme was a real copy. Not so. It too was 'created'. The difference was that while Bashir's documents contained information 'that could not be substantiated', the information contained in the Venables graphic was correct. Shown, but not allowed to film, the original document, Mark Killick had read its entire contents into a tape recorder and used that, word for word, as the basis for his graphic. Nevertheless, while the Corporation might be 'confident of its veracity', it was defending something viewers had been led to think was a true copy of a document, when that was not strictly the case.

The moral to this tangled tale is simple: don't create, for any *Panorama* purpose, graphics that give the impression of being actual documents, when they are not.

Hall insists that the internal BBC row after the Diana interview did not damage Bashir – that it was his success that was the problem: 'Martin was definitely not in the dog-house; but how do you follow a scoop like that?' Certainly Bashir's next big interview[127] (with Louise Woodward, the British nanny convicted in the US of killing the baby in her care) was not in the same television league. And whatever Bashir's success, some producers now no longer wanted to work with him.

Bashir left *Panorama* in early 1999 to join ITV's new current affairs series *Tonight with Trevor McDonald*. There his first programme was another impressive and controversial prizewinner – an interview with the suspects in the Stephen Lawrence murder case. But, says one senior BBC manager of the time: 'I did not regard it as a tragedy when Bashir left the BBC.'

Martin Bashir has not responded to an invitation to give his own version of events surrounding his Diana interview for this chapter. Perhaps he will write about it himself some day. But in the absence of any plausible explanation he was wrong to do what he did. That cannot detract from the brilliance of his interview, with which Diana expressed herself completely happy.

chapter thirteen

⊕ Whither Panorama?

Embargoed

'If *Panorama* is being condemned to a hand-to-mouth existence it will rapidly become just one more actuality programme, less and less distinguishable from all the other reportage series that have been started (on both channels) since it first began.'[1] So wrote Editor David Wheeler in 1964, complaining that his budget of £2100 a programme was quite inadequate. It was a familiar theme. Four years later Editor David Webster was suggesting that mutiny might be on the cards if more cash was not forthcoming: 'Morale in *Panorama* has improved greatly, but is in danger of sliding down again as people feel we are not getting the backing we deserve.'[2]

In the 1970s Brian Wenham used creative accounting to rob some of his other programmes in the Current Affairs Group to fund *Panorama*'s international reporting. But by 1987 his successor, Peter Pagnamenta, was showing Bill Cotton, Managing Director, Television just how badly all Current Affairs had lost out over the previous decade.

Pagnamenta's figures showed that Current Affairs that cost £100 in 1975 was costing £236 ten years later. But the cost of Drama had risen much more – up from £100 to £632. And while Current Affairs was now getting a smaller share of the available cash it was at the same time having to fill much more air time than was Drama. John Birt put more money into a combined News and Current Affairs Directorate, but in 1989 all programmes were told to reduce their costs. As former Editor Peter Horrocks says: 'Some journalism got cut out.' What really hurt was that as *Panorama*'s budget came down, 'factual' series such as *McIntyre Uncovered*, made outside the News and Current Affairs Directorate, were in the money. A programme which investigated model agencies to see if they were exploiting their young clients was getting roughly three times as much as a *Panorama* trying to deal with issues that might be regarded as even more important.

The funding problem was eventually recognised. In July 2000 *Panorama* got an extra half million pounds a year, and since then it's received another half million. But that alone has not been enough. To ensure that remaining programmes are adequately funded *Panorama* has been forced to cut its output. In a *Times* article in May 2000 headlined 'Why less will be more', Horrocks (then *Panorama* Editor) wrote: 'Yesterday the BBC announced changes to *Panorama* that involve a substantial investment in original and investigative journalism. *Panorama* is redirecting the money saved by cutting its annual number of editions from 38 to 30 into a new drive for investigations . . . This development represents a reinvestment and reaffirmation of faith in current affairs by the BBC.'[3]

This was casuistry, double-speak. Rather than 'a reaffirmation of faith in current affairs' it was an abdication of responsibility. It demonstrated a decision not to fund *Panorama* properly throughout the year, and so to end its role as BBC Television's main weekly current affairs programme.

'It's such a betrayal,' says David Elstein, who worked for both *Panorama* and *This Week* before becoming a senior executive elsewhere in the television industry. 'What is the point of the BBC and public service broadcasting if you don't have a *Panorama*? . . . You need skill, resources, nerve, commitment and air time. We are watching humiliating and embarrassing blows dealt by cuts in the number of programmes.'

Running in three blocks of ten programmes, *Panorama* was now no more than just another occasional factual strand. The flagship was embargoed, not allowed to sail out for much of the year unless it was suddenly needed to deal with a crisis. And even when that moment came, with the terrorist attack in America on 11 September 2001, *Panorama* did not respond in the way it might once have done.

When BBC1 Controller Lorraine Heggessey called for a *Panorama* special on the night of the atrocity, Editor Mike Robinson demurred. He felt he must husband resources for a *Panorama* on the following Sunday. So the special was not made by *Panorama*, but by a scratch crew quickly assembled by Peter Horrocks, as Head of Current Affairs. Robinson does not accept that when crisis comes it must be *Panorama* that takes responsibility for whatever special programme is called for. 'It's not critical that a special is badged "*Panorama*",' he says; 'we came back on the air five days after September 11th – earlier than planned – with a programme that played to our strengths.'[4]

When the terrorists struck, reporter Tom Mangold was in America, making a film about armed police. Walking into the offices of the Baltimore *Sun* to film some interviews he suddenly saw, on the television screens in reception, a passenger plane flying into a skyscraper. Quickly on the phone to *Panorama* in London to find out what he was required to do, he was told to call back later. He did, but still received no brief. Through the day a surreal scenario developed as Mangold went on shooting camera pieces for his own essentially timeless programme while the world was gripped by the minute-by-minute drama of one of the biggest stories ever. Though less than an hour's drive from Washington (where the Pentagon had been hit), Mangold and his team were never sent into action; a *Panorama* reporter who has made more programmes about defence, intelligence and terror than anyone else in Britain was simply not called on. Though on the spot, he was not asked to contribute either to the Current Affairs special that night, or to the *Panorama* the following Sunday – or offered to News or any other programme which might have used him in the crisis. Instead, at a time when scores of BBC journalists were flying into America in a specially chartered plane, Mangold and his crew were allowed to fly back to Britain. This is not the *Panorama* of earlier years.

Looking through the window

What about the viewers? Does anyone any longer want to look through that window on the world that once seemed so revealing?

As *Panorama* sailed away from lively magazine in the early 1960s to ponderous single-subject programme in the first half of the 1970s a good part of the audience waved it goodbye. An audience that had in 1962 often touched 10 million declined to less than half that. So it was that in 1992 Editor Glenwyn Benson could argue: '*Panorama*'s audience is the same average now as it has been since 1975 – around 4 million.'

In October 2000 *Panorama*, for four decades a Monday evening fixture, was shunted off to late on Sunday night. The audience, which had been running at an average of 3.4 million in the year before the move, dipped lower. At an average 3.2 million, *Panorama*, says Mike Robinson, has been 'holding its own'. Research shows a *Panorama* increasingly watched more by older, middle class men, and less by younger people.

Scuppered?

In March 2001 the Royal Television Society gave *Panorama* and people closely associated with it for many years no fewer than three major prizes. The Judges' Award went to Peter Taylor for his trilogy on Northern Ireland – 'Provos', 'Loyalists' and 'Brits'. It was, said Will Wyatt, presenting the prize, 'a classic piece of television . . . a set of programmes that set standards and that will be referred to for many, many years'. Journalist of the Year was John Ware: 'a professional irritant in the very best journalistic tradition'. And Programme of the Year was Ware's *Panorama* report 'Who Bombed Omagh?', made with producer Eamon Hardy.[5] As the citation said, it was 'a quite extraordinary piece of television journalism combined with television film-making of the highest quality'.

These awards seemed to reassert the importance – and potential – of *Panorama*. Yet 'Who Bombed Omagh?' was the last programme to be transmitted on the traditional Monday before *Panorama* was shifted to the 'graveyard slot' on Sunday night.

The BBC says that this is the best hope of keeping *Panorama* afloat, on active service. 'What we're asking people to do is change the habit of a lifetime,' says Lorraine Heggessey. 'This is reacting to the TV climate we find ourselves in . . . we're trying to give *Panorama* a fighting chance.' Really? Going out late on Sunday night, not on the air for much of the year, how can *Panorama* flourish under the conditions now imposed upon it? Far from being given the kiss of life, surely *Panorama* is now more like some poor victim of *peine forte et dure*, in which heavy stones were laid one by one upon the sufferer until, despite all his efforts, he could breathe no longer and expired. Yet, while *Panorama* gasps for air, the very people, like Heggessey, who are carrying out this sentence proclaim their 'passionate commitment' to a programme which is 'a crucial part of the schedule.'[6]

In September 2001 the BBC announced that money for two extra programmes would be given to *Panorama* and that out of the total of 32, four would be hour-long specials running at 9pm on a weekday. 'I'm delighted by this move,' Peter Horrocks emailed his staff, 'as it means that the best of *Panorama*'s journalism will get the space and prominence that it deserves.'[7]

Is that really what it means? Isn't it rather this: that the Controller of BBC1 wants a few really popular *Panorama* programmes which she hopes will not damage the evening's viewing figures too much and will at the same time demonstrate that *Panorama* has not altogether been banished from weekday peak time?

If *Panorama* can be allowed out on parole from its Sunday night prison four times a year, why not every week? It's a simple issue. If the BBC cannot nerve itself to risk its ratings, and schedule one serious current affairs television programme like *Panorama* once a week in peak time, then why should the Corporation be entitled to the £2.5 billion of Licence Fee money that currently sustains its privileged status?

For the first time in its history BBC1, under Lorraine Heggessey, has been attracting a bigger share of the viewers than ITV. But beating ITV at its own game is not what the BBC is for. Director General Greg Dyke is a man of energy and enthusiasm. He believes in a BBC that is about programmes, not corporate structures; a BBC that he wants, in his words, to do 'wonderful things'. But today his BBC seems to be trying to deliver a commercial service at the licence payers' expense. That will not help *Panorama* – or indeed the BBC – survive. Enjoying the right to live off a poll tax like the Licence Fee requires, in return, a commitment to public service broadcasting. That means making the best programmes – in every area – and then trying hard to get people to watch and listen to them. What is required is to make good programmes popular and popular programmes good.

In current affairs this means putting out well-made, authoritative programmes about important subjects, in peak time, on a regular basis. Clearly there has to be a balance in the programmes offered. Tilt too relentlessly towards 'serious' subjects and programmes will end up so demanding that few will want to watch them. Tilt too far the other way and the programmes will be 'popular' only because they rely on an undemanding agenda of crime, violence, sex and royalty.

Recently, *Panorama* has occasionally mistaken Tinseltown values for current affairs. 'The fall of *Panorama* (BBC1 Sunday) from serious news programme to flimsy infotainment is now complete,' wrote the *Guardian*'s television reviewer about 'September 11th: a warning from Hollywood'. In this 'special edition for Oscar night', as it was billed, *Panorama* contrasted the failure of Western security services to prepare for terrorist attack with 'eerily prophetic' films from the 'dream factory', illustrated with clips from these violent blockbusters. 'The way it was done', wrote Gareth McLean, 'was tasteless and dumb. As a piece of quality journalism it ranked alongside the *Panorama* they did on spaghetti trees, but at least that one was an April fool.'[8] As an item in a magazine-style *Panorama* – like the one which had included the 'spaghetti tree' – this story would have been acceptable. As a full-length programme it was not. The primary purpose of *Panorama* is to make good current affairs programmes – not chase ratings with tales from Hollywood.

'In the end people watch television for entertainment,' says Horrocks.[9] That's a rather a gloomy assessment from the Head of Current Affairs, and not entirely accurate either. People watch television to be informed as well as entertained. It's obvious that audiences for serious current affairs are always likely to be smaller than they are for light entertainment, drama, or some documentaries; and it may be, as Dyke and Heggessey argue, that even in peak time *Panorama* would not get much bigger audiences than it does now. But that is the Licence Fee bargain; that is what public service broadcasting entails: offering a healthy mixed diet of information and education as well as enter-tainment; trying to get people to enjoy orange juice as well as Sugar Puffs, at the same table, at roughly the same time. To hide a programme away, sending *Panorama* to skulk out late on a Sunday night, suggests that the BBC, while afraid to kill it off, is prepared to let *Panorama* just wither away. At best, it's like pushing a patient to a side ward, where aggressive treatment directed towards recovery stops, and palliative care is offered instead, until the end comes.

'I think the potential is still there to do many of the things it's done in the past,' says *Panorama*'s present Editor, Mike Robinson, bravely. 'We can still make waves, we can still be noticed, we can still do journalism people out there wish we hadn't done – and we should do more of it ... I am saying we haven't yet found anything the BBC hasn't let us do. That is a change in the mood music; you know that if you are doing awkward journalism the BBC will give you space to do it.' This is good to hear, especially after the John Birt years when the mood music often seemed sombre, if not downright depressing. It is only fair to say that in July 2002 the BBC announced that *Panorama* was among the programmes likely to benefit from an extra £1 million being provided for investigative journalism.

But Robinson seems to accept that the prospect of *Panorama* returning to weekday peak time on BBC1 is, under the present regime, unrealistic; and he's probably right. In January 2002, in the Council Chamber at Broadcasting House, Dyke was interviewed in front of an audience about his plans and policies by the *Today* programme's former presenter Sue MacGregor. Afterwards, beneath the portraits of his predecessors – from John Reith to John Birt – the Director General answered questions from the audience. He made it quite clear that he did not think there was any longer a role for a regular peak-time *Panorama* – or similar programme – on BBC 1, and suggested that television needed to find other ways of covering topics once regarded as *Panorama*'s territory.

Perhaps that can be done. 'There is no divine law that says *Panorama* should go on for ever and ever,' says Nick Hayes. 'Good journalism will come out in one way or another. *Panorama* has been an effective medium, but people will find other ways to tell the stories that need telling. If we have to wave goodbye to *Panorama* we will do it without too many tears.' Hayes speaks as a *Panorama* producer who became Editor of *World in Action*. That programme has disappeared. So too has *This Week*. They have been replaced on ITV by *Tonight with Trevor McDonald*, with a much more obviously popular agenda. Is it really so certain that, were *Panorama* to sail away into the sunset, other programmes would appear, ready and able to tackle the important issues of our time?

When *Panorama* set out in 1955 on its first serious voyage of discovery it had the ocean to itself. Wherever it sailed there was no other vessel in sight, and wherever it dropped anchor, it was the only ship in the harbour. Roam where it might, it was alone. And when it returned home its crew had pictures to show and tales to tell that people gathered round their television sets had never seen or heard before. No wonder then that *Panorama* was popular.

Almost at once came competition. *This Week*, 'the poor man's *Panorama*', was quickly fitted out and launched. *World in Action* followed. And then there was ITV's drama and light entertainment. But, while much of the television audience abandoned *Panorama* for the lively programmes on ITV, millions stayed loyal.

And *Panorama* did not surrender. In March 1957, 18 months after he had relaunched it, Producer Michael Peacock had this to say:

> Early in February *Panorama* had the largest audience of any programme in Great Britain – eleven and a half million viewers, and the following week found it in second place in popularity. Here is a curious phenomenon: a current affairs programme which sets out to be informative and is on the whole a pretty serious one, attracting more viewers than most programmes based on pure entertainment. What is the secret of *Panorama*'s success? It may well be our choice of items – there is usually something to interest everyone; it may be our team of contributors – they all have their own admirers; it may be the way we present the material, or the fact that we appear every Monday evening so that people get into the habit of viewing every week; or indeed it may be our *Panorama* signature tune which still makes my spine tingle although I have heard it so often I ought to be heartily sick of it.[10]

Nearly 50 years ago *Panorama* could succeed in attracting and holding a large audience, even in the face of fierce commercial opposition. So why is there such reluctance to let it do battle today?

Compare Michael Peacock's *Panorama* with how *Panorama* is today: it is no longer a magazine programme, so that if you don't fancy this week's single story you're less likely to stay watching; there is no longer a recognisable team of 'contributors', in-vision reporters with character and charisma with whom you can identify; the programme is now transmitted late on a Sunday night and is on for only 32 weeks of the year; as for its signature tune, that is now cut to just a few bars of the familiar theme presumably for fear that viewers will switch off before the programme proper starts. It's as if the BBC had taken all the elements Peacock thought important to *Panorama*'s success and carefully done just the opposite. It seems positively perverse.

Today's *Panorama* team includes journalists – reporters and producers – as talented as any in its history. But it could do with more, and there are not enough people of the right quality prepared to join a programme which seems to be unloved by the BBC itself.

A course to steer?

So how could *Panorama* be given new life for the new century? First would come a commitment to put the programme back in peak time on a weekday for, say, 48 weeks of the year; second, the resources that would help it justify its prominent place in the schedules – the sort of budget a popular factual series enjoys. Now comes the hard bit – what kind of programme would it be?

Nearly half a century ago, Michael Peacock found that a magazine programme led by a first-class team of highly visible reporters worked well – even up against ITV's entertainment programmes. That still seems a good model, and it's one that America's *60 Minutes* has found very successful. A magazine offers variety to attract more than one kind of audience, and it has the flexibility to go for longer items or even a single subject as often as is justified. As for the old argument that, given the existence of a comprehensive BBC News and *Newsnight*, a magazine doesn't make sense, that is in the end a matter of authority. *Panorama* can be again what it once was, the flagship to which all turn for the most important messages. And, when crises occur, let *Panorama* work with News to give the context and analysis of the story that BBC Current Affairs should offer. A presenter on the Richard Dimbleby model is not essential to this format, but would be welcome if he or she could be found. Perhaps Jeremy Paxman might bring his talent back to *Panorama*, where he first made a national reputation as a television journalist.

Of course such a programme need no longer be called *Panorama*. Rather than renovate the old hulk, perhaps the BBC will think it better to send *Panorama* to the breaker's yard and launch a new ship under a new name. But it doesn't seem sensible to abandon such a well-known brand. Is it really too late, nearly half a century on, for the Lords of the Admiralty in Broadcasting House to send this signal to the flagship: that *Panorama* will return to peak time on BBC1; that it will be sufficiently well funded to explore and explain the world we live in, week in, week out; and that it will recruit more people who can report their conclusions with on-screen authority? Then the BBC will be adding to that reputation for public service broadcasting which remains its only justification for the Licence Fee. Then *Panorama* will again be, as so often in its 50-year history, a programme about which we can all – viewers and *Panorama* people alike – feel pride, and never paranoia.

⊕ Postscript

Almost a year has passed since those concluding words were written, but still no signal has reached *Panorama* to order the flagship to a new station.

According to Editor Mike Robinson BBC research shows that people still have tremendous trust in the *Panorama* 'brand': the programme is seen as thorough, passionate, and determined. Viewers like the tag line 'exposing the truth', and that is the aspect of *Panorama* that Robinson now emphasises. *Panorama*'s job, he says, is essentially scrutiny, close examination of the use and abuse of power, often after lengthy research.

Many programmes in 2002–3 were good examples of that: the two-part 'A Licence To Murder', which drew on years of *Panorama*'s investigative journalism to expose collusion between the intelligence services and loyalist murder gangs in Northern Ireland; 'The Corruption of Racing', which showed up the humiliating failure of the Jockey Club to regulate the sport of kings; 'The Secrets of Seroxat', which highlighted the often harrowing side-effects of this widely prescribed anti-depressant; 'The Chicken Run', which detailed the food industry's repellent methods of filling chicken products with ever more water; and 'Fiddling the Figures', which exposed the tricks of health professionals claiming to meet NHS targets.

These programmes, and others, stood comparison with *Panorama*'s output at any time in the past. But when it came to covering an important news story (like the Iraq war) *Panorama* found it harder to make a significant and distinctive contribution. 'The Battle for Basra' seemed to follow where news crews had already covered much of the ground; and instead of delving deeper into hot topics like the Euro, *Panorama* often took cover in the studio bunker, with rather predictable debates and discussions that added little to a better understanding of the issues.

Mike Robinson has now been Editor of *Panorama* for longer than nearly all his predecessors, and clearly feels that the programme – with an average audience of around three million – is once again on an even keel. Aboard the flagship the disaffection among the crew provoked by the move to late on Sunday night has subsided. '*Panorama* has weathered that storm', says Robinson. But he concedes that though viewers now know pretty much when his programme is on – 'after the News', they don't think the mood of a Sunday evening is right for *Panorama*. And this remains the central issue. Much of *Panorama*'s journalism is good, and some excellent. But what is the point of that if it's not at the right place in the schedule?

In February 2003 the BBC published a little booklet which was sent to two thousand 'influential people' in Britain. Ten programmes had been selected from each month of the previous year to demonstrate the 'range and distinction' of BBC Television. *Panorama* featured no less than eight times in this booklet – far, far more often than programmes from any other strand. BBC bosses obviously think 'influential people' will be impressed by the emphasis they place on *Panorama*. But if they really think it is so good, why don't they schedule *Panorama* where a peak time audience has a chance to see it?

In April 2003, the BBC Governors published 'Looking Ahead', their annual 'BBC Statements of Programme Policy'. In it they emphasised the importance of putting programmes like *Panorama* in the middle of the schedule, not on the edge of darkness: 'The diminution of current affairs on commercial channels makes the BBC's commitment to serious journalism at the centre of popular television and radio networks more critical than ever.'

If they all think *Panorama* is so good, if they really believe that 'serious journalism' should be 'at the centre of popular television', then why don't they do something about it? Why don't they put our BBC Licence money where their mouth is? Why don't they assign the flagship a more prominent station in the fleet where it can be seen by all to be leading the fight for the best in television journalism against increasingly commercial competitors? What is the point of Governors and BBC executives 'talking up' *Panorama* if they are not prepared to give it real promotion?

Says a senior Governor: 'At least four times a year we're asking Greg and his colleagues 'why won't you play *Panorama* in peak time?' They tell us '*Panorama* will be damaged by the competition and get even smaller audiences if we do'. We're not yet sufficiently convinced that they're wrong to order them to put *Panorama* back in peak time'.

If the BBC is too nervous to let *Panorama* risk its ratings in the open seas of peak time, why does it continue to bang the drum so loudly in its support? Because it knows *Panorama* is a powerful reminder to the public of the high standards the BBC must demonstrate if it is to continue in its present form. 'The BBC', says Mark Thompson, Chief Executive of Channel 4, 'has a tendency to re-discover old-time religion once every ten years as it enters the run-up to Charter renewal'. What a pity it would be if all these pious protestations of support for *Panorama* turned out to be so many puffs of wind that die away as soon as the new BBC Charter is secure.

11 November 2003 will mark *Panorama*'s fiftieth birthday. This should be more than the occasion for a party; it's surely the perfect cue to look through *Panorama*'s window over the years at how Britain and the world have changed during the past half-century, and how those changes have been reported. Yet the BBC was initially against the idea of any special programme at all.

Said Lorraine Heggessey, Controller of BBC1: 'We've given the 50th anniversary a lot of thought and have decided it's best to commemorate with press and PR activity rather than with a programme.' So *Panorama*'s half-century was to be marked not with anything of substance, but with 'press and PR activity'. *Panorama* was being valued not so much for itself and what it has achieved as for the part it could play in bolstering the Corporation's image.

As the anniversary approaches, it looks as if the BBC has had second thoughts and will, after all, produce some sort of programme to mark the occasion. That is welcome, but not enough. Call it paranoia, but the author's pride in *Panorama* is tempered by doubts as to whether it is, any longer, right at the heart of the BBC.

Notes

Chapter one

1 The script incorrectly shows the month as December, rather than November

2 BBC Oral History Archive, Stephen Bonarjee interviewed by George Scott, 1 April 1980.

3 Grace Wyndham Goldie: *Facing the Nation*. The Bodley Head, 1977.

4 BBC Written Archives Centre [hereafter WAC], T32/266/2, 22 June 1953.

5 WAC, T32/266/2, 22 September 1953.

6 WAC, T32/266/2, 29 September 1953.

7 WAC, T32/266/2, 12 October 1953.

8 Bonarjee recalls working on attachment to Television Talks in offices in London's Marylebone Road.

9 *Radio Times*, 6 November 1953.

10 WAC, T32/266/3, 27 November 1953.

11 WAC, *Panorama*, 11 November 1953.

12 Dr Sargant was not named except as 'a physician', in accordance with the medical profession's ban on 'advertising'.

13 WAC, *Panorama*, 11 November 1953.

14 WAC, *Panorama*, 11 November 1953.

15 WAC, T32/266/3, *Audience Research Report*, 24 November 1953.

16 WAC, T32/266/3, 19 November 1953.

17 WAC, T32/266/3, *Audience Research Report*, 24 November 1953.

18 WAC, T32/266/3, 23 November 1953.

Chapter two

1 Max Robertson: *Stop Talking and Give the Score*. Kingswood Press, 1987.

2 WAC, T32/266/4, *Audience Research Report*, 30 December 1953.

3 Robertson insists that, whatever the programme records may say, the elephant's name was Jessie.

4 WAC, T32/266/16, 6 January, 1954.

5 WAC, T16/204/1, 3 February 1954.

6 Queen's Bench Division, 27 July 1976.

7 Michael Barsley: *Behind the Screen*. André Deutsch, 1957.

8 *Ibid*.

9 Asa Briggs: *The History of Broadcasting in the UK*. Oxford University Press, 1979.

10 Barsley: *Behind the Screen*.

11 WAC, T32/266/4, September 1954.

12 WAC, T32/266/16, 5 August 1954.

13 WAC, T32/266/16, 13 August 1954.

14 WAC, T32/266/16, *Audience Research Report*, 5 November 1954.

15 WAC, T32/266/13, 21 October 1954.

Chapter three

1 Sir Geoffrey Cox: *Pioneering Television News*. John Libby, 1995.

2 Grace Wyndham Goldie.

3 As late as 1967 Reith could tell Malcolm Muggeridge that television had been 'to the hurt of this country; of the world'.

4 Cox: *Pioneering Television News*.

5 *Ibid*.

6 Leonard Miall: *Inside the BBC*. Weidenfeld and Nicolson, 1994.

7 Grace Wyndham Goldie: *Facing the Nation*. The Bodley Head, 1977.

Chapter four

1 Max Robertson: *Stop Talking and Give the Score*. Kingswood Press, 1987.

2 WAC, T32/266/1, 3 June 1955.

3 WAC, T32/266/1, 22 June 1955.

4 Jonathan Dimbleby: *Richard Dimbleby*. Hodder and Stoughton, 1975.

5 *Ibid*.

6 WAC, 1c, Richard Dimbleby, 2 June 1955.

7 WAC, 1c, Richard Dimbleby, 3 June 1955.

8   WAC, 1c, Richard Dimbleby,
    4 July 1955.
9   A guinea was worth £1 1 shilling. So,
    with 20 shillings in the pound, 80
    guineas was worth £84.

Chapter five

1   Sir Ian Trethowan: *Split Screen*. Hamish
    Hamilton, 1984.
2   John Grist: *The Century before
    Yesterday*. Unpublished family history
3   BBC Oral History Archive, Rex
    Moorfoot interviewed by Frank Gillard,
    7 October 1992.
4   Michael Barratt recalls Wyndham
    Goldie saying to him, after a rather bad
    studio interview: 'This contract of
    yours, when does it end?'.
5   Woodrow Wyatt: *Distinguished for
    Talent*. Hutchinson,1958.
6   Cawston became seriously ill and had to
    leave the programme. He later became
    one of the BBC's most successful docu-
    mentary filmmakers.
7   *Radio Times*, 16 September 1955.
8   Grace Wyndham Goldie: *Facing the
    Nation*. The Bodley Head, 1977.
9   Leonard Miall: *Richard Dimbleby,
    Broadcaster*. BBC, 1966.
10 Sir Robin Day: *Grand Inquisitor*.
    Weidenfeld and Nicolson, 1989.
11 Sir Geoffrey Cox: *Pioneering Television
    News*. John Libby, 1995.
12 WAC, T32/1, 191/3, 20 November 1956.
13 Asa Briggs: *The History of Broadcasting
    in the UK, vol. 5*. Oxford University
    Press, 1995.
14 WAC, *Panorama*, 5 November 1956.
15 Robert Rowland, '*Panorama* in the
    Sixties', in Anthony Aldgate, James
    Chapman & Arthur Marwick (eds.):
    *Windows on the Sixties: exploring key
    texts of media & culture*. I.B. Tauris, 2000.
16 WAC, T32/1, 191/4, 12 March 1957.
17 WAC, T32/1, 191/4, 14 March 1957.
18 *Daily Sketch*, 5 February 1957.
19 *Daily Record and Mail*, 5 February 1957.

20 *Daily Mail* 5 February 1957.
21 Jonathan Dimbleby: *Richard Dimbleby*.
    Hodder and Stoughton, 1975.

Chapter six

1   WAC, T32/1, 191/1, 19 September 1955.
2   WAC, T32/1, 193/1, 19 September 1955.
3   Woodrow Wyatt: *Confessions of an
    Optimist*. Collins, 1985.
4   WAC, T32/1, 191/2, 15 September 1955.
5   *Ibid*.
6   WAC, T32/1, 191/2, 16 September 1955.
7   Crawley was the first Editor of ITN
    when ITV began in September 1955.
8   WAC, Woodrow Wyatt,
    20 December 1955.
9   WAC, Woodrow Wyatt,
    29 December 1955.
10 WAC, T32/1, 191/2, 10 January 1956.
11 WAC, T32/1, 191/2, 4 April 1956.
12 WAC, Woodrow Wyatt,
    16 September 1957.
13 WAC, Woodrow Wyatt,
    23 December 1957.
14 WAC, Woodrow Wyatt,
    31 December 1957.
15 WAC, T32/1, 191/3, 23 October 1956.
16 Ian Trethowan, a current affairs
    presenter, became Director General
    in 1977.
17 In early contracts these people would be
    called 'speakers'.
18 WAC, *Panorama*, 17 September 1956.
19 For Lewisham North
20 WAC, *Panorama*, April 25 1960.
21 WAC, Board of Management minutes,
    21 March 1960.
22 The vote went up by 40 per cent,
    Wyatt later claimed, sufficient to
    defeat the Communist candidates
    for all three posts.
23 WAC, *Panorama*, 14 May 1956.
24 WAC, T32/1, 191/2, 17 May 1956.
25 *Sunday Times*, 15 December 1957.
26 *Truth*, 20 December 1957.
27 He was elected MP for Leicester
    Bosworth in 1959.

28   WAC, *Panorama*, 22 February 1960.

29   *The Times*, 17 & 27 February 1960.

30   WAC, Board of Management minutes, 29 February 1960.

31   *This Week* began in January 1956.

32   Sir Robin Day: *Grand Inquisitor*. Weidenfeld and Nicolson, 1989.

33   6 August 2000.

34   Day: *Grand Inquisitor*.

35   Ludovic Kennedy: *On My Way to the Club*. Collins, 1989.

36   Richard Seare, *Daily Mirror*, 19 December 1961.

37   Robin Day: *Television: a personal report*. Hutchinson, 1961.

38   Michael Wall, *Listener*, 18 February 1960.

39   WAC, T32/1, 191/3, 24 July 1956.

40   By now Head of Television Talks.

41   WAC, T16/59/2, 14 May 1962.

42   WAC, T32/516/1, 9 May 1962.

43   WAC, T32/516/1, 15 May 1962.

44   WAC, T32/516/1, 23 August 1962.

45   Later the subject of 'Jeffrey Archer – A Life of Lies', *Panorama*, 19 July 2001.

46   WAC, T16/59/2, 7 September 1962.

47   Wyatt: *Confessions of an Optimist*

48   *The Times*, 24 March 1984.

49   Glenwyn Benson, Editor, *Panorama*.

50   'Conspiracy or Coincidence?', *Panorama*, 16 June 1986.

51   Special programme, BBC1, 19 August 1986.

52   Grace Wyndham Goldie: *Facing the Nation*. The Bodley Head, 1977.

53   Kennedy got on to the floor of the convention hall disguised as a state delegate. A splinter from the banner he was carrying gave him a bad case of blood poisoning.

54   Jonathan Dimbleby: *Richard Dimbleby*. Hodder and Stoughton, 1975.

55   Television, Richard Sambrook, Director, BBC News, January 2002.

56   WAC, Box 737, 1990.

57   Dennis Potter: 'In My View', *Daily Herald*, 13 July 1963.

58   'The Story of Child B', *Panorama*, 26 October 1995.

59   'Prisoners of Their Past', *Panorama*, 1 July 2001.

60   'Towards Zero Hour', *Panorama*, 12 December 2001.

61   'Lethal Force', *Panorama*, 9 December 2001.

62   Aidan Laverty and Thea Guest

63   Jeremy Murray-Brown: 'Unshackling the TV Reporter', *New Society*, 27 May 1965.

64   WAC, T32/119/8, 24 July 1962. Grace Wyndham Goldie seems to have meant Brian Redhead, not Redpath.

65   WAC, Michael Charlton, 11 May 1963.

66   'Journal of a War', *Panorama*, 13 June 1966.

67   William H. Stoneman, *Washington Post*, 17 June 1966.

68   Komer, writing to Lord Normanbrook, Chairman of the BBC, addressed him as 'Governor, British Broadcasting Company'.

69   Later in his broadcasting career Charlton made an 'oral history' series on post-war European diplomacy for Radio 3.

70   Peter Fiddick: 'Far Too Long', *Guardian*, 2 February 1971.

71   1 September 1963.

72   In 1969.

73   WAC, T5J8/265/2, 13 January 1965.

74   *Radio Times*, 12 October 1967.

75   It might have had something to do with Mulligan's reputation as an outstanding rugby international.

76   Philip Whitehead, *Listener*, 14 September 1973.

77   Elizabeth Cowley, *Evening Standard*, 4 September 1973.

78   Stuart Hood, *Listener*, 20 December 1973.

79   Shaun Usher, *Daily Mail*, 22 January 1974.

Chapter seven

1   Not until Michael Peacock's return to the programme in 1969 was *Panorama*'s boss given the title 'Editor'.

2   WAC, Woodrow Wyatt, 18 June 1958.

3   WAC, T32/1, 191/4, 10 September 1958.

4 Grace Wyndham Goldie: *Facing the Nation*. The Bodley Head, 1977.

5 Sir Robin Day: *Grand Inquisitor*. Weidenfeld and Nicolson, 1989.

6 Later Saltman would join Thames Television, where from 1989 to 1991 he was Editor of *This Week*.

7 The Bernard Levin Interviews, BBC 2, 3 May 1980.

8 Robert Rowland, '*Panorama* in the Sixties', in Anthony Aldgate, James Chapman & Arthur Marwick (eds.): *Windows on the Sixties: exploring key texts of media & culture*. I.B.Tauris, 2000.

9 Bush House was the production centre for BBC External Services.

10 Rowland, '*Panorama* in the Sixties'

11 *Ibid.*

12 Ludovic Kennedy: *On My Way to the Club*. Collins, 1989.

13 'The White Tribe of Africa', *Panorama*, four programmes in January 1979.

14 'Journey into Darkness', *Panorama*, 27 June 1994.

15 WAC, Board of Governors minutes, 4 December 1975.

16 Nicholas Bethel, *The Times*, 10 December 1975.

17 'Who Really Killed Kennedy?', *Panorama*, 6 March 1978.

18 'Israel's Secret Weapon', *Panorama*, 20 August 1979.

19 'A Blind Eye to Murder?', *Panorama*, 20 February 1978.

20 'Called to Account – How Roberto Calvi Died', *Panorama*, 20 December 1982.

21 'The Best Days?', *Panorama*, 21 March 1977.

22 'Yesterday's Men', BBC Current Affairs, 1971.

23 'High School', directed by Fred Wiseman, 1968.

24 Michael Davie, *Observer Review*, 6 March 1977.

25 Nancy Banks-Smith, *Guardian*, 22 March 1977.

26 *Daily Mail*, 22 March 1977.

27 *Evening News*, 22 March 1977.

28 On the night of transmission a fire destroyed one of Faraday School's portable classrooms.

29 A reference to John Birt's critique of television journalism in *The Times*, 28 February 1975.

30 Shaun Usher, *Daily Mail*, 22 March 1977.

31 Peter Night, *Daily Telegraph*, 22 March 1977.

32 *Observer*, 27 March 1977.

33 Broadcasting Complaints Commission, February 1979.

34 'The Friends Who Put Fire in the Heavens', *Panorama*, 16 October 1978.

35 'Karen Silkwood Deceased', *Panorama*, 5 March 1979.

36 'Project 706 – The Islamic Bomb', *Panorama*, 16 June 1980.

37 'Vietnam - Children of the Dust', *Panorama*, 9 January 1984.

38 'Grotties' were David Lomax's description of any foreign currency.

39 'The Deep Cold War', *Panorama*, 10 October 1977.

40 Nancy Banks-Smith, *Guardian*, 11 October 1977.

41 Sean Day-Lewis, *Daily Telegraph*, 11 October 1977.

42 'The Doomsday Doodlebug', *Panorama*, 13 September 1976.

43 Shaun Usher, *Daily Mail*, 14 September 1976.

44 'Terror International', *Panorama*, 13 January 1978.

45 'The Real War in Space', *Panorama*, 23 October 1978.

Chapter eight

1 Patrick Campbell, *Yorkshire Observer*, 16 November 1955.

2 Patrick Campbell, *Yorkshire Observer*, 14 December 1955.

3 WAC, T5J8/265/2, 15 July 1965.

4 WAC, T67/115/1, 12 February 1976.

5 Michael Wall, *Listener*, 18 February 1960.

6 Jonathan Dimbleby: *Richard Dimbleby*. Hodder and Stoughton, 1975.

7 *Ibid.*

8 Muggeridge attacked 'the Royal soap opera' in the *Saturday Evening Post*, October 1955.

9 Dennis Potter, *Daily Herald*, 13 July 1963.

10 'Flashpoint Cuba', *Panorama* Special, 23 October 1962. There was an audience of 12 million.

11 Paul Fox interviewed by Frank Gillard, BBC Oral History Archive, 30 November 1984.

12 *Panorama*, 17 February 1964.

13 Moorfoot became Editor of *Panorama* in April 1958.

14 WAC, 1c, Richard Dimbleby, 7 May 1958.

15 Clive James, *Observer*, 14 February 1982.

16 'Can We Avoid War?', *Panorama*, 10 May 1982.

17 Robert Kee, *The Times*, 14 May 1982.

18 Julian Barnes, *Observer*, 16 May 1982

19 The Conservative backbench Media Committee meeting on 12 May 1982 was chaired by Geoffrey Johnson Smith MP, who had himself briefly worked on *Panorama*

20 Press Association Report, May 12 1982.

21 Later, in the interview he gave the BBC's Oral History Archive in May 1984, the Chairman said he had received a personal letter from the Deputy Prime Minister William Whitelaw 'apologising for the discourtesy of a number of his colleagues, and saying he had told the Prime Minister that if she did not approve of what we were doing, if she thought the BBC was exceeding itself and behaving as traitors or whatever, the remedy was to get rid of the Chairman of the Board of Governors, and not to engage in a public slanging match. So he had made the constitutional position as he saw it, as the best friend the BBC has ever had, quite clear to the Prime Minister, who never thereafter uttered a public word of condemnation'.

22 Robert Kee, *The Times*, 14 May 1982.

23 WAC, T41/491/1, '*Panorama* 10th May and Its Consequences', 14 May 1982.

24 WAC, Press Office Briefing Note, 13 May 1982.

25 WAC, Press Office Briefing Note, 21 May 1982.

26 Then Assistant Head of Outside Broadcasts.

27 WAC, 1c, Richard Dimbleby, 11 September 1959.

28 WAC, 3a, Richard Dimbleby, 6 December 1960.

29 Peter Black, *Daily Mail*, 28 September 1965.

30 Philip Purser, S*unday Telegraph*, 10 October 1965.

31 4 January 1966.

32 ITN interview, 23 February 1956.

33 ITN interview, 29 June 1957.

34 *Lancashire Evening Post*, July 1957.

35 Day had stood as a Liberal.

36 WAC, Board of Governors minutes, 9 May 1960.

37 Robin Day: *But with Respect....* Weidenfeld and Nicolson, 1993.

38 'The Inquisitors', *Sunday Citizen*, 11 March 1964.

39 Day was a strong advocate of the tele- vising of Parliament, which finally came about in 1988 without any noticeable improvement to the standing of politi- cians in public opinion.

40 *The Times*, 24 February 1964.

41 Sir Robin Day: *Grand Inquisitor*. Weidenfeld and Nicolson, 1989.

42 Peter Black, *Daily Mail*, 4 May 1967.

43 *Panorama*, 25 September 1967.

44 Stanley Reynolds, *Guardian*, 26 September 1967.

45 *Panorama*, 20 January 1969.

46 *Panorama*, 16 October 1967.

47 Day: *Grand Inquisitor*

48 James Green, *Evening News*, 5 December 1966.

49 WAC, T5J8/265/2, 5 December 1966.

50 WAC, T5J8/265/2, 19 December 1966.

51 Milton Shulman, *Evening Standard*, 9 August 1967.

52 Broadcasting and the Public Mood. BBC, 1969.

53 *Daily Mail*, 21 January 1967.

54 *Television Today*, 30 November 1967.

55 Dennis Potter, *Sun*, 16 January 1968.

56 *Television Today*, 8 May 1969.

57 Julian Critchley, *The Times*, 17 May 1969.

58 28 January 1969.

59 Martin Jackson, *Daily Express*, 22 November 1971.

60 Richard Last, *Daily Telegraph*, 24 January 1972.

61 Most notably *The World at One* on Radio 4, from 1979 to 1987, and (on BBC1) *Question Time*, from 1979 to 1989.

62 WAC, 8, Robin Day, 3 August 1976.

63 WAC, 8, Robin Day, 3 September 1976.

64 WAC, 8, Robin Day, 22 July 1977.

65 WAC, 8, Robin Day, 27 September 1977.

66 Day: *Grand Inquisitor*.

67 Ivan Rowan, *Sunday Telegraph*, 30 January 1972.

68 Some of them, such as *Panorama* veterans Sir Paul Fox, Michael Charlton, Paul Hodgson and Robert Rowland, fellow members of the Garrick Club.

69 WAC, David Dimbleby, 27 April 1965.

70 WAC, David Dimbleby, 15 February 1965.

71 In 2001 David Dimbleby sold his newspaper company.

72 David Wheeler, *Listener*, 2 November 1978. Wheeler was reviewing *Panorama's* 25th anniversary programme.

73 WAC, BBC Press Release, 16 May 1982.

74 WAC, BBC Press Release, 15 May 1982.

75 *Daily Telegraph*, 27 May 1982.

76 'The Media War', *Panorama*, 18 October 1982.

77 Richard Ingrams, *Spectator*, 2 October 1982.

Chapter nine

1 Charles Wheeler would soon join Peacock as his 'co-Producer'.

2 WAC, T32/266/1, 3 June 1955.

3 WAC, T32/1,191/2, 10 January 1956.

4 Leonard Miall.

5 Michael Barsley, the previous *Panorama* Producer.

6 WAC, T32/1, 191/3, 24 July 1956.

7 WAC, T32/1, 191/4, 1958.

8 WAC, T32/1, 191/4, 14 March 1957.

9 Cecil McGivern.

10 WAC, T32/1, 191/4, 12 November 1958.

11 Neville Randall, *Daily Sketch*, 21 October 1958.

12 Frank Entwistle, London *Evening Standard*, 21 October 1958.

13 Not to be confused with Charles Wheeler, who had now returned to News.

14 WAC, T32/1, 191/4, 7 November 1958.

15 BBC Oral History Archive, Paul Fox interviewed by Frank Gillard, 13 November 1984.

16 WAC, T32/516/1, May 1963.

17 WAC, T16/204/2, 2 December 1963.

18 WAC, T32/1,191/8, 19 December 1961.

19 WAC, T32/1191/9, 11 August 1964.

20 WAC, T16/59/3, 31 March 1965.

21 'Mandrake', *Sunday Telegraph*, 27 June 1965.

22 WAC, T58/309/1, 17 February 1966.

23 WAC, T58/309/1, 6 May 1966.

24 Erik Durschmied.

25 WAC, T58/309/1, 7 June 1966.

26 WAC, T58/309/1, 8 June 1966.

27 WAC, T58/309/1, 13 June 1966.

28 WAC, T58/309/1, 16 June 1966.

29 Philip Purser, *Sunday Telegraph*, 19 June 1966.

30 WAC, T5J8/265/2, 20 June 1966.

31 WAC, T5J8/265/2, 17 August 1966.

32 Sadly, it seems that this was only a joke.

33 WAC, T5J8/265/2, 21 September 1966.

34 WAC, T5J8/309/1, 20 July 1966.

35 WAC, T5J8/265/2, 15 November 1966.

36 WAC, T5J8/309/1, 17 November 1966.

37 Though Webster did eventually become Editor in July 1967.

38 WAC, Board of Governors minutes, 1 December 1966.

39 *Daily Telegraph*, 2 December 1966.

40 WAC, T5J8/265/2, 2 December 1966.

41 Associated-Rediffusion became Thames Television in 1968.

42 Jeremy Isaacs, Opinion, 1967.

43 James Green, London Evening News, 5 December 1966.

44 WAC, T5J8/265/2, 5 December 1966.

45 WAC, T5J8/265/3, 8 February 1967.

46 Milton Shulman, London Evening Standard, 9 August 1967.

47 Maurice Wiggin, Sunday Times, 21 July 1968.

48 T.C. Worsley, Financial Times, 18 December 1968.

49 Robert Rowland, 'Panorama in the Sixties', in Anthony Aldgate, James Chapman and Arthur Marwick (eds.): Windows on the Sixties: exploring key texts of media & culture. I.B. Tauris, 2000.

50 Southern Rhodesia had – illegally – made a unilateral declaration of independence (UDI) in November 1965.

51 WAC, T5J8/265/2, 9 July 1968.

52 Julian Critchley, The Times, 17 May 1969.

53 Wenham became Editor of Panorama in December 1969.

54 BBC Oral Archive, Brian Wenham interviewed by Frank Gillard, 21 April 1988.

55 Panorama, 9 August 1971.

56 Daily Mirror, 19 October 1970.

57 Panorama's running time was increased to 60 minutes on 14 September 1970.

58 WAC, BBC Press Service, 28 August 1970.

59 Rowland became Editor of Panorama in January 1972.

60 'The Cost of Eating', Panorama, 12 March 1973.

61 Nancy Banks-Smith, Guardian, 13 March 1973.

62 London Weekend Television's Weekend World, started by John Birt, was first broadcast on 1 October 1972.

63 Mary Malone, Daily Mirror, 25 January 1972.

64 Pearson Phillips, Daily Mail, 9 March 1971.

65 Report of the Committee on the Future of Broadcasting, Cmnd 6753, March 1977.

66 WAC, Memo from Peter Pagnamenta to the Panorama team, 28 August 1975.

67 'Sir Alec at Seventy', Panorama, 2 July 1973.

68 Panorama, 1 March 1976.

69 Shaun Usher, Daily Mail, 16 March 1976.

70 'A Traffic in Babies', Panorama, 15 March 1976.

71 Michael Cockerell letter, 17 July 1979.

72 'The Boys in the Bush', Panorama, 17 April 1978.

73 'Iran's Moslem Dream', Panorama, 5 February 1979.

74 'Who Killed Georgi Markov?', Panorama, 9 April 1979.

75 'Otrag - The Friends Who Put Fire in the Heavens', Panorama, 16 October 1978.

76 'Ambassador Jay', Panorama, 3 October 1977.

77 David Wheeler, Listener, 2 November 1978.

78 Roger Bolton: Death on the Rock and other stories. W.H.Allen, 1990.

79 Penny Junor, London Evening News, 3 September 1979.

80 'The IRA's Open Door', Panorama, 3 September, 1979.

81 Bolton: Death on the Rock and other stories.

82 WAC, BBC News and Current Affairs minutes, 17 July 1979.

83 WAC, T41/492/1, 1979.

84 Daily Telegraph, 9 November 1979.

85 WAC, R1/46/4, 20 December 1979.

86 Ian Trethowan, the Director General, had suffered a heart attack on 1 October 1979.

87 WAC, Board of Management minutes, 19 November 1979.

88 18 November 1979; signatories included Peter Woon, John Wilson, Alan Protheroe, Desmond Wilcox, Paul Bonner, Tony Crabb and Christopher Capron.

89 At Carrickmore, Jeremy Paxman and David Darlow had been filming with freelance Paul Berriff as their cameraman.

90 9 November 1979.

91 In October 1988 a Government Direction on Broadcasting did indeed ban members of Sinn Fein from speaking for their Party on television.

92 WAC, Board of Governors minutes, 22 November 1979.

93 WAC, R2/32/3, Appendix to Board of Management minutes (79) 39, 19 November 1979.

94 WAC, Board of Governors minutes, 22 November 1979.

95 WAC, T41/492/1, 14 September 1979

96 BBC Chairman's statement, *Broadcast*, 26 November 1979.

97 Sean Day-Lewis, *Daily Telegraph*, 19 November 1979.

98 Bolton: *Death on the Rock and other stories*

99 'The Tory Treatment', *Panorama*, 17 September 1979.

100 WAC, R2/32/3, Board of Management minutes, 26 November 1979.

101 'The Third Man', *Panorama*, 7 July 1980.

102 WAC, C66, RS5, Board of Management minutes, 14 July 1980.

103 WAC, R78/2, 810/1, 14 July 1980.

104 'The Chinese News Machine', *Panorama*, 15 September 1980.

105 'A Dying Industry', *Panorama*, 14 April 1980. Peter Taylor reported on expanding sales of tobacco in the Third World.

106 WAC, T41/491/1, TD15, 17 September 1980.

107 WAC, T41/491/1, TD15, 22 September 1980.

108 WAC, T41/491/1, 15 January 1981

109 Roger Bolton, *New Statesman*, 31 October 1986.

110 *Panorama* had given the sound of the Governor General's interview to BBC Radio, so had not committed the unforgivable journalistic crime of sitting on the news.

111 The first *Panorama* at the new time of 9.30pm was transmitted on 18 February 1985.

112 Paragraph 54, Chapter 6, 'Conclusions', Young Conservative Report, January 1984.

113 Also reported by Michael Cockerell

114 Interview in BBC staff magazine *Ariel*, 29 February 1984.

115 Peter Carter-Ruck: *Memoirs of a Libel Lawyer*. Weidenfeld and Nicolson, 1990.

116 Later the BBC's Political Editor.

117 *Daily Mail*, 16 March 1984.

118 Tony Crabb, 21 October 1986.

119 Marmaduke Hussey: *Chance Governs All*. Macmillan, 2001.

120 *Ibid.*

121 Carter-Ruck: *Memoirs of a Libel Lawyer*.

122 WAC, R78/2,810/1, 27 March 1984 .

123 WAC, R78/2,810/1, 18 April 1984.

124 Bette Davis as Margo Channing in *All About Eve*, 1950; script by Joseph Mankiewicz.

125 28 April 1986.

126 Richard Last, *Daily Telegraph*, 20 May 1986.

127 WAC, Television Programme Review minutes, 4 February 1987.

128 WAC, Board of Management minutes, 9 February 1987.

129 'Londoner's Diary', London *Evening Standard*, 20 August 1987.

Chapter ten

1 Kendall McDonald, London *Evening News*, 27 October 1958.

2 WAC, I/C-38/279 T32/1, 399/1, October 1958.

3 WAC, T32/1, 191/3, 2 August 1956.

4 WAC, T32/1, 191/3, 22 October 1956.

5 WAC, T58/349/1, 3 January 1967.

6 Back at the BBC, Anne Tyerman became Editor, Political Documentaries. Her contract was ended in February 2002, when the BBC decided to do politics differently. She is now an independent producer.

7 *Panorama* producer Jane Drabble later became BBC Director of Education.

8 'The Media War', *Panorama*, 18 October 1982.

9 'The Marketing of Margaret', *Panorama*, 13 June 1983.

10 'The Jewish Pawns in Russia's Game', *Panorama*, 25 March 1985.

11 Mary Kenny, *Daily Mail*, 26 March 1985.

12 An innovation of Pagnamenta's in 1975.

13 Calderwood notoriously chose as the unofficial working title for a *Panorama* film about the Pope's visit to Colombia 'Kiss My Ring in Bogota'.

14 Butch Calderwood and Robin Ivor: *Don't Shoot, I'm Only the Cameraman*, unpublished memoirs, 1993.

15 Erik Durschmied: *Don't Shoot the Yanqui: the life of a war cameraman*. Grafton Books, 1990.

Chapter eleven

1 *The Times*, 26 May 1971.

2 *Guardian*, 30 October 1971.

3 *News of the World*, 21 November 1971.

4 *Sunday Telegraph*, 31 October 1971.

5 'Babies on Benefit', *Panorama*, 20 September 1993.

6 Later, some did. *Daily Telegraph*, 17 September 1994.

7 *Guardian*, 13 September 1994.

8 *Daily Telegraph*, 23 February 1995.

Chapter twelve

1 Peter Mandelson, was the chief architect of New Labour's election victory in 1997.

2 'Have They Got News for You', *Panorama*, 30 September 1996.

3 'Iran: the barrels and the guns', *Panorama*, 1 October 1973.

4 WAC, Board of Governors minutes, 15 November 1973.

5 WAC, R78/2, 745/1, 29 November 1973.

6 *The Times*, 22 October 1973.

7 WAC, T32/1, 191/4, 29 January 1957.

8 WAC, T32/1, 191/4, 28 February 1958.

9 WAC, T16/59/2, 20 February 1962.

10 WAC, T16/716/3, 12 March 1962.

11 Assistant to the Director General

12 WAC, T32/1, 191/4, 27 October 1958.

13 WAC, T16/204/2, 1 January 1964.

14 *Ibid.*

15 'Will You Still Feed Me?', *Panorama*, 20 February 1989.

16 'Going Critical: your nuclear future', *Panorama*, 2 July 1979.

17 6 September 1979.

18 31 October 1979.

19 *The Nuclear Power Debate*, BBC1, 8 January 1980.

20 WAC, Audience Research Report, 1 February 1980.

21 Letters, *Radio Times*, 26 January 1980.

22 WAC, R78/2,745/1, 17 July 1962.

23 WAC, R78/2,745/1, 18 July 1962.

24 WAC, T16/716/3, 17 July 1962.

25 WAC, T16/716/3, 18 July 1962.

26 WAC, T16/716/3, 20 July 1962.

27 *Ibid.*

28 'Do You Want to Know a Secret?', *Panorama*, 2 April, 1979.

29 WAC, Board of Governors minutes, 27 September 1979.

30 Draft reply from acting Director General to British Safety Council, 17 August, 1979.

31 'The Heart Changers', *Panorama*, 17 March 1980.

32 D. Wainwright Evans & I.C. Lum, *Lancet*, 26 April 1980.

33 John Garfield: 'Personal View', *British Medical Journal*, 11 February 1978.

34 Diagnosis of Brian Death, Conference of Royal Colleges and Faculties of the United Kingdom, October 1976.

35 *Ibid.*

36 Memorandum on the Diagnosis of Death, January 1979.

37 John Searle & Charles Collins: 'A Brain-Death Protocol', *Lancet*, 22 March 1980.

38 'Transplants - Are the Donors Really Dead?', *Panorama*, 13 October 1980.

39 In Denmark the tests included an angiogram, to show that blood was no longer circulating through the brain.

40 The Removal of Cadaveric Organs for Transplantation, A Code of Practice, October 1979.

41 H.K. Beecher: 'After the "definition of irreversible coma"', *New England Journal of Medicine*, 1969.

42 'Transplants – Are the Donors Really Dead?' *Panorama*, 13th October 1980.

43 WAC, BBC Audience Research, 11 November 1980.

44 Richard Last, *Daily Telegraph*, 14 October 1980.

45 'An Appalling *Panorama*', *British Medical Journal*, 18 October 1980.

46 *The Times*, 16 October 1980.

47 Christopher Pallis, *British Medical Journal*, 18 October 1980.

48 Donald Gould, *New Scientist*, 23 October 1980.

49 Chris Dunkley, *Financial Times*, 25 February 1981.

50 D. Alan Shewmon, MD, Professor of Pediatric Neurology, UCLA Medical School: '"Brainstem Death", "Brain Death", and Death: a Critical Re-evaluation of the Purported Equivalence', *Issues in Law and Medicine*, Vol.. 14, No. 2, 1998.

51 At that time MI5 headquarters.

52 MI5/MI6: 'The right to privacy and the need to know', *Panorama*, 23 February & 2 March 1981.

53 Sir Ian Trethowan: *Split Screen*. Hamish Hamilton, 1984.

54 *The Times*, 28 February, 30 September & 1 October 1975.

55 Charles Leadbetter, *New Statesman*, 18 July 1997.

56 Michael Tracey: *In the Culture of the Eye: ten years of Weekend World*. Hutchinson, 1983.

57 WAC, R78/2,810/1, 9 June 1987.

58 29 April 1987.

59 Very strangely, the tapes of the McDonald interview disappeared from the BBC and the interview was therefore never included in the 'Spycatcher' programme.

60 The ACTT, the film technicians' union, powerful in ITV, had long insisted on crews much larger than necessary for current affairs filming.

61 22 July 1987.

62 20 July 1987.

63 Simon Freeman: 'The BBC Gets Camera-Shy', *Spectator*, 8 August 1987.

64 *Spectator*, 22 August 1987.

65 Chris Horrie & Steve Clarke: *Fuzzy Monsters: fear and loathing at the BBC*. Heinemann, 1994.

66 Steven Barnett & Andrew Curry: *The Battle for the BBC: a British broadcasting conspiracy*. Aurum Press, 1994.

67 'The Two Hundred Million Pound Rip-off', *Panorama*, 8 February 1988.

68 Paul Woolwich resigned from the BBC in February 1988. He later became Editor of Thames Television's *This Week*.

69 Rajiv Gandhi was later assassinated by a Tamil terrorist.

70 'India's Pilot Prime Minister', *Panorama*, 18 January 1988.

71 Compare the complaint by the Indian High Commission in 1962.

72 Later, in 1993, in a speech to the Radio Academy, Mark Tully spoke of the 'climate of fear' John Birt had created in the BBC

73 *Guardian*, 20 April 1988.

74 *Guardian*, 22 April 1988.

75 In June 1988 the author joined the Independent Broadcasting Authority, where he was given responsibility for ensuring truth and impartiality in news and current affairs on ITV and Channel 4.

76 'Unsafe Convictions', *Panorama*, 24 February 1992.

77 'Hot Property', *Panorama*, 18 July 1988.

78 'Death on the Rock', Thames Television, 28 April 1988.

79 3 October 1988.

80 *Daily Express*, 3 October 1988.

81 *Daily Telegraph*, 7 October 1988.

82 *Private Eye*, 14 October 1988.

83 *Observer*, 23 October 1988.

84 'Behind the Desert Shield', *Panorama*, 15 January 1991.

85 22 February 1991.

86 9 March 1992.

87 'Crisis at the Coalface', *Panorama*, 2 March 1992.

88 The author reluctantly accepts Shah's denial of the story that while working on the London Weekend Television religious programme *Credo* he once included a graphic headed 'God's Options'.

89 16 March 1992.

90 20 March 1992.

91 Alastair Campbell, *Daily Mirror*, 10 March 1992.

92 John Naughton, *Observer*, 15 March 1992.

93 Roger Bolton: 'Truth, the BBC and a Betrayal of Trust', London *Evening Standard*, 10 March 1992.

94 'Sliding into Slump', *Panorama*,4 May 1992.

95 Paul Gent, *Daily Telegraph*, 5 May 1992.

96 Glenwyn Benson.

97 'The Price of Power', *Panorama*, 16 May 1994.

98 'Bad Timing: political constraints on BBC journalism', *Violations Paper 23*, Charter 88, November 1994.

99 Ernest Saunders.

100 'Who Pays for the Party?', *Panorama*, 8 October 1990.

101 Lord Wyatt, formerly *Panorama*'s Woodrow Wyatt, was arguing that a statutory obligation of impartiality should be placed on broadcasters.

102 *Independent*, 9 October 1990.

103 Steve Clarke, *The Times*, 29 January 1992.

104 Georgina Henry, *Guardian*, 12 March 1992.

105 From the film *The Wizard of Oz*, 1939.

106 Michael Leapman, *Independent*, 25 November 1992.

107 Glenwyn Benson, *Independent*, 27 November 1992.

108 Glenwyn Benson, Editor, *Panorama*, 'Report to the Controller, BBC1', 18 June 1993.

109 Russell Twisk, *Observer*, 1 August 1993.

110 Jane Thynne: 'Inside Track', *Daily Telegraph*, 14 August 1993.

111 'An Ordinary Boy', Kilroy TV/*Panorama*, 6 September 1993.

112 Richard Brooks, *Observer*, 12 September 1993.

113 'Forcing the Peace', *Panorama*, 8 February 1993.

114 'The Swamp of Civil War', *The Times*, 10 February 1993.

115 Glenwyn Benson, *The Times*, 17 February 1993.

116 'The Case of India One', *Panorama*, 27 September 1993.

117 'The Manager', *Panorama*, 16 September 1993.

118 'The Norway Channel', *Panorama*, 13 September 1993.

119 Brenda Maddox: '*Panorama*'s Triumphant Return to Form', *Daily Telegraph*, 29 September 1993.

120 Andrew Cuff: '*Panorama* Hits the Mark on an Upward Swing', *Guardian*, 8 November 1993.

121 In 1989 intimate telephone conversations between Prince Charles and Camilla Parker Bowles, and between Diana and James Gilbey, had become embarrassingly public.

122 Mike Robinson became Editor of *Panorama* in October 2000.

123 16 November 1995.

124 BBC Public Affairs, 21 November 1995.

125 According to Suter, the BBC was relying on the note from Diana.

126 WAC, BBC Press Service, *Panorama* Statement, 13 April 1996.

127 'Louise Woodward', *Panorama*, 22 June 1998.

Chapter thirteen

1 WAC, T32/1, 191/9, 3 February 1964.

2 WAC, T58/265/3, 19 January 1968.

3 Peter Horrocks, *The Times*, 12 May 2000.

4 'The World's Most Wanted', *Panorama*, 16 September 2001.

5 'Who Bombed Omagh?', *Panorama*, 9 October 2000.

6 Lorraine Heggessey, Controller, BBC1, March 2001.

7 13 September 2001.

8 Gareth McLean: 'Crash and Burn', *Guardian*, 25 March 2002.

9 Leigh Holmwood: 'Looking after Affairs', Broadcast, 19 April 2002.

10 Michael Peacock: 'The BBC Window on the World', *Radio Times*, 15 March 1957.

Index